NICKLAUS THOMAS-SYMONDS is the Labour Member of Parliament for Torfaen and a frontbencher. He is a Fellow of the Royal Historical Society and is the author of *Attlee: A Life in Politics* (I.B. Tauris).

'[a] lucid, well-researched biography… This is a warts and all biography, written by an Oxford academic, but mercifully free of academic jargon. It offers a balanced assessment of a complicated man.'

Chris Mullin, *Observer*

'Thomas-Symonds distances himself both from the Nyolatry of early biographer Michael Foot and the castigation of right-wing successors whose chief objection to Bevan is that he was a socialist. He offers a genuine understanding of Bevan's political philosophy, of how his democratic socialism differed from the state-imposed model of the communists who were his sparring partners in his home town of Tredegar… [Bevan] is well served by this closely argued political biography.'

Jad Adams, *Independent*

'…deftly examining the structural circumstances in which Bevan operated… [*Nye*] offers a convincing account of how Bevan threw the leadership away… an unrivalled perspective on Bevan's life and political career adding much to the historiography on post-war Labour politics.'

Patrick Diamond, *Times Literary Supplement*

'Symonds is an assiduous researcher, and particularly informative on Bevan's early life and career.'

Paul Johnson, *Standpoint*

'*Nye* is a well-written reassessment of the political life of Bevan, and Thomas-Symonds demonstrates why his reputation remains high among a younger generation of Labour politicians and activists.'

Keith Simpson, *Total Politics*

'This is a gripping new analysis of one of the most controversial, but also one of the most charismatic, figures in recent British history.'

Kenneth O. Morgan

'The 70th anniversary of the NHS in 2018 brings into sharp focus its creator, Nye Bevan. His work helped to give us our most precious asset – health care as a human right for all of our lifetimes. I warmly recommend Nick Thomas-Symonds' biography for its fascinating analysis of this quite remarkable life.'

Jeremy Corbyn

'…what marks this book out from many other Bevan biographies is the intimacy of this young South Walian lawyer's understanding of Nye's background, which so profoundly shaped his values and purposes throughout his life. Above all, Nick Thomas-Symonds comprehends Bevan's central, propelling quality of audacity.'

Neil Kinnock

'This is essential reading for everyone who wishes to understand the quintessentially benign but audacious rooted character of Nye's generation of organic working class intellectuals who helped civilise our postwar world, and who should continue to inspire us today.'

Hywel Francis MP

'If you only read one book on Nye Bevan then, for its objectivity and illumination, make it this one.'

**Dai Smith, Raymond Williams Research Chair
in Cultural History, Swansea University**

'A very readable and well researched study of one of the true political giants of the twentieth century. This book will be a useful addition to the canon of labour history and British political history more generally.'

**Matthew Worley,
Professor of Modern History, University of Reading**

'A lively account of Bevan's political career that is well written and carefully researched.'

**Paul Corthorn,
Senior Lecturer in Modern British History, Queen's University Belfast**

Nye

The Political Life of Aneurin Bevan

NICKLAUS THOMAS-SYMONDS

foreword by

Neil Kinnock

I.B. TAURIS

LONDON · NEW YORK · OXFORD · NEW DELHI · SYDNEY

For my grandparents, my parents, Rebecca,
Matilda Olwyn, Florence Elizabeth Mary, and Ellie.

I.B. TAURIS
Bloomsbury Publishing Plc
50 Bedford Square, London, WC1B 3DP, UK
1385 Broadway, New York, NY 10018, USA
29 Earlsfort Terrace, Dublin 2, Ireland

BLOOMSBURY, I.B. TAURIS and the I.B. Tauris logo are
trademarks of Bloomsbury Publishing Plc

Revised paperback edition published in 2018 by I.B. Tauris & Co. Ltd
First published in paperback in 2016 and hardback in 2015 by I.B. Tauris & Co. Ltd
First published in Great Britain 2018
Reprinted 2017, 2018, 2019 (twice), 2020 (twice), 2021

A catalogue record for this book is available from the British Library.
A catalog record for this book is available from the Library of Congress

ISBN: HB: 978-1-7807-6209-8
PB: 978-1-7845-3562-9
ePDF: 978-0-8577-2525-7
eBook: 978-0-8577-3499-0

Printed and bound in Great Britain

To find out more about our authors and books visit
www.bloomsbury.com and sign up for our newsletters.

Contents

List of Illustrations

Preface to the New Edition

On 4 July 1948, the night before the National Health Service came into existence, Aneurin Bevan, Minister of Health and Housing, spoke at a Labour Party rally in Manchester and declared, with justification, that Britain had assumed the 'moral leadership of the world'. Capturing the values that underpin our health care system, Bevan declared that the services available would be provided on the basis of need, not wealth, and deal with people as they presented themselves for treatment, making no judgements about them, their behaviour or their lifestyles. The free market should not be allowed to create inequalities of health provision between richer and poorer areas: the service should be of a universally high standard across the country. Bevan's vision was one of compassion in action.

The years since the publication of this book have demonstrated to me the value of the National Health Service in a stark way. My son, William, who was born on 17 September 2016, was taken seriously ill at the age of seven weeks with chronic kidney failure, requiring five operations in five months at the Noah's Ark Children's Hospital for Wales. My mother Pamela, whom I lost on New Year's Day 2018, had been diagnosed with cancer in January 2016. Thanks to her treatment on the National Health Service, she was able to live long enough to see William recover from the intense period of surgery he needed and to become the engaged, energetic, happy one-year-old that he now is.

After the European Union referendum campaign of 2016, the 'Vote Leave' red bus has become infamous for the unfulfilled promise of extra money on its side: 'We send the EU £350 million a week: let's fund our NHS instead.' Yet it is indicative of the status of the National Health Service that, as an institution, it was regarded as having the emotive power to attract voters to the cause 68 years after it was set up.

At the 2017 Conservative Party Conference, Jeremy Hunt, speaking from the platform as Secretary of State for Health, sought to downplay Aneurin Bevan's role in the creation of the health service, in order to claim credit for the Tories. (I responded to Hunt's speech with an article in the *Independent* on 4 October 2017: 'Jeremy Hunt is so bad at his job that he's now resorted to rewriting the history of the NHS'.) Hunt played a video before declaring: 'That was the Conservative health minister in 1944, Sir Henry Willink, whose White Paper announced the setting up of the NHS. He did it with cross-party support.' It is correct that Sir William Beveridge's 1942 report, *Social Insurance and Allied Services*, assumed there would be a 'national health service', which idea Willink adopted. But there was a significant difference between a 'national' health service and the National Health Service that Bevan created.

One of Bevan's critical contributions to the shape of postwar health care provision was his decision to nationalise the hospitals. Willink would have left hospitals in the hands of local authorities and voluntary groups. Within the Labour Cabinet, Herbert Morrison, who, as leader of the London County Council, had run a wide-ranging health care service, argued for local authorities to keep control of their existing hospitals but was defeated by Bevan. All of Bevan's skills of creativity, drive and tenacity were in evidence in his careful negotiations with the British Medical Association to ensure that sufficient numbers of doctors participated in the new service to make it work.

The acid test of the Tory position on the foundation of the National Health Service was the vote in Parliament in the debate on its core principles. The then Conservative opposition voted against Bevan's 1946 National Health Service Bill at second reading in the House of Commons, though the measure passed by 359 votes to 172. There was no cross-party support across the despatch box from the Tories.

None of this, however, diminishes the central point. Bevan's National Health Service is still so popular with the public that politicians from across the political spectrum *want* to be associated with it. It is a unique national institution that is there for those who need it. As a Member of Parliament, I know that there can be instances where people or their relatives do not receive the standard of service they deserve, and it is vital that those cases are brought to the attention of those in authority within the National Health Service to ensure that lessons are learned where needed. But this should not detract from the fact that over-whelming numbers of people, when they find themselves relying on the National Health Service, when their lives are in danger or they require non-urgent treat-ment, are given the help they need. The National Health Service is not a mere monument: it is a living institution made up of its dedicated, outstanding staff who provide care around the clock. Those who work in our National Health Service have made it what it is today, and we should always thank them for their remarkable commitment to public service, often carried out in the most difficult of circumstances.

It is a matter of great pride to me as chair of the Aneurin Bevan Society to be playing a role in the celebrations that will mark the 70 years that have passed since 1948. In one sense, this is uplifting, but in another, the feeling is a sobering one. The Conservative–Liberal Democrat Coalition government's Health and Social Care Act of 2012, emphasising 'competition' in health care, the fragmentation it has brought about, and spending restrictions under the Conservative austerity programme since 2010, mean that our marking of the 70th anniversary of the National Health Service has to be a reminder that Bevan's values must be fought for in every generation. Ironically, given that Bevan was opposed to devolution, it is in the nation of his birth, Wales, that his values remain best preserved, as the Welsh Labour government has shielded the health care system from the legislative changes across the border in England.

The great challenge of my generation will be how to solve the problem of the funding of social care for future generations, as more and more people live longer lives. As we debate these issues, we should not forget, however, the role of the National Health Service in improving the health of the population to produce this longevity: increased lifespans may present policy challenges but are to be celebrated.

If the rise of populist politics teaches us anything it is that we should never assume that the political battles of the past are won. Issues from previous generations that were debated and then resulted in advances for our people and became settled policy can no longer be put to one side as unimportant. The public affection for the National Health Service is unquestioned, and it still frames our public debate on health care as a right, not a luxury. But that does not mean that it will still command such respect in 20 years' time. It falls upon all of us who believe in its transformational power over people's lives to continue to make the case for it. This imperative is even more pressing as the time before the National Health Service existed moves towards the edge of living memory. We take our free health care for granted at our peril.

I was privileged to spend two years of my life writing about Aneurin Bevan: a great, fascinating politician who inspired me. Bevan could use words to persuade and move people, crafting some of the finest oratory this country has ever produced. But he would have been the first to say that mere words are not enough. He translated his principles into positive action that changed people's lives. These two lessons, of fine speech-making allied to constructive achievement, form a guide for anyone in a position of leadership in communities up and down the country.

In issuing this edition of my biography to coincide with the 70th anniversary of the National Health Service, I hope to provide an opportunity for people to find out more about Bevan, his beliefs and the struggle to create a health service that is there for us all. Anniversaries can be more than mere markers of time if we ensure that they also give us a moment to reflect. Now is the time to pause and consider the magnitude of what Bevan achieved. As the leader of the Labour Party, Jeremy Corbyn, puts it on the cover of this book: 'The 70th anniversary of the NHS in 2018 brings into sharp focus its creator, Nye Bevan. His work helped to give us our most precious asset – health care as a human right for all of our lifetimes.'

NICKLAUS THOMAS-SYMONDS MP
ABERSYCHAN, APRIL 2018

Preface

The interest generated by the publication of the hardback edition of *Nye: The Political Life of Aneurin Bevan* is evidence of an enduring fascination with the creator of the National Health Service. In the book's concluding paragraph, I quoted two of Bevan's contemporaries, Dai Price and Jack Thomas, both of whom testified to Bevan's special aura as an individual. One very interesting point put to me by the Rt. Hon. Rhodri Morgan, former First Minister of Wales, is whether the name *Aneurin* contributed to Bevan himself feeling special, thereby contributing to his sense of destiny.[1]

Morgan's account is that Nye was named after Aneurin Fardd ('Aneurin the Poet'), who was born Aneurin Jones in 1822. Jones, who died when Nye was a young boy, in 1904, was a friend of his father, David Bevan. Jones lived in the Gwent Valleys for a time, before emigrating to America and spending a period as Superintendent of the New York Parks. Jones was heavily involved with Eisteddfodau, at which David Bevan himself won prizes.[2] 'Aneurin' is itself a corrupted version of 'Aneirin', the name of the great Dark Ages Welsh poet.[3]

Bevan always had great self-belief and a sense of purpose; I do not discount the possibility that his parents' choice of first name contributed to this. Indeed, it is fitting that his name had a literary genesis given his own passion for the arts. The name also has distinctively *Welsh* literary roots. This again brings into sharp focus Bevan's relationship with Wales. The popularity of events promoting the biography across the UK suggest that Bevan remains significant as a *British* politician. Bevan's beliefs were certainly more about the class struggle, with problems common to the *British* working class, than identity politics, but that is not to say that his own identity was not highly important. As I argue in Chapter Three, Bevan was a 'Monmouthshire Man' representing a particular Welsh tradition from the eastern side of the South Wales coalfield. His speech on the eve of the

1958 Royal National Eisteddfod at Ebbw Vale remains crucial in this respect. *The Times* reported that Bevan saw the very holding of the Eisteddfod in Ebbw Vale as 'an expression of the reunification of Monmouthshire with Wales'. [4] In calling for an end to the use of the phrase 'Wales and Monmouthshire' Bevan was locating his own Ebbw Vale constituency in *one* Wales.

Morgan cites the significance of Rhymney, one of three towns in Nye's constituency of Ebbw Vale symbolised by his three memorial stones in South Wales. Rhymney was known throughout Bevan's time as a Member of Parliament as the last Welsh-speaking town in Monmouthshire. [5] The unity Bevan was calling for between the anglicised Monmouthshire and Welsh-speaking Wales was mirrored in his own constituency between Rhymney on the one hand, and Tredegar and Ebbw Vale on the other.

Morgan also points to the similarity in background between Bevan and Soviet leader Nikita Khrushchev. [6] Khrushchev had worked in the Hughesovka coal mines and been involved in industrial action too. Bevan's speech opposing unilateral nuclear disarmament at the Labour Party Conference in Brighton in 1957, covered in Chapter 16, was preceded by a visit to the Soviet Union, and discussions with Khrushchev. Such shared early experiences could certainly have helped to build a personal rapport.

In publishing this paperback edition I am also pleased to take the opportunity to add clarity to three points picked up by readers. Firstly, Owen Hatherley drew attention to the text giving the wrong impression of the date of the Ukrainian famine. [7] Secondly, Morgan raised the fact that Richard Thomas & Baldwins Ltd, owners of the Ebbw Vale Steelworks in Bevan's constituency, was left in public ownership when steel was re-privatised by Churchill's government in 1953. [8] I have dealt with both points in the text. Thirdly, Michael Hill, a retired Professor of Social Policy, set out the role of local authorities under the National Assistance Act 1948. [9] The Act, as I argued in Chapter 12, plugged gaps in welfare provision. Speaking in the House of Commons during the Second Reading Debate of the Bill, Bevan set out that despite the legislation already passed by the Attlee government, the old Poor Law regime, with its handouts from the 'Poor Law Guardians', and its workhouses, had still not been fully eradicated:

> there will still remain, after all these things have been done, 400,000 persons on outdoor relief, and 50,000 in institutions. There thus remain, after we have bitten into the main body of the Poor Law, these residual categories which have to be provided for. This Bill, therefore, must be seen as the coping stone on the structure of the social services of Great Britain. [10]

Bevan's approach had significant long-term consequences. He took a strong line on the division between central and local responsibilities: 'The Government approach the problem from the angle that they wish to see the whole residual problem in two special categories. They wish to consider assistance by way of monetary help made a national responsibility and welfare a local responsibility.'[11] This gave 'all the poor law cash-giving powers to the National Assistance Board as a "national agency", the only responsibility it gave to local authorities was the residual residential care.'[12] This is of more than mere academic interest; with our ageing population, adult social care remains one of the great policy challenges we face. It is a matter of debate whether there will, in the longer term, be a National Health and Care Service (as proposed by the Labour Party at the 2015 General Election), or a more locally-based service, and how provision will be funded. Certainly, however, the Welsh government's joined-up approach to health and social care points a way forward.

Such policy considerations now regularly occupy my thinking. For I will never forget the year that has passed since this biography was first published. I was selected as the Labour Party candidate for my home constituency of Torfaen, adjacent to Bevan's own Ebbw Vale constituency, on 7 March 2015 and, just two months later, in the early hours of 8 May 2015, I was given the extraordinary privilege of representing the people of my valley in the House of Commons when I was elected their Member of Parliament.

In recent months, I have often recalled Bevan's advice to a newly-elected MP:

> His first impression is that he is in church. The vaulted roofs and stained-glass windows, the rows of statues of great statesmen of the past, the echoing halls, the soft-footed attendants and the whispered conversation, contrast depressingly with the crowded meetings and the clang and clash of hot opinions he has just left behind in his election campaign. Here he is, a tribune of the people, coming to make his voice heard in the seats of power. Instead, it seems he is expected to worship; and the most conservative of all religions – ancestor worship.[13]

There is definitely an ecclesiastical feel to the Palace of Westminster. As a historian I cannot help but be fascinated by the rich history of the place, yet at the same time I studiously avoid being overly-reverential to the past. Much has changed for the better since Bevan uttered these words. For a start, his advice was expressed in the masculine form, as there were so few female Members of Parliament in his time. I am proud to sit with 99 women on the Labour benches in the Commons, but I also know there is much more to do to reach a 50:50 gender balance in Parliament.

There are of course lessons from the past to apply to the great challenges of the future, but Parliament is not a place to be overawed by the surroundings. One other Bevan missive also sticks in my mind: 'Election is only one part of representation. It becomes full representation only if the elected person speaks with the authentic accents of those of who elected him.'[14] I will always try to speak in the authentic accents of the people of Torfaen.

NICKLAUS THOMAS-SYMONDS MP

ABERSYCHAN, NOVEMBER 2015

Foreword

I must have been about 11 when I asked my retired grandfather, 'Gramp, which pit did you work in?'

'First, Ty-Trist,' he said, 'and then I moved to the largest colliery in the world, Pochin.'

Surprised at this, I said, 'But that doesn't seem all that big to me.'

'I didn't think so either,' he said. 'But if all those who say they worked with Nye Bevan really did, it must have been the biggest bloody pit on earth!'

Then he told me why so many men made the claim that they'd shared a workplace with Aneurin Bevan. He was the schoolboy who had dared to stand up to his terrorising headmaster, the lodge chairman elected at 19, the Pochin checkweighman chosen by his fellow workers, the councillor locked in weekly combat with the lackeys of the town-owning Tredegar Iron and Coal Company, the Medical Aid Society committeeman helping to manage collective contribution for individual care, the leader of the Council of Action – the 'Tredegar Soviet' – that ran the community in the destitute seven months of the 1926 strike. Nye, my grandfather told me, was the young MP who battered Tories and timid Labourites, who outrageously lambasted Churchill at the height of his wartime dominance; who used – and acknowledged – information from my uncle Bill, a young artillery officer who, like thousands of other servicemen, fed Bevan with briefings from the front line; who secured temporary release from war work for my aunt Dorothy so that she could care for her dying mother. He was the housing minister who insisted on high standards for council accommodation, the blessed bringer of the National Health Service, the often bloodied but always unbowed scourge of exploiters, bullies and any enemy of justice... and much more.

From that conversation on, Aneurin Bevan joined Gilbert Parkhouse, the Glamorgan and England batsman, Ken Jones, the Wales and British Lions wing,

John Charles, 'Il Buona Gigante', of Leeds United, Juventas and Wales, and Merthyr's Eddie Thomas, British and European welterweight titleholder, in my boyhood pantheon of champions.

He stayed there through my adolescence as I saw him (you never merely 'heard' Bevan) speak to packed, electrified Workmen's Hall meetings and read *In Place of Fear*. In my adulthood, Nye's best friend Archie Lush and my beloved comrades Michael Foot and Geoffrey Goodman gave me a deeper understanding of the strengths and shortcomings of this practical, pragmatic, patient, impulsive, politically poetic genius.

That admiration endures. Indeed, it has been reinforced through the years of political and personal experience and is now further refreshed by this biography written by Nick Thomas-Symonds. His research is admirably thorough, his approach is candid and free of hagiography, his treatment of personalities and events swirling around Bevan is illuminating, and his perceptions are incisive and fluently expressed. But what marks this book out from many other Bevan biographies is the intimacy of this young South Walian lawyer's understanding of Nye's background, which so profoundly shaped his values and purposes throughout his life.

Above all, Nick Thomas-Symonds comprehends Bevan's central, propelling quality of audacity.

From his truculent assaults on the Tredegar bosses to his furious, frequently trenchant criticisms of wartime leaders when the reality of peril subdued others; from his certainty – publicly expressed even before the fall of France in 1940 – that the war would be won and Labour must prepare for that outcome to his success in establishing the NHS through guile and slogging determination, compromise and assertiveness; from his forays into decolonisation and his arguments for non-alignment to his support for a nuclear-armed Britain – apostasy to his closest comrades – Bevan was bold.

Some of his bravery came from adversity and, naturally, could be bloody-minded. Much of it came from belief in his own capability and sometimes exposed him to the charge of arrogance – 'men in public life,' he declared, 'need thick skins or an aristocratic temperament,' and he exhibited both, without baring his wounds in public. Most of his courage came from conviction. His democratic socialism was firmly based on the axiomatic certainty that 'free people can use free institutions to solve the social and economic problems of the age, if they are given the chance to do so'. His concept of freedom was cultural and spiritual as well as constitutional. The institutions which could – if fully employed with rigour – energise and safeguard that freedom were those of the parliamentary system. Giving and sustaining the 'chance' for people to be intellectually, vocationally, economically and politically empowered to control their conditions and their destiny was his life's ambition, and his lifetime's work.

To pursue these aims, Aneurin Bevan used his full armoury of articulacy. As a writer, he was brisk and, like most radicals, slightly more measured in print than in spirited speech. As an orator, he was a sight to behold and a sound to summon up the blood.

Bevan was never a ranter, and he despised the demagogic style (and content) of extremist fulminators. He was a debater whose preference was to identify and shred his opponents' strongest points, a teacher who painted word pictures to enlighten or stir his audience, an advocate who would mix forensic detail with rousing declamation, a polemicist who sometimes overstated his case in breach of his maxim that 'if truth be pushed too far it can fall into error' – and suffered damage as a result.

He was an unusually – possibly uniquely – accomplished speaker who, unlike others, could demonstrate brilliance in all of the public arenas then available to pre-TV political communicators. In Parliament, he excelled in the tumult of a crowded Commons or in the almost conversational close combat of a standing committee. He commanded the conference platform – often delighting the spell-bound adoring, sometimes over barracking hostility. At party rallies and on the Trafalgar Square plinth he was compelling as he battled, in those pre-admission-ticket days, with hecklers, the elements and unreliable loudspeaker systems.

His voice was neither sonorous nor particularly resonant. Its tone and rhythm flowed with his vocabulary and emphasis, and his forward-leaning body and jabbing forefinger carried the same current.

From the dark depths of solemnity and in a near-whisper he would rise very gradually, through a fusillade of illustrations and – with a warning grin – jokes, to a crescendo of incredulity and scorn. The occasional sibilant stutter would add to the machine-gun delivery and then, having given the moral or message, he would ram it home with a forceful, damning, dismissive or revelatory conclusion. He could use sweet charm or rhetorical acid, deploy understatement and risk abusive overstatement, be reconciling and impulsive, demonise and satirise – and all of the time he sought to give effect to his credo that a political leader in a democracy 'must articulate the wants, the frustrations, the aspirations of the masses. Their hearts must be moved by his words, and so his words must be attuned to their realities.'

No better advice was ever given to Labour representatives. That rooted belief in the direct, palpable connection that must be made between leaders and the needs and hopes of people and their communities was at the core of Bevan's parliamentary socialism. He was convinced that all major political and economic decisions should be compatible with the well-being of human society and taken through accountable means, and – to him, like fellow believers – the essential purpose of collective action and provision was to enable personal emancipation. 'If the policies of statesmen, the enactments of legislation, the impulses of group activity, do not have for their object the enlargement and cultivation of the individual life,' he wrote, 'they do not deserve to be called civilised.' And being uncivilised in conditions which permitted enlightenment was, to this former miner and one of ten children who left schooling at 13, among the most hideous of offences.

It is, of course, unlikely that – on our continent at least – we shall see Aneurin Bevan's assembly of attributes again. Times, conditions, challenges and expectations shift, backgrounds and experiences alter and – as he recognised – political tools 'have to be renovated and sometimes discarded for others more apt'. What is obligatory for socialists, therefore, is not to cling to dogma or to mistake rigidity for fidelity to the body of guiding principles. It is to 'achieve passion in action in the pursuit of qualified judgements [...] knowing how to enjoy the struggle while recognising that progress is not the elimination of struggle but rather a change in its terms'. The unbending determination to do that, and to conceive and implement enabling and liberating policies that came from it, defined Bevan.

In his poem 'Out of Gwalia', Bevan's friend and constituent, the Rhymney poet Idris Davies, wrote of 'a soul on fire':

A prophet great in anger and mighty in desire.
His words shall move the mountains and make the floods rejoice,
And the people of his passion shall lift the golden voice.
A prophet out of Gwalia shall rouse the heart again, give courage to the bosom
And beauty to the brain.

This is an accurate portrait of Aneurin Bevan. His words and deeds live on.

NEIL KINNOCK, WESTMINSTER, 2014

Acknowledgements

I would like to thank my two excellent researchers: Thomas Braithwaite for his detailed work, and Chris Booth for his superb efforts. I would also like to thank my friend John Dunbabin, emeritus fellow of St Edmund Hall, Oxford, who read the first draft in great detail and provided such useful feedback. I am grateful to Lord Kinnock for writing the foreword to this book and for being so generous with his time in providing an interview. The late Tony Benn, Lord Healey, Lord Touhig and Dr Hywel Francis MP were also kind enough to give me interviews. Robert S. Cornish (great-nephew of Clement Attlee) took the time to write to me. Professor Dai Smith has been extraordinarily helpful, giving me an interview, corresponding with me and granting me permission to quote from the extensive papers he was given by Michael Foot, which are now deposited in the Richard Burton Archives, Swansea. Indeed, I should also place on record my thanks to Elisabeth Bennett at the Richard Burton Archives, and my gratitude to Sian Williams at the South Wales Miners' Library for her assistance, particularly with locating and referencing oral source material. Professor Smith also pointed me in the direction of Susan Demont's 1990 thesis, 'Tredegar and Aneurin Bevan: A society and its political articulation 1890–1929'. Susan is a former student of Dai's, and he was the supervisor of the work. Astonishingly, this fine piece of research is still unpublished. I have contacted Susan and thanked her for all the help the thesis has given me, but I would also like to thank her again here. Darren Treadwell at the People's History Museum, Manchester, provided great assistance. I also thank Colin Harris and the archivists at the Bodleian Library, Oxford, together with those at Nuffield College; the archivists at the Modern Records Centre, University of Warwick; at University College, London; at the Open University, Milton Keynes; at the Gwent Archives, Ebbw Vale; and at the British Medical Association, Tavistock Square. I would also like to thank Megan

Fox, who was so generous with her time in helping me collect material for this book. Her grandfather was in the Query Club, and she very kindly took me to interview two of Aneurin Bevan's Tredegar contemporaries, Dai Price and Jack Thomas. I was very sorry to hear that Dai and Jack both passed away in 2012. I am very grateful to Jaselle Williams, the great-granddaughter of Aneurin Bevan's brother William Bevan, her parents, Councillor David Williams and Jane Williams (Aneurin Bevan's great-niece), and Margaret Bevan. Margaret ('Betty') married William's son, 'Little Nye'. They have all provided me with their recollections and given invaluable access to the papers in their possession. These were originally the papers of Aneurin Bevan's sister, Arianwen Bevan-Norris, who served as his secretary for a period. Jo Godfrey, at I.B.Tauris, was a constant source of support and advice, as was Alex Middleton at the editing stage. I should also like to express my deep gratitude to Geoffrey Goodman. Geoffrey was an incredible source of information and support in the writing of this book, providing me with numerous interviews and commenting on drafts. His involvement undoubtedly improved the quality of my work significantly. I was very saddened when he passed away in September 2013. I can only hope that this book is a fitting tribute to his contribution to producing it. Any faults or errors in this work are, however, my responsibility alone.

Introduction

On Sunday, 4 November 1956, nearly 30,000 people gathered at a large demonstration in Trafalgar Square organised by the National Council of Labour. The main speaker on the platform was Aneurin Bevan, then the Labour Party's Shadow Colonial Secretary. From his hard manual work as a miner underground when he was a teenager, he had an imposing physique. His dark suit contrasted with his side-parted, white–grey hair. He was a towering presence alongside other Labour speakers, including the MPs Tony Greenwood and Edith Summerskill. The rally marked the launch of a campaign against the Conservative government's policy in Egypt. Months earlier, on 26 July, the Egyptian Republic under Colonel Nasser had nationalised the Suez Canal. The prime minister, Anthony Eden, responded with military force, and, on 31 October, Britain and France began a campaign to recapture the canal with a bombing campaign. It later emerged that the two countries had reached a secret agreement with Israel, which had invaded through the Sinai Peninsula two days previously. Protesters carried 'Law, Not War' banners, which, according to *The Times*, formed a 'small forest' above the crowd.[1]

Bevan spoke with his head bent slightly forwards, an accusatory stance emphasised by the use of his hands at important points of his address. His finger-pointing added to the drama of his speeches. He spoke without notes, having practised in his usual way – by marching up and down in private, trying out his best lines on his close friends. Bevan did not believe that Nasser was right. He also thought that Israel had been provoked by the Egyptian leader's actions. But he felt that, by using force in an attempt to solve the 'Suez crisis', as it became known, Eden had stained Britain's international reputation and lowered the country's standing in the world. The use of force was highly dangerous: 'we are dealing with an international situation where there is so much inflammable material around that at any time general war can break out.'[2]

It is one of the few Bevan speeches that has been recorded and is still widely available to listen to.[3] He was on top form, and roused the crowd before him: 'It is a sad, sad story that is unfolding before our very eyes at the present time. A very sad one indeed. I myself feel despondent – really despondent – about the situation into which we have been got, when some young Tories say, "Ah, we are giving the lead."' A man in the crowd shouted back: 'The lead to where?' Bevan always dealt well with interventions. He shot back: 'Yes, the lead back to chaos, back to anarchy, and back to universal destruction. That's not the lead we want. This policy of the British government is a policy of bankruptcy and despair.' Military success would 'only prove that we are stronger than the Egyptians. It won't prove that we are right.'

Bevan was the master of the political barb. The policy of the Labour Parliamentary Committee ('Shadow Cabinet' in modern terms) was to refer the matter to the UN, and against the use of military force. Eden had, however, acted without UN authority, and Bevan seized on some rather unwise remarks from the prime minister on the effect of the invasion: '*Sir* Anthony Eden has been pretending that he is now invading Egypt in order to *strengthen* the United Nations. Every burglar of course could say the same thing, he could argue that he was entering the house in order to train the police.' He adopted a mocking tone: 'So, if *Sir* Anthony is sincere in what he is saying, *and he may be, he may be* […] then he is too *stupid* to be a prime minister.' The stress on words starting with the letter 's' was a result of Bevan's stammer, a childhood problem that he had strived to conquer. Sometimes – as in this section of the speech – it served to enhance the effect Bevan created, since it introduced a natural emphasis on certain key words. However, he also often used non-obvious words, avoiding those that brought out the problem. Thus, he made the charge later in the speech that the Conservative government had 'besmirched [not 'sullied'] the name of Britain'. Another of his oratorical weapons was humour:

> Many Tory newspapers today are saying: 'Ah, well maybe we are judging too soon. It may be that Eden will get it all over with and then we can breathe a sigh of relief.' That's what the Germans said about Hitler. They said: 'Ah, well, he may be a liar, but will he be a successful liar?'

As the crowd roared with laughter, Bevan swept on: 'They said he is a bully, but will he be a successful bully? They were perfectly prepared to accept his morality, so long as he gave them the prizes.'

Bevan was a man of substance, and the thrust of his critique of the government's use of force was that, while Egypt might be weaker than Britain, equally, there were other countries much stronger than Britain. Even if you accepted the case for bullying (which Bevan did not), there was little point unless you were the strongest bully in the playground: 'Are we prepared to accept for ourselves the logic we are applying to Egypt? If nations more powerful than ourselves accept the absence of principle, the anarchistic attitude of Eden, and launch bombs on London, what answer have we got?' If force was the 'arbiter to which we appeal, it would be at least common sense to try and make sure beforehand that we have got it.' Eden was not only wrong, he was incompetent:

> Even if you accept that abysmal logic, that decadent point of view, and if you are going to appeal to a court whose answer you are going only to accept if it is in your favour, you might take care to pack the jury beforehand. But of course we can't do that.

He wound up powerfully. Losing his temper was to bring him problems at times during his political career. But when he became angry during his speeches, it had an emotive effect: 'I say to *Sir* Anthony, I say to the British government, there is no count at all upon which they can be defended.' He reached his peroration: 'They have made us ashamed of the things of which formerly we were proud. They have offended against every principle of decency and there is only one way in which they can begin to restore their tarnished reputation and that is to *get out, get out, get out!*'

Less than four years after this great speech, Bevan was dead, succumbing to stomach cancer on 6 July 1960, at the age of 62. There was an outpouring of national mourning, with glowing tributes from the press. The *Daily Herald* reported that 'MPs weep in the Commons', and that, in the South Wales Valleys, there was 'sorrow at every street corner'.[4] The *Daily Express* lauded Bevan: 'Farewell, Bright Spirit [...] Unmanageable, Incalculable, Adored – and Hated [...] Bevan *was* the history of Socialism.'[5] Michael Foot led the tributes in the left-wing weekly *Tribune*: 'Aneurin Bevan was unique. There was no one else even remotely like him.'[6] Bevan's stature in the national consciousness has grown over time. In the BBC's *100 Greatest Britons* poll of 2002, Bevan was placed third-highest of the six twentieth-century politicians who made the list, coming in at 45th, with only Margaret Thatcher and Winston Churchill ahead of him, in 16th place and first place, respectively.[7] On St David's Day 2004, it was announced that Bevan had been voted the greatest ever Welsh person in an online poll.[8] The legend of Aneurin Bevan is one of powerful, emotional oratory and political fearlessness: a willingness to stand up for what he believed in any circumstances, and, if necessary, at great personal cost. In 2011, even such disparate modern columnists as William

Rees-Mogg and Caitlin Moran referred to Bevan's speech-making and political bravery. Rees-Mogg, commenting on US President Barack Obama's speech in Westminster Hall on 25 May 2011, declared: 'The natural orator who can speak like Cicero or the elder Pitt has scarcely been heard at Westminster since the generation of Winston Churchill and Aneurin Bevan.'[9] Moran, in her message to the world's 7 billionth person in November 2011, wrote: 'I pray that you will rise from wherever you are born to acquire great wisdom, bravery and kindness. That you become some incredible mixture of Glinda the Good, Nye Bevan, Obama and Gandhi.'[10] Bevan's name is frequently cited at Labour Party Conferences: to take one example, it was mentioned by no less than five different speakers before lunch on the first day of the Welsh Labour Party Conference of 2012.[11]

The most important aspect of Bevan's lasting reputation is his statesmanship. For he was a great British statesman, the twentieth century's most outstanding government minister who never held the office of prime minister. The National Health Service that he created on 5 July 1948 is no mere monument to his success. Rather, it is a living, breathing example of his democratic-socialist principles, applied pragmatically to bring a better life for his fellow citizens. With a budget of over £108 billion, the modern-day NHS is the world's largest publicly funded health service, employing more than 1.7 million people and providing health care to over 63 million people in the UK.[12] Such is the scale of Bevan's achievement that the central principle of the NHS, care free at the point of delivery on the basis of need regardless of wealth, is uncontested by any major political party over 60 years after the service's foundation. No politician dare promise outright privatisation of the NHS. Still improving the lives of millions of people in the twenty-first century, the NHS is the Labour Party's greatest achievement. Appointed Minister of Health and Housing by Prime Minister Clement Attlee after Labour's landslide election victory was declared on 26 July 1945, Bevan persuaded the reluctant medical professionals to join the service and make it work. His own description of the struggle to establish the NHS has entered the national lexicon: the doctors had their mouths 'stuffed with gold'.[13]

Of those ministers who did not hold the office of prime minister in the postwar era, perhaps only another South Wales politician, Roy Jenkins, with his social reforms as Home Secretary from 1965 to 1967, can compete with Bevan's achievements.[14] For Bevan was, above all, a man of power. The second paragraph of his only book, *In Place of Fear*, is a succinct expression of the central importance of power to his political life: 'A young miner in a South Wales colliery, my concern was with the one practical question: where does power lie in this particular state of Great Britain, and how can it be attained by the workers?'[15] His life has been described as one long search for power. The famous story is of him walking in

Tredegar, when his father pointed out a member of the local Urban District Council as a man who possessed power. Remembering this, Bevan secured election to the Urban District Council. However, in a discussion with a clerk to that council it was explained to him that power had now moved to the county council. Bevan was soon elected to the county council but found no power there either, being told that power actually lay with the government in Parliament. Bevan was then elected to Parliament in 1929, but when he got there he found again that, like a bar of soap, power had slipped from his grasp and that it was actually monopolised by the Treasury bench.[16] Bevan sought power for a purpose. He was at ease with power; he could use it for the benefit of working people; he was a skilled negotiator. His famous remark that people who stood in the middle of the road were run down could be misleading. He *could* compromise when he needed to; and, above all, he could apply his socialism in practice.

Bevan was also a deeply controversial figure. During the Second World War he became the principal opponent of the coalition government, the leader of the opposition in all but name. Although it may be argued that Churchill should still have been held to account, even in wartime, with the lives of friends and relatives being lost every day in the fight against Nazism, Bevan's stance was always going to be impossible for the public to accept. Bevan and his wife Jennie Lee regularly received parcels of excrement through their letter box.[17] Famously, in his speech at the Labour Party rally of 4 July 1948, on the eve of the launch of the NHS, Bevan attacked the Conservative Party in visceral terms. Talking about his childhood in Tredegar, Bevan almost spat out his disgust, saying that 'no attempts at ethical or social seduction, can eradicate from my heart a deep burning hatred for the Tory Party that inflicted those bitter experiences on me. So far as I am concerned they are lower than vermin. They condemned millions of first-class people to semi-starvation.'[18] Conservative activists formed 'Vermin Clubs', and Herbert Morrison lamented that Bevan's words 'did much more to make the Tories work and vote [...] than Conservative Central Office could have done.'[19]

It made him a hate figure among many Conservatives. When he spoke in public, he was often heckled, with the word 'vermin' thrown back at him by the crowd. When he stood against Hugh Gaitskell for the party leadership in 1955, an anonymous Conservative correspondent (who preferred him to Gaitskell) illustrated the level of animosity towards him: 'Although I hate you like poison (since I am one of the "vermin" you would like to exterminate) I would much rather see you in Attlee's place than that pseudo-intellectual upstart.'[20] In the 1950s, Bevan was the authentic socialist bogeyman of the right-wing press, seeking control of the Labour Party and the country to implement his left-wing vision. On the eve of the 1955 general election, the *Daily Sketch* tried to scare voters with the prospect of Bevan as prime minister, reporting a plot to depose Attlee if Labour won.[21] When Bevan was elected Labour Party treasurer on 2 October 1956, *The Times* called it 'real evidence of the hold Bevan has on the Socialist Party'.

For so polarising a figure Bevan has attracted a small number of biographies. The first was by Vincent Brome, published in 1953. Interim biographies can provide authentic first-hand impressions denied to the later historian. Yet Brome had an uncomfortable relationship with Bevan himself, frustrated at his subject's reluctance to endorse his book in any way.[22] Perhaps Brome's difficulties with Bevan contributed to the book's poor critical reception.[23] There was a second biography published in 1961, a year after Bevan died, by an American, Mark Krug. Krug characterised Bevan as a 'cautious rebel' and sought to explain the Bevan phenomenon to an American audience. Krug is able to capture the American suspicion and dislike of Bevan's socialism.

It is typical of Bevan that his two major biographers should have such conflicting views. Michael Foot's monumental two-volume study of Bevan, published in 1962 and 1973, and covering 1,164 pages, is the greatest partisan political biography written in the twentieth century. It is a rich primary resource for historians. Written with verve and passion, Foot's conclusion captures Bevan's impact on his followers: 'For Socialists, for those of us who heard him speak and talk and argue and who shared his political aspirations, he was the man who did more than any other of his age to keep alive the idea of democratic Socialism.'[24] Foot's friendship with Bevan gave him an insight that all Bevan's other biographers lacked. At the same time, this friendship – and personal hostility to Gaitskell – makes him part of the Bevan story. Objectivity is necessary for an assessment of the Foot–Bevan relationship, particularly in the difficult period after Bevan's repudiation of unilateral nuclear disarmament in his speech at the Labour Party Conference in Brighton in October 1957, an issue that divided the two men politically and personally. One major difference between Bevan and Foot was their attitudes to power. Bevan – like his fellow Welshman David Lloyd George – was an outsider but with an instinctive grasp of ministerial power and how to utilise it. Foot was an instinctive rebel. Indeed, so keen is Foot to place Bevan in the dissenting tradition that the first chapter of his biography opens with a quotation from William Hazlitt: 'It is hard for anyone to be an honest politician who is not born and bred a dissenter.'[25] Moreover, Foot's biography was inevitably going to be subject to amendments: the first Attlee Cabinet papers, for example, did not enter the public domain until 1975, two years after the appearance of Foot's second volume.

Jennie Lee's well-written *My Life with Nye* appeared in 1980, illuminating not only Bevan's personal life but also the breadth of his intellectual and cultural interests. As his wife, she had provided him with great emotional support, and the book brought out Bevan's softer side. There was not only his tenderness towards her, but also his caring attitude to her parents, who lived with them from the late 1930s onwards. It also revealed his strong desire for privacy as his every move became subject to press scrutiny in the 1950s.

When the next major biography of Bevan, by John Campbell, appeared in 1987 it drew a bleak conclusion about his life's work. Its approach was captured in the title, *Nye Bevan and the Mirage of British Socialism*. For Campbell:

> The sad [...] fact which the biographer has to face is that Bevan's life – the immense achievement of the National Health Service notwith-standing – was essentially a failure, not because of the machinations of pygmy rivals but because his great gifts were for all his life in thrall to an erroneous dogma.[26]

Campbell's argument is that Bevan was not a rebel but a genuine man of power and that, because his political philosophy was defeated, he must therefore be written off. Campbell is certainly right to identify Bevan as a man of power, but wrong to see him as a failure.

In Campbell's defence his biography was written in the mid 1980s, at the height of Thatcherism, when vast swathes of British industry were privatised. The Attlee government's nationalisation was firmly rejected as a policy prescription both by the government of the day and by the electorate, which elected the Conservative Party for the third consecutive time in the year of the publication of Campbell's book. There was even doubt about the Labour Party remaining as the main centre-left party in British politics. Campbell himself had written an interim biography of Roy Jenkins in 1983, who had cofounded the Social Democratic Party (SDP) in 1981, before forming the Alliance with the Liberal Party, to seek to supplant the Labour Party as the main contender for government against the Conservatives.[27]

There is also an attractive simplicity in Campbell's position. The argument for the historic determinism of a transition to socialism – whatever that means – has weakened time after time as Western liberal capitalism emerges from its periodic crises strengthened. The West triumphed in the Cold War. Even Communist China now has its own brand of so-called 'state capitalism'. Yet Bevan stands out from other twentieth-century politicians *because* of his overarching, developed political philosophy allied to his constructive political skills. As Barbara Castle put it: 'Nye's mastery of parliament was not merely based on his command of oratory: it was due to his power to express Socialism in philosophic rather than narrow party terms.'[28] It is the fact that Bevan had the audacity to express himself in such terms that allows Campbell's criticism to be made at all: in one of his outstanding features lies his apparent downfall.

There is an argument that Karl Marx should not be dismissed out of hand, along the lines of the remark allegedly made by China's first prime minister, Zhou Enlai, who, when asked in the mid-twentieth century about the significance of the 1789 French Revolution, said that 'it was too soon to tell'.[29] Perhaps in view of the global financial crash of 2008 it is unsurprising that thinkers should revisit Marxist principles. Terry Eagleton, in his 2011 book *Why Marx Was Right*, asks: 'was ever a thinker so travestied?'[30] Eagleton argues that Marx 'was even more hostile to the state than right-wing conservatives are and saw Socialism as a deepening of democracy not as the enemy of it. His model of the good life was based on the idea of artistic self-expression.'[31] There is certainly something in this analysis, but it would be ineffective to defend Bevan on the chance that a transition to socialism may still occur hundreds of years hence.

Rather, Bevan's beliefs themselves need to be examined. He admired the Marxist critique of capitalism, but it was a critique better exemplified by another of his favourite authors, the Uruguayan José Enrique Rodó, whose *Ariel* distinguishes between capitalist materialism and the human spirit, providing a critique of the US. Bevan often read aloud from Rodó's *The Motives of Proteus*, emphasising its argument that society should not be uniform, or governed by a lowest common denominator, but seek to raise every individual to the fulfilment of their potential. While Bevan would happily describe himself as having been educated in Marxism, he was not a Communist. Bevan could easily have joined the Communist Party, but did not do so. His friend Arthur Horner, president of the South Wales Miners' Federation (SWMF) from 1936 to 1946, and then secretary of the National Union of Mineworkers (NUM) until 1959, was a Communist. Horner and Bevan were engaged in a decades-long dialogue, with Bevan attempting to persuade Horner to join him in the Labour Party, and Horner seeking to persuade Bevan to join the Communist Party. Bevan was also deeply uncomfortable with the certainties of Communism. As he often remarked to his friend, the journalist Geoffrey Goodman: 'You cannot bring forward the future and impose it now.'[32]

The debate over public ownership has also skewed modern perceptions of Bevan. The commitment to nationalisation in Sidney Webb's 1918 version of Clause IV of the Labour Party Constitution was replaced by Tony Blair in 1995. Blair had succeeded where Bevan's old rival, Hugh Gaitskell, had failed. Gaitskell had argued that the identification of public ownership as the central purpose of socialism was the product of a 'misunderstanding about ends and means'. Further nationalisation was not crucial to creating a more equal society.[33] It now appeared that Gaitskell had been right all along: his problem was only that he was a man ahead of his time. There is no doubt that Bevan passionately believed in public ownership. As he put it in his book *In Place of Fear*: 'The conversion of an industry to public ownership is only the first step towards Socialism. It is an all-important step, for without it the conditions of further progress are not established.'[34] With Clause IV changed, Bevan now seemed not only obsolete, but apparently on the wrong side of history. Yet such analysis is to misunderstand Bevan's position.

Firstly, Bevan did not see the Attlee government nationalisations as a panacea. He was strongly critical of Herbert Morrison's model of using boards to run the nationalised industries with ministers taken out of the day to day administration: 'the boards of our nationalized industries, in their present form, are a new and potentially dangerous problem, both constitutionally and socially. We still have to ensure that they are taking us towards Democratic Socialism, not towards the managerial society.'[35] Secondly, it would be unfair to characterise Bevan as thinking that all businesses should be under public ownership. He put it best himself in what was to be his final conference speech in 1959: 'If it is said that we lost the election because of our belief in public ownership, then 12,250,000 people voted for us because they believed in public ownership. It is not a bad start-off, is it?'[36] But crucially, he added: 'I believe in public ownership but I agreed with Hugh Gaitskell yesterday: I do not believe in a monolithic society. I do not believe that public ownership should reach down into every piece of economic activity.'[37] The basic idea was an echo of a speech Bevan had given a decade earlier, at the party conference of 1949: 'It is of no advantage at all to a Socialist that private enterprise should be languishing.'[38] He made a key distinction between immediate priorities and ultimate goals. In the 1950 general election, which Labour won with a tiny majority of five seats, the party had promised to nationalise only sugar beet manufacturing and sugar refining, the cement industry and, if necessary to 'assure vital national interests', sections of the chemical industry. The party held a conference in Dorking on 20 and 21 May 1950 at which they discussed the election result. The case Bevan put for nationalisation was a pragmatic one. He argued that the *commitment* to nationalisation had to be retained, otherwise the Labour Party could be outflanked to the left. If nationalisation were abandoned, he was sure Arthur Horner would win the Rhondda Valley parliamentary seat as a Communist. The firm commitments on sugar and cement should be retained; to abandon them would be to sound a retreat. There was a strong logic to the proposals, since both industries were private monopolies, with sugar even having statutory protection. Thus, while he argued for the principle of further nationalisation, he also argued that a list should be drawn up of those private enterprises that would *not* be nationalised, to provide reassurance. He gave the example of industries mostly 'under the personal control of the proprietor', such as small engineering firms and shops.[39] Herbert Morrison noted, wryly: 'If I had made this proposition Nye would have accused me of being a Tory.'[40] For Bevan, the *vision* of the society he wanted to create was the key. That was why the existing promises should not be abandoned: 'How can we put forward an ethical appeal if we leave our wounded on the battlefield?'[41] At the same time, he was a realist. His famous remark was that the 'language of priorities is the religion of socialism'.[42] As he put it: 'If there is something wrong with an industry, it ought not to be necessary for us to take the whole of it over. It might even not be necessary to take any of it over.' He saw the elimination of restrictive practices and monopolies in the private sector – 'those restrictions that prevent private enterprise from playing its proper part' – as important.[43]

It is a major error to see Bevan in the late 1950s as a deluded swimmer with his arms hopelessly flailing against the capitalist tide. He certainly disliked the materialistic society of the 1950s. For him, the desire for private consumer affluence flew in the face of the social good: 'This so-called affluent society is an ugly society still. It is a vulgar society. It is a meretricious society. It is a society in which priorities have gone all wrong.'[44] Neither had he accepted defeat in his arguments for socialism. There is a confessional section in the final paragraphs of Bevan's 1959 Labour Party Conference speech. Perhaps this was because, as the *Daily Express* claimed on his death, he already sensed that his life was drawing to its close, even though overt physical symptoms of his stomach cancer had not yet manifested themselves.[45] Bevan was a fighter to the end:

> Are we going to accept defeat? [...] Are we going to send a message from this great Labour Movement, which is the father and mother of modern democracy and modern socialism, that we in Blackpool in 1959 have turned our backs on our principles because of a temporary unpopularity in a temporarily affluent society?
>
> Let me give you a personal confession of faith. I have found in my life that the burdens of public life are too great to be borne for trivial ends. The sacrifices are too much, unless we have something really serious in mind; and therefore, I hope that we are going to send from this Conference a message of hope, a message of encouragement, to the youth and to the rest of the world that is listening very carefully to what we are saying.[46]

However, Bevan was not an intransigent ideologue, either in the application of his political philosophy or in the tenets of the ideology itself. As Barbara Castle put it:

'Nye had no use for rigid ideologies. He was a free spirit with too creative a mind to be trapped in any dogma which prevented him from questioning its validity.'[47]

Bevan believed in a positive role for government and public spending: 'We will never be able to get the economic resources of this nation fully exploited unless we have a planned economy in which the nation itself can determine its own priorities.'[48] From his time as a miner, he recognised the necessity of collective action. However, this was not to be at the expense of individuality: Bevan wanted each and every person to flourish and develop. This is captured in his remark: 'The purpose of getting power is to be able to give it away.' One reason that he was inspired by Rodó was the latter's emphasis on individual fulfilment. Bevan's idea that the individual is powerless in the face of the financial power of large corporations has a modern resonance. Perhaps the challenge for the twenty-first century is not to write off this creed: to use Bevan's phrase, to ask not how British people can conquer the 'commanding heights' of the domestic economy, but how the world's citizens can exercise democratic control over the 'commanding heights' of the global capital markets.

Even as Bevan's reputation hit the low of the Campbell biography, its rehabilitation also began. For Bevan's pursuit of power was not indicative of an overriding personal ambition. Nor was he inflexible. Rather, he had a keen recognition of the need to translate principles into practice. This was well captured by Kenneth O. Morgan in his essay on Bevan in his 1987 work *Labour People*: 'He was unusual, almost unique, in the Labour Movement in combining strong socialist principles with rare creative gifts of practical statesmanship.'[49]

Dai Smith then started work on a biography of Bevan. Michael Foot provided him with papers that now fill seven boxes in the Richard Burton Archives in Swansea. Foot's original biographical drafts can be found in those boxes, along with newspaper cuttings and other original papers that have been utilised here. Of particular use are the interviews conducted by Hywel Francis, who later served as MP for Aberavon, and others with Bevan's contemporaries, including his great friend Archie Lush. That Smith did not complete the book is undoubtedly a loss to the historiography on Bevan. But the work Smith did produce, *Aneurin Bevan and the World of South Wales*, is an outstanding addition, contextualising Bevan's career in the culture of the South Wales Valleys. For Smith: 'Imagining Aneurin Bevan's culture is an essential pre-condition to comprehending his politics.'[50]

On the 100th anniversary of Bevan's birth, in 1997, Smith, along with other writers, from Will Hutton to Barbara Castle and Alan Watkins, contributed essays to *The State of the Nation: The Political Legacy of Aneurin Bevan*, edited by Geoffrey Goodman, covering topics from the birth of the NHS to Bevan's relationship with Wales, his leadership potential and his legacy. A further short, balanced biography of Bevan was written by Clare and Francis Beckett in 2004. Most recently, in 2011, Kenneth O. Morgan produced another fine essay on Bevan, locating him – largely – in the mainstream of Labour politics. For Morgan, Bevan 'remains a giant in Labour's Valhalla – but a giant as much of the centre ground as of the left'.[51]

This biography is produced for three main reasons. The first is to attempt to move beyond the two views adopted by Foot and Campbell. The analytical space between the two biographies is vast. Foot may at times lapse into hagiography, but, equally, the life of the creator of the NHS should not be castigated as a failure on the Campbell thesis. Secondly, this book has the benefit of new material, including the official papers that were unavailable to Foot and of the additional documents Foot provided to Smith, together with the aforementioned interviews conducted with Bevan's Tredegar contemporaries by Hywel Francis. Aneurin Bevan did not leave a set of his own personal papers, but the documents left by his sister, Arianwen Bevan-Norris, who served as his secretary for a period, have proved quite a find. With this material, this book seeks to demonstrate the central importance of Bevan's local political experience to understanding his political career, which has been neglected by his biographers. To take one example, Campbell argues: 'Bevan was a county councillor for only a year.'[52] This is not even factually correct: Bevan was actually a county councillor for two periods between 1928 and 1934, the first for three years, and the second for just over two years. Thirdly, this book seeks to demonstrate why Aneurin Bevan remains relevant in the twenty-first century, although it is not uncritical.

In doing so, it seeks to rise to the challenge Bevan laid down to all historians when he said that all history was gossip, with the political autobiographies and biographies the least truthful. Bevan was a historical giant. Recognising his great achievements is a central part of understanding his story. It is crucial to understand Bevan the man, and the role of those close to him – not just his family and his wife Jennie Lee, but his best friend Archie Lush, Michael Foot and others. Bevan was a complex man. His judgement could be in error. Yet recognising his faults is to recognise all the elements that make up the kaleidoscope that is the political life of Aneurin Bevan.

Part I

Boy to Man, 1897–1919

Chapter 1

The Welsh Valleys Childhood, 1897–1911

'I never used to regard myself so much as a politician as a projectile discharged from the Welsh Valleys.'[1] With that pithy phrase, Aneurin Bevan captured the significance of his childhood. The generic description 'Welsh Valleys' is an over-simplification. There is a common industrial heritage in iron and coal, but small and distinct communities are scattered on the hillsides around the pitheads. As Dai Smith puts it: 'The coalfield is a tablecloth shaken vigorously and frozen unexpectedly. It is everywhere the same cloth, it is everywhere a different part of that cloth.'[2] Aneurin Bevan was born on 15 November 1897 in Tredegar, which is located at the top of the Sirhowy Valley, on the eastern side of the South Wales coalfield. Sirhowy is one of three valleys running almost parallel north to south, with the Rhymney Valley to the west and the Ebbw Valley to the east. Only the Eastern Valley then lies before the Monmouthshire countryside. Aneurin's childhood world was certainly local to Tredegar, but common features of the whole Valleys tablecloth are visible throughout his British political career.

Most distinctively, there was the Welsh Valleys lilt in his speaking voice, with its distinct rhythm, stress placement and timing. Bevan's critics often sought to place a negative South Wales image on him. He could never have been, for example, a 'Tito of Tonypandy', as some in the British Medical Association labelled him during the negotiations to create the NHS.[3] He never lived there; neither did he even live in the vicinity of the Rhondda Valley. Tonypandy was associated with the riots of 1910–11, and was well known as a cradle of public disorder. Churchill also called him the 'minister of disease' and always pronounced his name Bev-*anne*. This was not simply to distinguish him from Ernest Bevin. It was also a mocking of his Valleys accent. Yet the accent was crucial to Bevan's oratorical prowess. He had a unique voice. It was distinct from that of another great Welsh orator, Lloyd George. Lloyd George was from Llanystumdwy, and very much a product of 'Welsh Wales', with a very strong *Welsh* accent on the vowels, but without the Valleys lilt. Aneurin Bevan's oratory was suffused with genuine argument, pregnant pauses, vivid imagery and wit. He could shout and soothe as the mood took him. Yet beneath these fine oratorical qualities was the crucial ability to connect emotionally with his audiences. As David Brooks put it in his 2011 book *The Social Animal*: 'Politics isn't primarily about defending interests. It's primarily about affirming emotions.'[4] The connection was dependent upon style: Aneurin Bevan usually spoke without notes. That is not to say that he had not thought about his speeches beforehand, but the ability to speak directly, with full eye contact and without the careful wording of a pre-prepared text, gave him a magnetic quality. His audiences would be transfixed. But the connection is ultimately about substance. Bevan embodied the self-educated working class. The South Wales Valleys were a tough place in the Edwardian age in which he grew up: the working classes lived in a time of low life expectancy, high infant mortality, cramped houses, poor sanitation and long working hours. This is not to convey a sense of a 'poor boy made good' but to understand that Aneurin Bevan's working-class background gave his later utterances – particularly on the welfare state – an authenticity. In 1925, his father David Bevan was 'choked to death by pneumoconiosis' (a lung condition caused by his long-term inhalation of coal dust), but no compensation was paid to him as it was not classified as an industrial disease under the Workmen's Compensation Act.[5]

The society Bevan grew up in was not defined by deprivation. Rather, he thrived on all the different opportunities and experiences that were provided by the South Wales Valleys. Smith captures this: 'in place of the cliché of things, of pit-head, wheels and cloth caps, I propose the sense of a culture that emphasised self-understanding and irony and maturity and the self-confidence and hope that occurred in the process of the making of this dynamic society.'[6] Indeed, Bevan's oratory was perhaps least impressive in his native home. As Raymond Williams said:

> I never trusted Aneurin Bevan for the cynical reason that it takes one Welshman to know another. He comes from only 20 miles away and I'd heard so much of that style of Welsh speaking since the age of two that I was never as impressed with it as other socialists were.[7]

While the *common* industrial struggles of the early-twentieth-century South Wales coalfield certainly shaped the children who grew up in it (and, indeed, shaped the voting patterns of the South Wales Valleys for further generations), that does not mean that every childhood was identical. There is, in any event, almost always a difficulty in drawing firm conclusions about the childhoods of working-class politicians in this era, because there is a lack of primary evidence. The texture of relationships between children and parents is far harder to gauge without, say, letters and diaries. Contrast Winston Churchill, born to a son of the seventh Duke of Marlborough at Blenheim Palace, about whose childhood there is a plethora of available letters and papers. There is little in the way of direct contemporary evidence on the nuances of Bevan's childhood.

The broad narrative is, however, well known. Aneurin was the sixth child of ten. His father David was a Baptist and his mother Phoebe a Methodist, though this distinction within Nonconformity was of little importance to Bevan himself, who later described both his parents as Methodist.[8] Aneurin was one of only six children who survived into adulthood. The eldest, David John, died at the age of eight; then there was Blodwen; William George; Herbert Luther, who died in infancy; Myfanwy; Aneurin himself; Margaret May, who died in 1917; the twins Iorwerth and Idris, though Idris died at birth; and the youngest Arianwen, to whom Aneurin was particularly close in his adult life. Until Aneurin was eight the family lived in a four-roomed house at 32 Charles Street, Tredegar. There was nothing unusual about a family of this size living in such a property at this time in the South Wales coalfield. Nor was the family particularly large by the standards of the time.[9]

While the chapels were central to the Tredegar that Bevan was born into, his childhood coincided with the era in which the politics of the South Wales coalfield shifted decisively. Six days' work and then a visit to chapel in Sunday best was the norm. A 26-year-old evangelist, Evan Roberts, claimed to have had two visions of the Holy Ghost and, in 1904, started a movement of prayer for the outpouring of the spirit. Roberts was from Loughor, a small estuary town to the west of Swansea, but the Welsh religious revival he sparked off went far and wide. Bevan was too young for it to have had any significant impact on him, but men such as Noah Ablett, Arthur Horner and James Griffiths were all deeply affected, convinced along with many others that their society was changing dramatically.[10] Even that central plank of Nonconformity, temperance, was under threat. Smith described Merthyr at this time: 'Here public houses were built of such a gargantuan dimension that they implied the thirst for alcohol was insatiable, and it was, while chapels were thrown up as if they were going out of fashion – and they did.'[11] The Liberal Party, rooted in Nonconformity, fell out of fashion as well. The spread of socialist ideas among the working class in South Wales, together with a rising class consciousness, led – through the industrial struggles, the First World War and the Voting Reform Act of 1918, which provided every adult male over the age of 21 with a vote – to the Labour Party's historic ascendancy over the politics of the South Wales coalfield, which remains even into its post-industrial era. David Bevan exemplified this transition from Liberal to Labour. In the West Monmouthshire constituency he had voted for the Liberal candidate Sir William Harcourt, and it was only in 1906 that he first voted for Tom Richards, who was the miners' nominee.[12] David Bevan received Robert Blatchford's socialist *Clarion*, recently founded in 1891, every week.

David Bevan was an aesthete and good with his hands.[13] In 1906, the family moved to the larger 7 Charles Street, which had seven rooms, to which David Bevan added an additional room. He also installed the first gas stove in the street, a bathroom, an inside toilet and hot water.[14] The house was bought with the family's own money, though there is a dispute as to how much it cost. Michael Foot records the amount paid as £130 with the help of a mortgage.[15] Campbell notes that in 1937 Bevan remembered the sum as £40.[16] David Bevan had a 'Welsh Wales' heritage with ancestors from Carmarthenshire. He belonged to the Welsh cultural organisation Cymmrodorion, and won prizes at Eisteddfodau. He did not, however, teach his children Welsh. Nor would the language have been of great practical use in the English-speaking Welsh industrial Valleys. Aneurin's mother, Phoebe, was from the Prothero family. She was from Tredegar, but her father John was a blacksmith from Hay-on-Wye who had moved to find a job at the Bedwellty Pits.[17] Phoebe Bevan brought order and discipline to the family home. She made ends meet by buying in bulk. In one room there was a chest of drawers in which she kept old and new clothes. When she went shopping to Newport, Cardiff or Bristol she would pick up bargains that she stored in the chest for future use.[18]

An enduring mystery of Bevan's childhood is how he developed his distinctive stammer. One explanation is the bullying he suffered at school. Lord Kinnock states: 'Even in the 1950s, when he faced political difficulties, Bevan would refer jokingly to a teacher and say nothing was as bad as dealing with that teacher. The stammer was a defence mechanism.'[19] Though Bevan's sister Myfanwy won a scholarship to the local grammar school, all the Bevan children first attended the Sirhowy Elementary School. The headmaster there, William Orchard, was Bevan's tormentor-in-chief. It is unsurprising that Bevan felt bullied. On one occasion, Orchard even struck Bevan's chin. That is not to say Bevan did not fight back: he reacted to the physical assault by stamping on Orchard's corns. Bevan even lobbed an inkwell at his headmaster after Orchard had mocked another boy for being absent due to his brother taking his turn to wear the shoes they shared that day. Orchard then kept Bevan in a lower class for a year.

Michael Foot puts it slightly differently, however. For him, the stammer might have provoked the bullying, but the bullying was not its cause.[20] There are two other possible explanations for the stammer. The first is that it was a reaction to the trauma of being forced to write with his right hand, as happened during this era (Bevan was left-handed). The second was suggested by Phoebe Bevan, who was convinced that he developed it by imitating an uncle who came to stay while he was at 7 Charles Street.

John Campbell asks whether Phoebe Bevan was overprotective, but there is little evidence to support this. Aneurin, like many South Wales Valley sons, may well have been what was called a 'Mam's boy', but this is meant in a positive sense: he was close to his mother.[21] He was lucky to have the parents he did. Phoebe kept a good home. She was well organised, with tasks allocated to each of her children. Aneurin's was to cut the bread. She also demanded certain standards of behaviour, with punctuality expected at mealtimes and gossip about the neighbours banned. Myfanwy remembered her mother as 'dominating but not domineering'.[22] Aneurin took his passion for books from his father who, despite working from daybreak to dusk in the pit, was able to introduce Aneurin to a lifelong love of reading. David Bevan loved poetry and taught his children to sing, bequeathing to Aneurin a love of the arts that never left him. As a government minister, he passed legislation to allow local authorities to provide money for the arts, including provision of theatres.[23] Aneurin was less keen on mathematics, and later remarked: 'Any fool can see that two and two make four but it takes a real capacity to stretch it to five or, better still, six or seven.'[24] David Bevan also clearly demonstrated to the young Aneurin that he could engage in cultural pursuits alongside practical political activities: he was an active trade unionist as treasurer of the local miners' lodge.

During his final months at Sirhowy Elementary School, Aneurin had a job working as a butcher's boy at Davies' in Commercial Street, Tredegar. He received 2s. 6d. a week and spent the money on boys' magazines including the *Magnet*, the *Gem* and the *Penny Popular*.[25] David Bevan, for reasons that are unclear, banned all three publications from the house. Perhaps he had sound left-wing judgement. George Orwell, writing in 1939, excoriated the *Magnet* and the *Gem* for their snobbish portrayal of public-school life and right-wing politics: 'their basic political assumptions are two: nothing ever changes, and foreigners are funny.'[26] Whatever the reason, the ban was ineffective: Bevan stored his magazines under Sirhowy Bridge.

He also joined the Sirhowy Bridge lending library. His favourite author was Jack London, whose dystopian novel *The Iron Heel* was published in 1907. Aneurin was fascinated by London's description of the wealthy 'oligarchy' ('Iron Heel') in the US and of how it retained power until a revolution that changed society and brought about a 'Brotherhood of Man'. He found the writings of other American socialists equally congenial. As he put it many years later:

> Insofar as I can be said to have had a political training at all, it has been in Marxism. As I was reaching adolescence towards the end of the First World War I became acquainted with the works of Eugene V. Debs and Daniel De Leon of the United States. At that time I was reading everything I could lay my hands on. Tredegar Workmen's Library was unusually well stocked with books of all kinds.[27]

The timing here does not fit: Bevan was well past adolescence toward the end of the First World War (he was 21 four days after the armistice). Debs and De Leon were also different types of socialist. De Leon saw no purpose in reform of capitalism, without wholesale replacement of the economic system itself, being hostile to what he saw as compromises, such as the provision of old-age pensions.[28] In contrast, Debs did see merit in making specific demands to improve workers' lives (including pensions), and stood five times for the American presidency. Nonetheless, it was unsurprising that both men inspired Bevan. Debs denounced the First World War, and was, as a consequence, imprisoned for obstructing conscription on 14 September 1918. Debs argued passionately for public ownership; De Leon was similarly critical of the lack of freedom of the individual under private ownership. But, despite his taste for reading, Bevan did not show any particular ability in his formal education. He did not even try for secondary school, so he started work at Ty-Trist Colliery at the age of just 13 in November 1911.

Chapter 2

The South Wales Coalfield, 1911–19

C oal production from the South Wales coalfield reached its peak just before the First World War. The saleable output in 1913 was 56.83 million tons.[1] The miners had also gained significant victories. The House of Lords' Taff Vale Judgement of 1901 meant that unions faced a drain in funds since they could be subject to actions for damages in respect of any strike, but this was reversed by the Trade Disputes Act of 1906. Similarly, the Osborne Judgement of 1909 had declared the union levy from workers' pay packets for political activity to be illegal, but this, in turn, was reversed by the Trades Union and Trade Disputes Act 1913.

The Miners' Federation of Great Britain (MFGB) had formally affiliated to the Labour Party in 1908. Yet the SWMF faced two significant issues. The first was about leadership: class collaboration or class conflict? The second was about organisation, and the tension between local autonomy and collective strength. The SWMF had been founded in October 1898, at the end of a six-month-long wage strike. At that time there were seven district unions in the coalfield. The wages in each were governed by the 'sliding scale' where the earnings of miners were directly related to the rising and falling market price of coal. This created a common interest between workers and employers, but had not provided a living wage. The 'sliding scale' was eventually abolished in 1903, but the union leader who exemplified the idea of working with the employers, William Abraham, known as 'Mabon', the first president of the SWMF, remained in place until 1912. Mabon, the epitome of respectability, had been elected as a Liberal–Labour MP for the Rhondda in 1885, and remained in Parliament until 1920.[2] Mabon's successor, William Brace, had been a leading campaigner against the 'sliding scale' and had been elected MP for South Glamorganshire in 1906.

The pamphlet *The Miners' Next Step*, published in 1912, provided a stringent critique of the conciliation policy: 'The old policy of identity of interest between employers and ourselves [ought to] be abolished, and a new policy of open hostility be installed.'[3] Written by the 'Unofficial Reform Committee', its principal author was Noah Ablett, who had a great influence on the young Bevan. The tenth of 11 children, Ablett was born in the Rhondda in 1883. While working as a miner, he won a scholarship to Ruskin College in Oxford, where he studied from 1907 to 1909. In March–April of his final year, Ablett was part of the students' strike. Founded in 1899, Ruskin was a working men's college, but the strikers saw it as supporting the existing capitalist order rather than setting down a Marxist challenge to it. They set up a new Labour College in north Oxford, which then moved to London as the Central Labour College. Its funders included the SWMF, and its effect on the class consciousness of the South Wales coalfield was profound. It 'inspired a new growth of rank-and-file militancy', with many Welsh miners active among the 'Ruskin Rebels': in addition to Ablett, there was Ted Gill, Frank Hodges, Noah Rees and W. H. Mainwaring.[4]

When Ablett returned from Oxford, he ran Marxist classes, principally in the Rhondda and Cynon valleys. He had already formed the Plebs' League in January 1909, which promoted Marxist ideals, and which could count Rees, A. J. Cook and Mainwaring (whom Cook had defeated for the post, and who later became Rhondda East MP in 1933) among its activists. In 1910–11, the miners were defeated in the Cambrian Collieries dispute in the Rhondda. This bitter quarrel, which led to the Tonypandy Riots, had been caused by the tonnage rates set for a coal seam at Naval Colliery, Penygraig, being too low to enable the miners to earn a set living wage. From the summer of 1911, the Unofficial Reform Committee set to work on a programme distinct from that of the SWMF. Many former Ruskin and Central Labour College students attended Unofficial Reform Committee meetings. Many of them were also active in the Plebs' League.[5]

The Miners' Next Step was evidence of a new generation revolting against the old order. It was extremely critical of the miners' leaders, and expressed grave doubts about the whole concept of leadership. For the leader 'prevents the legislative power of the workers'.[6] The problem was that the miners' leaders developed their own self-interest: 'Think of the tremendous power going to waste because of leadership, of the inevitable stop-block he becomes on progress, because quite naturally, leaders examine every new proposal, and ask first how it will affect their position and power.'[7] Ablett denied that he was a syndicalist: 'I call myself an industrial unionist and not a syndicalist.'[8] This may or may not be a meaningful distinction, for Ablett certainly believed in industrial democracy: 'To have a vote in determining who shall be your fireman, manager, inspector, etc., is to have a vote in determining the conditions which shall rule your working life.'[9] Either way, as the miners' historian Robin Page Arnot put it, the pamphlet gave rise to a 'blaze of horrified publicity first in the *Western Mail*, then in *The Times* and then in the other press'.[10] Bevan was inspired by the idea of workers achieving power through their own industries: 'Going to Parliament seemed a roundabout and tedious way of realising what seemed already within our grasp by more direct means. As a South Wales leader of great intellectual power and immense influence, Noah Ablett, put it, why cross the river to fill a pail?'[11] Bevan did, however, lose faith in this creed in the 1920s, particularly after the failure of the General Strike in 1926: 'These dreams of easy success did not survive the industrial depression of the twenties. Mass unemployment was a grim school, industrial power was just what the unemployed did not possess.'[12]

The Cambrian Collieries defeat also starkly illustrated the difficulty of acting locally without wider support in the coalfield. Still, vested interests opposed collective action. Local miners' agents were powerful figures who did not want to cede power to a central committee. The miners themselves also looked first to their own pits: 'Since the colliers' wages depended heavily on the local customs and price list that is locally negotiated, his first defence, he felt, had to be at this level. Only half of the monthly contribution of 1*s*. went to the new central executive.'[13] Bevan's life in Tredegar *was* the local pits. As he put it himself:

> Greek mythology had it that each tree was inhabited by a spirit – called I believe a dryad – which died when the tree died. The pit is to the mining village what the tree is to the dryad. When the pit dies the village dies too; when the pit is ill, the village groans. Each is interwoven with the life of the other.[14]

The impact that mining had on the young Bevan cannot be overestimated, transforming him from boy to man. When he started he was still attending Sunday school, moving to the Congregationalist chapel from the Baptist school. When he finished, to attend the Central Labour College, he was a seasoned, well-known trade unionist and rebel, experienced not simply in employment relations in the coalfield, but in the real, everyday grind of being a miner. As he put it: 'Here down below are the sudden perils – runaway trams hurtling down the lines; frightened ponies kicking and mauling in the dark, explosions, fire, drowning.' Rather than feeling pleasantly tired as a result of physical exercise, the miner is exhausted by 'a tiredness which leads to stupor [...] particularly of the boy of 14 or 15 who falls asleep over his meals and wakes up hours later to find that his evening has gone and there is nothing before him but bed and another day's wrestling with the matter.'[15]

Speaking in the House of Commons years later, Bevan recalled: 'I started in the pit when I was 13 years of age, and I do not remember any meal which I had for the following seven years that I did not fall asleep over.'[16] Aside from walking, his physical activity after work was swimming: 'When I was a boy those who wanted to learn to swim went to the mountain pools and tarns, which were also a great depository of dead dogs [...] We were swimming in a soup of decomposing carcasses.'[17]

Bevan's use of the soup image was a typical oratorical device, but there is an element of truth here: in tougher times working-class families did find themselves having to drown their own pets.[18] Bevan later scoffed at the idea that physical education should be suggested to colliers who would be tired from hard labour underground: 'To suggest physical training to those engaged in the mining industry is utterly fantastic.'[19] Bevan was always a fighter, and overcame his exhaustion to broaden his self-education. Often borrowing a thesaurus from the library, he recited poetry, including Keats, Shelley, Wordsworth and Shakespeare, on the hills above Tredegar. By doing this, he conquered his stammer and gained a wide vocabulary. This command of language became a weapon in his political armoury. As health minister, he often had to defend the issue of the cost of the NHS from a Conservative attack. On one occasion, as various Tory MPs made speeches of complaint in the House of Commons, Bevan taunted them for their lack of cheer, using a word from Thomas Gray's poem 'Elegy written in a country churchyard': 'The Tory party used to represent itself as a *jocund* party [my emphasis].' When the MPs failed to understand, he told them they did not understand English any more.[20]

The Plebs' League provided Bevan with a regular Marxist education. Sidney Jones, a thoughtful man who was the chairman of the miners' Abernant and Llanover Joint Lodge, gave fortnightly classes at Blackwood. After the publication of the first volume of his Bevan biography, Michael Foot received a letter from a correspondent who claimed that Jones was the greatest influence on Bevan in his formative years.[21] Bevan not only attended Jones' lectures but he also was a regular visitor for discussions at Jones' home. Bevan is said to have learned the 'telling pause' feature of his oratory from Jones. Jones had attended the Central Labour College and taught Bevan 'a realistic doctrine of revolt'. Perhaps it was from Jones that Bevan learned his pragmatism. Harold Finch, later MP for Bedwellty, who was a contemporary of Bevan's at the Jones classes, saw them as having played a 'very useful part' in his development. Certainly the evolution of Bevan's note-free oratorical style would have been assisted by some of the exercises. For example, students would be given books, which included classic novels such as Charlotte Brontë's *Jane Eyre*, to read over a week or two, and asked to produce a 20-minute summary from memory. Finch noticed that the stammer was improving and that Bevan was gaining in confidence. He was widely read, and, for Finch, 'the star of the class'.[22]

A further influence was Walter Conway. Conway was a miner, born in 1875, who was elected in 1909 to the Bedwellty Board of Guardians and who became Secretary of the Tredegar Medical Aid Society. Conway held classes on 'social science', which Bevan attended. He also gave Bevan advice on dealing with his stammer. Conway told him: 'If you can't say it you don't know it': in other words, prepare your speeches and research the subject in detail.[23] Throughout his political career, Bevan followed this advice, not only preparing but practising his speeches, usually pacing back and forth, often trying out what he wanted to say on his friends. Bevan considered Conway's words to be the 'best advice I ever had'.[24]

It would be unfair to suggest Bevan was anything other than a hard worker. However, this is not to say that his political enemies did not later try to damage his image by attacking him for his behaviour while in the mines. In 1949, *Time* magazine launched a visceral attack, quoting 'one of his former bosses', who said that he was a 'bad little brat'. The (nameless) boss continued: 'he would lie down right there beside the tubs rather than do one stroke.' Bevan would only do what was 'absolutely necessary to earn his minimum wage'. He tried to influence others to be equally difficult and asked the question, 'why should *we* sweat our guts out to fill the capitalists' bellies?' Apparently nothing could be done with him.[25] Bevan was certainly not lazy, but he was an out-and-out rebel.[26] He shared the view about the 'well-to-do' expressed in Rhondda author Gwyn Thomas' novel, *The Alone to the Alone*: 'they seemed to have a lot more of everything than we had, except sense.'[27] He and his brother William lasted only a few years at Ty-Trist, and after a falling-out left to go to Bedwellty New Pits. Bevan's work ethic was demonstrated by the fact that he and his brother were soon earning the highest wages in the pit. Yet a disagreement with the deputy manager (who asked why Bevan was leaving early, only to be told that he was on his way to see the miners' inspector in Newport to report on goings-on at the pit) meant that Bevan and his brother were moved on to the Whitworth Colliery, where Bevan refused to use second-hand timber to secure his stall for the holidays, believing that it would be unsafe. Bevan was then sent out of this latest workplace for a refusal to unload a rubbish dram. Although Bevan was able to prove that he had been victimised, it was something of a pyrrhic victory as the Tredegar Iron and Coal Company sent him to Pochin, which was known locally as a 'bad pit'.

By the end of 1916, Bevan, at the age of just 19, was the chairman of his miners' lodge. He demonstrated his belief that collective strength was crucial by working to create the Tredegar Combine Lodge, which amalgamated 12 pits around the town. The lesson was a simple one, and he had read it in *The Iron Heel*: 'It was the expiring effort of organized labour. Three-quarters of a million miners went out on strike. But they were too widely scattered [...] They were segregated in their own districts and beaten into submission.'[28] In 1917 he was a local delegate to an SWMF meeting in Cardiff. In June 1919, he was an SWMF delegate to the Labour Party Conference in Southport, and supported a resolution to nationalise the coal mines.[29] For Bevan the local coal-owners epitomised all that socialism had to conquer. The pits were less places of work than the tools of the wealthy. Like *The Iron Heel*'s oligarchs, the coal-owners held all the instruments of power. The only viable response was collective action. This would not subsume individuals, but release them to achieve their full potential: 'the hope of individual emancipation was crushed by the weight of accomplished power.'[30]

There is much debate on the issue of Bevan's call-up papers in the First World War. Herbert Henry Asquith's wartime coalition government had introduced conscription for unmarried men in January 1916. When Bevan's time came, the Tredegar Iron and Coal Company had stopped the day's wages of a miner who had ceased work and taken home the dead body of one of his colleagues. This precipitated a strike, and Bevan was away seeking support in other parts of Wales. While he was absent, the call-up papers arrived and his sister Blodwen threw them on the fire. After Bevan had returned, two policemen called at the family home while his sister Margaret lay dying. Bevan was concerned about his ill sister being disturbed and went with the policemen. He was eventually kept at Tredegar police station overnight. He initially argued that there was an error: he knew that the call-up quota for his local colliery was 30 and that he was 31st on the list. He was bailed, and when the case was brought before magistrates a month later Bevan produced a medical certificate confirming he had nystagmus, a miner's disease of the eyes that had been caused by working in the dark. Bevan was opposed to the war, as were many others on the left. He remarked that he would choose his own enemy, and his own battlefield. The incident did not damage Bevan in the way that being a conscientious objector in the Second World War would have done. After all, with his anti-war stance, he was in good company in the Labour movement. Ramsay MacDonald had resigned the party leadership in August 1914 on account of his pacifism. Moreover, there was a wider movement in favour of peace, given intellectual depth by the argument that the will of the people should prevail over warring governing elites.[31]

Four days after the guns fell silent on the Western Front on 11 November 1918 Bevan turned 21. Soon after, in 1919, Tredegar's Labour Party was formed, and he was immediately adopted as one of the four candidates for the West Ward council elections of April 1919. Bevan was well known, both because of his reputation as an agitator and as a result of his remarks after the call-up papers case. He was defeated in the election, but not deterred. Later that year he sat an examination for the SWMF scholarships to the Central Labour College, a natural step forward from his classes with Jones and Conway. He won one, and Bevan the autodidact was now to enter formal education, leaving South Wales in autumn 1919 for two years in London.

Part II

The Making of
Aneurin Bevan, 1919–34

Chapter 3

Local Politics, 1919–28

The period of almost 15 years between Bevan's attendance at the Central Labour College in the autumn of 1919 and his standing down as a county councillor in the spring of 1934 were the most important in his life in terms of shaping the politician he became. Reflecting on his career, and that of Bryn Roberts, the runner-up to him in the Ebbw Vale parliamentary selection of 1929, Bevan himself identified this period as key: 'Our ideas were fashioned, and our political motivations fixed by our common experiences in the years between the two Great Wars.' They were 'both haunted by the knowledge of the fine men and women whose lives were broken by the long years of unemployment and poverty that shadowed the Welsh valleys'.[1] There were two tracks, the industrial and the political, temporarily running parallel in Bevan's life, and much of his later behaviour is explained by his experiences over this period.

Bevan was angry at what he saw as the Westminster government's indifference and failure to tackle these problems that blighted his local communities. His anger was partly a matter of nature – that was how he was – but his experiences gave an edge to it that he never lost. He was bitterly frustrated by the fact that people were treated like this, and he laid the blame for the deep poverty he saw around him on the organisation of society and the way its resources were mobilised. The state was an instrument of the propertied classes, and government was stacked in their favour. Later, he sarcastically remarked that: 'This island is made mainly of coal and surrounded by fish. Only an organising genius could produce a shortage of coal and fish at the same time.'[2] The feeling was so deep because Bevan saw the impact of government policies directly on his friends and family, not least his father, with pneumoconiosis. The 1920s also confirmed that Bevan was no rebel doomed to wander in the wilderness with only his doctrinal purity to comfort him. He *applied* his socialism in practice; he himself sought to improve people's lives, not least as the chair of the Council of Action, which virtually ran Tredegar during the General Strike. Crucially he eschewed the Communist Party as a solution to society's problems. That burning sense of injustice and the need to find a workable solution are what made Bevan tick as a politician.

Bevan's 1920s existence in Tredegar should not, however, be seen through rose-tinted spectacles. The environment he existed in also shaped his temperament. It was a tough place to survive in: meetings could be so heated that they were on the edge of physical violence. The atmosphere could sometimes bring out the worst in him. In one incident, Bevan went to see W. D. Woolley, who was from 1923 the Tredegar Iron and Coal Company's general manager, to ask for a job. Bevan was treated badly, left on the mat outside the door, then told that there was nothing for him. By this time Bevan was a member of the Tredegar Urban District Council. According to his Tredegar contemporary, Oliver Powell, Bevan retorted: 'Woolley, in future remember there is a handle to my name. And when you address me in the future, it is Councillor Bevan, and don't you bloody well forget it.' Bevan was not satisfied with only a verbal volley, and stormed up to Markham Pit to get the workers out. One worker, however, was less than convinced by Bevan's motives, and called him a 'bloody twister', leading Bevan to throw himself into the crowd with his fists flying, and his friends had to usher him out.[3] That said, he managed to keep the Markham miners on strike for a week. Bevan's great friend Archie Lush criticised Foot's biography for not having brought out Bevan's temper, which could be vicious: 'I recall his fights (physical) [...] I recall the time when he failed to get a unanimous vote in the DLP [Divisional Labour Party] and how he rushed up to those who voted against him.'[4] Neither could Bevan ever afford to allow his speeches to lose direction or to lose the crowd. His impetuousness could be a problem. He had a habit of interrupting other speakers, which could cause irritation.[5] Once, he was humiliated at a conference in Cardiff organised by the Labour Party at the old Cory Hall. Bevan's speech was simply too long, causing another attendee to stand up and ask, 'What is this, Mr Chairman, Tennyson's Babbling Brook?' Bevan was hurt, and it served as a reminder that Walter Conway was right: impetuous speaking without proper preparation carried enormous risks.[6]

From 1919 to 1921, Bevan lived a dual existence, both locally in Tredegar and at the Central Labour College in London. There are two very different views of Bevan's period at the Central Labour College. Foot takes at face value Bevan's later claim that his time there was a complete waste. He apparently disliked the college routine of waking early and set mealtimes. Foot even manages to portray the one major result of Bevan's attendance at the college, the improvement of his stammer, in a less than positive way: 'He took elocution lessons from Miss Clara Bunn who recalls him reciting William Morris under her instructions. His own real remedy was to hurl himself into speeches or arguments. To the question – "how did you cure the stutter, Nye?" – he replied, "by torturing my audiences." Direct evidence for Bevan disliking the disciplines of life at the college and staying up late into the night debating with fellow students rather than attending formal lectures also comes from the principal at the time, W. W. Craik. For Craik, Bevan still had a lingering dislike of school.[7] Yet George Phippen, from the Rhondda, another recipient of an SWMF scholarship, who was at the college at the same time, felt Bevan not only broadened his horizons, but also developed his self-confidence.[8] He points out that Bevan was able to roam beyond the essential subjects of sociology, economics, philosophy and history, as outside lecturers taught on a range of diverse subjects, including local government, the French Revolution, literature and even the history of London itself. Bevan also went out to evening classes that the college paid for. Together with Phippen, he attended sessions on finance, banking and foreign exchange in Fulham. Even Harold Finch, who noticed Bevan's marked development in Sidney Jones' Blackwood classes, concludes that it was while in London that 'much of his stammer disappeared'.[9]

But there remains a case to be made for this period as an important one in Bevan's intellectual development. That he was still reading voraciously is demonstrated by the books he purchased in London while a student there. These included Joseph Dietzgen's *Philosophical Essays on Socialism and Science*, Ernest Untermann's *Marxian Economics*, the second and third volumes of Marx's *Das Kapital*, Adam Smith's *The Wealth of Nations*, Lester Ward's *Outlines of Sociology*, Charles Darwin's *Origin of Species*, some Dickens novels and Edward Carpenter's *Towards Democracy*.[10] The range of this list demonstrates Bevan's developing intellectual curiosity. Dietzgen's work would have held a particular appeal, since he was self-educated, and propounded a theory of dialectic materialism with the economy as the major driver in societal change.

A strong influence over the Central Labour College was Noah Ablett, who was chairman of the board of governors, and whose ideas permeated the teaching. Jim Griffiths, who was a student at the same time as Bevan, took notes in which it was argued that the Fabian Society no longer dominated Labour thought; rather, it was 'industrial unionism'.[11] Bevan could not have asked for a better peer group in terms of political potential. The Central Labour College intake of 1919 was very strong. Alongside Bevan were not only Griffiths and Ness Edwards, who would be elected Labour MP for Caerphilly in a by-election in 1939, but also Bryn Roberts. Other students during this period included Will Coldrick, Jack Williams and Charlie Brooks, who also became Labour MPs. When Bevan returned to Tredegar in 1921, he assisted Sidney Jones with classes, as did many Central Labour College students.

Also instructive are two articles Bevan contributed to *Plebs*, the magazine of the Plebs' League. The first was written in 1920, and was a report of 'The South Wales "Textbook" Conference' held in Cardiff. Bevan placed great emphasis on supporting the 'class movement' and took pleasure in the presence of delegates from many different organisations and areas: 'The miners, as usual, turned up in force, and so did the railwaymen, practically every NUR [National Union of Railwaymen] Branch in the South Wales area being represented. But the most cheering feature [...] was the presence of so many delegates from other organisations.'[12] Bevan's second article, a critique of *The Communist Manifesto*, is erudite and evidence of his intellectual maturity.[13] Bevan did argue that the next revolution would have to concentrate on destroying 'all private property relations' since the current ruling class possessed so much property that it could be seen as its personification. However, it is also clear that Bevan *did not* see the tract as definitive and unchanging: 'because tactics must always be sought in the conditions immediately at hand, the Manifesto is today tactically valueless, except in so far as persistent stress of first principles is of tactical importance.' He added: 'we should be misunderstanding the spirit of its authors if we attempted for one moment to give its findings the rigidity of a dogma or to make it anything like a touchstone for all time.' Bevan did not see a further revolution as inevitable. Far from it, in fact: he knew that it depended on people's attitudes: 'want and misery alone don't make for a revolution. There must also be present either actual means of amelioration, or potentialities of such sufficiently developed to be recognised. The will to revolution is abortive without the means to give that will effect.' The essential conclusions he drew in this article about *The Communist Manifesto* proved to be central planks of his thinking throughout his political career. He was concerned that the working classes, and their leaders, had *not* seized opportunities when they had been presented.

For Bevan, the first practical example illustrating his analysis was the behaviour of the leaders of the 'Triple Alliance', which consisted of the MFGB, the National Transport Workers' Federation (NTWF) and the National Union of Railwaymen (NUR). Bevan drew significant lessons from this. For Bevan, it was not the might of the state that led to the decision of the leaders of the NTWF and NUR not to strike in support of the miners on 'Black Friday', 15 April 1921, ending the Triple Alliance; rather, it was the failure of the union leaders to consider the consequences of exercising their industrial power. After the First World War and, in particular, the Russian Revolution of October 1917, the prime minister, David Lloyd George, took the prospect of a revolution in Britain very seriously. In his book *In Place of Fear*, Bevan relays a story told to him by the MFGB president, Robert Smillie. Smillie, the transport workers' leader Robert Williams and the railwaymen's leader Jimmy Thomas met Lloyd George together in 1919. The prime minister told the three men that the government was at their mercy, and would be defeated by a strike. But, he added tellingly, 'if a force arises in the state which is stronger than the state itself, then it must be ready to take on the functions of the state, or withdraw and accept the authority of the state.' He asked the three men if they had thought about this, and if they were ready. Smillie told Bevan that they knew they were beaten from that moment. Bevan saw this moment as enormously significant, even more important than the General Strike: 'After this, the General Strike of 1926 was really an anticlimax. The essential argument had been deployed in 1919. But the leaders in 1926 were in no better theoretical position to face it.'[14] Bevan's criticism is not so much that the union leaders were charmed or duped by the Welsh Wizard; instead, it was the fault of the leaders themselves, and, indeed, an expression of the culture of the workers themselves: 'The workers and their leaders paused even when their coercive power was greater than that of the state. The explanation must be sought in the subjective attitude of the people to the extension of the franchise and all that flows from that.'[15] For Bevan, the workers had been too deferential.

The government had taken over the mines during the First World War. Not only had there not been any question of closing uneconomic pits, as all coal that could reasonably be extracted was required for the war effort, but also the miners' wages were not subject to market fluctuations. In addition, the SWMF had in wartime conditions been able to secure a number of demands. Even before the government took control of the South Wales coalfield in December 1916, the Board of Trade had mediated a dispute between the unions and the coal-owners, resulting in a formal agreement on 18 April 1916 for a 'closed shop': all colliery workers had to be members of a recognised trade union. While this did not guarantee the SWMF an increase in membership, as it was one of three such unions, it was a step forward; and, indeed, by February 1921, the membership of the federation stood at over 200,000.[16] However, after the war, there were inevitable questions, not just about working conditions and wages in the economic aftermath, but also about whether the private owners should regain control. When the miners demanded a wage increase, a six-hour day and nationalisation, Lloyd George responded with the offer of a Royal Commission chaired by a High Court judge, Sir John Sankey. The Sankey Commission produced two reports: the first, published on 20 March 1919, recommended a wage increase of two shillings per shift and a restriction of the working day to seven hours; the second recommended nationalisation, though a minority of the commission favoured privatisation. Lloyd George announced that the government accepted the minority view on 19 July 1919. On 31 March 1921, the coal mines returned to private ownership, and any miners who did not accept the wage cuts of the new coal-owners were locked out. The miners' determination during the three-month lockout was to no avail. The demand for a national system of setting wages was lost, with settlements agreed by district.[17]

Bevan's problem during the lockout was that, when he was supposed to be studying at the Central Labour College, he had been unable to resist being back in Tredegar, where the action was. He even chaired a Tredegar miners' meeting during the week that ended with 'Black Friday', when the executives of the NTWF and the NUR announced that they would not recommend strike action in support of the miners.[18] During a time of acute economic distress, the miners were financing Bevan's education. The local Tredegar Valley District Executive of the SWMF therefore wrote to the Central Labour College for an explanation. For neither Bevan nor the other student from the same district, Sam Fisher, had even turned up for the summer term. The reply gave an assurance that permission had been granted in order for Fisher and Bevan to provide help to the SWMF, but the miners were not impressed: 'He was throwing his weight about and the people didn't like it at all. He was interfering and he had no standing with the men actually, but he was always on the platform [...] he wouldn't let go. He was distinctly unpopular.'[19] The funding of Bevan and Fisher was an issue: there was a shortage of money to pay their summer term grant as some of the miners' lodges had not made their contributions to the specific fund used for sending locals to the Central Labour College. A proposal to pay the grants from the general funds of the Tredegar Valley District was narrowly defeated.[20] Bevan would not receive his grant, even if he had been inclined to return to London, which he was not. Making enemies is perhaps inevitable in any political context, let alone the early interwar period in the South Wales coalfield. Even in his own lodge, Bevan 'had tremendous enemies, who hated his guts but they hadn't the intellect [...] to use their hatred.'[21]

One period of Bevan's life that has become legend is the near three-year phase of unemployment he suffered on his return from the Central Labour College to Tredegar. Central to the credibility of his concern for the unemployed, particularly in his early years in Parliament, was the fact that he had been unemployed himself, and had experienced the indignity of having to rely on the earnings of his sister Arianwen. When he spoke on the means test in Parliament, his own experiences lent weight to his arguments: 'There were three of us in the family, my mother, sister and myself, and I was an applicant for extended benefit. I had exhausted my claim to what was then called uncovenanted benefit.' Bevan's sister, Arianwen, was employed as a stenographer, and 'because her earnings, divided by three, came to 11s. per head of those in the family, benefit was disallowed for myself and my mother'. He concluded: 'I can understand the bitterness in the breasts of people up and down the country today, because of my own sense of humiliation when I had to go home and tell my mother, "In future we will have to live upon my sister's earnings".'[22] This cannot have referred to the early 1920s. Bevan's father did not die until 1925, so the three-person household containing him, his mother and his sister would not have existed. His father would have lived there, too; by that time David Bevan's health was failing and he had left the pits to become an insurance agent. Thus, the story can only refer to the second, short period of unemployment Bevan endured when Bedwellty New Pits were closed and he lost his job there as checkweighman in 1925. He remained out of work until the following year, *after* his father's death.

There is a suggestion that the reason for Bevan's unemployment when he returned from the Central Labour College may not have been his inability to find work. Rather, he had no intention of working and actually only wanted to further his position in the SWMF. There is direct evidence that, when he returned to Tredegar, he made a formal enquiry of the Tredegar Valley District as to whether or not he had to be employed underground to qualify for membership.[23] The combine confirmed that he did not. Some evidence in support of this view is provided by his Tredegar contemporary, Oliver Powell, who says that Bevan only applied for a job with the Tredegar Iron and Coal Company *after* losing the chairmanship of the Tredegar Combine Lodge in 1924.[24] One fellow student at the college remembers Bevan receiving a compensation payment for his nystagmus, which he is said to have passed on to his family.[25] If this were the case, Bevan was unfit for work in any event. Yet set against all this must be the evidence of Bevan *seeking* work (for example, his approach to W. D. Woolley discussed earlier) and the inherent implausibility of the idea that he deliberately made himself unemployed and willingly suffered the humiliations that entailed: Bevan even took work on the Urban District Council labour scheme as pipe-layer and trench-digger on pain of losing his unemployment benefit if he did not.

Rather than a deliberate conspiracy to avoid work, Bevan's family, particularly his mother, who was worried about the stormy lodge meetings her son was regularly at the centre of, wanted him to become a barrister, as he had developed significant expertise in advising people on the system of poor relief in operation.[26] Since many of the unemployed were miners, the Tredegar Valley District was heavily involved in assisting unemployed claimants. Bevan represented some unemployed men before the local employment committee. He and Harold Finch divided cases between them, and advised on likely questions that claimants would face.[27] However, while Bevan certainly had the adversarial skills for the Bar, he might well have struggled with the 'cab-rank rule' of having to take any case offered to him, regardless of who the client is: it is difficult to imagine him providing soaring advocacy on behalf of a coal-owner.

There is also a ring of truth in the story Bevan tells in *In Place of Fear* about being deeply moved by the plight of those who were forced by the economic circumstances into emigrating, and that he, in his more desperate moments, had an urge to do so himself. Bevan was one of the leaders of a march by the unemployed on the Bedwellty workhouse. Based in Tredegar, the workhouse was the regular meeting place of the Poor Law Board of Guardians. The real target of the ire of the unemployed was not actually the guardians themselves, but the health minister, Neville Chamberlain, who was only willing to offer the guardians loans to assist with relief if the rates were cut. During the period when the guardians were trapped in the workhouse (two days and two nights), Bevan was standing in the yard with another of the leaders of the march, from Blaina, who was emigrating and asked Bevan to go with him. Bevan was overcome by emotion: 'His words moved me profoundly, for he was a man for whom I had an affection amounting to love, and I felt my eyes flooding.' However, Bevan refused to go: 'if all the young men leave, who is to continue the fight, and I can't bear the thought of seeing them win over us.'[28]

Bevan's response to the 1921 defeat was to form the Query Club over the winter of 1921–2. Members wore badges shaped as question marks. The membership was very selective, and never more than 20. At this early stage, Bevan, as the leading light, was joined by local friends such as Eddie Howells, Oliver Jones, Oliver Powell, the Brain brothers and councillors Rhys Davies and J. B. MacPherson. Only those dedicated to 'the cause' were accepted.[29] But what was 'the cause'? What was the Query Club seeking to do? It was obviously not an intellectual group seeking to debate ideas. Indeed, there is a suggestion that the members were less well versed in Marxism than their frequent quotations from Marx would suggest: Archie Lush claims that the first 27 pages of the Tredegar library copy of *Das Kapital* were dirty, while the remainder of the pages remained clean.[30] The purpose was to utilise all the local political and industrial machines against the Tredegar Iron and Coal Company. The pits were the defining force in the local community, and so the pit lodges and the local district were natural targets, but there were other bodies, too. There was the Workmen's Institute, which included the library, the Medical Aid Society, the Hospitals' Committee, and the Trades and Labour Council. Politically, there were the ward and divisional Labour parties, together with, in the local-government structure of the time, the Tredegar Urban District Council, and, beyond that, Monmouthshire County Council. One major problem in tracing the development of the Query Club is that there are no formal membership records to show precisely what the extent of its influence was. However, those people who are known to have been members certainly took up positions of responsibility in the various community bodies that dominated Tredegar. Oliver Powell was on the Workmen's Institute Library Committee from 1922, and later became its chairman, in 1932. In 1923 Bevan also became chair of the Ebbw Vale Constituency Labour Party (which included, alongside Ebbw Vale, Tredegar and Rhymney). He also took the chairmanship of the local Trades and Labour Council.

Around the same time, Bevan also moved into the Tredegar Medical Aid Society, and served on the Hospitals' Committee. There the Tredegar Iron and Coal Company was influential, with formal representation on committees, having contributed funds to the building of the local cottage hospital, completed in 1904. Founded in 1890, members paid a contribution (miners and steelworkers paid three pence in the pound, for example) to the society in return for health care free at the point of delivery. Much has been made of the Medical Aid Society as a model for the NHS, and, indeed, its principles of operation are very similar, save that the NHS was paid for from general taxation, not specific contributions. Bevan's formative experience in providing health care was undoubtedly the Medical Aid Society. One of the doctors employed by the society, A. J. Cronin, went on to write two novels about coal-mining communities: *The Stars Look Down* in 1935 and *The Citadel* in 1937.

Archie Lush was Bevan's closest friend throughout his life, but he was not one of the original Query Club members. Lush, who like Bevan was unemployed for a period in the early 1920s, initially joined the Communist Party. He fell out with them on the apparently trivial issue of how to approach the selling of the *Socialist Worker*. Lush thought the number of copies sold was more important than the insistence that he stand on a specific pitch. There is no definitive date for when Lush joined the Query Club, but it is reasonable to assume that it was around the time that he became secretary of the Ebbw Vale Divisional Labour Party, in 1924.[31] Bevan was already the chairman, and it is unlikely that he would have allowed Lush to become secretary without a fight had he not already been in the Query Club.[32] The significance of this cannot be understated. Local party secretaries are powerful because they have the potential to control the local political machine, by dint of their access to information and correspondence and their control of meeting structures and agendas. Throughout his parliamentary career, Lush always watched Bevan's back, protecting his interests locally. Bevan and Lush clicked immediately, bound by a shared interest in books and learning. Indeed, Lush became chairman of the Workmen's Institute and Bevan – naturally – chair of the Library Committee, and they also used the institute to play billiards in the evenings after meetings were over. The expansion of the library, and the thousands of volumes it stocked by the end of the 1920s, was a testament to the positive influence Bevan had on his community.[33] It was also with Lush that Bevan walked the mountains, and went on holiday, be it to Cornwall or North Wales. They formed a close and strong bond; all the time they spent together was also made possible by the fact that Bevan had no girlfriend. Lush has said that there were girls, 'a girl in Pontypool' and 'nurses in Abergavenny', but nobody special, and it was only when he later met Jennie Lee that Bevan really brooded about a woman. However, what is fascinating about the Bevan–Lush relationship is not only its closeness – they were best friends in the truest sense – but also the dynamic, with Lush as the junior partner.[34]

Lush was a man of great talent in his own right. Having attended a Balliol College summer school, Lush went up to Jesus College, Oxford. He was a teacher and lecturer who served from 1944 to 1964 as Monmouthshire's chief inspector of schools, and was also chairman of the Welsh Hospital Board. Lush's own explanation is that he was not personally ambitious for a political position, and preferred exercising influence: he liked deciding things before meetings with Bevan. That said, the thought of his own advancement most certainly did cross his mind. There were limits to Lush's loyalty, specifically in relation to the Labour Party itself. Had Bevan ever walked away from the party, Lush would not have been alongside him. Lush *did* think about standing against Bevan in Ebbw Vale if Bevan ever left the Labour Party. His view was that if Bevan stood as an independent for Ebbw Vale, he would win the first election but would find it difficult in any subsequent election if Lush himself were the Labour candidate. When, in 1932, Oswald Mosley formed the 'New Party', Lush told Bevan he could not follow him if he joined.[35]

In April 1922, Bevan was elected to the Tredegar Urban District Council. This local-government experience gave a structure and discipline to his political activity that had not always been present before. The *South Wales Argus* carried the results for the four-member Tredegar West Ward on 8 April 1922: an independent, Reg Jones, topped the poll with 726 votes; two other independents were placed second and third: Dai Morgan with 630 and W. Powell with 620; then Bevan came in fourth with 596. It was hardly a stunning victory, but Bevan was elected, and had a public platform. He had no formal power, as there was an independent majority on the Urban District Council until 1928. Yet, in this six-year period, Bevan showed himself not only to be a fiery debater, but also to have a strong practical streak. The annual general meeting took place on 25 April 1922; Bevan started as he meant to go on. There was a clash between geographical precedent and seniority: a member of the Tredegar West Ward was in line for the chairmanship, but the members were all new, so Bevan proposed that a member of the Georgetown Ward be chairman and a West Ward member be vice chairman; this was seconded and carried 12–3.[36] The meeting was so controversial that it had to be adjourned and continued two days later. Bevan was having a good year. He capped it in December by regaining his position as chairman of the Tredegar Combine Lodge. Also, having failed to be elected checkweighman at Ty-Trist No. 1, Bevan was elected to the same post at Pochin No. 2. This was the one position elected by the miners themselves, though it was paid for the mine-owners. Ablett had been elected to the same role in 1912 at Maerdy Pit. The job was to ensure that the amount of saleable coal being produced was not artificially reduced or increased in order to manipulate the market price.

Bevan's role as a councillor was a constant in his life in a way that his union status was not. For his progress as a union official was hit by frequent setbacks. Having regained the chairmanship of the Combine Lodge, he lost it again two years later, to another Tredegar urban district councillor, William Allen, in a close contest: Bevan received 1,132 votes to Allen's 1,321.[37] Bevan then regained the chairmanship in December 1925. However, he twice failed to be elected to the SWMF Executive, and fell out with his old tutor, Sidney Jones. In October 1924, Bevan was second to Jones by 1,274 votes in a three-cornered contest (Jones topped the poll with 4,724 votes); in June 1927, he lost by 896 votes.[38] Jones and Bevan's voting strengths lay in different areas: Bevan, obviously, in the Tredegar District, and Jones in the Llanover Pit, Oakdale and Wyllie. There is one argument that Jones' district was simply more numerous, and yielded more votes. There is, however, another, darker explanation: the campaigners for both men were guilty of stuffing ballot boxes, but Jones' followers were far more effective at this form of cheating. His ballot-riggers would, allegedly, submit six 'votes' for their candidate at a time, while Bevan's would only put in one fake ballot at a time.[39]

All outstanding debaters need good opponents. Bevan's great rival in the council chamber was an independent, Councillor Bowen. One very revealing Bevan–Bowen debate was on the issue of the Tredegar Urban District Council 'scavenging department', which was responsible for sweeping the streets. Bowen wanted to 'contract out' the service. Bevan opposed this on the grounds that the priority of a public health authority was the well-being of local people, whereas for a contractor it would be pure profit. Bowen proposed that the council invite tenders for a 12-month period to ascertain the cost; Bevan proposed an amendment that no case had been made out for any change in the system. To find a way forward, the sanitary inspector was called in, and he confirmed that contractors had been used before, and that they had neglected street-cleaning in favour of other, more lucrative work. After the sanitary inspector had answered questions, Councillor Bowen's seconder, Councillor W. E. Jones, withdrew, and Bowen could not find a replacement. Bevan's motion was carried with only Bowen recorded as having voted against.[40] One view, put forward by Susan Demont, is that Bevan took an 'essentially pragmatic approach which won him a degree of grudging support from his political opponents and almost certainly created far more opportunities for him to participate in council business than simple oppositionalism would have done'.[41] Indeed, Bevan did not *always* oppose Bowen. On 20 April 1926, Bevan was noted as 'supporting' (though not proposing or seconding) Bowen's nomination to become vice chairman.

Bevan's major priorities were housing and general public health. On his first election in 1922, he immediately became a member of the Health and Housing Committee. Today, it is almost a cliché to refer to the terrible living conditions during this period, but they were a reality of daily life for many working people. The regular health reports for Tredegar tell a sorry story. One weary quotation from the 1928 report from the medical officer of health sums it up: 'Suffice it to say that nearly all housing evils, such as over-crowding, cellar dwellings, tent and van dwellings, and old dilapidated houses, are still with us.'[42] This is not, however, to suggest that the Valleys towns were helpless slums; far from it. There was widespread homeownership. As Minister of Health from 1919 to 1921 in the postwar Lloyd George coalition government, Dr Christopher Addison had pushed through the Housing and Town Planning Act 1919, and his drive for new housing and slum clearance had had a particular impact in Cardiff and Swansea. Addison's progress was, however, swiftly halted by the retrenchment in the public expenditure that occurred as a result of the government's adopting of the recommendations of Sir Eric Geddes' Committee on National Expenditure in the early 1920s – the so-called 'Geddes Axe'.[43] Then there was John Wheatley's Housing (Financial Provisions) Act 1924, a fine legislative achievement of the first Labour government of 1924. This increased the government subsidy paid to local government to build houses for low-paid workers. Strong communities thrived in the Valleys.

The approach Bevan took to housing on the Urban District Council was the very same one he took as Minister of Health and Housing from 1945 to 1951: he did not believe in lowering the standards of housing provided for working people in order for more houses of a lower standard to be built more quickly. The previous Labour council's homes were built 12 per acre, with three or four bedrooms and a parlour. The independents changed this to 16 per acre and took away the parlour. One independent councillor justified this on the basis that people complained that the previous design was not suitable for working men. This drew a sharp rebuke from Bevan, who said he was 'sick of hearing the phrase "working men's dwellings" as if a working man's house should be a rabbit warren. A rabbit warren house led to a rabbit warren life': the Housing Committee was putting the need to cut expenditure above all other considerations, including artistic merits.[44]

In the local elections of April 1928, Labour finally won a majority on the Tredegar Urban District Council, taking ten of the 16 seats. The party had done well across the South Wales coalfield. Bevan took the powerful seat as chair of the Finance Committee, and was immediately faced with the stark realities of power. In opposition, he had often railed against the low level of the rates, arguing for an increase in order to carry out improvements: indeed, Labour's Urban District Council manifesto had promised an increase. However, he did not see the purpose in raising the rates to a level that the already squeezed working class of Tredegar could not pay. So he proposed that the existing rate of three shillings should be frozen. Bowen slammed Bevan's speech as the 'most slippery' he had ever heard.[45] Bevan was less concerned about consistency than he was about pragmatism.

Despite – or perhaps partly because of – his debating style, in which he regularly savaged opponents, Bevan earned respect on all sides. At the meeting of 18 June 1929, ten councillors paid warm tribute to him when he resigned following his election to Parliament. These included Councillor Bowen, who said that Bevan was the first Tredegar-born man to enter Westminster, that he hoped he would 'prosper' and that 'he was sure he would be an asset to the Parliamentary Division and to Tredegar'. On behalf of the officials, the clerk predicted 'a brilliant Parliamentary career'. Bevan's final speech in response was to call for an open-air swimming bath in the district.[46]

Bevan described his time on the Urban District Council as the 'most instructive portion of my life'.[47] But he had also continued with his other union and community activity. The stand-out year was 1926, when Bevan was a central figure in Tredegar during the General Strike. An issue for the coal industry in the 1920s was increased foreign competition, particularly as Germany and Poland recovered after the First World War and could again produce coal. In 1925, the two-year Franco-Belgian occupation of the Ruhr coalfields to enforce postwar German reparations payments also ended. The problem was exacerbated by the decision of the Chancellor of the Exchequer, Winston Churchill, to adopt the gold standard at the prewar parity. This arguably provided stability and protected savers, but the rate chosen was probably too high, affecting exports and needing high interest rates to support it. When the coal-owners and the workers clashed over hours and pay, the Conservative government initially bought time, agreeing to a temporary subsidy and a Royal Commission under the Liberal Herbert Samuel. This concession has since been dubbed 'Red Friday', 31 July 1925. However, it did not avert the conflict, and when the Samuel Commission reported in March 1926, the miners still faced the prospect of longer hours and lower wages, which the coal-owners sought to impose through a lockout. The Trades Union Congress (TUC) announced a general strike on 1 May 1926, which began on 3 May and lasted nine days; however, the miners continued on strike for a further seven months thereafter.

In Tredegar, Bevan became the chair of the Council of Action, which had effective control of the town, and was largely responsible for organising the distribution of food. By then, he had enormous popularity: on 6 April 1925, he had been re-elected to the Urban District Council, topping the poll in the Tredegar West Ward with 1,131 votes.[48] He had also been elected checkweighman at Bedwellty Pits, and was the Tredegar disputes agent. Bevan was also developing his own administration to deal with his many responsibilities. The Bevan family moved from Charles Street to Commercial Street, and Bevan used the front room of the new property, Beaufort House, as his office. His sister Arianwen worked as his secretary. During the General Strike itself, Bevan attended an extraordinary meeting of the Urban District Council on 10 May, and gave a stark demonstration of his power. The Tredegar Iron and Coal Company had written to the Urban District Council indicating that they had made arrangements to deliver coal to the workhouse, the hospital and the cottage homes, but that the locomotive drivers were refusing to move wagons of coal on the orders of a 'Council of Action'. Bevan left the Urban District Council meeting to speak to the 'Council of Action' and returned with a written 'permit' permitting the movement of five wagons of coal. The permit expired the next day.[49] Independent councillors regretted the fact that, in organising the Council of Action, the local Labour Party was already one step ahead of them. They felt the Urban District Council *as a whole* should have taken the lead, but 'as things had gone so far they could do no more [...] Councillor Bevan has been too smart for us. We have been absolutely whacked!'[50]

Bevan publicly burned the *Western Mail* on Waunpound, the mountain between Ebbw Vale and Tredegar: the newspaper not only supported the coalowners but also attacked the miners' leader, A. J. Cook, for 'the criminal stupidity of his speeches'.[51] This story has, perhaps, obscured the very practical battle Bevan had to prevent the *Western Mail* from being distributed in Tredegar. Oliver Powell's account is that Bevan took aside 14 men, including Oliver Jones, who was told to ensure that nobody was hurt. Since the railwaymen were on strike, road transport was the only viable means of delivery. Hence the men placed a single plank across a barrel to create a roadblock. When the taxi containing the newspapers eventually turned up, there was no violence, and the taxi turned around and left. For Powell, Bevan did 'some extraordinary things' in the battle against the mine-owners. In order to prevent coal being extracted and sold from 'coal holes' he had knocked out all the supporting timber and made them useless; he had 'stopped practically all the sale of coal from the patches'.[52]

Bevan was also a frequent delegate sent by the Tredegar Combine to MFGB special conferences during the General Strike. One miner wrote to the *Merthyr Express* to complain: 'Mr. Bevan goes to London and I go to the soup kitchen.'[53] Bevan argued for a twin-track approach: driving the lockout forward with a view to complete victory over the coal-owners while also considering the possibility of a negotiated settlement. This pragmatism was to bring him into conflict with Arthur Horner, with whom he clashed publicly at the November MFGB special conference. If Horner could show 'that to continue with consequent collapse and disintegration is the best condition for us, then let us accept that with our eyes open. I am certain even our friend Horner would not claim at the end of the month to be in any stronger position than we are now.' Horner said he did claim precisely that, and Bevan had to respond:

> You might claim it, but nobody would give you what you claim. I say
> that as I see it, we have reached the meridian of our negotiating power,
> if we believe that our men are in favour of a negotiated settlement,
> then it would be better for the Miners' Federation.

Bevan was concerned about the areas of South Wales where Poor Law relief had ceased.[54] In his autobiography, *Incorrigible Rebel*, Horner admitted: 'I knew when I was beaten. I knew that the only policy in view of the attitude of the Conference was to get the best possible terms.'[55]

Bevan still steered away from Communism, even during this most difficult of periods. The National Minority Movement had been founded in 1924. Communist-dominated, its president was Tom Mann and its secretary Harry Pollitt. Its ostensible intention was to foster unity across the working class, but it aimed at a radicalisation of the trade union movement, and sought 'to secure the creation of a General Council of the T.U.C. with real power to direct, unite and co-ordinate the struggles and activities of the trade unions'.[56] During the General Strike, a Minority Movement conference was called on 30 August 1926 to try to reduce the number of 'blacklegs' returning to work. However, just as there was no significant Communist influence on Bevan's Council of Action, so too did he keep the Communist Party element of the Minority Movement at arm's length. Bevan's attitude to the Minority Movement is instructive: he believed in the aim of working-class unity, but not Communism. He was willing to *associate* with the movement, but not formally join it.[57]

The steady flow of men returning to work did, however, weaken the position of the miners. Some 70,000 men had deserted the union cause during the seven months of the strike from 1 May until 30 November 1926, when the result of the ballot on giving the miners' leaders authority to negotiate a settlement was announced: 50,815 in favour; 27,291 against.[58] Defeat hung over the final negotiations between the coal-owners and the miners, who were left with district agreements in each area, rather than any form of collective agreement. The miners ended up in the worst of all worlds: alongside the longer hours were lower wages; A. J. Cook's call of 'not a penny off the pay, not a minute on the day' rang hollow. Worse still, strikers, particularly lodge officials, were victimised and blacklisted.

At the end of 1926, miners could be forgiven for thinking that they were in a weaker position than ever before. The SWMF produced a report on conditions in the various districts after the lockout, and it illustrates that the boot was on the foot of the mine-owners. Men who had been active in the stoppage itself were often discriminated against, being told that there was no work available for them.[59] Vindictiveness against the strikers was not confined to the mine-owners, either. The government passed an anti-trade union law, the Trade Disputes and Trade Union Act 1927, which outlawed general and secondary strikes, and made the political levy paid by trade union members to the Labour Party subject to a 'contracting in' provision, overturning the 'contracting out' provision of the Trade Union Act 1913, in an attempt to reduce Labour Party funds. There was an air of depression over the South Wales coalfield. A notebook survives of the minutes of the Tredegar Combine Committee of 1928 and reveals such controversial issues as whether or not married men should have the place of single men in the workforce. One minute bleakly records: 'things are more black than ever.'[60]

Bevan certainly saw the 1926 defeat as pivotal: 'The defeat of the miners ended a phase, and from then on the pendulum swung sharply to political action. It seemed to us that we must try to regain in Parliament what we had lost on the industrial battlefield.'[61] But this quotation should not be taken to confirm that, as of the defeat of the miners in 1926, Bevan made a firm decision that he wanted to be a Labour MP. Secondly, the defeat did not alter his views on Communism. His friend Oliver Jones remembered that he 'rarely spoke of "revolution" except during discussions of an abstract nature [...] He never waited for the beat of a distant drum.' Bevan told one Communist Party member: 'Your difficulty is that you've got your eyes fixed too much on Moscow and not enough on Markham.'[62]

The simple view is that Bevan – in his search for the location of true political power in Britain – had concluded that he should leave the field of industrial conflict and attack in a different territory: Parliament. However, a totally different account is given by Archie Lush. According to Lush, in the year he became an MP, 1929, Bevan 'was not keen on being an MP, he was a syndicalist.'[63] Lush was convinced that Bevan's ambition was still to be the president of the SWMF. Foot's argument is that this 'might easily have occurred but for the opening which appeared, partly by accident, in the representation of the Ebbw Vale constituency.'[64]

The deselection of Evan Davies was anything but accidental. Lush recalls his frustrations with Davies, in particular over his failure to attend local meetings. Worse still, he was also a poor attender at the House of Commons, and had managed only ten recorded contributions in Hansard during his entire parliamentary career.[65] Lush's view is that Bevan was ambitious, but not in a personal sense: 'ambitious to get hold of a machine for a purpose, yes.' In support of this, Lush takes on himself the responsibility for the decision to seek to deselect Davies: 'It was me who was getting fed up with Evan Davies [...] And I was the fellow running the machine [...] I don't say I had to push hard [that is, work hard to persuade Bevan] but quite honestly if I hadn't moved against Evan Davies, Bevan wouldn't have done anything.'[66] There is always a suspicion that Lush would want to present Bevan in a positive light, as a man free from selfish ambition. Also, for Bevan to have Lush as the one openly pushing to deselect Davies has all the hallmarks of a political strategy of 'deniability': let your friends do the dirty work, and make sure your own hands stay clean. Yet there is a sterile element to this debate: it is unnecessary to bend over backwards to present Bevan as personally unambitious. Even if he was personally ambitious, this is hardly inconsistent with a political career in which he was able to achieve positive outcomes for people. Rather, Bevan's parliamentary career supports the idea that his own fate was often not the overriding priority in his political judgements. To take just two examples that will be discussed in later chapters, Bevan's anti-Churchill stance during the Second World War and his resignation from the Attlee government in 1951 were not the calculated actions of a politician principally interested in grasping his way up the greasy pole. The unspoken element here is whether Bevan wondered if *he*, had he become a trade union leader, could have done better than the leaders of the Triple Alliance in 1921. That would explain Bevan's reluctance to become an MP. The industrial weapon was not blunted; rather, it was ineffective in the hands of those who had held it.

Evan Davies was a sitting target, as he sometimes showed an alarming lack of judgement. On 1 March 1927, 52 men and boys were killed in an explosion at the Marine Colliery, Cwm, evidence that in the aftermath of the miners' defeat, the coal-owners took a blasé approach to safety, sacrificing it in the name of speeding up production. Prime Minister Stanley Baldwin visited to express sympathy, and, unsurprisingly given the outcome of the General Strike, was given a very hostile reception. Bizarrely, Davies apologised to Baldwin for what he dismissed as the behaviour of 'a few irresponsible youths'.[67] This was particularly ill-judged, since mining so dominated the politics of Ebbw Vale that the SWMF nominee would be automatically selected by the local Labour Party as the candidate. Indeed, Lush's first move was to ask the SWMF Executive to give an opportunity for other candidates to challenge Davies.

Permission was granted for an open contest, and altogether there were six candidates nominated. The three main contenders were Davies, as the sitting member, Bevan and Bryn Roberts, who was from the Rhymney Valley. The other three candidates included George Davies, another Ebbw Vale man, and T. Rowley Jones and W. G. H. Bull: Rowley Jones and Bull, as candidates from nearby constituencies, were always at a disadvantage against the locals.[68] Bevan topped the first ballot with 3,066 votes. Roberts took 1,816 and Davies came in a poor third with 1,533. George Davies took a creditable 1,061 votes, while Jones and Bull fell out of the contest with 328 and 225 votes respectively. The order of the three candidates at the top of the ballot was, however, set. George Davies' vote fell to 730 on the second ballot, with Bevan increasing his vote to 3,809. Roberts managed only a modest increase in his vote, to 2,208, and Evan Davies still trailed him with 1,859. On the third ballot, Bevan powered home with 5,097 votes. Roberts took 2,626 and Evan Davies' vote fell back to 1,710.[69] There is a strong suggestion that Bevan's supporters continued the ballot-rigging practices of the election for the SWMF Executive. Writing to Michael Foot just after the publication of the second volume of his Bevan biography, Lush commented darkly: 'I still feel that the Cromwellian warts have been left out [...] His contempt for certain people who had assisted at the ballot for selection (our Watergate). Probably because he might have had a conscience.'[70] This hints at Bevan's later shame for the events in the selection, which may well have expressed itself in his distancing himself from some of those who actually stuffed the ballot boxes.

Whatever the machinations, it turned out that Bevan had every reason to avoid being directly implicated in Davies' downfall. The sitting MP took his deselection very badly, and took to the pages of the *Morning Star* to criticise his former colleagues in the Ebbw Vale Divisional Labour Party. Not missing an opportunity to rile Bevan, the *Western Mail* printed the four articles Davies had contributed to the *Morning Star*.[71] But Ebbw Vale was a solidly Labour seat. The first MP, Tom Richards,[72] had been unopposed in 1918, as had Evan Davies when he first took the seat in a by-election in 1920. Davies had easily defeated a Conservative candidate in the 1922 general election, taking 16,947 votes to his opponent's 8,952. Davies won again in the 1923 general election, albeit with a slightly smaller majority against a Liberal candidate, with 16,492 votes to 8,639. Davies was again unopposed in 1924.

In keeping with the general pattern of the 1929 general election, the Labour vote in Ebbw Vale was higher than in the previous 1920s elections. Bevan topped the poll with 20,088 votes; the Liberal candidate came a distant second, with 8,924. William Brace's nephew, Mark Brace, stood for the Conservatives and took 4,287 votes.[73] Bevan would now join the ranks of Labour MPs from the South Wales coalfield. John Campbell argues that, 'Taken as a whole, with notable exceptions, the miners' MPs have been the solid ballast of the Parliamentary Labour Party, not its stars or leaders; they have been marked by moderation, loyalty and a certain dullness.'[74] There are problems with this analysis. The first lies in the assumption that the Welsh mining MPs were all the same. The actual *valley* the MP was drawn from was relevant. The contrast between Bevan himself and James Griffiths (presumably another 'notable exception' in the Campbell thesis) illustrates the differences that existed between Welsh mining MPs.

Griffiths was elected to Parliament some seven years after Bevan, becoming Labour MP for Llanelli in a by-election in 1936. Both were certainly stars of the party: both rose to become its deputy leader, both were architects of the welfare state (Griffiths was Attlee's choice as Minister of National Insurance in 1945), and both were Cabinet ministers. Griffiths was a Welsh-speaker from the Amman Valley on the western edge of the South Wales coalfield; Bevan was from the anglicised eastern half and spoke only English. Griffiths was passionately pro-devolution.[75] In contrast, Bevan saw problems as being universal across the British working class, and placed less emphasis on the specific Welsh context. During the first Welsh day debate in the House of Commons on 17 October 1944, Bevan argued: 'Wales has a special place, a special individuality, a special culture and special claims,' and accepted that there was an argument for devolution. But, for him, there was 'no special solution for the Welsh coal industry which is not the solution for the whole mining industry of Great Britain'. He added: 'There are sheep on the Welsh mountains, and there are sheep on the mountains of Westmorland and in Scotland, but I do not know the difference between a Welsh sheep, a Westmorland sheep and a Scottish sheep.'[76]

This is not to say that Bevan was somehow less 'Welsh' than Griffiths; rather, their respective views are evidence of the rich diversity of tradition and opinion not simply across the whole of Wales, but on the South Wales coalfield. In 1958, the Royal National Eisteddfod was held at Ebbw Vale. Bevan, as the local MP, and an English-speaker, was unable to preside over a day's events because of the 'all-Welsh' language rule. Instead, he presided over a hymn-singing meeting prior to the formal opening of the festival. His guest was his friend, the African American actor–singer Paul Robeson. Bevan was a Monmouthshire man, Monmouthshire being the predominantly English-speaking area of south-eastern Wales. Monmouthshire had been treated as an English county in statutes since Henry VIII's Act of Union with Wales in 1535. Specific references to Wales in

Acts of Parliament usually referred to 'Wales and Monmouthshire'. Bevan reflected on this division, seeing the fact that the Eisteddfod was being held in Ebbw Vale as symbolic: 'If the spirit of the Eisteddfod is to become universal then the walls dividing nations must be broken down.'[77] Bevan called for the end of the use of the phrase 'Wales and Monmouthshire'. Monmouthshire *was* part of Wales, as 'Nature intended it to be', according to one local historian.[78] For Bevan was a proud Welshman. He just happened to come from a distinct Welsh tradition. As the historian Kenneth O. Morgan puts it, Bevan and Griffiths embodied '*different aspects* of the same Welsh Labour ethic [my emphasis]'.[79]

Two more instructive comparisons emerge from consideration of not simply the Welsh mining MPs, but the Welsh mining leaders as a whole. Firstly, there were those who joined the Communist Party, and those who joined the Labour Party. Secondly, there were those who had careers almost entirely in the trade union movement, and those for whom trade union officialdom was the precursor to becoming an MP. On both counts, the appropriate comparison with Bevan was Horner. Born in Georgetown, Merthyr Tydfil, on 5 April 1894, Horner rose from membership of the SWMF Executive to succeed James Griffiths as federation president in 1936. In 1946, he became the general secretary of the newly formed NUM, which had succeeded the MFGB on 1 January 1945. Horner stood unsuccessfully for Rhondda East as a Communist in 1929, 1931, at a by-election in 1933 when he came within 3,000 votes of Labour candidate W. H. Mainwaring, and in 1935. Horner's career demonstrated what could be achieved through the industrial route to power: just before Horner's last union conference as general secretary in 1958, the *Daily Herald* said that he was 'once described as the most powerful man in Britain – because he could have stopped all coal production'.[80] Horner and Bevan shared an essential humanity, and an ability to debate and reason with people of very different views. Bevan was able to sit around the dinner table of Max Beaverbrook in the 1930s with other guests such as the arch anti-socialist Tory MP Brendan Bracken; Horner had sat around the death-bed of his close friend A. J. Cook in 1931, with Sir Oswald Mosley and Walter Citrine – general secretary of the TUC for over for over 20 years – who was no friend of the Communists.[81] Yet Horner and Bevan's political philosophies were very different. Horner *was* a Communist, in label and substance; Bevan was not.

The *valley* each man was from was important. Horner's formative political years were spent in the Rhondda. Initially drawn there by religion, Horner had trained as an evangelist in the small Protestant group the Churches of Christ. He worked as a haulier for a local grocer's in Llwynypia and moved to Ynyshir in 1913, where Noah Ablett had grown up. It was in the Rhondda that Horner developed his close friendship with A. J. Cook. Later, Maerdy became known as 'Little Moscow', but there were no equivalents to Ablett or Cook in Tredegar. Rhondda's voting habits displayed a marked Communist streak. In Rhondda East, after the last of Horner's candidacies in 1935, a Communist stood at every subsequent general election for the constituency until the seat was merged with Rhondda West to form one seat for the first 1974 general election. In 1945, Harry Pollitt came within 1,000 votes of defeating the sitting Labour MP, W. H. Mainwaring. In contrast, during the period that Bevan's Ebbw Vale constituency existed, from 1918 until its abolition for the 1983 general election, not one Communist candidate even stood for Parliament. Bevan and Horner shared a long-lasting close friendship. As Archie Lush put it, Horner was 'pretty close [to Bevan] all the time'.[82] Later in their careers, they even shared common enemies: Bevin and his successor as general secretary of the Transport and General Workers' Union (TGWU), Arthur Deakin, allegedly kept Horner off the General Council of the TUC, and it was Deakin and his allies who were determined to deny Bevan the leadership of the Labour Party in the 1950s.[83]

A further comparison is with Bryn Roberts, another son of the South Wales coalfield, born in Abertillery in 1897. Denied the Ebbw Vale seat, Roberts became, in January 1936, at just 36, the leader of the National Union of Public Employees (NUPE). When he died in 1964, the union had over 220,000 members.[84] Bevan said of their 1929 contest:

> After this Bryn continued on his way in the trade union movement and I was launched into politics. Our roles could quite easily have been reversed. That I won was due to nothing more flattering to me than that Tredegar has a larger population than Rhymney where Bryn was the Miners' Agent.[85]

This may or may not be the major reason for Bevan's victory, but the central point here is sound. Bevan and Roberts *could*, as it were, have been the 'other way around', but Bevan's selection in Ebbw Vale was the key event in his not continuing in the SWMF.

The election campaign itself was uneventful. Bevan had not even canvassed for support: he never needed to throughout his tenure as an MP. Instead, he used his oratorical skills to address large public meetings in main areas such as Tredegar, Ebbw Vale, Rhymney, Abertysswg, Trefil, Beaufort and Cwm.[86] In his victory speech, on the balcony of Tredegar Town Hall, he cited the 'solidarity of the Labour Party' and was optimistic about a Labour government: 'The workers were at last awakening to a realisation of the power which lay in their grasp and were beginning to use it.'[87] That optimism, however, was not to last.

Chapter 4

Monmouthshire County Council and Parliament, 1928–34

A neurin Bevan was first elected to Monmouthshire County Council on 5 March 1928 for the Tredegar Central Division, taking 727 votes to his Anti-Socialist opponent R. S. Grierson's 590.[1] Contrary to what is often thought, he did not step down when he was elected an MP in 1929. In fact, he lost his seat in 1931 to an independent, Joseph Davies.[2] Then, when the member for Tredegar West, Edward Moon, passed away, Bevan won re-election by a landslide on 22 February 1932, taking 1,532 votes to his independent opponent D. Emlyn Harris' 365.[3] He did not, however, stand in the election of 5 March 1934. Bevan's experience on Monmouthshire County Council was formative, but he never dominated the arena in the way that he had the Tredegar Urban District Council.

Bevan did make distinctive contributions. For example, on 5 December 1928, attending both the Education Committee and full council, Bevan raised the issue of the overcrowding at Dukestown School, Tredegar. His major problem was his declining attendance, caused by his parliamentary commitments. Prior to his election to Parliament in May 1929, Bevan attended ten of 16 council meetings, including his first at County Hall, Newport, on 1 May 1928. Afterwards, in the 22 months prior to losing his council seat, he only managed to attend four of 28 meetings.[4] He only ever attended committee meetings that were on the same day as full council was held.[5] Monmouthshire County Council operated principally through its committee system: once reports had been discussed in committee and recommendations made to full council, they tended to be either wholly adopted, or endorsed with only minor changes. Thus, by limiting his committee attendance, Bevan was also limiting his influence. The most powerful figures tended to be those with experience, in particular the aldermen who were chosen by the council itself and not subject to the triennial local elections. The leading Labour figure was Arthur Jenkins, father of Roy, an alderman who served on five different committees. Jenkins was an accomplished councillor of local fame. He had served a three-month prison sentence for inciting pickets and had a rapturous homecoming in the streets of Pontypool, for which he was elected MP in 1935. He was also an exceptionally close Parliamentary Private Secretary to Clement Attlee, and might have gone on to greater things had he not died at the age of 62 in 1946.

Elections had, by law, to be held every three years, and in November 1930 were set for 2 March 1931. Bevan made no noticeable contribution in his last pre-election meeting, on 25 February 1931.[6] The date of 2 March was a canny choice, since it was the day before the rates were fixed for the next year.[7] Bemoaning a turnout of 50–60 per cent, the *Western Mail* complained: 'The Socialist party, the party of misrule and extravagance, not only retained its hold on the administrative machine but experienced an accession of strength.'[8] There was a net Labour gain of six in Glamorgan, and one in Monmouth. However, the *Western Mail* reported gleefully: 'The Independents succeeded in unseating Mr Aneurin Bevan, MP, in Tredegar Central, the successful candidate being a retired police constable.' Bevan lost by 560 votes to 557 to Joseph Davies.[9]

It was a very narrow defeat that rankled with Bevan. In one sense, he could have few complaints, given his sporadic presence in the council chamber. Neither was he able to be in Tredegar throughout the campaign, and the Central seat was a difficult one from the Labour point of view. However, his defeat was also a sharp reminder of the central battle in Welsh Valleys local government during this period. Labour councils, grappling with social problems, needed more money so there was inevitable pressure to push up the rates. On the right, there was a desire to argue 'value for money' in keeping the rates down. The 'Conservative' label was not generally used by candidates of the right, who either called themselves 'ratepayers', 'anti-socialists' or 'independents'. One special meeting of Monmouthshire County Council, on 13 August 1928, had to be called because the authority was struggling to finance free school meals, despite the medical department having found that many children were malnourished.[10] Yet the *Western Mail* continuously savaged Monmouthshire County Council for its extravagance.[11] Bevan, however, did not have to wait long for his redemption, and was back in the council chamber by the end of February 1932. But his level of attendance did not improve in this second spell as a councillor, which ended on 5 March 1934 when Alfred Barrett succeeded him. Over the two years, Bevan attended only nine of 32 council meetings.[12]

The period as a Monmouthshire county councillor did, however, give Bevan a direct insight not only into the chronic underfunding of local government, but also into its inadequacy in dealing with the issue of health. Neville Chamberlain's Local Government Act of 1929 had provided for 'block grants' for local authorities calculated on the basis of a number of factors, including not only population but also indicators of deprivation such as unemployment levels. Ostensibly this was an improvement on the previous system of percentage grants, which favoured richer local authorities, since the greater the resources of the authority, the more Exchequer funding it received. But this did not solve Monmouthshire County Council's funding difficulties. It was an area of high social deprivation (with the exception of its rural eastern side on the English border), and funding was inadequate. The council's accountant bemoaned the high levels of unemployment, and how that lowered rateable values, reducing the council's ability to raise money.[13] The financial estimate for the year ending 31 March 1933 makes grim reading. Spending for 1931–2 had overshot to £927,057 against an estimate of £893,709. The Exchequer grant expected covered just over 50 per cent of the projected spending for 1932–3. Health was chronically underfunded.[14] Bevan was acutely conscious of these monetary difficulties, and the vulnerability of local government to cuts in central-government funding, when he took the decision to nationalise the hospitals in his creation of the NHS.

Bevan also used his knowledge as a councillor to try to effect government policy. One issue that arose only months into his first term as an MP related to a Monmouthshire police constable who had been dismissed. On duty at a local colliery, the officer was meant to ensure that wood that was of use was not removed; colliers were only allowed small pieces of wood for personal use in reasonable quantities. The colliery manager thought the officer too lenient, and Bevan told the private secretary of the Labour Home Secretary, J. R. Clynes, in a meeting on 2 September 1929: 'The only explanation which can be found locally of the acceptance by the Tribunal of the evidence of a colliery manager and his wife and the rejection of the testimony of 27 working miners is class bias on behalf of the Tribunal.' Bevan felt the case would generate criticism, and that the chief constable and the Home Secretary could attract a condemnatory resolution from Monmouthshire County Council if the decision was allowed to stand. Clynes replied to Bevan on 6 September 1929 that he was 'much impressed by the sincerity' of Bevan's representations but that the case had been 'duly disposed of in the manner provided by the Statute'.[15]

It was a Monmouthshire County Council issue that was to bring Bevan into conflict with Herbert Morrison for the first time. Bevan and Morrison were to develop a long-standing political rivalry. In 1931, Morrison was the Minister of Transport. Monmouthshire County Council ran 'Direct Labour Schemes', employing workers to build and repair roads. The council wanted to set fair rates of pay in the district, but Morrison objected, insisting on a competitive tendering process rather than the council paying what it considered reasonable.[16] At Westminster, speaking on the issue of prolonging transitional payment to the unemployed, Bevan highlighted the pressure this put on local government: 'Monmouthshire County Council reduced their scale of public relief at the time of the introduction of transitional payments because had they continued the county would have been bankrupt in a fortnight.'[17] Yet for all the problems faced by local councils, there was an unmistakeable sense that the Labour Party was progressing at local level. For a short period, this had seemed to be the case nationally as well.

The general election of 1929 was a landmark for the Labour Party. For the first time, it became the largest party in the House of Commons, albeit only as a consequence of having a more efficiently distributed vote than the Conservatives. This was, however, a minority government, and it was always going to be a difficult parliament for the Labour prime minister, Ramsay MacDonald, taking office for the second time; the Liberals, with 59 seats, held the balance of power. The Cabinet MacDonald appointed had members of long experience in the party. Aside from Clynes, a previous party leader who was given the Home Office, Arthur Henderson, another former leader, was given the Foreign Office. Both had served in the first Labour government of January to October 1924, as had Philip Snowden, who again became Chancellor of the Exchequer. The man tasked with finding a solution to the problem of unemployment was the general secretary of the NUR, one of the leaders of the Triple Alliance in 1919–21, Jimmy Thomas, who was appointed Lord Privy Seal.

This was not merely an otherwise competent government overcome by the adverse economic weather, though that is the impression sometimes given, particularly by MacDonald, who, in April 1930, bemoaned the 'economic blizzard' raging after the Wall Street crash during the last week of October 1929.[18] The government was also a prisoner of its leaders' own political strategy. MacDonald's aim, ever since Labour had first become the official opposition at Westminster after the general election of 1922, had been to establish the party as the main centre-left alternative to the Conservatives in a two-party system; and to do this he had to ensure that Labour was seen as credible on the economy. Central to this strategy was Snowden, who took a very orthodox economic line: strongly in favour of free trade (he was to resign from the National Government in 1932 over the imposition of tariffs), turning his face against government borrowing.

As a new MP, Bevan was a passionate spokesman for the plight of the unemployed. There *had* been a radical programme put forward to tackle this. The Liberal MPs had been elected on a pledge made by the leader, Lloyd George, on 1 March 1929, to bring unemployment down to a normal level within a year.

The pamphlet, *We Can Conquer Unemployment*, is a cogently argued document. Robert Skidelsky is glowing in his praise: 'intellectually the most distinguished that has ever been placed before a British electorate'.[19] Ably assisted by John Maynard Keynes, Lloyd George's proposals represented a bold vision, with a particular emphasis on constructing roads: £145 million on trunk, rural, district and ring roads, providing total employment for 350,000 people. The key to the proposals was the funding: the money would all be borrowed. The historian Ross McKibbin has defended the second Labour government for not adopting these proposals, and points out, credibly, that there was no guarantee of support from the Liberal MPs for such a programme, particularly since the bulk of them were later to advocate 'sound finance' in support of the National Government from August 1931. McKibbin also argues that the pre-Second World War state itself did not have the capacity to do any more than 'marginally influence' the economy, due to its small budgets and an inflexible administrative heritage.[20]

The proposals also flew in the face of the Labour strategy: to support them meant not only an admittance that the party they were trying to supplant had the more credible policies, but also that Snowden would have to support extensive borrowing, which would undermine the Labour claim of being responsible in office. Yet, at the same time, the proposals were a means of attack on the one issue that was not simply more of a concern than any other for Labour politicians of the interwar era; it was also the defining domestic issue of the period. Lloyd George mocked the Labour dilemma during the 1929 election: 'The Labour Party could not make up its mind whether to treat the Liberal plan as a freak or to claim its paternity.'[21] Labour's response, *How to Conquer Unemployment: Labour's Reply to Lloyd George*, drafted by G. D. H. Cole, attacked the proposals on the basis that they would only provide a temporary solution, and that they would necessitate borrowing.

While there were sound political reasons for not adopting the Lloyd George plans, the problem of unemployment became so pressing that Bevan himself was to ask on the floor of the House of Commons why MacDonald and his colleagues had not carried out the proposals in *We Can Conquer Unemployment*. There was, however, a further explanation aside from political strategy: neither Keynes nor Lloyd George was a socialist. As Ben Pimlott puts it, Keynes appeared a 'false and dangerous prophet' to those looking for the end of capitalism: 'His remedies were intended to modify and revitalise capitalism not to replace it.'[22] Bevan knew this, but the immediacy of the unemployment problem and what was politically possible would also have been in his mind. As McKibbin states: '*Politically* [my emphasis], the real contribution of Keynes was to suggest that governments did not have to stand helpless in the face of cyclical movements in a capitalist economy: thus the Labour governments did not have to wait for "socialism".'[23] This was the impact on Bevan: he wanted *positive government action* to alleviate unemployment.

In Parliament, Bevan's first question, fittingly, was on unemployment insurance, asking the government on 10 July 1929 if it intended to introduce legislation to address 'iniquities' in the way it was administered. The government confirmed it did not. Six days later, he spoke in Parliament for the first time. The speech was made on an impromptu basis, and followed none of the traditional conventions of maiden speeches. There was no tribute to Bevan's predecessor (though, in the circumstances, it would have been interesting to see how Bevan described Evan Davies' nine years in Parliament); neither were there favourable remarks about the constituency. Bevan was even interrupted as he spoke. He spoke on 16 July, a Tuesday, in a debate on the Development (Loan Guarantees and Grants) Bill. MacDonald's government had introduced the bill to provide a subsidy to local authorities and public-utility undertakings, for capital development work to provide employment. The issue was close to Bevan's heart, and he was moved to speak by what he perceived as the cynical, coordinated behaviour of the Conservatives and Liberals against the minority Labour government:

> I would not have intervened in this Debate, as this is my first effort, were it not for the fact that we have listened to some extraordinary speeches from the benches opposite, and I think it is necessary to point out that this is the first example of what we are to expect in the form of collusion between the Tories and the Liberals in obstructionist tactics.

He emphasised unemployment as the defining issue of the times, and attacked the Tories and Liberals for their chicanery:

> The desire of the Tories and the Liberals to assist the Government in solving what they declared to be the most pressing problem of modern times is to be found in the fact that they take the first opportunity to embarrass the Government when the Government are engaged in that effort.

It was appropriate that the two main opposition speakers he responded to were such giants of twentieth-century British politics: Churchill and Lloyd George.

He turned first to Churchill, saying that it was the second time he had heard him speak: 'The first time he was in the role of bogeyman of the country, over the wireless, and on the second occasion he was the entertainer of the House of

Commons.' Bevan rounded on him: 'his chameleon-like character in politics is founded upon a temperamental disability. He fills all the roles with such exceeding facility that his lack of political stability is at once explained.'[24] He added that Churchill's position was that the schemes are 'negligible and will have no effect'; Churchill interrupted: 'I said that the effect would be negligible.' Bevan brushed him aside: 'The right hon. Gentleman said the schemes themselves are negligible as remedies for unemployment, which is about the same thing.' Next he turned to Lloyd George, and pointed up his disagreement with Churchill. While the latter had criticised the scheme, which the Lord Privy Seal, Jimmy Thomas, had introduced into the Commons, for lacking ambition, Lloyd George had also criticised the government for its adventure: 'seeking powers so elastic, so ambitious, and so audacious, that hundreds of millions of pounds might be spent within their circumference without asking the House at all'.[25]

While the speech stands more as a 'first' speech than as a maiden speech following convention, Bevan did still refer to his experiences in local government in South Wales: 'Speaking as one with some experience of local authorities, we have had during the last two years great difficulty in obtaining any grants for schemes from the late Government.' Bevan returned to the theme of housing provision: 'What hon. Members opposite really want is that private enterprise shall set up new industries where it likes in any part of the country, and that the poor people shall migrate to those industries, and have to put up with the bad housing conditions that would exist.'[26] He finished with a flourish: 'When we have the opportunity of making our report to the country, we shall claim that we have had our eyes on the needs of the people, and not on the acrobatics of Parliamentary tactics.'[27]

A week later, on 23 July, Bevan finally came face to face in debate with the scourge of the Poor Law Guardians, Neville Chamberlain. He excoriated him: 'The worst thing I can say about democracy is that it has tolerated the right hon. Gentleman for four and a half years.'[28] He decried Chamberlain's previous effort to soften the effects of the Poor Law with the introduction of tests in the workhouses, by which people were told they could no longer receive relief unless they did 'test work': 'I know cases of colliers who had to walk four or five miles in the morning to do work connected with building walls, cracking stones and weeding turnips.' Bevan virtually spat out his disgust: 'I never thought it possible that any man from a detached position in this House could encourage an administration so in-human, but after listening to […his…] speech […] I am not at all surprised.'[29]

Bevan also made a number of interventions on the Coal Mines Bill. The measure sought to provide national planning in the coal industry, with individual mines given production quotas. Bevan favoured the bill on practical grounds, as the package of measures included a reduction in miners' hours but with money made available to maintain miners' pay at the current level. He attacked Lloyd George directly, accusing him, in opposing the bill, of using 'his Parliamentary position for the purpose of trying to put new life into the decaying corpse of Liberalism'.[30] He challenged the opposition MPs to face the consequences of voting against the bill. Not only were they voting for lower wages, they would be 'voting at the same time for an increase in the number of accidents in the collieries [...] whenever you make it more difficult for the piece-worker underground to earn a decent wage, you ask him to devote himself to output at the expense of safety in the colliery'. He then returned to his specific attack on Lloyd George: 'It is always characteristic of Liberal hypocrisy to pay lip-service to these things, and refuse to face the consequences that follow from them. We say that you cannot get from the already dry veins of the miners new blood to revivify the industry. Their veins are shrunken white.' Bevan mocked Lloyd George for his frequent expressions of sympathy for the miners, followed by the use of 'all your Parliamentary skill, all your rhetoric, in an act of pure demagogy to expose the mining community of this country to another few years of misery.'[31]

The symbolism here cannot be overstated. Bevan consciously attacked the Welshman who had laid the foundations of the welfare state during the Edwardian period. There was an unmistakeable sense of the mantle of Welsh radicalism passing down a generation. Lloyd George was deeply shocked, as the muddled reply he gave demonstrates. He sought on the one hand to give a magisterial put-down from the old master to the young pretender, but on the other struggled to deal with the ferocity of Bevan's speech. Bemoaning a 'very bitter personal attack', he struck an 'elder statesman' note: 'I regret that he should have marred what otherwise, if I may say so as an old Parliamentarian, was a very able speech, by imputing mean motives to other people.' He then fell back on the weak argument that 'we are all doing our best for those we represent in this house', before eventually finding his point: 'It is not so easy a problem as my young friend imagines.' Lloyd George's issue was that fixing a high price for coal could have an effect on costs in other industries, which might then have to reduce wages for their own workers, but he struggled to get into his stride.[32]

Despite his misgivings about the MacDonald government, Bevan made no openly critical speeches about the Labour administration until his patience finally snapped on 4 November 1930, 17 months after the government was formed. Bevan said the key issue, when the government faced the electorate, would be the failure to do more for the then 2 million unemployed:

> This is the first time [...] I have spoken critically of the Government on the Floor of this House, but [...] Parliament has a right to expect an

answer [...] If there is no shortage of money – and we are told in the City and [...] told here that there is plenty of money for investment [...] the Government can find the money.[33]

The speech was evidence of Bevan's disappointment with the failure of the government to tackle what he saw as the great issue of the time. Other Labour politicians were also frustrated. Oswald Mosley, then Chancellor of the Duchy of Lancaster, wanted to introduce a retirement plan, raise the school leaving age to 15 and to create a public works scheme. The rejection of Mosley's memorandum setting out these ideas led to his resignation from the government on 21 May 1930. That same day he informed the Parliamentary Labour Party (PLP) that he would be moving a motion in the party in criticism of the government's policies on unemployment and calling for bolder action. The PLP met the following evening, at 8 p.m. in Committee Room 14. Bevan and John Strachey canvassed for support for Mosley's position. What Bevan actually said in the meeting is not recorded, but Hugh Dalton records the proceedings as follows:

Bevan was vocal on behalf of Lord Oswald but Ebby Edwards [miner and MP for Morpeth 1929–31] went for him and threatened to have this reported to the M.F.G.B. [Joshua] Ritson [Miner and Labour MP for Durham, 1922–31, 1935–45], at one time a little under Lord Oswald's influence, says 'we've muzzled Bevan.'[34]

The later speakers in the meeting included MacDonald and Henderson, who wound up the debate some two and a half hours after it started, at 10.30 p.m., with a conciliatory speech, arguing that MacDonald would now have more time, not being preoccupied with the London Naval Conference, and that he would now take charge of unemployment.[35] The Mosley motion was spectacularly defeated, by 210 votes to 29.

What is curious is why Bevan pursued what he must have known was a hopeless cause. During Henderson's speech, Bevan was seen speaking to Strachey and Mosley as the numbers of votes on either side were totted up. Mosley, having been told that there were 50 in support, decided to proceed. Dalton commented, witheringly: 'Lord Oswald is the worst tactician of the age!'[36] Nonetheless, Bevan continued to associate with Mosley, and remained part of his inner circle. Over the 1930–1 New Year, with Strachey, another Labour MP, William Brown, and the former Marxist Allan Young,[37] Bevan co-wrote *A National Policy: An Account of the Emergency Programme Advanced by Sir Oswald Mosley MP*, which became the New Party's formal programme on its launch in February 1931. There was a particular emphasis on tackling unemployment, including funding housing schemes and reducing expenditure on armaments.[38]

What drew Bevan to Mosley? By any standards, it was a risky association. The *Western Mail* gleefully reported the resignation of the Mosleyites from the PLP.[39] On 10 March 1931, the party's National Executive Committee (NEC) unanimously excommunicated Sir Oswald Mosley, John Strachey, Oliver Baldwin, Dr Robert Forgan, the MP for West Renfrew, and Lady Cynthia Mosley. Later, on 26 April, Arthur Greenwood spoke against Mosley in a speech at Stoke-on-Trent: 'Mosleyitis is a disease of short duration; it is like measles.'[40] Closer to home, at a May Day rally at Blackwood in 1931, Charles Edwards MP attacked Mosley, as summarised by the *South Wales Argus*: 'Sir Oswald's attitude, he said, gave the impression that he had never entered the Labour Party to help it, but to attack it from within.'[41]

Lush's view is that Mosley's appeal to Bevan lay in his frustration with MacDonald. When Lush raised the issue of him leaving the Labour Party for the New Party, Bevan snapped back: 'You don't think I'm bloody going there, do you?' Lush is lightly critical of Bevan's tendency to mix with people who were not miners' leaders. Strachey, for example, is described by Lush as 'purely intellectual'.[42] He was the son of an editor of the *Spectator*, educated at Eton and Magdalen College, Oxford. Yet alongside the 17 Labour MPs who signed the 'Mosley Manifesto' of 1 December 1930 is the signature of A. J. Cook, who *was* a miners' leader.[43] There was a general desperation about the existing political system, not confined to abstract thinkers. Even Clement Attlee, who succeeded Mosley as Chancellor of the Duchy of Lancaster, spoke about the end of capitalism: 'We do not believe in the capitalist system [...] we should like to see it ended.'[44]

Bevan did *not* judge people purely on background; he judged on ideas, as his relationship with Mosley, the baronet's son who defected from the Conservatives, later with Beaverbrook, and, indeed, with the privately educated Michael Foot himself, showed. In *My Life with Nye*, Jennie Lee recounts the story of Bevan's friendship with a young Tory who also became an MP in 1929, Edward Marjoribanks. Marjoribanks sat for Eastbourne, and was the stepson of the first Lord Hailsham. He had first approached Bevan after his attack on Lloyd George.[45] Bevan enjoyed debating with Marjoribanks, an Eton- and Oxford-educated barrister, and it was through him that he met Beaverbrook. Marjoribanks, at Beaverbrook's invitation, took him to dinner, and Bevan's association with Beaverbrook began. Bevan became close to Marjoribanks, who confided in Bevan that he was dreading his forthcoming wedding because he felt he was impotent. Tragically, Marjoribanks died at the age of 32 in April 1932. He shot himself in the gun room of the Hailsham country residence, either deliberately or accidentally. Bevan was deeply upset, and bitter that Marjoribanks' stepfather had not treated him with more sympathy.[46] Far from deliberately avoiding the company of those from a different social background, Bevan thoroughly enjoyed discussion and debate with them. After all, Mosley did offer radical ideas to deal with the unemployment problem. That said, once Mosley formed the British Union of Fascists, Bevan was very clear about his opposition to what he stood for. He even debated with him on whether fascism or socialism was the superior political system at the Cambridge Union in February 1933.[47]

Without Mosley, the second Labour government limped on during 1931. The government eventually fell when the Cabinet was unable to agree to cuts in unemployment benefit. The government was under pressure to adopt deflationary policies and balance the budget. Moves were needed to preserve government credit and to persuade the New York banks that it was safe to lend: 'foreign credits – needed to stop the haemorrhage of gold from London – could only be obtained by heavy reductions in government expenditure, particularly in unemployment insurance.'[48] MacDonald resigned, and then, on 24 August 1931, agreed to form a 'National Government'. The ten-strong Cabinet included Snowden, Jimmy Thomas, by now Dominions Secretary, and the Lord Chancellor John Sankey. These Labour members were joined by four Conservatives – Stanley Baldwin, Neville Chamberlain, Sir Philip Cunliffe-Lister and Sir Samuel Hoare, and two Liberals – Sir Herbert Samuel and the Marquess of Reading. On 26 August, the Labour Party NEC, the General Council of the TUC and the consultative committee of the Parliamentary Labour Party met and issued a joint manifesto declaring that the new government was 'determined to attack the standard of living of the workers'.[49] Two days later, the Parliamentary Labour Party met with members of the General Council of the TUC also present, and Arthur Henderson became leader in place of MacDonald.

The 1931 general election was Labour's worst since 1918. On 27 October, the party was reduced to 52 seats, taking just over 30 per cent of the popular vote. The National Government had won a landslide victory, with 67 per cent of the popular vote. The Conservatives were the dominant force, winning a massive 473 seats, a record for any political party in Britain during the twentieth century. MacDonald's new National Labour Party won 12 seats, the National Liberals 35 and the remainder of the Liberals 33. Labour's only saving grace was the Liberal disarray: the *total* number of Liberal seats was above that of Labour, but the total Liberal vote share was far less than that of Labour and there were even four independent Liberals sitting on the opposition benches with Labour. Bevan was spared any active part in the election in the Ebbw Vale as he was fortunate to be unopposed.

After the election, the immediate issue that caused division in the National Government was free trade. On 4 February 1932, the government introduced the Import Duties Bill into the House of Commons, which set a general tariff of 10 per cent on imports. Later that year, at the Imperial Economic Conference in Ottawa, Britain's dominions agreed on a system of imperial preference, which effectively placed trade barriers around the Empire. The Home Secretary, Herbert Samuel, and his 'Samuelite' Liberals left the government. Bevan attacked the 'food taxes' imposed by the Ottawa agreements strongly: 'We say it is an unforgivable crime of the Government to have gone to Ottawa to impose additional burdens upon poor people at this time.'[50]

Bevan's main attacks on the National Government were, however, on its domestic policy, and its treatment of the poor and unemployed. For, as Philip Williamson observed in his authoritative *National Crisis and National Government*, the first King's Speech of the new government did not mention the words 'unemployment' or 'employment' for the first time since 1928. MacDonald's Cabinet committee structure 'treated unemployment as a secondary matter'. Public works schemes were dismissed.[51] Bevan drew on his own experience to put the case against the government. He argued against a proposal to reduce benefit the longer the period of unemployment went on: 'During the first six months, the resources of the family have not become entirely exhausted, but later on everything in the family has to be renewed – clothing and the most expensive parts of the household equipment – and that has to be done out of depleted resources.'[52]

Bevan was consciously the voice of the unemployed, commenting in another debate two months later on the plight of those who were out of work during the cold winter months: 'I shall stick to my past and I am not ashamed of it [...] It would be a disaster and it would be a disservice to the House if the feelings of those were not allowed to find an echo within these walls.'[53] Bevan's attitude to the National Government was summed up in a speech he made in a later unemployment debate on 10 December 1931. Recognising that the government had more authority to carry out a plan than a single party administration, and the ability to 'set aside any vested interests which may stand in the way of [...its...] execution', he saw the weakness in the government's state of mind, that it was not prepared to use its enormous power: 'Has there been any indication of the production of a Government plan? Is it not obvious that the Prime Minister is merely fobbing off the House of Commons with one tit-bit after another in the hope that time will come to his rescue?'[54]

A principal target of Bevan's attack was the hated means test. Introduced in September 1931, it sought to reduce the cost of unemployment benefit by obliging claimants to use up the income of other family members before claiming a 'transitional benefit' (as Neville Chamberlain's 1927 Unemployment Insurance Act termed it) available after the 15-week national-insurance period introduced by the Liberal government's landmark 1911 National Insurance Act. For families, this meant a humiliating investigation into household assets and finances. As Bevan said, its purpose 'was not to find the parasites'. Rather, it had three aims. The first was the obvious one of saving taxpayers' money;

> secondly, to throw the main burden of the maintenance of poor people on to the shoulders of their families, and, thirdly [...] to drive the unemployed to such a condition of destitution as will make it easier to reduce the standards of life for the working classes of this country.[55]

Bevan also complained to the Ministry of Labour that the needs of illegitimate children not in the same household as the claimant were not taken into account.[56]

The brilliance of Bevan's parliamentary oratory was complemented by fine initial work as a new constituency MP. He continued to take up the cause of the miners whenever he could. In March 1931, with the Labour government still in office, the MFGB national conference had demanded amendment of the Coal Mines (Minimum Wage) Act 1912. In late April, the miners' MPs, including Bevan, together with an MFGB deputation, met ministers, including MacDonald and Henderson, but again received no firm commitment.[57] Unsurprisingly, the *Western Mail* took a strong line against the miners for seeking to circumvent the 'arbitration award which governs miners' wages in this part of the country'. On 20 April 1931, Bevan was among the miners' MPs who met Manny Shinwell, then the Secretary for Mines, with another MFGB deputation. Tom Richards and A. J. Cook put the case for the miners: the 1914 earnings level plus a cost-of-living increase to be the minimum for the proposed Minimum Wage Bill. There should also be a guaranteed weekly minimum wage of £2 per day for workers and £2 10s. for pieceworkers. Shinwell refused to reveal to the press what the decision of the government was.[58]

With the National Government in office, the left started to splinter as it despaired of the political and economic situation. Henderson remained as party leader in name only until he resigned in October 1932, since he had lost his parliamentary seat in 1931. Attlee, along with Stafford Cripps and George Lansbury, Solicitor General and First Commissioner of Works in the second Labour government respectively, shared the leader of the opposition's room at the House of Commons and carried the burden of responding to the National Government in parliamentary debates. The trio moved Labour policy decisively to the left away from the MacDonald–Snowden economic orthodoxy of the 1929–31 government.

Attlee himself argued for the abolition of the House of Lords, and put the case for positive state action to tackle unemployment and organise industry.

Within the wider Labour Party, the Mosleyites were not the only group choosing to go their own way. Formed in 1893, the left-wing Independent Labour Party (ILP) had been a foundation stone of the Labour Representation Committee in 1900, and had initially affiliated to the Labour Party, as it became known, in 1906. Those ILP members who remained in the party formed the Socialist League. Stafford Cripps became a prominent figure in the league, as, later, did Michael Foot. The fate of the ILP pointed up another consistent aspect of Bevan's character, namely his belief in the Labour Party itself as a vehicle of progress for the working class. The ILP unquestionably had a left-wing agenda that was appealing to Bevan. In February 1931, James Maxton even issued the text of a Living Wage Bill. But, in August 1932, under the chairmanship of Fenner Brockway, the ILP finally decided to disaffiliate from the Labour Party. Bevan's remark to Jennie Lee, herself a committed ILP member, when they discussed this is revealing. Quoting Hamlet to Ophelia, he told her, 'Why don't you get into a nunnery and be done with it? Lock yourself up in a separate cell away from the world and its wickedness. My Salvation Army lassie. Poor little Casabianca [...] I tell you, it is the Labour Party or nothing.'[59] Bevan felt the ILP were going down a blind alley. Furthermore, he felt no emotional pull to the ILP as a consequence of his involvement in local politics. The ILP had never been a force in Tredegar's politics in the way it had in Merthyr Tydfil's, for instance, for which ILP founder Keir Hardie had sat as MP from 1900 to 1915.[60] Once the ILP had disaffiliated, Bevan visited Lee at home, and she considered pretending she was not there. She eventually decided to let him in and get the argument over and done with.[61]

The events of 1931 had a profound effect on Bevan's thinking. Writing anonymously, he contributed a passage to *The Coming Struggle for Power: An Examination of Capitalism*, published in 1932 by Strachey.[62] This piece is evidence of the immediate, and most important, lesson that he drew, which was that the gradualist approach of Labour's governments in the 1920s, 'which requires that private enterprise shall continue reasonably successful [*sic*] whilst it is being slowly and painfully eliminated', was futile. The Labour Party would not be allowed to reform capitalism, since the interests of capital and labour could not be reconciled. To reassure private enterprise meant breaking the promise of socialism to the workers, whose support would be lost. Bevan accepted the general view held in the Labour Party at the time that the government had been brought down by a 'bankers' ramp' of international capitalists. Second, he felt it 'reasonably certain' that there would 'never be another Labour Government in England except in conditions of economic crisis and consequent mass unrest'. He felt the very election of another Labour government would cause such conditions, since it would be 'charged with menace to the whole capitalist interest'. Third, in such a situation, he was pessimistic that even a majority Labour government could do anything constructive without dropping its gradualist approach, since it 'would pause irresolutely between the two alternatives' of abandoning gradualism and adopting socialism, or abandoning socialism with the aim of 'reassuring private enterprise in order to get a breathing space'. In short, should there ever be another Labour government, it could only be successful if it abandoned gradualism and introduced socialism. Bevan did not define the 'socialism' he envisaged in this passage, and neither did he go so far as others, such as Stafford Cripps, were to in the 1930s in their criticism of Parliament as an effective instrument for economic change. Cripps was later to argue that, once elected with a popular mandate, *nothing* should then obstruct a socialist government carrying out its programme. For Bevan, it was not Parliament that was at fault, but the policy of the Labour leaders.

Later, in 1952, in *In Place of Fear*, he devoted a chapter to the role of Parliament, and, having by then served in Cabinet in a majority Labour government, gave a more considered view. He criticised MacDonald as a 'pitiful strategist' who was like Mr Micawber in Dickens' *David Copperfield*: doing nothing and waiting for 'something to turn up'. He recalled meeting MacDonald in 1930. Bevan was going to propose a resolution at the meeting of the PLP drawing attention to the national crisis and the need for a special national party conference. All MacDonald could say to persuade Bevan to withdraw the motion (which he did not) was that the economic recovery was 'just around the corner'. Bevan claimed MacDonald and Snowden saw the role of Parliament as 'ameliorative, not revolutionary'. In contrast, he saw Parliament as 'the most formidable weapon of all'.

Immediately after 1931, Bevan's pessimism about the prospects of there ever being another Labour government reinforced his ongoing interest in seeking power via the industrial route. It was a battle Arthur Horner was still fighting manfully. The *Western Mail* denounced Horner's Mardy as 'a Communist-ridden stronghold in the Rhondda Fach, which has become known as "Little Moscow" by the number of Bolshevists who reside there.' At the conclusion of a trial for unlawful assembly at the Glamorgan Assizes on 24 February 1932, Horner, a 'pestiferous fellow', was among the 29 people convicted, and was sentenced to 15 months' hard labour; the *Western Mail* bemoaned the 'easy sentences inflicted upon these desperadoes'.[63]

Once Adolf Hitler became German chancellor on 30 January 1933, Bevan looked for cooperation across the left in order to be able to defend the working classes from the Nazi menace. The Communist Party and the ILP had sought a programme of common action with the Labour Party itself, but the NEC had rejected any cooperation. Bevan sought to create Tredegar Workers' Freedom Groups, which would promote physical training. Despite their paramilitary inspiration (from the Vienna Schutzbund, which was organising against the Nazis), they acquired no weapons. Bevan *did* see a role for the Freedom Groups on a national scale, not simply in Tredegar. There was a flurry of interest in the idea. Bevan had stayed with John Strachey over Easter 1933 and had become very excited about its potential; he even offered to go to Mardy to discuss it with Arthur Horner.[64] Given that they were not exclusively Labour Party groups, they were vulnerable to capture by the Communist Party. The badge worn by members of the Tredegar Workers' Freedom Group resembled a coffin, and Brendan Bracken mercilessly mocked Bevan for his 'Coffin Clubs'.[65] The *Western Mail* was similarly unimpressed by Bevan, even going as far as to describe him as a 'Cymric Hitler'.[66]

The proposal for some sort of 'resistance movement' was not attractive to the locals of Tredegar. There was a great camaraderie between the miners, but they were not about to become some sort of paramilitary organisation. On one occasion, Bevan was leading the Freedom Group, mostly colliers, across the Welsh mountains, to encourage physical fitness. Archie Lush and the rest of the marchers sat down for a rest and Bevan continued regardless before realising what had happened. Amidst the laughter, Lush told him: 'You see, Nye, an important element in military strategy is that the general must never go too far ahead of his troops.'[67] As it turned out, this marked a final note in Bevan's involvement in local politics in Tredegar. For, while he always remained deeply attached to the Tredegar he had grown up in, his life was about to become permanently based in London.

Part III

Establishing Himself on the National Stage, 1934–45

Chapter 5

London and Jennie Lee

In the early 1930s, there was an unmistakeable sense that Bevan was at a cross-roads in his life. Jennie Lee captures this: 'In spite of his brilliant parliamentary debut and left-wing stance, I was in two minds about him. For one thing I did not like some of the company he kept. He delighted in the [Max] Beaverbrook ménage and talked exuberantly about slumming in the West End.' She posed the key question: 'Was he too clever by half? Would he stand the pace or had he the makings of another Victor Grayson?'[1] Like Bevan, Grayson had been a brilliant orator, and had won the Colne Valley by-election as an ILP candidate in 1907. Yet Grayson developed a drink problem, and lost his seat in the general election of January 1910. He drifted away from his more pacifist political colleagues on the left by backing Britain's involvement in the First World War. He then disappeared in murky circumstances in 1920 after threatening to expose the scandal of the then prime minister, David Lloyd George, selling honours.

Bevan most certainly did not develop a drink problem in the early 1930s, but he was broadening his horizons, keeping new company and adjusting to parliamentary life. At this time, Lee was having an affair with a fellow ILP member, the married father of four, Frank Wise. Wise was over 20 years older than Lee; they had been immediately attracted to one another after Wise was elected to Parliament for Leicester East in 1929, only weeks after Lee won North Lanark in a by-election, becoming the youngest MP. Wise and Lee never lived together, but Wise was the love of Lee's life.[2] She was devastated when he died suddenly of a brain haemorrhage while out for a walk in November 1933. Lee herself was a formidable politician. Fenner Brockway, admittedly not a neutral observer as a fellow ILP member, was a great admirer, and wrote this in 1942: 'Jennie is in my opinion far and away the ablest woman who has been in the House of Commons.'[3]

The one criticism levelled at Bevan at this time was that of Walter Citrine, who saw Bevan regularly at meetings of the trade union group of Labour MPs who kept close links with the TUC: 'He excelled as a critic but, in contrast to

Ernest Bevin, creative thought at that time was not his strongest characteristic. He would present any number of difficulties to any proposition which came from official sources, but seldom put forward any proposals of a constructive character.'[4] Bevan *could* have developed into a mere left-wing critic shouting regularly from the sidelines. That he did not was due to his self-confidence and commitment to what he believed in. He knew how he wanted society to be. It was this set of core beliefs that gave him, even at this early stage in his parliamentary career, the strength to withstand the criticism that he knew would come from his association with someone like Beaverbrook. Beaverbrook was the newspaper giant of his time. He had purchased the *Daily Express* in 1916, and then founded the *Sunday Express* in 1918. In 1923, he added the *Evening Standard* to his collection. He was unpredictable, and prone to mercurial behaviour. In addition to his fascination with systemic power, Bevan also had an interest in powerful individuals. What he wrote to Beaverbrook on 11 March 1932 expresses Bevan's thinking perfectly:

> As one who hates the power you hold, and the order of life which enables you to wield it [...] I hold you in the most affectionate regard, and confess to a great admiration of those qualities of heart and mind which, unfortunately, do not appear to inspire your public policy.[5]

Bevan moved in the Beaverbrook set because it provided interesting and exciting conversation. Bevan was widely read, with a mind that roamed over many different intellectual fields, and enjoyed the debates enormously. He saw great value in developing his arguments and ideas through discussion. His famous phrase was 'This is my truth, tell me yours', an invitation to others to debate with him. He called good conversation 'star tapping': moving from the known world to the unknown, developing and refining ideas through talking, often late into the night. For the embrace of Beaverbrook extended far and wide across party divides. Beaverbrook had, of course, played a part in securing the premiership for Lloyd George in December 1916. He was then, later, involved in fomenting Conservative rebellion against the Lloyd George coalition, and close to Andrew Bonar Law, who succeeded Lloyd George as prime minister in 1922. Beaverbrook actually drove Law to the famous meeting of the Conservative Party at the Carlton Club on 19 October 1922, at which it was decided to fight the coming general election as an independent party, rather than as a coalition.[6]

The association illustrates the Beaverbrook trait of having friendships on different sides of political divides. This same trait is in evidence in the 1930s with Brendan Bracken and Bevan sharing Beaverbrook's company. Bracken held the Paddington North parliamentary seat from 1929 until being defeated in the Labour landslide of 1945. He served as Minister of Information from 1941 to 1945 and was briefly First Lord of the Admiralty in Churchill's caretaker government of 1945. Ostensibly Bracken had a classic English public-school background, and was briefly the headmaster of the Hertfordshire independent school Bishop's Stortford College. But he was actually Irish, born in County Tipperary into an Irish nationalist family; his father Joseph was a member of the Irish Republican Brotherhood. His great friendship in politics was with Winston Churchill, and he was an outspoken anti-socialist who recommended himself to Beaverbrook as not only fascinating company in his own right, but also the ideal sparring partner for Bevan. The Beaverbrook dinner parties were undoubtedly intellectually stimulating affairs. The guest list was not entirely composed of professional politicians, either. Other regulars included the journalist and writer Arnold Bennett, another Beaverbrook protégé who had served in the Ministry of Information in the First World War at Beaverbrook's suggestion. Bevan missed out on regularly crossing swords with Bennett, who died of typhus in March 1931, but was regularly in the company of another Beaverbrook favourite, H. G. Wells.

In accepting Beaverbrook's hospitality, Bevan's lifestyle and tastes *themselves* provoked criticism. Even the historian Robert Crowcroft, writing in 2011, dismisses Bevan as a 'Welsh miner turned bon viveur and social climber'.[7] Brendan Bracken's remark about Bevan's champagne socialism was first recounted in the *Evening Standard* by Churchill's son, Randolph, on 8 August 1958, the day Bracken died at the age of 57 from oesophageal cancer. Bracken is said to have berated Bevan in the drawing room of Beaverbrook's Stornoway House: 'You Bollinger Bolshevik, you ritzy Robespierre, you lounge-lizard Lenin. Look at you, swilling Max's champagne and calling yourself a socialist.' Michael Foot was given an alternative account of the incident by Frank Owen, who was also present. In this version of the story, Bevan claimed that it was his right to enjoy fine wine, and told Bracken: 'The best I ever had from you, by the way, Brendan, I'd call bottom lower-class *Bolshevik* Bollinger.'[8] We will never know for certain what was said. Both accounts could be accurate. Bevan's remark might well have been the response to Bracken's attack. Both remarks have the ring of authenticity. Bracken was savaging Bevan for arguing for the redistribution of money and property from the richest while enjoying the fruits of wealth. Bevan, however, thought people from his working-class background had the same right as those from privileged backgrounds to enjoy the finer things in life, and his needling of Bracken for providing poor champagne was a typical flourish with which to finish his point. There is much to be said for Bevan's argument. On the Bracken view, it seems that all those on the left who argue for redistribution must themselves live in sackcloth to avoid charges of hypocrisy. Nobody criticises Winston Churchill's lifestyle with its champagne breakfasts and love for brandy and cigars. Rather, the cigar is a defining Churchillian feature. Bevan may have liked the finer things in life, but he could take the Beaverbrook circle for what it was: a group chosen by Beaverbrook to promote lively discussion.

Bevan's association with Beaverbrook was not lifelong. Beaverbrook's biographer, A. J. P. Taylor, thought that his subject and Bevan did not see each other after 1943. Beaverbrook did not believe that the bombing of Germany on its own would lead to victory. He argued for a second front in Western Europe, and resigned as Minister of War Production in February 1942, after only 15 days in post, in order to put the case publicly. The similarity with Bevan's views at this time is unmistakeable, though Beaverbrook was a close confidant of Churchill and Bevan was Churchill's arch-critic. But the common cause over the second front could not bridge the gap that had opened up between Bevan and Beaverbrook over Churchill. Bevan had *always* been cautious in his dealings with him, in any event. After Bevan's marriage to Jennie Lee, Beaverbrook made the couple an offer of a country cottage on his Cherkley estate. Bevan, admittedly with some pressing from Lee, refused on the basis that it 'would be politically indiscreet'.[9] There is even a suggestion that Bevan was once sent a cheque by Beaverbrook that he returned, but Taylor was unable to find any proof of this when he was writing his Beaverbrook biography.[10] In contrast, Michael Foot is a stoical defender of Beaverbrook. He devotes the longest chapter in his book *Debts of Honour* to Beaverbrook, and saw him as a 'surrogate father'.[11]

There is perhaps a deeper reason why Bevan did not rely on Beaverbrook in the way Foot did. At his 70th birthday celebrations in 1949, Beaverbrook remarked that Foot's problem was that 'he [...] never had a self-starter'.[12] There is much truth in this, but it should not be read as Foot being a man totally devoid of personal ambition. After all, Foot stood twice for the leadership of the Labour Party, in 1976 and 1980. Rather, the point was that Foot, while highly capable, was often inspired to great heights by others. After Bevan introduced Foot to Beaverbrook in the autumn of 1938, Foot produced some great writing, including, ironically, *Guilty Men*, which he co-wrote with Frank Owen and Peter Howard, assailing the appeasers of Nazi Germany when Beaverbrook himself had been in favour of the Munich Agreement of September 1938. Bevan admired others, of course, but his inspiration, his burning desire to change society, came from within. His self-starter had been constructed in Tredegar before he became an MP.

The political reality should not be neglected, either. There were inherent political dangers in associating too closely with a maverick like Beaverbrook. In his response the next day to Churchill's infamous election broadcast of 4 June 1945, in which he argued that a socialist government would need some sort of

'Gestapo', Attlee used the spectre of Beaverbrook to frighten voters: 'the voice we heard last night was that of Mr Churchill, but the mind was that of Lord Beaverbrook.' This set the tone for the Labour government's collective view of Beaverbrook. Beaverbrook became something of a pariah for both main parties, as the Conservatives were also deeply suspicious of his behind-the-scenes advisory role to Churchill in contributing to the 1945 general-election defeat. In staying away from Beaverbrook, Bevan was taking the politically sensible course. He knew the dangers of the association throughout, and when he realised that it had become politically toxic, particularly after 1945 when he was a Cabinet minister, he never returned to Beaverbrook. He was deeply committed to his work as a Cabinet minister.

He also became deeply committed to Jennie Lee. Bevan had shown little sustained interest in women before Lee, though his Tredegar contemporary Oliver Powell records that Bevan had an interest in some of the Tredegar Workmen's Institute Library's more erotic titles. He was particularly keen on the multi-volume *The Arabian Nights Entertainments*, in particular a French version that had been translated by Powis Mathis.[13] Despite her relationship with Frank Wise, Bevan pursued Jennie Lee from his early months in Parliament.

Born in 1904 on the Fifeshire coalfield to James Lee and his wife Euphemia, she was seven years younger than Bevan, but from a similar background. James Lee was a miner and a local ILP chair. The ILP speakers who visited and spoke included James Maxton. Unlike Bevan, she was not wholly self-educated. Her mother, the strong homemaker, always wanted the very best for her daughter, and supported her throughout her education. Highly intelligent and fiercely independent, Lee left to study for five years at the University of Edinburgh, achieving an MA, law degree and teacher's diploma. Bevan adored his mother-in-law, who became known as 'Ma Lee' from the first time he got to know her when he and Lee visited her parents in Lochgelly after the Edinburgh party conference of 1936.[14] James Lee was initially wary of Bevan. However, he warmed to him after Bevan chided Lee for bringing her father cheap cigars back from one of her lecture tours to America.

Bevan and Lee had first had a serious conversation on the House of Commons terrace in the summer of 1929. Lee thought his suit was awful, a dreadful combination of a Nonconformist Welsh minister and ambitious stockbroker. (Actually, his mother had bought it from the Tredegar Co-operative!) Putting this aside, they discussed James Lee's pacifism during the First World War, and his syndicalist outlook. Both were keen on political action, having witnessed the 1919, 1921 and 1926 industrial defeats. Lee said they had so much in common they could be brother and sister. Bevan gleamed mischievously: 'With a tendency to incest.'

Bevan was smitten with her. She was a strong, passionate socialist who stood out as a young, attractive, dark-haired woman in a male-dominated Parliament. Bevan's sister Arianwen, who was now dealing with his constituency correspondence in Tredegar, took a different view. She visited Bevan in the Commons and he asked her view of Lee while she was on her feet, speaking. Arianwen took an immediate dislike: 'her jaw is too heavy,' and was less than pleased when Bevan pushed her to help Lee with her typing. But Bevan's relationship with Lee blossomed. While she was still with Frank Wise, Bevan called in at Lee's London flat and went on country walks with her. He had spent the 1931 general-election campaign with Lee in North Lanark, and even went to Leicester East to help Frank Wise, but was nonplussed when told that there was nothing for him to do.[15]

It was Clement Attlee, in his characteristically taciturn way, who declared that Bevan's problem was that, in a wife, he needed an emollient, but actually ended up with an irritant. There is something in this. For Lee always retained her strong ILP heritage. The 1932 choice of disaffiliation from Labour indicated that the group preferred the doctrinal purity of the wilderness to the grubby compromises of actual political power. It is no surprise that she fell for Frank Wise, a Cambridge-educated, intellectually self-confident ILP-er who was keen to assist the Russian government. Wise held directorships in Soviet companies, and advised the Soviet Trading Mission on developing exports. Indeed, the Bevan–Lee differences were also palpable in their attitudes to Russia. In September 1930, Bevan visited Russia with John Strachey and George Strauss. He was impressed by certain aspects, including the 'simple austerity' of the study used by Lenin during the Russian Revolution. The men were taken to a textile works, the 'Factory of the Red Banner', which had a crèche attached, and were told that women were allowed two months' paid leave before and after childbirth. They were also informed that the schoolchildren of parents on low salaries were entitled to free school meals: 'Health to the children is the best monument to Lenin.' With the process of 'collectivisation' of smaller farms ongoing (*artels* being aggregated into *kolkhozy*), Bevan and his companions also visited three villages in south-western Russia: Mechetenskaya, Kagalnitskaya and Bataysk.[16] The latter two both had small hospitals (with 15 beds and 35 beds, respectively), which naturally found favour with Bevan. Finally, the visit took in the construction site of a new dam on the River Dnieper, which was designed for electricity generation and to increase navigability at low water. On their return, the three published *What We Saw in Russia*.[17] But Bevan was not blind to the hardship he saw. The 'de-kulakisation' campaign of repression of more affluent farmers was described as the 'liquidisation of a class', and Bevan was told of the exclusion of kulak children from schools.[18] There is no evidence he ever saw the Ukrainian famine that began two years later.

He remained optimistic. Bevan *did* praise Russia, and, along with many on the left, wanted the Russian Revolution to 'succeed' in the eyes of the world. Speaking in the House of Commons in 1932 on the Hours of Employment (Limitation) Bill, Bevan was responding to the argument that the working day should not be made shorter. His argument was that, over the preceding 150 years, productivity had vastly increased. He praised Russia: 'Why can Russia organise her hours of labour and still sell goods successfully against the rest of the world?'[19] Neither did he shy away from criticising Russia; his view is aptly summarised in his dictum that while Britain was a slave to the past, in Russia they were slaves to the future. Lee, in contrast, even after Stalin's show trials of the 1930s, was still arguing for the Soviet Union, and was less critical. Her short book, *Our Ally Russia: The Truth*, was published in 1941. This was despite Bevan being provided with at least one trial transcript.[20]

Bevan had started sharing Lee's one-bedroom flat in Guilford Street, London, only weeks after Frank Wise's death. The cynic might say he moved in quickly. He finally secured Lee's agreement to marry him at a dinner at the Café Royal in May 1934. He chose the very best meal, telling her: 'You can always live like a millionaire for five minutes.' That summer, he travelled to America for the first time before returning in September to announce the engagement. Acutely aware of events in Germany, he had originally intended to spend a week in New York on behalf of the Relief Committee for the Victims of German and Austrian Fascism. Lee was a committee member, and the purpose of the trip was to participate in a mock trial on the Reichstag fire of February 1933, which Hitler had exploited to tighten his grip on power in Germany. John Strachey had been the first choice of the committee, but could not be persuaded to take on an unprofitable task. Bevan was his replacement, and, in the event, was away for two months. After New York, he travelled across to the east coast on a speaking tour to raise money for the committee.[21] He enjoyed the intellectual climate. Unlike on his next visit to America 23 years later, he was impressed by the quality of the debate on great issues of the time.[22]

The wedding itself was characteristically idiosyncratic. The ceremony took place at Holborn Registry Office on 25 October 1934. There were two invited witnesses: naturally Bevan's was Archie Lush, and the other was a friend of Lee's, Marion Balderston. Lee wore no hat and no gloves, bought no new coat, and chose to wear no wedding ring despite liking rings. There was great interest from the press, and Beaverbrook's *Daily Express* covered the wedding the next day.[23] Bevan's family was represented by his brother William, who attended out of loyalty to Nye, despite his disapproval of Lee. He was an accomplished politician himself, charismatic like his famous brother. He, too, left the mines, and became a milkman, going on to become an alderman on Monmouthshire County Council.[24] He was a figure of some authority. Don Touhig, later the Labour MP for Islwyn, was a young councillor on the new Gwent County Council when William, whom he had never met, ticked him off for not lighting the coal fire in the members' room at County Hall, which was the duty of the first councillor in the building each day.[25] Yet Lee was annoyed when William asked for beer, rather than champagne, at the wedding reception afterwards at The Ivy.[26] Bevan and Lee never had any children themselves. Bevan is said to have wanted 'a brood or none', though it seems Lee did have a miscarriage. She is said to have made clear that she did not want children:

> She said she had made this plain from the beginning: no children to get in the way of her work, to which she was dedicated. She had practised birth control successfully since her student days, but should there be any accidental pregnancy she had no doubts about what she should do. She would have an abortion, in Holland.[27]

It was an 'open' marriage. After Bevan's death, Lee told Michael Foot's wife Jill: 'I do hope Nye had some nice affairs.'[28] Bevan was certainly attracted to Barbara Castle, though there is no evidence that they had a sexual relationship. Born Barbara Betts in 1910, she was a pretty, blue-eyed redhead with strong left-wing convictions. Castle broke new ground for women in a male-dominated political world. As one of only 21 female Labour MPs elected in 1945, she went on to serve as a Cabinet minister in the governments of Harold Wilson. She was a strong, brave political operator. Once, she called into the flat shared by Bevan and Lee to find him alone listening intently to Beethoven's *Eroica*. Fond of 'physical conversations', he made an 'amorous pass' at Castle from which she extracted herself with some embarrassment before leaving. Nonetheless, she saw him as a political genius and a 'guiding light'.[29] Lee disliked Castle, and was her competitor not only in politics, but in clothes and looks as well.[30] Castle was no fan of Lee, either. In the early 1950s, exasperated by Bevan taking major decisions without consulting her or his other 'Bevanite' political allies, Castle lashed out at what she called Lee's 'Nyedolatry'. She thought that Lee reinforced the worst in Bevan, and later bemoaned the ruination of men by 'doting wives'.[31] Castle was openly in tears in the House of Commons when Bevan died.

Bevan definitely took advantage of the freedom within his marriage to Lee, as set out by her biographer, Patricia Hollis. He took Lee's university friend Suse Saemann to dinner at the Commons before spending the night with her in the Savoy Hotel. He even put his arm around Michael Foot's wife Jill and tried to touch her while she was driving. Jill asked him what he was doing, and what he would do if he was seen by the police. Bevan quipped back: 'Officer, I would say, how can you blame me?'[32] There has been a suggestion that Bevan was bisexual, but beyond an alleged homosexual act with Tom Driberg, there is little evidence to support this.[33] Lee herself seems to have tired of having affairs.[34] Perhaps because of her previous relationship with Frank Wise, she took the view that they were no longer worth it.

Bevan's sister Arianwen became one of Lee's strongest critics. Bevan's relationship with Lee certainly *did* cause a rupture with Tredegar. Bevan's marriage meant the end of Arianwen's role as his secretary. He stood down as a Monmouthshire county councillor a matter of weeks after moving in with Lee. His trips back from London to attend council meetings were no longer required. Arianwen did not mince her words. For her, Lee was 'a terrible woman'. The sheet justifying this charge was, as far as Arianwen was concerned, a long one.[35] The Bevan family had also received an anonymous letter about Lee's affair with Frank Wise, which was hardly a good start. Bevan's mother did not like Lee, either.

After two years living together in London, Bevan and Lee bought their first home together. For all his enjoyment of the social scene in London, Bevan never enjoyed living in the city. He preferred the space of the countryside. Lane End in Brimpton, close to Reading, was a picture-postcard Elizabethan thatched rural cottage with a near three-acre garden. Bevan and Lee bought it, and thoroughly enjoyed renovating it, including the installation of an open log fire.[36] However, Bevan's mother immediately took a dislike to Lane End (on the basis that it was not a solid stone cottage) and the fact that Lee did not intend to refurnish it. Lee paced the lane outside and told Bevan he had to choose between her and his mother. Bevan chose Lee, who returned to the house.

In contrast, Bevan got on famously with Lee's parents. James and Ma Lee came south of the border to live permanently with Bevan and Lee in Lane End. Lee's younger brother Tommy was in Australia, and the arrangement made sense. Neither Bevan nor Lee wanted to come home to an empty house when the other was away. Bevan had his parliamentary duties and Lee, having lost her seat in Parliament in 1931, was often on lecture tours abroad. James Lee was reluctant to leave home, but the tipping point was his health, as he had been in and out of hospital. Conscious of his own father's death, Bevan feared for James Lee if he went back down the pits, and urged Lee to persuade him. This seems to have worked, as James Lee lived until the age of 74, dying in 1952. He and Bevan often spoke until late into the night. James Lee often waited up until Bevan returned home from the Commons. But James Lee seems to have pined for his Scottish mining community. He and his daughter had often engaged in banter, but Bevan once chided Lee for going over the top with her father, and urged her to be more respectful. Being in his daughter's home and in a way relying upon her, James Lee became distant from his daughter. Though Lee and her father certainly reconciled before his death, it was Ma Lee who was in her element. A superb cook, she adored looking after Bevan and Lee. She actually outlived Bevan, dying in 1962.[37]

Meanwhile, the ill feeling between Lee and the Bevan family led to other petty incidents. On one occasion in the late 1950s, by which time Bevan and Lee had purchased Asheridge Farm in Buckinghamshire, Lee told Arianwen to put away the plates after she had not only cooked but also done the washing-up; Arianwen refused. Lee, however, threatened to drop the plates on the floor if she did not comply. Arianwen's criticisms of Lee range from the serious charge that Lee did not look after Bevan properly when he was ill, to disapproval of Lee's refusal to agree to Bevan having a large dog on the basis that her parents might be afraid of it. In 1938, after nine years in Parliament, Bevan had accumulated enough money to help his mother buy a house in Queen Square, Tredegar. It had been the town's workhouse in the nineteenth century, a fact that would not have been lost on Bevan. Lee had, however, already put her foot in it by suggesting that, as they did not have a great deal of money, the Bevan family might be better off with a council house. The Bevan family were horrified at the suggestion. When Mrs Bevan died, her Queen Square house in Tredegar went to Arianwen. Perhaps unwisely given the family situation, when Bevan and Lee sold Lane End after the Second World War and lived instead solely in London, they decided occasionally to stay with Arianwen in Tredegar on the basis that they then need not buy a second home in the country. Lee, with her usual knack of upsetting Arianwen, duly sought to dust her rooms with Arianwen's very best pillowcase.

At times, Bevan himself did not help the situation. Once, in August 1950, he refused to go to Tredegar because one of his nieces, a daughter of Arianwen, would be there as well. Lee's attempts at pouring oil on troubled waters do not read particularly well, and her letter to Arianwen playing for sympathy rings a little hollow:

> We are not youngsters with the world all before us, able to go off and live in hostels or even hotels [...] Always we are pursued by insensitive rubber-neckers. They simply cannot understand that the more public work people do, the more profound is their need of privacy at times.

Lee adds: 'We do not even have our room unless there is a tranquil easy atmosphere in the whole home.' If she and Nye were more selfish, they 'would insulate ourselves and be unaffected by others under the same roof. As it is we cannot help but be aware, responsive and so invaded.'[38] Bevan and Lee did not want to be put in a position where they would feel they had to make the effort with their niece. There is a clash of lifestyles here. Bevan and Lee were human beings having to deal not just with the public gaze but with a ferocious hatred from certain quarters. This is not to say that Arianwen did not understand the pressures on Bevan. Of course she did, and it was her caring for him that fuelled her dislike of Lee. However, Bevan's unwillingness to spend the weekend with the niece was seen as a slight to the whole Bevan family. The problem was the very fact that it was *an effort* to spend time with his niece.

Yet, ultimately, the fascination in this marriage is only relevant to the extent that it affects the interpretation of Bevan's political life. Lee was clearly a central figure in his life who gave him great emotional support. Whatever criticism is made of Jennie Lee, she was Bevan's choice and there is no evidence other than that she made him very happy. He loved her precisely *because* she was a strong, independent woman.

Chapter 6

Working-class Unity, 1935–9

T he general election of 14 November 1935 was the most recent in which the government received over half the popular vote. The National Government took a commanding 432 seats in the House of Commons. Labour took 37.9 per cent of the vote, and 154 seats. The Liberals trailed with only 20 seats. With Clement Attlee as caretaker leader, Labour had gained just over 100 seats, which was certainly a recovery on its 1931 position, but still nowhere near its 1929 total of 288 seats, and nowhere close to a parliamentary majority.

Bevan won a landslide victory in Ebbw Vale, against a single, Conservative opponent, taking 25,007 votes (77.8 per cent) to 7,145. This result was the first in a consistent pattern for Bevan in his constituency. The difference from his 1929 contest was the absence of a Liberal candidate. In fact, the national decline of the Liberal Party proved to be the only event that affected Bevan's constituency vote in any significant way, in the sense that the Liberals never again ran a candidate. The Liberal performance in 1929 proved no more than a temporary mini-revival. There was no renewal even after the Samuelite ministers had left the National Government. After 1935, Bevan fought five more elections, in 1945, 1950, 1951, 1955 and 1959. In each contest, he only faced the one opponent, a Conservative, and his vote varied only between 79.3 per cent and 81 per cent. Similarly, turnout only varied between 82.6 per cent (in 1935 and 1945) and 87 per cent (in 1951).[1] For all the major political and social changes, both domestic and international, in the 25-year period that Bevan remained in Parliament after his 1935 victory, Ebbw Vale's voting pattern never changed: four out of every five voters always voted for Bevan. Over the course of his parliamentary career, he was also a good constituency MP, building on his enthusiastic start. He took time to deal with the issues raised to him by his constituents. This is not to say that he *visited* South Wales on a regular basis. When his local party told him they wanted to see more of him, he told them that they must 'pay the price of your success' in having such a high-profile MP.[2] But while only parts of his constituency correspondence survive, the evidence available suggests that he dealt with matters conscientiously and effectively.[3]

The steelworks was a common source of complaint. Steel-making had ceased in October 1929, so, naturally, in the early 1930s, he put the case for steel-making in Ebbw Vale forcefully. On 6 February 1932, in Tredegar, Bevan addressed a conference of ten local authorities to highlight the risk of areas of Monmouthshire becoming derelict as local industries closed down. This gave the issue prominence in the national press.[4] In a letter to Leslie Hore-Belisha, then Secretary to the Treasury, on 21 September 1933, he argued that locals were 'living in a township which is under sentence of death and with the spectacle of a huge steel plant slowly decaying in its midst'. After work resumed, different problems arose. Bevan took up the issue of dust pollution, but the Ministry of Supply would not divert resources from the war effort to remove a locomotive coaling station that was causing the problems.[5] When collieries, including Ty-Trist, closed in 1959, Bevan – successfully – took up the case with the Ministry of Power for the miners who had worked there to have transport arranged for them to other pits.[6] Improving local roads had been a long-standing issue for Bevan.[7] He may not have visited Ebbw Vale every week, but he could never be accused of neglecting the issues that mattered to local people.

In contrast to Bevan's rock-solid position, Lee, standing for the ILP in 1935, was in a far more difficult position in North Lanark, as the Labour Party ran an official candidate against her. This split the Labour vote, and allowed the Conservative, William Anstruther-Gray, to take the seat. She and Bevan knew how difficult it was going to be once the Labour candidate entered the fray; Bevan wrote from Tredegar on 5 November 1935: 'Cara mio, I cannot say how sorry I am that McAlister is standing, but I was afraid of it all along.' Bevan, in pessimistic pre-election mode, thought things were difficult in Ebbw Vale with the tinplate producers Richard, Thomas & Co. having bought the steelworks. The managing director, Lady Firth, was 'spending her time in Ebbw Vale, stirring up as much trouble as she can'. He added, with a touch of gallows humour:

> in the event of my being defeated in Ebbw Vale I am looking forward to being supported by your £400 a year for North Lanark. In the event of us both being defeated I have arranged for a barrel organ. I think that would be O.K. for us because you look alright with a shawl over your head, and your Gipsy blood will come in first class.[8]

The first issue for the PLP to settle in the aftermath of the defeat was the leadership. Attlee, who had been the sitting tenant during the election campaign, after George

Lansbury's resignation, won the leadership on 26 November 1935. His principal opponent was Herbert Morrison, who had been elected to lead the Labour group on London County Council in 1933 and became leader of the council after the Labour victory in 1934; Morrison held that post until being appointed Minister of Supply in the wartime coalition of May 1940. In the first ballot, Attlee took 58 votes, Morrison 44 and Arthur Greenwood 32. Greenwood dropped out, and the final result was Attlee 88, Morrison 44.[9] William Golant, who published an article about Attlee's emergence as leader, quotes the historian A. L. Rowse: 'One observer closer to the events suggests that "Bevan directly influenced the 1935 election for the leadership by pressing trade union MPs to vote for Attlee. The election of either Morrison or Greenwood would have alienated one-third of the party. Attlee alienated none."' Golant concludes: 'Though there is no corroborating evidence of Bevan influencing MPs the general point is valid.'[10] Morrison's conception of nationalised industries run by a state board was a problem for union-sponsored MPs.[11] There are alternative explanations proposed by Morrison and his leading supporter, Hugh Dalton. Morrison and Dalton both claim that Greenwood was the Freemasons' candidate, and there was an agreed strategy of his voters switching to Attlee on the second ballot. Morrison and Dalton both argue that the Labour MPs who had served in the 1931–5 Parliament voted for Attlee (Morrison had lost his seat in 1931), and Dalton also felt that there was a sense that, if Morrison were elected, he would hang on to the leadership, but that Attlee would only be a temporary appointment.[12]

Writing in *Tribune* on 16 December 1955, when Attlee stepped down as leader, Bevan expressed his admiration for Attlee's political intuition. He argued that it accounted for his success as party leader and for his positive relationship with the party rank and file: 'They have felt safe with him even if at times he seemed too slow, too modestly cautious.' This judgement was made with the benefit of hindsight, looking back on Attlee's 20 years as leader, and is not direct evidence about what Bevan thought at the time. Bevan's view of Attlee was to change over time. Yet it is difficult to conclude that he voted for anyone other than Attlee. Morrison had been out of Parliament from 1931 to 1935, and Bevan's only contact with him tended to turn into conflict. Bevan had argued with Morrison (and Ernest Bevin) at the 1934 party conference over the NEC's proscription of the Relief Committee for the Victims of German and Austrian Fascism on the basis that it was 'auxiliary or subsidiary' to the Communist Party. Bevan's motion to change the NEC's harsh policy on dealing with the Communist Party and its associated bodies was soundly defeated by 1,820,000 votes to 89,000.[13]

Bevan's parliamentary speeches continued in the same vein as in the 1931–5 Parliament. He developed his attack on the means test, and his speeches employed a combination of aggressive rhetoric and technical skill. He understood the position of the unemployed only too well. When the National Government had introduced the means test in September 1931, existing Public Assistance Committees of local authorities had been given responsibility for assessing the needs of applicants for unemployment payments. However, such 'transitional payments' were funded by the Treasury, not by local government. A Royal Commission headed by Holman Gregory reported in November 1932, and recommended that these payments, which became known as 'unemployment assistance', should be provided by a service separate from local authorities. Neville Chamberlain, by now Chancellor of the Exchequer, readily accepted the proposal, and Part II of the Unemployment Act 1934 established a statutory commission, the Unemployment Assistance Board. Structured with a board of six members along the lines of the BBC, it was proposed that it would have its own staff. Any unemployed person who was not insured would be covered by the board; local authorities were left only with the sick and aged, and those who were temporarily in workhouses.[14] Speaking on 22 June 1936, Bevan attacked the lack of democratic accountability of the new Unemployment Assistance Board:

> It seems to me that if the House of Commons has reduced the persons I represent to such impotence, what is left for them to do? I am not going to use exaggerated language, but I ask hon. Members opposite to tell me what they think these people can do. You have deprived them of any voice anywhere.[15]

For him, the staff would be 7,000 unelected officials whose every decision could not possibly be controlled by Parliament.

There had been demonstrations in South Wales in early 1936 since the initial proposals, funded partly by the Treasury's Unemployment Assistance Fund, and a local-authority contribution, meant that many people would be worse off. Bearing in mind the public protests, Bevan concluded angrily. He said he was not going to use 'exaggerated language', but if the regulations did make conditions worse for the people he represented he hoped they would 'behave in such a manner that you will require to send a regular army to keep order [HON. MEMBERS: "Shame!"] I say that without the slightest hesitation. Hon. Members sit on those benches in cynical indifference to what has happened.'[16]

Bevan's detailed knowledge made his speeches far more than loud protests. One speech in the Commons on 15 February 1938 illustrates this. After the protests in 1936, the government had not introduced the Unemployment Assistance Board's new payment scales until late 1937, with fewer cuts. Bevan was concerned about the Labour Party's position of seeking the extension of unemployment insurance to different categories of people: 'there is a very excellent leverage in the hands of the Government which will cause them to do it more and more as time goes on, because the more the categories of insurance the more the Treasury is going to be relieved of the obligations of maintaining unemployed people.' What Bevan meant is that the scheme of unemployment insurance was funded partly by the insured workers themselves, who made contributions to it. While the government and the employers also contributed in industries that were covered (agricultural workers had recently been added), Bevan felt that: 'The general result of extensions of this sort is to unload on to the shoulders of the working class the burden of maintaining unemployed members of the working class.' Bevan correctly identified that the main difference between the unemployed person entitled to a period of unemployment insurance and the unemployed person who was not was the means test: 'What I want to do is to minimise and modify and ultimately abolish the means test so that all workers who are unable to find employment shall receive maintenance at the expense of the Treasury and not of the contributions of the rest of their fellow workers.'[17]

Bevan also was much involved outside Parliament. Such was the atmosphere of the interwar period in Britain that consideration was given to charging Bevan for sedition for the contents of a speech he made opposing the means test. On 19 June 1936, Bevan had delivered a typically strident address against the means test, sharing a platform with Aberavon MP William Cove and the outspoken Swansea preacher Reverend Leon Atkin, who became a Labour councillor that same year. There was a march from the Aberavon municipal buildings to Aberavon beach, where Bevan spoke for 30 minutes. Judging the speech is extremely difficult, since the only extracts that exist are in a letter sent by a local police inspector to a superintendent at the county police office. The contents obviously seek to paint Bevan in a negative light, and it is difficult to avoid the conclusion that there are gross exaggerations in the letter. Bevan is alleged to have said that the National Government was 'the cause of the suffering of the working people of this country'. That is entirely plausible, as is the suggestion that he overheard the prime minister, Stanley Baldwin, saying in the Commons lobby that the means test 'will lick the Reds'. Bevan may well also have said that in 1931 the government would not borrow £1 million for unemployment benefits but would now borrow £300 million for armaments. However, it is incredible that he called for violence: 'if you are forced to join [the army] by the Means Test, don't forget when you get rifles issued out to you, what forced you to join the Army, and then you will know what way to use these rifles.' Bevan may well have used what could be termed violent *phrasing*, but he had no record of calling for physical force. Secondly, given the conclusions he had drawn about the events of 1926, it is very doubtful that he would have wound up by saying, 'Stand up for your Trade Unions and bring about a general strike if the means test is passed'. The negative tone of the letter is confirmed by the suggestion that speakers failed to excite the 2,200-strong crowd, which included women and children.[18] The chief constable of Glamorgan, Lionel Lindsay, wrote to the Director of Public Prosecutions, Sir Edward Tindal Atkinson, within 48 hours, on 21 June, calling Bevan 'one of the worst agitators in South Wales and Monmouthshire. For him to use such language on such an occasion [...] is, to put it mildly, grossly seditious.'[19] The matter was dealt with as a matter of urgency at the highest level, and Atkinson wrote to Lindsay 36 hours later, on 24 June, confirming that the Attorney General, Sir Donald Somervell, had decreed that 'it would not be advisable to institute proceedings against Mr Bevan for using seditious words on the strength of one passage which occurred in the course of his political speech'.[20] Perhaps Somervell, a barrister, knew the wide-ranging legal ramifications of seeking to prosecute MPs for single passages in their public utterances. If one were to be prosecuted, where would a line be drawn? This episode is indicative not of a serious effort by the National Government to silence Bevan, but of his power as an orator and the fear of local police that he *could* influence people. If the crowd had been unaffected, as the initial letter on the matter claimed, it is doubtful that there would have been such concern.

Alongside Bevan's fight for the poorest was developing a growing antagonism with some trade union leaders. He was also starting to come into increasing conflict with his two later rivals in the Attlee government, Morrison and Bevin, who was at this time general secretary of the TGWU. Writing in the *New Statesman* in May 1936, G. D. H. Cole argued for a 'British People's Front' and a planned economy to deal with the threat of fascism, which was about to be starkly demonstrated when the Spanish Civil War began on 17 July 1936. Rebel army officers under General Franco revolted against the 'Popular Front' left-wing coalition government. The war became a proxy conflict between left and right on the continent of Europe, with fascist Germany and Italy supporting Franco, and Soviet Russia supporting the government. The conflict was a key issue at the Labour Party Conference, held in Edinburgh in October. Attlee and Bevin both declared for non-intervention. Bevan was concerned about the effect of the fall of the Spanish government on France, where, he felt, the Popular Front government would soon follow.[21] The issue was, however, a complex one. Fighting between the citizens of the same country carried risks in itself, but the danger of intervention was that the war might escalate into a general European conflict. Furthermore, the French socialist prime minister, Léon Blum, was in favour of non-intervention as he would struggle to hold together his governing coalition, which included the centre-right. Yet Mussolini was helping Franco: non-intervention effectively meant the end of the Spanish government as the side receiving less outside help. Bevan was right, and Attlee changed position in a matter of weeks.

Bevan was in favour of what he considered to be working-class unity. That same summer, the Left Book Club was founded by Victor Gollancz, Harold Laski and John Strachey. Members would be supplied with books on a monthly basis, and the club was sympathetic to the idea of Communist affiliation to the Labour Party. Bevan himself had visited Arthur Horner after the Rhondda East by-election of 28 March 1933. Horner, as a Communist, lost to the Labour candidate, the local miners' agent, W. H. Mainwaring, who was the driving force behind the expulsion of Horner's Mardy Lodge from the SWMF.[22] Bevan told Horner that he would have spoken on his behalf, *had he stood as a miners' candidate*.[23] Bevan spoke at Cory Hall in Cardiff at a meeting of working-class organisations called by the South Wales and Monmouthshire Division of Trades Councils. Bevan declared that capitalism was doomed and that it had already declared war on democracy.[24] His view at the time was that Communist affiliation would lead to a 'spiritual reawakening of the British Working-Class movement'.[25] He was reflecting the views of the SWMF, which had not only voted in support of affiliation, but elected Horner as president in April 1936. Bevan did not, however, maintain a consistent view on Communist affiliation. He also saw Communists as an electoral enemy of socialists. In the 1950s, he praised the Italian Socialist leader Pietro Nenni, with whom he formed a close personal bond, for his work in gaining votes at the expense of the Communists.[26] Nenni's Italian Socialists had allied with the Communists in the immediate aftermath of the Second World War, but freed themselves. But in the 1930s, Bevan saw political sense in coordinated political activity. He asked why a

> first-class piece of work like the Hunger March has been left to the initiative of unofficial members of the Party, and to the Communists and the ILP [...] Consider what a mighty response the workers would have made if the whole machinery of the Labour Movement had been mobilised for the Hunger March and its attendant activities.[27]

Morrison's dislike of the Communists related not only to their attacks on his administration at London County Council, but also to their entryist tactics: 'Local party after local party was weakened, good men and women were discouraged by the organised activities of Communist factions stirring up trouble.'[28] Bevin was particularly concerned about the role of Communists in unofficial strikes, which he believed they fomented to the detriment of the wider trade union movement. In the event, the vote at the Labour Party Conference in Edinburgh in October 1936 went against affiliation by the large margin of 1.728 million to 592,000. The vote marked a break between Morrison and George Strauss, who had argued for it. At that time Strauss was MP for Lambeth North and a member of London County Council. Morrison removed him as chair of the Highways Committee and vice chair of the Finance Committee.[29]

It was the money of Strauss and Cripps that went to the founding in January 1937 of *Tribune*, which was to play such a large part in Bevan's political life.[30] Bevan's conflict with the trade unions was to continue through the pages of *Tribune*. Take this article on 12 August 1938: 'Big wage problem faces the T.U.C.' Bevan made a generalised attack on the trade unions: 'There are eighteen million workers in Great Britain. They are wage-earners. The kind of life that they and their families live is determined by the amount of wages they earn.' He then moved on to the plight of the unemployed: 'almost two million of them, living on standards below subsistence and kept there because it is considered wrong to give them as much as they could by working.' Bevan criticised unions for acting individually at the expense of raising wages for the working class as a whole: 'In short, what is wanted is a policy for all workers, irrespective of the occupation they follow. For only in such a policy will they feel their identity of interest and find their strength.'

There was a mutual suspicion between much of the left and many trade union leaders. Walter Citrine was vehemently opposed to the Socialist League and puzzled by the behaviour of Stafford Cripps: 'Like many others, I was perplexed to understand how a man of such legal eminence could utter such irresponsible drivel, characteristic of the tyro in public affairs.'[31] Citrine had met leading members of the league, including Cripps and Cole, at the London School of Economics on 3 July 1933. Cripps said that government aims would, on the whole, be carried out through Orders in Council, minimising the parliamentary scrutiny and opposition that primary legislation would bring. Cripps even envisaged a Labour government extending its life beyond the maximum five years prescribed by the Parliament Act of 1911. Cole openly criticised the parliamentary method for carrying out fundamental change, saying that it was useful only for gradual change. Citrine also asked Cole about a view he had expressed that all property worth over £1,000 should be confiscated by the state on death. Citrine wryly remarked that he 'did not think this was the way in which the middle class would be converted'.[32] Bevan did not share the pessimism of Cripps and Cole on the effectiveness of the parliamentary system.

On 24 January 1937, the Communist Party combined with the ILP and the Socialist League to launch a 'Unity Manifesto' in the Free Trade Hall, Manchester, with Cripps, Bevan and Horner among the signatories calling for class conflict rather than class collaboration. Labour's NEC prohibited association with the Communist Party. On 24 March 1937, the committee decided that members of the Socialist League would not be entitled to Labour Party membership from 1 June. With its membership falling, the league held a dissolution conference in Leicester on 15 May. As the historian Paul Corthorn concluded, this was a 'major blow. For the remainder of the 1930s the Labour left would take a different – and markedly less cohesive – form.'[33]

On 7 October 1938, *Tribune* carried a front-page view from Bevan, who said that the

> Tories in the House of Commons are scared of Chamberlain's policy. They feel they are back to 1914 once more, faced by a Germany made immensely more powerful by seven years of National Government rule. The ruling classes are demoralised to an extent that would have appeared incredible a few months ago.

He added: 'The initiative is passing to the Labour Party and it has only to be grasped with courage and energy to transform the present hopeless situation.'[34] Labour policy on defence had shifted decisively in the late 1930s. After the pacifism of George Lansbury, party leader from 1932 to 1935, Attlee had set up a Labour defence committee on becoming leader himself. Labour, with Hugh Dalton particularly prominent as foreign-affairs spokesman, moved slowly towards a policy of rearmament. Bevan was opposed to the party's change of policy in July 1937 on voting against the arms estimates. He did not think socialists should vote to give the national government arms.

As a vehement anti-fascist, Bevan was, however, increasingly critical of the Chamberlain administration. He was more in tune with Attlee when he opposed Neville Chamberlain's Munich Agreement. Hitler had annexed Austria to Germany in the *Anschluss* of 12 March 1938, and then demanded the annexation of the Sudetenland, the ethnically German part of Czechoslovakia. Neville Chamberlain flew to Munich to meet Hitler, and, on 30 September 1938, agreed to concede the Sudetenland to Germany declaring, famously, on arriving back at Heston Aerodrome, that he had secured 'peace for our time'. The following month, Cripps sought an immediate cross-party 'Popular Front' alliance between anti-appeasement MPs in the Conservative Party and Labour Party to remove Chamberlain, of which Attlee was allegedly in favour.[35] Bevan's visit to Spain in

January 1938 as an invitee of the Spanish government had also fortified him in his passion for events in Spain, and he was horrified when Chamberlain recognised the Franco government in February 1939. Yet his friendship with Beaverbrook remained strong, despite the latter's *Daily Express* supporting Chamberlain's attempts to secure peace. Bevan had never been attracted to Beaverbrook's views, in any event. He was attracted to sparkling conversation with those he saw as interesting, including the more raffish Tories, and had no time for the cold, austere Chamberlain.

Meanwhile, Bevan and Cripps had become firm political friends. While their relationship was to deteriorate when they were both Cabinet ministers, the late 1930s was the high watermark of their allegiance. Bevan saw Cripps as a political older brother, a principled voice of the left who was unafraid to stand up to authority, even on his own side. That is not to say that their perspectives were the same. One major difference between Cripps and Bevan was their attitudes to religion. Bevan was agnostic. In contrast, Cripps had been brought up by his father, Charles Cripps, later Lord Parmoor, as a High Church Anglican. After he returned from his period as British ambassador to Moscow, Cripps served for a time in the War Cabinet. Churchill is said to have once remarked: 'There, but for the grace of God, goes God!' Cripps also had direct influence in bringing Foot into contact with Bevan. Foot had been a contemporary of Cripps' son at Oxford, and Foot's first job in Liverpool as a shipping clerk was in a company in which the Cripps family had a majority holding. Bevan helped Foot in return. It was in the offices of *Tribune* that the friendship between Foot and Bevan was forged. Barbara Castle takes the view that Bevan, seeing the potential in Foot, 'turned the chrysalis into a butterfly'. Firstly, Bevan bought a machine to apply ultraviolet rays to Foot's debilitating eczema. Secondly, he recommended him to Beaverbrook, as a result of which Foot was offered a job on the *Evening Standard*.[36]

On 9 January 1939, Cripps wrote to the Labour Party general secretary, then the former journalist James Middleton, seeking an NEC meeting to discuss a memorandum he had prepared on a Popular Front, suggesting that, in the exceptional circumstances of the time, Labour should negotiate with other parties of the left. By this time, the situation in Spain had worsened. Franco's troops were in the Barcelona suburbs. The NEC rejected the memorandum, and, exasperated by Cripps' continued organisation of campaigns outside the party, demanded that he pledge loyalty to the party constitution and withdraw the memorandum. Cripps would not back down. Bevan became one of his staunchest advocates. At an 'Arms for Spain' meeting in the Queen's Hall on 25 January 1939, the day of Cripps' expulsion, Bevan declared his allegiance: 'If Sir Stafford Cripps is expelled [...] for wanting to unite the forces of freedom and democracy they can go on expelling others. They can expel me. His crime is my crime.' He despaired of Parliament: 'It can be stirred from outside, but only from outside.'[37] Cripps formed a 'Petition Committee' for a Popular Front, and the NEC responded by indicating that all those who backed it would be in danger of expulsion. Bevan was duly expelled on 31 March 1939.

Chapter 7

The Second World War, Part I: 1939–42

T he Second World War made Aneurin Bevan a household name. On the maxim that all publicity is good publicity, Bevan had a good war. When Neville Chamberlain declared war on Nazi Germany in a radio broadcast on 3 September 1939, Bevan, having been expelled, was not even a member of the Labour Party. Six years later, he held one of the most important Cabinet posts at perhaps the most crucial time in the twentieth century, responsible for the nation's postwar health provision and housing. Aside from the effect on Bevan's political prospects, there is a wider democratic case to be made for his actions. His attack on the wartime coalition government had two separate strands. The first was the government's effectiveness at prosecuting the war; the second was civil liberties at home. To have provided a critique in these areas is hardly ignoble, and there is an argument that such opposition politics played a part in keeping Churchill and his ministers on their mettle.

Such judgement, however, has the benefit of hindsight. For Britain in the Second World War had an extraordinary sense of common purpose. Politically, this found expression not just in the coalition government itself but in the electoral truce declared between the main political parties for the duration of the war. Bevan's problem was that in expressing the views he did, he appeared to be doing more than holding the government to account from the opposition benches. He was striking a blow at the very heart of the nation's collective spirit. His position was made stark by the behaviour of the actual leaders of the opposition during the war. The position was held by, in succession, Hastings Lees-Smith, Frederick Pethick-Lawrence and Arthur Greenwood, who carried out the role only in order to ensure that parliamentary business proceeded smoothly, which would have been difficult had the post been left vacant. None of them saw themselves as questioning and opposing the government on a regular basis.

For all the controversy that was to dog Bevan, his start to the conflict was remarkably low-key. It was at Lane End Cottage that Bevan and Lee heard confirmation of the outbreak of war, on the one o'clock news on BBC Radio. Lee recalled:

> We had discussed this so often and so much. Now at last it had come. Our enemy Hitler had become the national enemy. All those who hated fascism would have their chance now. They would have their chance to fight back. No more one-sided massing of all the wealth, influence and arms of international reaction against the workers of first one country then another.

She then sets out how Bevan reacted. He was pacing: 'He stopped walking up and down to rummage in a corner among a disorderly pile of gramophone records. He found what he was looking for. He found records we had not dared to play for more than a year: the marching songs of the Spanish Republican armies.' He became restless, and went to London. When he returned, he told Lee that he sensed a different mood: 'Funny driving today, says he. Everyone went a little faster, more erratically, more recklessly.'[1]

By early December 1939, Bevan had been readmitted to the Labour Party, having applied for readmission the day after his expulsion. He always believed in the Labour Party as the only effective machine for progress in British politics, and did not wish to be outside the fold for any significant period. The reaction to the expulsion episode also marked his first visible move out of the shadow of Cripps. Bevan, Strauss and Cripps had written to the Labour Party NEC offering to sign undertakings that applied to all members in terms of criticising party policy, but reserving the right to participate in free discussion. The executive placed the matters in the hands of a subcommittee, which sought an apology, together with a blanket acceptance of party rules and policy and a declaration not to participate in campaigns against party policy. Cripps rejected this out of hand, and was, in the event, not readmitted to the Labour Party until 1945 when Attlee appointed him President of the Board of Trade. Bevan was more pragmatic, and, with the support of the SWMF, he and Strauss agreed on a compromise formula: 'to refrain from conducting or taking part in campaigns in opposition to the declared policy of the Party; but this declaration does not interfere with my legitimate rights within the Party Constitution.'[2] The virulence of the *Western Mail* often undermined its own effectiveness, and here it was no different, as it railed against the voters of Ebbw Vale, who it thought would in any event re-elect Bevan when an election came: 'This escapade would cost him his seat in many parts of the country, but in Ebbw Vale we suppose it counts for political righteousness.'[3]

In the early part of the war, two issues in particular led Bevan to attack the government in the Commons. The Home Secretary, Sir John Anderson, had introduced a battery of emergency powers that Bevan thought unduly compromised civil liberties. Also, in a precursor to his later wartime parliamentary battles, he berated the government for leaving in place the hated means test. When Churchill became prime minister on 10 May 1940 and retained Chamberlain in his War Cabinet, Bevan was incensed that he should remain. Yet Bevan played no role in the fall of Chamberlain. Bevan was not even called to speak in the famous Norway debate, which commenced on Tuesday, 7 May 1940. Germany had invaded Norway on 3 April. On 2 May, the troops Britain had put ashore to repel the invaders had to be withdrawn. On an adjournment motion, the government majority fell from over 200 to just 81, with 41 Conservative MPs voting against the government. The two crucial interventions in the debate were from Leo Amery and David Lloyd George. Amery famously quoted Oliver Cromwell when he dismissed the Rump Parliament in 1653: 'You have sat too long here for any good you have been doing. Depart, I say, and let us have done with you. In the name of God, go.' Lloyd George told Chamberlain to 'sacrifice the seals of office'.[4]

The historian Max Hastings effectively sums up the problem with Bevan's conduct during the Second World War. Describing Bevan as a 'dogged class warrior', Hastings writes that, on the one hand: 'Throughout the war, Bevan upheld Britain's democratic tradition by sustaining unflagging criticism of the government.' On the other: 'His figures were accurate, but his scorn was at odds with the spirit of the moment – full of gratitude, as was the prime minister.'[5] Michael Foot compares Bevan with Charles James Fox, Prime Minister William Pitt the Younger's great rival in the late eighteenth and early nineteenth centuries. While Foot concedes that Bevan did not see the Second World War as 'unjust and unnecessary' in the way that Fox saw the French Revolutionary and early Napoleonic wars of Pitt, he sees a remarkable comparison between the two men, 150 years apart, in their critique of the British war effort.[6]

It would be churlish to suggest that there are not elements of comparison here, not least in the obvious sense of Fox's critique of Pitt's conduct of the conflicts. Bevan fulfilled a similar role in opposition to Churchill. No doubt Fox and Bevan both possessed extraordinary charisma that gave them circles of devoted followers, and both were first-rank orators. However, this analysis can be overstated. Fox's biographer, L. G. Mitchell, puts his finger on it:

Fox had little or no interest in the exercise of power [...] Having influence gave him pleasure, in that it sometimes allowed him to promote or reward his friends, and to pursue single issues like the slave question, but that was the extent of it. He was quite incapable of mastering the detail of a question.[7]

In this major respect, Bevan could not have been more different. He did not seek power as a means of assisting others up the greasy pole, but he was fascinated by it, and had an outstanding ability to master detail. Bevan does not belong in the Foxite dissenting tradition.

If he was not wholly some latter-day Fox, the question arises as to how best to characterise the wartime Bevan. He was not, as Robert Crowcroft describes him, 'the era's biggest hypocrite'.[8] He was not a blinkered critic of Churchill. He justified himself to Archie Lush on two bases: 'Hey listen boyo […] if Churchill is knocked down with a bus tomorrow what will we do, write to Hitler and say we give in?' He added: 'Look, it is after the war this fellow [Churchill] is going to be dangerous, if we make him into a God.'[9] These are valid arguments. Concern about the over-reliance on one man, Churchill, and the political danger Churchill posed to the Labour Party after the war, was common sense. Also, as a consequence of two incidents, Churchill was seen as an enemy not only of the British working class as a whole, but more specifically of the South Wales miners. During the 1926 General Strike, Churchill was highly aggressive towards the strikers, and was content to see tanks on the streets.

Aside from this general belligerence towards working people, there was a specific charge against Churchill relating to the Tonypandy Riots, when he was Home Secretary in Asquith's Liberal government. The story grew in the South Wales coalfield that Churchill had 'turned the guns on the miners'.[10] This may be inaccurate. The chief constable of South Glamorgan sought troop reinforcements after rioting broke out close to the Ely Pit on 7 November 1910. Churchill apparently held the infantry at Swindon and the cavalry were only allowed as far as Pontypridd, on the confluence of the Rhondda and Taff rivers, and not in the Rhondda Valleys themselves. Only as the troubles continued did Churchill send a detachment of the Lancashire Fusiliers into the Rhondda itself, where they remained stationed for almost a year.[11] But, even if the Lancashire Fusiliers did not face the strikers across the barricades, nonetheless, the Glamorgan Constabulary did, and Churchill was always in the background with the threat of troops.

Bevan was not an admirer of Churchill as a politician, and thought Lloyd George the greater man.[12] The wartime coalition, not only headed by Churchill, but bestrode by him as the man whose oratory had repelled Hitler in the summer of 1940, was a natural target for Bevan. But his behaviour was not motivated purely by this personal dislike and political rivalry. Nor should it be seen as an exercise in pure egotism. Like George Orwell, Bevan believed passionately in the transformational potential of the Second World War. Writing in 1940, in an essay entitled 'My country right or left', Orwell argued: 'Only revolution can save England, that has been obvious for years, but now the revolution has started, and it may proceed quite quickly if only we can keep Hitler out.'[13] In his 1941 essay 'The lion and the unicorn', Orwell was optimistic that change was under way:

> The English revolution started several years ago, and it began to gather momentum when the troops came back from Dunkirk. Like all else in England, it happens in a sleepy, unwilling way, but it is happening. The war has speeded it up, but it has also increased, and desperately, the necessity for speed.[14]

Bevan concurred. He saw the defeat of Hitler as a necessary (but not sufficient) step on the road to socialism. Labour had to realise that the tide of history was moving in its direction, and ride on it to victory in the first peacetime general election. Bevan most certainly did not restrict his criticism to the wartime government's plans for the peace, but, once it was obvious that the D-Day landings had established a beachhead in Normandy, it was to that that he almost exclusively directed his fire.

Bevan was a natural advocate for the underdog. His whole argument about civil liberties in wartime was an expression of his desire to argue for the plight of the underprivileged, for those who lacked power. He recognised that there had to be a restriction on civil liberties for the war effort. If anything, though, that wartime compromise made the task of monitoring civil liberties even more pressing. He was, naturally, most concerned with the rights of working people, especially the miners, but he should not be seen purely as a class warrior. In fact, while they were never personally close, Bevan's criticisms of the wartime coalition have a great deal in common with those made by Orwell. Nobody applies the blunt criticism of 'class warrior' to the great Orwell. Instead, Orwell's line of argument has been referred to as 'revolutionary patriotism', a label he first applied to himself in *Tribune* on 20 December 1940. Orwell wrote regularly in *Tribune* from the spring of 1943, and had his own broad 'As I please' column from 3 December 1943, though Jennie Lee also wrote the column later in the war. As an elected politician, Bevan was far more prominent than Orwell in his criticisms, making him a more obvious target for venom, but also the 'class warrior' tag attaches less easily to the Eton-educated Orwell.

As the Allies approached victory, Orwell and Bevan were at one on two issues. First, they opposed wholesale punishment of the German people and the insistence on unconditional surrender.[15] Second, they were disgusted at the Soviet Union's adopting of the mantle of a colonial great power, treating the peoples of Eastern Europe as mere subjects as Stalin carved up the territory with Churchill and President Roosevelt. Orwell's anti-Stalinist stance found expression in his famous political allegory *Animal Farm*, published on 17 August 1945, just 48 hours after the Japanese surrender. Orwell and Bevan respected each other and allowed each other the freedom to express their views. One description of *Tribune* weekly editorial meetings is as follows: 'rather like a stage play by Harold Pinter, with Bevan and Orwell speaking in monologues about what each would be writing for the next issue.'[16] Where Orwell and Bevan parted company was on Labour's electoral prospects in 1945. Orwell predicted a small Conservative majority.[17] This may be because of a difference in assessment on social change in Britain. Orwell did not comment on the British domestic political situation in *Tribune* from 1943 onwards because 'he had long since given up his high hopes of 1940–1 that Britain was on the verge of a socialist revolution'.[18] Bevan remained convinced that a postwar Labour government could drive through a radical socialist programme.

If the conflict could be won militarily, there would be a great opportunity to build a new world. That same argument had formed the basis of Jennie Lee's book, *To-morrow Is a New Day*.[19] It was a further reason for attacking Churchill: the Britain that Bevan wanted to emerge from the war was not an extension of the 1930s but under a different Tory peacetime prime minister. For Labour to grasp the opportunity after the war, he realised that Churchill's personal popularity would be a major obstacle. In the autumn of 1940, Neville Chamberlain was dying of cancer. Mindful of Lloyd George's weakened position after the First World War, when he was left without the leadership of any party, Churchill seized the Conservative Party leadership. Bevan saw the political danger immediately, as the 'Tory caucus drapes itself in the national flag'.[20] But even Bevan acknowledged the greatness of Churchill's speeches in the late spring and summer of 1940.[21] The issue was not Churchill's leadership of the nation in this most testing of periods, but that the prime minister was not the man to lead Britain in the new world *after* the war: 'Mr Churchill ennobles retreat and can rally the nation to make its stand here in this island, but he cannot unfold for us the plans for victory.'[22]

Bevan philosophised deeply on the battle, and, having never held ministerial office, identified strongly with other thinkers. There is a revealing account of a conversation with Bevan in the diary of Harold Nicolson. On 4 December 1941, three days before the Japanese attack on Pearl Harbor, Bevan told Nicolson that:

> *we intellectuals* are in a difficult position [my emphasis]. Our tastes
> attract us to the past, our reason to the future. Hitherto we have been
> able to appease this conflict since our tastes were still able to find their
> outlets, whereas our reason could indulge in the picture of the shape
> of things to come.

Bevan saw that money and travel were two of the pleasures lost in the war, and felt that there was 'a tendency therefore for the weaker souls to escape to mysticism. Their reason tells them that the future is right, but it is agony for them to lose the past.'[23] According to Nicolson, the two men Bevan identified as having suffered this fate were the philosopher C. E. M. Joad, who was becoming famous for his performances on the wartime BBC Radio discussion show, *The Brains Trust*, and the novelist Aldous Huxley, who was by then learning spiritual practices at the Hollywood-based Vedanta Society of Southern California, founded by the Indian philosopher and monk Swami Prabhavananda. Bevan apparently thought that Nicolson himself was too courageous to go the same way. The same could be said of Bevan himself. That did not, however, prevent him being mocked for his passion for intellectual discussion. Morrison was unsympathetic: 'In Bevan [... his...] background had produced an undue sense of bitter grievance combined with a desire to be highly intellectual and a master of strange words. He was a bit of a hybrid: half proletarian and half intellectual.'[24]

Throughout the war, Bevan had a regular outlet for his views: *Tribune*. Its pro-Soviet editor, H. J. Hartshorn, was replaced in early 1940 by Raymond Postgate, who was much more in line with the pro-war socialist view. For British socialists who looked to the Russian Revolution for inspiration, the Nazi–Soviet Pact had been difficult to bear. The Nazi foreign minister, Joachim von Ribbentrop, and his Soviet opposite number, Vyacheslav Molotov, signed the agreement on 23 August 1939. Together with its secret protocol, it carved up Eastern Europe between Germany and the Soviet Union, and allowed Germany to invade Poland the following week, having already squared Stalin. In terms of realpolitik, there was a strong logic to this. Stalin had moved the Soviet border a couple of hundred kilometres to the east, and prevented the Soviet Union becoming isolated by a pact between the Nazis, France and Britain. This did not, however, obscure the stark reality that Communist Russia was now arm in arm with the fascists. Writing in August 1941, Jennie Lee sought to explain the actions of Stalin on the basis of the isolation the Soviet Union had been subjected to by European nations during the interwar period.[25] This is one explanation, but it did not prevent Bevan from strongly criticising Stalin's invasion of Finland on 30 November 1939. He and Lee respected each other's independent views. Then, when Hitler eventually turned on Stalin and launched Operation Barbarossa on 22 June 1941, it gave clarity to the position of the left. Now support could be given to Stalin in his fight against fascism. Two days later, Bevan argued for the opening of a second front in Western Europe in the House of Commons, and took to the pages of *Tribune* arguing for aid for Russia.[26]

Bevan, Strauss and Victor Gollancz formed *Tribune*'s editorial board, and then, in early 1942, Bevan took over as editor himself. As he was busy in Parliament, Bevan needed someone else to carry out the administrative side of the job. That person was Jon Kimche, a Swiss Jew who had written for the *Evening Standard* and came on Michael Foot's recommendation. Kimche was soon joined by Evelyn Anderson. Born to a German Jewish family, Anderson had strong anti-Communist views. She was shortly joined by George Orwell, who became *Tribune*'s literary editor in 1943. Bevan remained in the role until 1945. He was a good journalist. His articles were pugnacious and well argued. While they were not written with the sole motive of promoting discussion, they certainly fulfilled the purpose of expressing a strong opinion and provoking a reaction in the reader. That was not, however, the standard by which Bevan wanted his work to be judged. His *Tribune* articles were an extension of his critique of the wartime coalition outside Parliament; in Parliament, his speeches were his weapon. Writing every week alongside his many other engagements hardly gave him significant time to reflect on his contributions, but the act of having to write out his articles meant that, inevitably, his *Tribune* pieces were more considered than some of his parliamentary interventions.

It was on the issue of Russia that Bevan had his first wartime clash with Herbert Morrison, who had replaced Sir John Anderson as Home Secretary. Ironically, it was on a matter upon which they agreed. Bevan saw the strategic necessity of the Soviet Union entering the war at an early stage, and did not accept the British Communist Party position of 'revolutionary defeatism', which held that the proletariat had nothing to gain from a capitalist war. Bevan had savaged the *Daily Worker* in *Tribune* on 13 September 1940 for assisting Hitler. Morrison, on the same basis, closed down the newspaper in January 1941. Bevan was outraged, and denounced Morrison in the House of Commons. His argument was that Britain's love of liberty found expression in its tolerance of organs such as the *Daily Worker* in this most testing of times, and that that evoked admiration, particularly in the US: 'The Home Secretary by his action has now deprived us of that precious asset. He has made a present to our enemies of the fact that we feel so insecure that we can no longer permit the liberty that this newspaper was enjoying.'[27]

At times during the war, despite his position as Churchill's tormentor-in-chief, Bevan did carry out tasks at the request of the government behind the scenes.

On one occasion, he went with the Catholic MP Dick Stokes to Ireland to see if the Taoiseach, Éamon de Valera, could be persuaded to allow a British troop presence to deter a potential German invasion. De Valera was, however, immovable, and may even have remembered Bevan's admiration for Sinn Fein figures like De Valera's great rival, Michael Collins.[28] Similarly, at the request of Brendan Bracken, then Minister of Information, Jennie Lee went to America in late 1941 to drum up support for the British war effort. However, there was no friendliness with Morrison away from the public gaze. Bevan's attack on the suppression of the *Daily Worker* was entirely authentic, and based on a sound civil-liberties footing. But his feud with Morrison as Home Secretary was more than political, as he discovered in the days after the Commons debate. Bevan had only garnered six votes in favour of censuring Morrison, but he had certainly got under the Home Secretary's skin. Worse was to come in early 1942. On 6 March that year, the *Daily Mirror* had published a cartoon by Philip Zec showing a merchant seaman in the oily wreckage of a ship with a caption linking this to the recent increase in petrol prices. Morrison did not, in fact, suppress the *Daily Mirror*, though he could have done under the emergency wartime regulations. Rather than do nothing either, Morrison took the middle course of issuing the newspaper with a warning. Bevan's subsequent attack on Morrison in the Commons on 26 March was vitriolic:

> I have heard a number of hon. Members say that it is a hateful paper, a tabloid paper, a hysterical paper, a sensational paper, and that they do not like it. I am sure the Home Secretary does not take that view. He likes the paper. He takes its money.

In a testy exchange, Morrison told Bevan not to make it personal, as someone 'closely connected' with him was also taking the *Daily Mirror*'s money. He was referring to Jennie Lee, who was at that time working as the *Daily Mirror*'s House of Commons representative. Bevan brushed him aside: 'Be as personal as you like.'[29] Bevan then waved a copy of the *Daily Mirror* from 1 February 1940 in which Morrison had penned an article, 'My report on what the people want'. Mockingly, Bevan added that this was part of a series that Morrison had written.

Morrison fumed about Bevan's behaviour, and the following month the PLP issued him with an official rebuke for his actions. Morrison had spoken at a meeting of the PLP against both Bevan and another of his critics, Bassetlaw MP Frederick Bellenger. The matter was referred to the PLP's Administrative Committee, which issued a statement expressing 'strong disapproval' of the personal attacks on Morrison by Bevan and Bellenger; these were in breach of the standing order that members should take 'special care' not to attack other members and were 'completely out of harmony with the spirit of fellowship within the party'. Worse still, Bevan became a victim of the very 'police state' mentality he was fighting against in Parliament, as MI5 kept him under surveillance.[30]

The Morrison–Bevan rivalry became increasingly fierce as the year progressed. One exchange, on 18 December 1941, was so heated that the Deputy Speaker of the House of Commons, Sir Dennis Herbert, had to suspend the sitting. Regulation 18B of the government's wartime emergency powers gave the Home Secretary the power to imprison dangerous citizens without trial. The Ministry of Information formed the view that a proposed BBC Radio broadcast on the provision was not impartial, and sought Morrison's view before banning it. Morrison's position was that he had only expressed a view, not actually banned it himself. Bevan went straight for him: 'The right. hon. Gentleman's cheek is sticking out.' Morrison asked Bevan what he was being accused of, and duly got his answer: 'It is obvious that the right. hon. Gentleman is talking with a very large tongue in a very distended cheek.' Morrison stuck to his guns and sought to distance himself from the actual decision itself: 'they asked our view and we gave it and they themselves came to the conclusion which they did, having been under no obligation to me.'[31]

There was a restlessness in the Labour ranks in December 1941. Forty rebels, including Bevan, had opposed an extension of conscription early that month. Bevan had also clashed with Bevin on 10 December on the issue of MPs not being exempted from National Service. Just days after the Japanese attack on Pearl Harbor, the debate reads like an oddly technical discussion at a time when there were greater matters of substance at stake: 'If the Minister of Labour directed me to do a job which I considered would interfere with my parliamentary duties [...] I would take no notice of his direction.' He added:

> It may be embarrassing for him to learn this, but I would consider that the direction given to me by my constituents was more impor- tant than his direction and that I should be, in fact, betraying the confidence imposed in me by my constituents if I took any notice of his direction.[32]

The debate was certainly entertaining. Bevan slapped down a Tory backbencher, the former Liberal Sir Edward Grigg, who asked whether, if Bevan joined the army, he would become an officer. Bevan remarked that he could overcome the disadvantage of not having been to Harrow or Rugby and enter the officer class. But the deeper point is that the debate marked a new strand in Bevan's line of attack on the wartime coalition: its decision-making processes, which neglected the role of Parliament.

Another significant bone of contention was India. Bevan sympathised with the aims of the anti-colonial Indian National Congress (INC), and its leader Jawaharlal Nehru. Later, in the 1950s, he would be welcomed to India by Prime Minister Nehru with open arms. In Nehru, a Cambridge graduate who had been called to the English Bar, and who was a self-confessed socialist, Bevan saw the potential for a socialist India. Like Bevan, despite – or perhaps because of – visiting the Soviet Union, he was a socialist but not a Communist. This piece by Nehru could have been written by Bevan: 'Russia apart, the theory and philosophy of Marxism lightened up many a dark corner of my mind. History came to have a new meaning for me.' Nehru was instinctively sympathetic to Marxist analysis, but suspicious of Russia ('The Bolsheviks may blunder or even fail because of national or international reasons, and yet the communist theory may be correct'), and disliked the Indian Communists: 'as soon as they leave their general principles and enter into details [...] they go hopelessly astray.'[33]

Bevan's position on India must be judged in context. In 1939, when Britain declared war, the viceroy of India, Lord Linlithgow, had declared India at war too, without even troubling to consult the Indian leaders. The INC withdrew from the provincial legislatures that had been set up under the Government of India Act 1935. The Indian Muslim leader Muhammad Ali Jinnah, on behalf of his party, the All-India Muslim League, saw the political sands shifting, and in March 1940 made his 'Lahore declaration' for a Muslim state, Pakistan. Later that same year, Linlithgow made what became known as his 'August offer' of an Indian-drafted constitution and a legislative assembly. This was rejected, and Gandhi stepped up his civil-disobedience campaign. Japanese forces might threaten the Raj, and Britain had to strike a very careful balance between maintaining the defences of India in the event of a Japanese attack, but also keeping onside the anti-imperialist American President Roosevelt, who compared the British position in India with the War of American Independence.[34]

The position in the Far East became more urgent in early 1942. On 10 December 1941, the battleship *Prince of Wales* and the cruiser *Repulse* had been sunk by Japanese aircraft in the South China Sea. The Singapore naval base fell on 15 February 1942. That prompted a reshuffle in Churchill's government. On 19 February, Attlee became Dominions Secretary and deputy prime minister. He also became the chair of the Cabinet's India Committee. Cripps, who had been sent to Moscow as ambassador in June 1940, became Lord Privy Seal. Increasingly concerned about the Japanese threat to British India, Churchill dispatched Cripps to the Raj to negotiate a settlement in March 1942. Cripps was a canny choice, with his expertise in Indian affairs and his contacts with the INC. If he could strike a deal with the party, that would be welcomed. If he could not, it was important to ensure that Britain should be able to demonstrate to Roosevelt that it had made the best effort it could to seek such an agreement.

The British War Cabinet was willing to commit to setting up an elected body to frame a new constitution for India once the war was over. However, during the conflict, the key issue for Britain was to be able to take responsibility for India's defence in order to protect its interests in the Far East. This latter requirement proved to be the sticking point. The most Cripps could offer was a change of wording: 'organising to the full the military moral and material resources of India with the cooperation of the peoples of India.'[35] Churchill confirmed to Cripps on 2 April that the War Cabinet was unwilling to alter the wording further, and that the Indians were using the defence issue to avoid reaching agreement.[36] Cripps continued to try to find a solution before confirming to Churchill on 10 April that all hope was lost. He left India two days later.[37]

Matters, at the high political level at least, had been on hold until the Cripps mission had concluded. In August 1942, Gandhi launched his 'Quit India' campaign. On 9 August 1942, Attlee ordered the arrest of Gandhi and Nehru. *Tribune* took a very critical line. On 14 August, it set out the plight of Indian workers (who were not in the armaments industry), and the problem of rising prices, together with that of the advancing Japanese army; the *Tribune* argument was to highlight these underlying problems that Attlee's arrests could not solve:

> Men like Nehru have made offer after offer to us only to be spurned. Congress tactics and even its policy may be questioned, but that is the concern of the Indians. Have we done what we could do to enable a settlement to be reached before it is too late again?[38]

Attlee's point was that a negotiated solution had been attempted and had failed. The arrests were illiberal, but a necessity in order to ensure that Britain had the capacity to defend India.[39]

The Indian issue not only brought Bevan into conflict with Attlee and Bevin; it also led him to criticise Cripps. Under a front-page headline of 'Ersatz leadership' on 21 August 1942, *Tribune* harried Churchill for his failure to make firm pledges to Stalin about opening a second front in Western Europe during their recent face-to-face meeting. It then attacked the Labour leaders: 'We have numerically the most organised Labour Movement this country has ever known [...] As yet it remains unrepresented in the Cabinet by Attlee and Bevin, *and also indirectly by Cripps* [my emphasis].'[40] Noticeably, Bevan offered no support to the suggestion that Cripps might be a better leader than Churchill. Cripps had returned from Moscow after his period as British ambassador on a high. *The Times* praised his 'political far-sightedness'.[41] There was cross-party disillusionment with the prime minister and, on 1 May 1942, *Tribune* had launched a sustained attack on Churchill's strategy for winning the war. There was a lengthy charge list put by Frank Owen, which included not only the failure to open up a second front in Western Europe, but also the Norway disaster of May 1940, the Balkan campaign of April–May 1940, the fall of Crete, and the loss of *Prince and Wales* and *Repulse*.

Bevan was initially optimistic when Cripps was appointed Leader of the House of Commons in February 1942. He thought Cripps could influence Churchill from within the War Cabinet. After all, Cripps, like Bevan, was an advocate for a second front in Western Europe to relieve the pressure on Russia on the Eastern Front, and Bevan, together with Strauss, was described by Dalton as Cripps' 'chief adviser' when he was appointed.[42] But within months, Cripps offered his resignation after disagreements with the prime minister about the government apparatus and structure of the War Cabinet, and became Minister of Aircraft Production outside of that body in November 1942. Bevan felt that Cripps had failed to assert himself. He speculated that Churchill had actually put the knife in. Cripps' political weakness was that he was not then a member of the Labour Party: 'lonely men are easiest murdered.'[43] As Bevan was later to say of Lloyd George in his later years as leader of the declining Liberal Party: 'even the most superabundant personal qualities are irrelevant if not associated with great mass machines.'[44] In any event, Bevan's relationship with Cripps was not damaged. For there is no direct evidence that Cripps thought he *could* seize the crown from Churchill; furthermore, he thought the viable alternative to Churchill was Anthony Eden, rather than himself.[45]

Bevan vehemently opposed Attlee's policy of Indian suppression:

> The death penalty is imposed on any malefactor who cuts the telegraphic wires. Collective fines are imposed on areas for suspected sabotage. Already a fine of £2,250 has been imposed on a village near Nagpur. A military officer over a certain rank can take life in trying to protect property.

In Bevan's defence, he could not be accused of criticism without offering a possible way forward: 'There is one section of the Congress which as yet is still in a minority, but which could overnight, as it were, win the leadership of political India: that led by Nehru.' Bevan urged the government to free Gandhi, and ask the latter to form a government for an independent India and put forward a treaty between all the Allied powers and India. This, he postulated, would constitute firm political action to deal with the political situation in India and would also allow Britain to maintain troops on the subcontinent. In *Tribune*, Bevan recognised the two central political problems: the INC saw independence as a precondition to organising the defence of India; and while its leaders remained under lock and key there would be no progress. Bevan's suggestion was to broaden the negotiations, and consult not just Indian organisations such as the INC, but also Chinese Premier Chiang Kai-shek, Stalin and Roosevelt.[46]

The political problems with India coloured Bevan's view of Attlee. On 2 October, in *Tribune*, Bevan attacked his party leader. While the article is notable for its reluctance to foment a personal rivalry, Bevan did not pull his punches. He made clear that he was not attacking Attlee *the man*, but the politician: 'Mr Attlee is a gentleman [...] but Mr Attlee is no longer the spokesman of the movement which carried him from obscurity to the second position in the land. This is a political fact, not a personal issue.' Bevan attacked strongly on India: 'in the name of Labour and Socialism he has underwritten one of the blackest documents that imperialist bigotry has ever devised – Mr Churchill's India effusion.'[47] Bevan's reluctance to attack Attlee personally was not only born of a reluctance to attack his own party leader in visceral terms. It also ensured that he maintained a division between personal relations and political disagreement. For all his disagreements with Attlee in the war years, Bevan never burned his bridges with him. He did have some personal admiration for Attlee, as even this most negative of articles demonstrated.

Had the events taken place in peacetime, Bevan would have been correct. The arrests were a blunt instrument that did not solve any of the underlying problems posed to Britain by the Indian demands for independence. Had there been more time, Bevan's suggestions for resolving the problems were sensible. However, what Bevan's articles gave little space to, well argued though they were, was the urgency of the situation facing Attlee. The British priority was the defence of India, and Attlee's actions have to be seen in that context. They were not his first choice of solution, but, in that first week of August 1942 when Gandhi stepped up his campaign, a negotiated settlement had been attempted and had failed on the one issue that the War Cabinet could give no further ground upon. Attlee's options were limited.

Meanwhile, in North Africa, Erwin Rommel was establishing his reputation as Germany's 'Desert Fox'. On the night of Tuesday, 26 May 1942, Rommel attacked British forces in Libya. Barely a month later, on 21 June, he accepted the surrender of the Allied forces at Tobruk. A censure debate on Churchill's strategy for prosecuting the war was set down for 1 and 2 July 1942. Days before, on 25 June, the previously Conservative-held seat of Maldon had fallen in a by-election to Tom Driberg, later a Bevanite, standing under the label of 'Independent Labour'. Rommel was closing in on the Suez Canal, and on the first day of the debate was less than 100 miles from Cairo. Bevan waited for his moment, and spoke first on the second day.

Bevan opened his speech by trying to deal with his weakest point: 'With regard to the morale of the troops, my hon. Friends and I would be loath indeed to do anything here which might have the effect of undermining the courage and resolution of our troops in battle.' He added the obvious point: 'It will never be possible for us, in this war, to move a Vote of Censure on the Government at a time when no battle is in progress. Battles are going to be continuous throughout the war.'[48] Bevan made a wounding remark that Churchill was more effective at winning debates than battles. He attacked the whole strategy of the conflict. Churchill did not appreciate the weapons and methods that would be used by the Germans: 'It is that primary misconception of the war which has been responsible for the wrong strategy of the Government, and, the strategy being wrong, the wrong weapons were produced.' Bevan used two specific examples: the failure to develop dive-bombers and not equipping the army with transport planes.[49] These were not the best areas to choose for criticism, which reflected Bevan's lack of expertise in the area. To the latter issue, Bevan devoted only two sentences, which was perhaps indicative of the weakness of the criticism. He made only two points: transport planes would have assisted in supplying troops in specific areas, and they would have enabled more supplies to be delivered by air, eliminating the exclusive reliance on the sea. While the argument itself has an obvious logic, it ignored the need to set priorities with available resources. Defending Britain in 1940 had required fighters, and bombers were needed for long-range bombing of Germany. In the event, under the US programme of Lend-Lease, by which the US supplied its allies with military aid between 1941 and 1945, Britain was able to benefit from American transport planes while continuing to concentrate its own resources. While Britain had not developed dive-bombers, there were strong arguments for not doing so. The Germans had used Junkers Ju 87 'Stuka' dive-bombers, though they had proved very ineffective in the Battle of Britain. Not only were Stukas slower than the RAF's bombers, as Max Hastings puts it in his history of the Second World War, *All Hell Let Loose*:

> A dive-bomber pilot attacking a 750-foot ship from astern, for instance, had only a 1.5-second margin of error in pressing his bomb release, which from abeam fell to a quarter of a second; it was a tribute to

the skills of German Stuka pilots that they inflicted severe losses on British convoys.[50]

While such arguments have the benefit of hindsight, there was contemporary knowledge as well. The Stukas were defeated by the RAF when the two came into contact, and Hitler took them out of the Battle of Britain. As for using dive-bombers against troops, the only use Britain could sensibly have made of them after the evacuation from Dunkirk was in North Africa.

The choice of these two examples was a rare blemish on an otherwise well-crafted speech. On the North Africa campaign itself there was merit in Bevan's criticisms. For example, Hastings sets out that Rommel had advanced almost 300 miles in three weeks after launching an offensive on 21 January 1942. The British Eighth Army commander, Neil Ritchie, had created a defensive 'Gazala Line' using brigade boxes defended by mines and wire: 'He intended Rommel to dissipate his strength assaulting these, then to commit British armour, as usual superior in numbers, to press his advantage.' Rommel did not fall for the trap. The so-called 'brigade boxes' were too far apart to support each other, and the German tanks were very skilled at manoeuvres, maintaining their distance from the range of the British guns.[51]

There is an argument that Bevan's opposition outside the government could have been used by Churchill to strengthen his hand inside it. After all, Churchill himself was deeply frustrated by the campaign in the Western Desert. In August, Churchill changed commanders, replacing Ritchie as Eighth Army commander with Bernard Montgomery and Sir Claude Auchinleck as Middle East commander-in-chief with Sir Harold Alexander. Churchill did not, however, view Bevan's contribution as constructive. He saw him as a 'squalid nuisance'. Whatever the great virtues of Churchill's wartime leadership, he was intolerant of criticism. This applied not only to Bevan, but even to Attlee, who gave Churchill nothing but loyal service. Attlee wrote a private note to him on 18 January 1945 criticising him for his inefficient conduct of Cabinet business. Churchill did eventually calm down after receiving the note, but his initial reaction of referring to his deputy prime minister as 'Atler or Hitlee' is telling.[52]

Bevan's analysis of the situation was that the army was 'riddled with class prejudice'.[53] In an echo of his remarks to Sir Edward Grigg in December 1941, Bevan argued that, had Rommel been British, he would have been a sergeant. Bevan also argued that Churchill needed to change the shape of his government: 'The Prime Minister, in the course of an evening, produced a whole series of brilliant improvisations, but he has not the machinery to carry them through.'[54] Bevan considered the seven-member War Cabinet one by one. He excluded the

Lord President of the Council on the basis that he was a civil servant rather than a politician. He felt Eden, as Foreign Secretary, was 'burdened by a complicated office'. Bevan reserved his strongest fire for Bevin, who, as Minister of Labour, nonetheless carried out speaking duties on the weekends: 'How can he master documents about the war? I do not think the right hon. Gentleman has ever claimed to understand much about the war – this is a serious matter – and in any case he has not got the time.'[55]

Bevan also savaged the Minister of Production, Oliver Lyttelton, for his lack of political experience. Lyttelton had only entered Parliament for the constituency of Aldershot in a by-election in 1940. His background was in business, having served as managing director of the British Metal Corporation.[56] Bevan was also critical of Attlee, as deputy prime minister, being given a specific department, the Dominions. He cited Lloyd George's advice that the War Cabinet should consist of six members, all without portfolios. He also slammed the Secretary of State for War, the former civil servant Sir Percy James Grigg, mystified that he had been brought into government in the first place. Bevan thought Grigg had been plucked from obscurity for no good reason, and proffered British soldiers' lack of recognition of his name as a serious weakness. Bevan also continued his argument for a second front: 'We cannot postpone it until next year. Stalin expects it; please do not misunderstand me, for Heaven's sake do not let us make the mistake of betraying those lion-hearted Russians.'[57] These were strong words. In contrast, Bevan said little about the value of the American alliance to Britain throughout the war. He was not blind to it, but still – at heart – wanted the workers' revolution somehow to succeed. As he put it in *Tribune*: 'the U.S.S.R. occupies a unique place in the affections of the workers of Britain. With all its imperfections the workers believe that the Revolution in Russia was the only thing of value that came out of the last war.'[58] In the event, there was no invasion of Western Europe in 1942, though there was the large-scale Dieppe raid in August, in which around two-thirds of the small, 6,000-strong invading force was lost, either dead, injured or taken prisoner.

Churchill defeated the vote of censure easily, by 477 votes to 27. The press reported his speech as a triumph. The day after the debate, on 3 July, *The Times* reported that, when the voting figures were announced, there was a loud cheer and Churchill left the Commons Chamber to an ovation. While, to its credit, *The Times* ran a full report on the debate, its main article did not mention any of Bevan's speech, but merely that he had seconded the motion of censure. But Bevan's performance was outstanding. His wide-ranging attack was indicative not only of his knowledge of the wartime situation, and the government itself, but also of his confidence and stature. Yet it did not mark a step on the ascent to a greater critique of the government's strategy for prosecuting the war. Rather, it should be viewed as the high point of Bevan's attack on that ground. As the war drew to its close, it was inevitable that Bevan should increasingly turn his attention to winning the peace. But it also became more difficult to criticise a winning team, as the Allies moved slowly but inexorably towards victory. Bevan was left with keeping up the pressure for a second front.

For Britain, the symbolic military turning point in the Second World War was Montgomery's victory at El Alamein in North Africa. Rommel's offensive was launched on 23 October 1942, and he eventually withdrew on 4 November. On 8 November, the Allies launched 'Operation Torch', landing in Morocco and Algeria, then controlled by Vichy France. The British and Commonwealth forces had once again reached Tobruk by 13 November. On 15 November, church bells all over Britain rang out to celebrate. As Churchill later put it: 'It may almost be said, before Alamein we never had a victory. After Alamein, we never had a defeat.' His words at the time were cautious: 'Now this is not the end. It is not even the beginning of the end. But it is, perhaps, the end of the beginning.'

The victory came a mere two months after Bevan had called for the end of Churchill's premiership. On 9 September, Bevan had spoken in the Commons of the 'major national disaster' of Churchill remaining in office: 'He is no longer able to summon the spirit of the British people, because he represents policies that they deeply distrust.' Bevan finished with a flourish: Churchill provided 'nothing but nostalgia over ancient battles and old ways that are dead'.[59] The speech was one of his worst of the war. It sounded spiteful, and, after all, at this time, Bevan had never run anything himself, so had no personal experience to add weight to his criticisms. He had no credible alternative prime minister in mind (again, he did not suggest Cripps) and, in any event it gave a hostage to fortune. Churchill, in desperate need of a military victory throughout 1942, only had to provide one to prove Bevan's argument wrong. It was a classic example of a credible Bevan criticism being lost in overstatement, namely that Churchill represented an outdated, Edwardian imperialist worldview.

Bevan spoke on El Alamein in the Commons on 12 November. His most memorable line was an indictment of Churchill's avoidance of taking personal responsibility for previous military setbacks: 'The Prime Minister always refers to a defeat as a disaster as though it came from God, but to a victory as though it came from himself.'[60] Bevan gave great credit to the troops on the ground: 'The penetration of that land-mine was an extraordinary feat.' Yet Bevan also put the battle into its broader context: 'The strategical consequences of the battle of El Alamein will be very important indeed, but I would like to ask hon. Members, when they start rejoicing, to keep some sense of proportion.' Bevan contrasted the military position in the Western Desert, where there were only 15 divisions ranged against Montgomery's forces, only four of which were German panzers, with the Eastern Front, where the Russians were facing 176 divisions. He was also against the ringing of the church bells as prematurely triumphalist.[61]

Bevan struck a discordant note in this debate, but his speech also pointed up the fundamental difficulty he faced throughout the war. One exchange was particularly telling. Sir Gurney Braithwaite, the MP for Holderness, who had served in the Royal Navy at Gallipoli in the First World War, had opened his own speech with a stinging attack on Bevan, saying that some men serving in the navy were so angry about his criticisms that they were willing to land him 'on some hostile shore'.[62] Bevan gave a spirited defence of his wartime stance, defending the rights of MPs to criticise military strategy despite not being specialists in the field: 'We are sent here because we are amateurs; not because we are experts. Representative government is government of the experts by the amateurs and always has been.'[63] He was undoubtedly right about this. If there is valid criticism of him, it is that, unintentionally, his views could be read as having the potential to sap British civilian spirit and troop morale, and, at times, his language was undoubtedly over the top. But Bevan's wartime experience gave him a national stature in British politics he had hitherto lacked. He was willing to take positions he believed in when others did not speak out. Personally, however, the price of taking such a stand was a high one.

Chapter 8

The Second World War,
Part II: 1943–5

The surrender of Field Marshal Friedrich Paulus, commander of the German Sixth Army in Stalingrad, on 31 January 1943, is often regarded as marking the turning point in the Second World War. Afterwards, the Germans were gradually driven back on the Eastern Front. Meanwhile, back at home, the plans for postwar reconstruction gathered pace with the publication, on 1 December 1942, of the *Report of the Inter-departmental Committee on Social Insurance and Allied Services*, which became commonly known by the surname of its author, the economist and Liberal Sir William Beveridge. The report had been commissioned by Labour's Arthur Greenwood, then chair of the War Cabinet's Committee on Reconstruction, on 23 June 1941.[1] Beveridge's 'five giant evils' of squalor, ignorance, want, idleness and disease were to enter the national lexicon, and his report became a bestseller.[2]

Writing in *Tribune* on 4 December 1942, Bevan welcomed the report enthusiastically. He correctly saw it not as a socialist blueprint, but as a plan to soften the rougher edges of capitalism: 'Sir William has described the conditions in which the tears might be taken out of capitalism.' However, Bevan thought the report had the potential to go much further. He always saw the central importance of property rights as the bedrock upon which the British ruling class had built its power, and felt that, in elevating the importance of welfare provision, Beveridge had, almost certainly unintentionally, threatened the authority of the monied classes: 'We should not be surprised, therefore, if all unconsciously by doing so, he threatens capitalism itself.' Bevan also saw in the report firm evidence for his argument that the war itself was a great motor for profound social change. He quoted Karl Marx's phrase, 'war is the locomotive of history'. This is not to say that Bevan did not have reservations about Beveridge. His fundamental belief about poverty was that it was a product of the structure of society and the economy, rather than the fault of the individual. David Lloyd George, as Chancellor of the Exchequer, had introduced the idea of 'insurance' in the National Insurance Act of 1911, as a compromise between the majority and minority reports that his Poor Law Commission had produced. The employee, the employer and the state all contributed. The majority had argued for a Victorian approach of no handouts to the poorest as this encouraged poverty, while the minority, among them Sidney and Beatrice Webb, argued for universal welfare. Much had changed since then. In the 1930s, Bevan had argued against the extension of insurance, as he did not believe that the working poor should have to contribute to their own benefits by way of contributions. Bevan remained very much in the 'minority report' tradition. But he saw the arguments for backing Beveridge, and thought that the Conservative Party would have difficulty in supporting it wholeheartedly. In that, he was absolutely right. In January 1943, Churchill's lack of enthusiasm for Beveridge was made clear by his withdrawing from circulation the summary of Beveridge by the Army Bureau of Current Affairs (ABCA), which had been set up both to raise the morale of the troops and to disseminate information. The government's principal reason for the withdrawal was that the pamphlet was too controversial politically. Given that a central purpose of ABCA was to educate service personnel on current events, and the Beveridge report had had such an impact, the decision was difficult to justify on an objective basis.

In contrast, the Labour Party seized the moment and endorsed Beveridge. The National Council of Labour, which was made up of representatives of the TUC, the Labour Party and the Co-operative Union, approved the Beveridge report on 17 December 1942. The NEC welcomed the report, and claimed it as the natural development of the arguments the Labour Party had been putting forward in previous months: 'its general framework conformed to the terms of the resolution approved at the last Annual Conference of the Party.' This consisted of comprehensive social security provision, cash payments 'whatever the contingency', family allowances and the National Health Service.[3] The wording of the resolution captured an important point. For Beveridge, and the reaction to it, showed that, politically, the general public was moving towards Labour. If a 'cradle to grave' welfare state was received this enthusiastically, that could only be good for the left-of-centre party in Britain.

Nonetheless, while formally committed to Beveridge, the coalition government refused to pass legislation immediately. Attlee and the other Labour coalition ministers held to the government line. In February 1943, in the parliamentary debate on the report, virtually all the Labour backbenchers – 97 – voted in favour of legislating immediately. In June 1943, at the party conference, Sydney Silverman MP put down an amendment to record 'profound distrust' of the government's commitment, and to urge the PLP to 'continue its efforts to secure immediate legislation' (though this was lost by 1,715,000 to 955,000 votes).[4] The second problem posed by Beveridge was party political. If the Labour Party was winning the battle of ideas, then it should capitalise on this, leave the wartime coalition and seek to win a general election. Ever since the Battle of El Alamein, Bevan had been arguing for the end of the electoral truce. At the 1943 party conference, Attlee contended that it was not the right moment to throw away the wartime unity. The war was still raging. Bevan's speech was measured: 'The suggestion that we should carry the resolution today withdrawing from the Government would give a false impression to the whole of the armed forces of Great Britain.'[5] Instead, Bevan sought a declaration that Labour should contest the postwar general election as an independent force. The vote that took place, however, was only on the *immediate* ending of the electoral truce, and that was easily defeated by 2,243,000 votes to 374,000.

The 1943 party conference marked the second occasion on which Bevan had argued for a commitment to ending the electoral truce. At the previous year's conference in May 1942, a resolution to end the truce had also been defeated, as had a resolution on having no compromise with the means test.[6] The issue of remaining in the coalition brought Bevan into direct conflict with Attlee, who dealt with the issue as a matter of party management. Bevan and Attlee had had a minor skirmish in the Commons in December 1942. Attlee, in typically clipped tones, had gently suggested to Bevan that he was 'so adept at pursuing lines, he pursues them so far that he generally finds himself back where he started. He is apt to become airborne in the last five minutes of his speech.' Bevan was never going to take that lying down, and swung back at the deputy prime minister: 'The right hon. Gentleman is usually sunk at the end of his.'[7] Yet Attlee agreed with Bevan on the purpose of the war. He did not see it as an opportunity for the old British imperialist order to reassert itself in the world.[8]

After the D-Day landings on the Normandy beaches on 6 June 1944, Bevan stepped up his arguments for resuming political hostilities. He feared that, as in 1918, the coalition government would continue into peacetime. This would entirely defeat what he saw as the central purpose of the war, the emergence of a new world order. Unless Labour was willing to reassert its independence, the opportunity for the left to put its ideas into effect in the unique postwar circumstances would be lost. Speaking on the BBC on 21 March 1943, Churchill offered a four-year plan for reconstruction put forward by a National Government of members drawn from the three main British political parties. Bevan thought that such a plan was manifestly not in Labour's interests, since it could win the postwar election. In contrast to his pessimism in 1931 that there would never be another Labour government – events had changed his mind – Bevan thought that the social effects of the war had produced a desire for change which would mean a large Labour vote.

Bevan also had direct feedback on the situation on the ground from Jennie Lee. As a consequence of the electoral truce, there were no Labour–Conservative contests in which to test the opinion polls. Into this vacuum stepped the Common Wealth Party, founded on 26 June 1942. It was a form of progressive party: 'The professional ethic and the ideal of service, rather than class interest, were the basis of its appeal [...] managers and workers were to own factories and cooperate in running them.'[9] Common Wealth candidates won at Eddisbury in April 1943, Skipton in January 1944 and Chelmsford in April 1945. Lee stood as an Independent Labour candidate in the Bristol Central by-election on 18 February 1943, with the support of the Common Wealth Party. She came second to a Conservative, Lady Apsley, the wife of the dead sitting MP, Lord Apsley, who had been killed in action the previous December. Lee discerned a left-wing tide in her packed election meetings, and felt she had only lost because of the heavy bombing of properties in the city, which meant that many working-class Labour voters were living outside the constituency, and did not return to vote. In contrast, the Tory business voters *did* return to vote, as they were then entitled to as property owners.[10] In his analysis of Labour's electoral prospects, Bevan was entirely right. As the historian Paul Addison put it: 'polls conducted by the British Institute of Public Opinion predicted a Labour victory on six occasions after June 1943.' However, since opinion polling was in its infancy, its conclusions were largely ignored.[11]

The PLP was certainly becoming more rebellious. In 1942, a coalition White Paper on 3 June had argued for a requisition of the coal mines, but fudged the question of common ownership. The following month, 63 Labour MPs voted against a low pension increase of 2s. 6d. a week. There was then the parliamentary debate on Beveridge in February 1943, mentioned above, which was the largest Labour rebellion during the whole war. Another rebellion followed before the party conference in June. In May 1943, the government's latest Pensions Bill offered no increase. A motion condemning this was put down by 40 Labour MPs, and, in the event, 59 Labour MPs rebelled in the subsequent vote.

On 17 April 1944, Bevin amended the Defence (General) Regulations, which had been introduced by the Chamberlain government in 1939 as part of the government's emergency powers to be exercised in wartime. His new regulation (labelled '1AA'), created a new criminal offence, to 'instigate or incite any other person to take part in, or otherwise act in furtherance of, any stoppage among persons engaged in the performance of essential services'. Those convicted faced five years' imprisonment, or a fine of £500, or both. At the same time, Bevin also amended regulation 1A, and outlawed peaceful picketing. Bevin had covered his back before introducing the measures, having consulted both sides of industry. Furthermore, the TUC supported Bevin and criticised Bevan for his opposition.

Part of Bevan's attack on Bevin was again on constitutional grounds: Bevin was, he argued, treating Parliament as an irrelevance. Bevan had chosen his ground carefully. Parliamentary procedure was not Bevan's strong point, though he did muster an effective answer to Bevin's question as to why he had not proceeded by way of formal parliamentary bill. Bevin's answer was simple: a statute carried a risk of permanence, whereas the wartime regulations were by definition temporary.[12] Bevan recalled his own childhood:

> I was a boy at the coal face myself and I did not like to have to go down the pit on a sunny morning. These little boys get together and one says to another, 'Look here, let us go back home.' I did it myself when I was a nipper. Is it to be five years' penal servitude because these boys have a nostalgia for sunshine?[13]

That was beautifully put. What was less elegant, and unwise, was Bevan's attack on Bevin for protecting trade union vested interests, the

> trade union official, who has arteriosclerosis, and who cannot readjust himself to his membership. He is defending an official who has become so unpopular among his own membership that the only way he can keep them in order is to threaten them with five years in gaol.[14]

Bevan then defended the rights of the non-unionised working classes against the unionised:

> George Bernard Shaw said, in 'The Apple Cart,' that the person in this country who is in the most strongly entrenched position, next to the King, is the trade union official. Between 7,000,000 and 8,000,000 organised workers and trade union officials are protected under this Regulation, but 13,000,000 unorganised workers have no protection at all.[15]

Bevan was one of 15 Labour MPs who voted against the measure; a further 73 abstained or were not even present in the House.[16] On 10 May, the PLP voted for a motion proposed by Manny Shinwell to refer the matter to a special committee made up of the Parliamentary Committee (the Shadow Cabinet) and the NEC. In the event, the NEC voted 20–8 to demand a written undertaking from Bevan to follow the party line in future. The SWMF showed great loyalty by backing Bevan personally. After all, Bevan had not discriminated between unions in his attack. The SWMF members formed one of the strongest unionised societies in the country, and Bevan had vented his spleen on protecting the non-unionised workers at their expense. Bevan repaid their trust by swallowing his pride and signing the required document. He saved face by justifying it on the basis of needing to stay in the Labour Party to fight against it continuing in the coalition into peacetime.[17]

In 1944, in developing his case against a postwar coalition government, Bevan published *Why Not Trust the Tories?* Quickly written, and only 89 pages in length, the tract is packed with Bevan's arguments against continuing the coalition after the end of the fighting. He compared the existing situation with 1918: 'The Election was rushed while the mood of exaltation following the victory still ran like a heady wine in the veins of the people [...] The first tocsin to be sounded was the need to maintain the same national unity which had served so well in the war years.'[18] Bevan argued that the Beveridge report was 'the most sensational political document of modern times'.[19] Yet the Tories had 'fought a successful rearguard action' to avoid immediate action on the proposals.[20] Bevan also attacked the White Paper on Employment, and his critique is worth considering in detail: 'Many Socialists have been pleased with the White Paper because it frankly admits that the system of free private enterprise, if left to itself, inevitably produces unemployment.' However, he said it was 'difficult to understand why we should be so delighted with the admission of a fact which is known to every man and woman in the country, most of whom have not had the advantages of the specialised education enjoyed by the advisers of the Government'.[21] Bevan's central attack was that 'the White Paper, being a Tory production, proposes to continue private enterprise after the war. In other words, it is proposed to keep in being a system which even its own supporters admit must inevitably and automatically produce unemployment.'[22] Bevan was disappointed with the language of the White Paper, which only *aimed* at a 'high and stable level of employment'. The White Paper also contained a proposal for each local authority to submit every year to the relevant central government department its plan for capital expenditure for the following five years. Government ministers would then intervene and amend the proposals on the basis of unemployment prospects. Bevan argued that this would create an unfair divide between public and private sector:

One of the worst consequences of this lunatic scheme is the uncertainty it will introduce into the public sector of employment, that is, the plans prepared by public authorities. They will be expected to keep back their own plans for increasing social amenities whilst Private Enterprise is having its unfettered fling.[23]

Bevan was not in favour of the approach of the White Paper because he saw it, rightly, as a means of supporting an existing capitalist system. In *Plan for Britain*, a 1943 Fabian pamphlet to which he contributed, he argued instead for full-scale nationalisation and the creation of a Supreme Economic Council for planning.

This is not to say that Bevan did not support the government when he approved of its proposals. The Conservative R. A. Butler's 1944 Education Act created a tripartite division of state schools: selective grammars, secondary moderns and technical schools, the last of which being geared more towards preparation for trades. In the 1950s and 1960s, Labour's Tony Crosland castigated the iniquities of the '11-plus' examination. However, the grammar schools seemed to offer working-class children the opportunity to compete with children from the remaining private schools. Bevan was particularly enthusiastic about the raising of the school leaving age to 15. If the war generally brought out Bevan's combative personality in Parliament, the Education Act debates showed his softer side. In one debate on 9 March 1944, he raised the issue of 'special agreement' (what would today be called 'faith') schools. Bevan declared himself sympathetic to the Catholic point of view (there was a concern that local-authority grants would restrict their religious freedom). He did not oppose giving further public money to Catholic schools, but argued (unsuccessfully) for a principle that the proportion of public funding should be in line with the extent of public control. Bevan recalled being a 'manager' (in modern-day parlance, a 'governor') of a Catholic primary school while a councillor, representing his local authority.[24] He was self-deprecating in recalling the discussions: 'As usual, I was in a minority.'[25] Later in that same debate, Bevan used his local-authority expertise to seek improvements in the legislation. Butler even took Bevan's point on board, and offered to meet him and amend his proposals if necessary. Bevan was concerned that if county councils were given the power to draw up instruments of governance of secondary schools, and excluded the possibility of representation on school governing bodies by other authorities (he had in mind Tredegar Urban District Council's subordinate relationship to Monmouthshire County Council), what could be done? If it was within the powers of the county council to set the rules, what redress was there? Butler said that he thought there was already a right of appeal in the bill for the aggrieved party to the minister, but, if not, he would insert one.[26]

Among Labour Party members, Bevan's political stock was rising. In 1944, he was elected to the NEC for the first time. The NEC consisted of 25 members nominated and elected in four sections. It had an affiliated trade union section with 12 members, a constituency section of seven members elected by the constituency parties, a women's section of five members elected by the whole party conference, and a section for socialist and cooperative societies and professional organisations, in which one member was elected by the affiliated groups. He had previously been reluctant to stand. As far back as 1935, the London Co-operative Society had offered to nominate him, but he worried about lacking the support necessary to secure election.[27] By 1944, he was well known among party members; of the seven available places in the constituency section, Bevan came in fifth. Above him were Harold Laski, Manny Shinwell, Jim Griffiths and Herbert Morrison. Hugh Dalton and Philip Noel-Baker came in sixth and seventh. In 1945, Bevan was re-elected in fourth place, and from 1946 onwards he was top every year, until 1954, when he stood instead for the post of party treasurer against Hugh Gaitskell. Bevan was highly popular among Labour Party members and activists. While members had no direct say during this period in choosing the party leader, or, indeed, in choosing the Parliamentary Committee, Bevan's election to the NEC marked a step forward in his career. He was still unpopular with the wartime ministers whom he had been criticising, though he remained close to Cripps, despite not having openly backed him for the premiership in his brief period of popularity in 1942. He was particularly disliked by Morrison, Bevin and trade union leaders such as Walter Citrine. But he had a mouthpiece in *Tribune*, and any Labour politician who was popular with the party as a whole could not be ignored by the leadership. It also meant that fellow MPs could not write him off as a firebrand. For Bevan was popular among their own constituency party activists, those members they relied upon for support and continuation as Labour candidates and MPs.

The issue of Labour's remaining in the wartime coalition came to a head on the first day of the Labour Party Conference in Blackpool, on 21 May 1945. Churchill had written to Attlee requesting the continuation of the coalition until the defeat of Japan, whenever that happened, rather than setting an end date in the autumn, which he understood to be Labour's preferred position. In a private session that afternoon, delegates considered the letter, and, putting aside Churchill's request for a commitment to remain in the coalition until Japan's defeat, only two voted to stay in government until the autumn. The mainstream Labour Party view had moved towards that of Bevan. Since victory in Europe in early May, Labour could legitimately leave the coalition without accusations of desertion before the task was complete. Attlee's reply carefully trod the line between avoiding a commitment to continuing the coalition into peacetime and not putting party politics above the needs of troops still on the fields of battle. Delegates approved his draft, which went no further than setting out that the coalition *could* continue until the autumn and that a July election would cause 'bitter resentment' among the forces.[28] Without a commitment from Attlee, Churchill duly called the election.

Bevan threw himself into battle. His speaking tour was the model for all of his future general-election campaigns. He addressed huge meetings all around the country, only returning to Ebbw Vale in the final days before the poll on 5 July. Lee had formally rejoined the Labour Party in late 1944, 12 years after the ILP's disaffiliation, and had been selected to fight the seat of Cannock. It was a large constituency, with a strong Tory vote in rural areas, but also a solid mining base. Lee was to win, and hold the seat until 1970. Naturally, Bevan visited to speak in support of her. He also went to Plymouth Devonport to speak for Michael Foot, standing in his hometown, who was to win a parliamentary seat for the first time. Bevan's campaign theme was power, and argued for the interests of working people against large corporations. His Ebbw Vale campaign literature was strongly worded. He characterised the election as 'a real struggle for power in Britain'. He argued: 'So the big employers want a scarcity of goods to keep up prices and plenty of unemployed workers to keep down wages. That state of affairs is a paradise for Big Business and hell for the mass of ordinary people.'[29] He also argued for a national plan for building houses for returning soldiers, an issue that was to become important later on when he was a minister. In Cardiff, days before the election, revisiting his scrutiny of the wartime coalition, he cautioned against 'hero-worship' of Churchill. Returning to his own constituency, he spoke in Cwm. Recalling the poverty and hardship of the interwar years, and eschewing narrow nationalism, he declared it an act of 'naked treachery' for a Welshman to vote Conservative.[30] Due to having to collect votes from service personnel still stationed all over the world, the 1945 results were declared three weeks after polling day, on 26 July. Labour took 47.8 per cent of the vote, winning 393 seats, an overall majority of 146. The Conservatives won only 213 seats and the Liberals 12. With a landslide victory of his own in Ebbw Vale, the only question was whether Bevan would be asked to serve in the first majority Labour government.

Part IV

Cabinet Minister, 1945–51

Chapter 9

The Labour Governments, 1945–51

C lement Attlee did not make a triumphant entrance into Downing Street. Rather, he had to face an immediate threat to his position from Herbert Morrison. Prior to the declaration of results, Morrison penned a letter to Attlee, and sealed it in an envelope with orders that it be given to him unopened. It contained a naked attempt to seize the leadership: 'I have decided that, if I am elected to the new Parliament, I should accept nomination to the leadership.'[1] Morrison's own explanation is that he was seeking to ensure that the party's 'democratic principles' were followed.[2] This is unconvincing. Morrison had been plotting in the weeks preceding this. The issue of the leadership had been canvassed with other Labour MPs. While there is no evidence that Morrison spoke directly to Bevan on the issue during this period, Bevan certainly discussed the leadership question. There is good evidence that he favoured Morrison as leader over Attlee. Morrison's biographers Bernard Donoghue and G. W. Jones claim: 'Aneurin Bevan followed Cripps in assuming that there would be a leadership election before forming a government and personally preferred Morrison to Attlee.' Donoghue and Jones' source for this assertion is George Strauss, whom they interviewed for their biography. Bevan stayed with Strauss at this time and had discussed the leadership issue several times on the telephone.[3] There is no reason to suppose that this is mistaken, and Strauss is a reliable contemporary source.

This may seem surprising, given the personal animosity between Bevan and Morrison. But there are two reasons why Bevan would back Morrison. First, Bevan had the ability to see beyond personal rivalry. There is an element in this, picked up in local politics of the 1920s, of 'leaving arguments in meetings': the ability to have bitter disagreements in the public arena but to retain a more objective personal judgement (indeed, it was this that Bevan was to lack later, during the events that led to his eventual resignation from the government in 1951). Bevan thought that Attlee had failed to assert himself in the wartime coalition. Morrison was nothing if not decisive as a minister, as Bevan could himself testify after the various battles. Second, Morrison and Bevan shared an agenda in 1945: the end of the wartime coalition. When Labour's NEC met on 19 May, it was Morrison who had argued for Labour's immediate withdrawal from the coalition, rather than remaining until the defeat of Japan.

The key events took place on the afternoon of 26 July, in Labour Party head-quarters at Transport House, where the party secretary Morgan Phillips met Attlee, Bevin and Morrison. It was Cripps' telephone call to Morrison to support his approach of waiting until the PLP met to choose the leader that, ironically, led to the most significant discussion taking place in Morrison's absence. Morrison left the room to take the call, and Bevin asked Morgan Phillips: 'If I stood against Clem, should I win?' Morgan Phillips said: 'On a split vote, I think you would.' Bevin turned to Attlee: 'Clem, you go to the Palace straightaway.'[4] This is not to suggest that somehow Attlee went to the palace on Bevin's bidding, but Bevin's support for him was one of the key features of the political landscape of the 1945–51 Labour Cabinet. He supported Attlee again during the 1947 currency crisis, which is discussed in a later chapter, and Attlee was deeply upset when he died on 14 April 1951. Bevin was the rock upon which Attlee built his leadership.

Bevin's lengthy trade union experience placed a great premium on loyalty. Employed by the Dockers' Union since 1911, he had played a major role in the merger of 14 unions into the new, giant Transport and General Workers' Union on 1 January 1922, of which he became the first general secretary. His experience was of seeking unity among his members. He was deeply suspicious of Morrison's manoeuvrings. In contrast, prior to his involvement in London local government, Morrison had had a varied working life. The son of a Tory police constable, Morrison started his working life in a shop, before becoming a telephone switchboard operator at Whitbread's. That led him into the National Union of Clerks, where he was active from 1910 to 1913, but it did not leave him with a lasting admiration for trade union camaraderie. Rather, the lesson he drew was that Labour needed to broaden its electoral appeal beyond the working class.[5] The newspaper he found work with in 1912, the *Daily Citizen*, folded in 1915. Such uncertainty in his life also heightened his intense personal ambition. Dalton heard, second-hand, that Attlee had told Bevin about Morrison's letter. Bevin replied: 'I won't have it. You leave him to me.' He then telephoned Morrison: 'If you go on mucking about like this, you won't be in the bloody Government at all.' But Bevin's support for Attlee was based on far more than denying Morrison the top job. He had a strong opinion on the ideal type of Labour leader. He told people to 'read history', citing Liberal prime minister

Sir Henry Campbell-Bannerman as an exemplar of managing a team of talented men. He was suspicious of personal leadership in the style of Ramsay MacDonald or Winston Churchill.[6] Attlee's switch of Hugh Dalton to the Treasury and Bevin to the Foreign Office was at least partly motivated by a desire to keep Morrison and Bevin apart.[7] Morrison was appointed Lord President of the Council and Leader of the House of Commons. This made Morrison second only to Attlee on domestic policy, and deputy prime minister. In his initial submission of ministers to the king, Attlee also included Arthur Greenwood, who became Lord Privy Seal, in effect a minister without portfolio, and William Jowitt, a former barrister, who was appointed Lord Chancellor. Finally, Cripps was appointed President of the Board of Trade.

The Attlee government has been seen as dominated in the first instance by the 'Big Five': Attlee himself, Bevin, Morrison, Dalton and Cripps. Cripps was still seen as the leader of the party's left by Attlee. Bevan had, after all, not held any office during the second Labour government of 1929 to 1931 or the wartime coalition. Speaking to Archie Lush on the night after the election results were declared, Bevan thought his prospects of being offered a place in the Labour government depended on Attlee's calculation as to whether he was better off having Bevan with him on the front bench than allowing him to be a critical voice from the back benches.[8] There is something in this, but there was more to Attlee's decision to appoint Bevan as Minister of Health and Housing than managing discontent. It was also an attempt to get the creative best out of Bevan. The major debate Attlee had over Bevan was not whether to put him the Cabinet, but whether he should be given education or health. Attlee's problem, ironically, was the number of new MPs on the Labour benches about whom he knew little. Despite a gain of over 100 seats from the 1931 electoral disaster, the Labour Party had still only won 154 seats in 1935. The 1945 election had seen 393 MPs elected, an enormous advance that left Attlee having to categorise the individuals on scraps of paper. He headed various columns 'Women', 'Lawyers' (which he subdivided into barristers and solicitors), 'Teachers', 'Dockers' and 'Young Men'.[9] He wrote out his choices in rough before finalising them on a 'Table of Political Offices' mounted on cardboard. While there were some obvious 'big players' to place, most Labour MPs had no previous experience of ministerial office.

Attlee pencilled in Bevan at education with Ellen Wilkinson at health, before changing his mind and swapping them.[10] This was a very significant change. Wilkinson, who had served as a junior minister in the wartime coalition, had a solid claim to Cabinet office. Known as 'Red Ellen' both for her shock of red hair and her politics, she was a doughty campaigner for working people, and had been one of the organisers of the famous 1936 march from her constituency of

Jarrow.[11] One of Bevan's great challenges in establishing the NHS was in winning the argument against Herbert Morrison on who should own and manage the hospitals: Bevan wanted to nationalise them, whereas Morrison, a stoical defender of local government, wanted local authorities to have responsibility for health services. Ellen Wilkinson was close to Morrison; she 'had long admired [... him...] to the point of love', though whether the careful Morrison would have risked the potential scandal of an actual affair is a moot point.[12] As Minister of Education, Wilkinson was content to leave the local education authorities in place. She would have been much more susceptible to the argument that the hospitals should remain under local-authority control. Bevan might have taken a different approach to education, but that is a matter of speculation. Attlee was not in favour of the abolition of private schools, and the government's main task was the implementation of the Butler Education Act. If there was a criticism, it was that the government did not implement the whole Butler tripartite system consistently. The division between grammar schools and secondary moderns was cemented into place, but secondary technical schools were neglected. Whether Bevan would have done any more on this can only be conjecture. George Tomlinson, a Christian pacifist with a strong interest in education, replaced Wilkinson after her tragic drug overdose in February 1947, and followed his predecessor's policy line. This all said, Bevan would have been far less comfortable with local-authority control over education than Wilkinson. He might even have won the argument with Morrison about raising the school leaving age even further, to 16 rather than 15. He had, in fact, shown a passing interest in the issue of the school leaving age as a Monmouthshire county councillor.[13]

No direct evidence survives as to why Attlee made this late change. Robert Crowcroft has argued that Attlee deliberately 'placed those who might pose problems – Bevan, Shinwell, Cripps, Wilkinson and, especially, Morrison – in roles about which the Labour Party would be sensitive.' Crowcroft even describes the NHS – oddly, given the scale of Bevan's subsequent achievements – as one of the government's 'truly thankless tasks'.[14] Yet such analysis fails to deal with why Attlee's thinking altered. It was also a self-sealing change since it was a direct swap. Attlee did not need to make the change in order to create a knock-on effect elsewhere. One factor does, however, stand out. Attlee genuinely believed that the Butler Education Act was so final that it had lifted the issue out of political competition. Was putting the crusading Bevan in charge of such a ministry the best use of his talents? Was he, after all, far more suited to the inevitable political battles ahead in establishing a National Health Service? This is not to say that Wilkinson would have been a poor health minister, but there is a powerful logic to Attlee's change of heart.

While Bevan may not initially have been part of the Attlee government's 'Big Five', he gradually emerged, along with Gaitskell, as a leader of the next political generation. The Attlee government is often seen as a group of older men, mostly born in the late-Victorian era. Attlee, Bevin and Morrison had all been born in the 1880s. Most members of the government were in their sixties and seventies. Bevan, at 48, was the youngest member of the Cabinet, until the advent of Gaitskell himself, who joined the Cabinet in October 1947 as Minister of Fuel and Power at 41. At the same time, Harold Wilson, a wartime civil servant and former Oxford don who had worked with Beveridge, entered the Cabinet as President of the Board of Trade at just 31.

Bevan formed a triangular rivalry of mutual hatred with Morrison and Bevin, each of whom, in 1945, outweighed him in terms of power and influence. However, as the government progressed, Bevan rose in importance as he became more experienced and senior. For example, in 1947, when Attlee restructured the Cabinet's economic machinery after the currency crisis, Bevan became a member of both the Economic Policy Committee and the Production Committee. By the time of Bevin's death in early 1951, Bevan had almost – but still not quite – achieved parity with his two rivals. Bevin despised both men, but if he had to choose between Bevan and Morrison (he would not have *wanted* to choose either), it would have been Bevan. When told that Bevan was his own worst enemy, Bevin quipped back: 'Not while I'm alive he ain't.'[15] Yet, when he was dying, Bevin was horrified to learn that he had been succeeded as Foreign Secretary by Herbert Morrison. When he first said that his chosen successor would have been Jim Griffiths, Attlee's former press secretary Francis Williams expressed surprise, to which Bevin responded: 'Well, Nye then. I'd sooner have had Nye than 'Erbert.'[16]

In terms of his time at the Ministry of Health, the far more significant of the two rivalries for Bevan was with Morrison, as they disagreed on policy. For a key period during the clash with Gaitskell, Morrison chaired the Cabinet during Attlee's absence, and Bevin was ill. Despite his declining health, Bevin did, however, make a point of coming down to the House of Commons to show his support for Gaitskell during the 1951 budget debate. Yet Bevan's relationship with Morrison was more complex than it at first appears. Even after their great parliamentary clashes in the Second World War, Bevan would have supported him for the leadership. Also, for all his machinations behind the scenes, Morrison was a consummate and constructive politician in his own right, with a key role in the success of the Attlee government. His Lord President's Cabinet Committee piloted the great nationalisation and welfare reforms through Parliament. Peter Mandelson, writing in defence of his grandfather, quotes Kingsley Martin, the then editor of *New Statesman*, who backed Morrison for the Labour leadership against Attlee in 1935, who said that Morrison was 'dynamic, open to ideas, keen to argue and above all keen that the party should succeed and win'. Martin had spoken to R. H. Tawney, who sought to emphasise that Morrison was actually more radical than he seemed, and characterised his politics as a kind of 'democratic cajolery which was very different from Bevin's autocratic bullying'.[17] The word 'bullying' is unfair to Bevin, but there were strong differences in style between the two men. Bevin was certainly the battering ram, Morrison the strategic plotter. Bevan was neither of these things. In Cabinet, he combined a mastery of detail with a forensic tenacity in argument. He was a great analyser of opposing arguments, willing to engage in impassioned discussion. It is tempting to read much into the similarity in their origins. Morrison and Bevan, both from large families, had overcome handicaps. Morrison was blind in one eye. Bevan had mastered his stammer. Bevin never knew the identity of his father and was orphaned as a child. All three had strong accents: Bevan's Welsh Valleys tones were joined around the Cabinet table by Bevin's West Country drawl and Morrison's cockney. Yet, in these three men, the British working class had thrown up three very distinct politicians.

In the immediate political battle within the Attlee Cabinet, with these two formidable rivals to contend with, Bevan needed allies. Bevan and Manny Shinwell, appointed Minister of Fuel and Power by Attlee, were often seen as similar by the press. In a draft of the second volume of Foot's biography of Bevan, the author included a sentence arguing that Shinwell and Bevan, with their left-wing reputations, were singled out for attack by the right-wing press, but wisely removed it.[18] Like Bevan, Shinwell had an ability to attract controversy. His remark, at the party conference in May 1947, that the Labour Party represented the workers and that other people did not matter 'two hoots', caused a press furore.[19] Shinwell also had a radical left-wing past, as an ILP-er and one of Glasgow's 'Red Clydesiders', and had even served a short prison sentence in 1921 for incitement to riot. He and Bevan may have been on the same side in certain arguments in Cabinet, most notably against Bevin's policy on Palestine (Shinwell's father was a Polish Jew), but they were not personally close. As Shinwell's performance in the fuel crisis over the winter of 1947 was to show, Bevan was far more at home with power. Over the course of the government, Bevan's greatest supporter was actually Attlee himself.

The central idea of Attlee's leadership style was *chairmanship* in its purest sense. He saw himself as a facilitator in the Cabinet's decision-making process, not a positive force. He saw his role as finding a consensus among his colleagues: 'I would sum up the essence of the Premiership by saying that there must be someone to take a decision. The decision that he must take is not that a certain course should be followed but that a decision must be come to.'[20] Attlee was brisk, and only allowed discussion with a purpose: 'Democracy means government by discussion, but it is only effective if you can stop people talking.'[21] Bevan's occasionally wordy speaking style might have been thought to irritate Attlee, but actually it did not. Attlee respected Bevan's mastery of policy detail.

The direct consequences of Attlee's leadership style for Bevan were twofold. In the first instance, Bevan was allowed the freedom to pursue his policies with vigour. Attlee allowed his ministers to get on with their jobs without undue interference. This is not to say Bevan had carte blanche; Attlee did intervene in the work of his ministers when he thought it necessary. Labour had also made various promises that ostensibly bound the government. The party was committed to implementing the Beveridge reforms. There was also the 1945 general-election manifesto, *Let Us Face the Future*, but Bevan agreed with its central message, that the poverty of the interwar years was a consequence of the economic system, with power concentrated in the hands of too few men. In short, Bevan had the ideal prime minister to allow him the political space to bring into effect the universal health care system he wanted to create. Secondly, when Attlee did have to arbitrate between Bevan's policy and the alternative (usually from Morrison), he backed Bevan. Attlee always retained a regard for Bevan, even after his rebellious behaviour in the 1951–5 Parliament, and he worked with Bevan in early 1955 to prevent him being expelled from the party for good.

In the early years of the government, Bevan also found an ally in the Chancellor of the Exchequer, Hugh Dalton. They had been on opposite sides of the defence debate in the Labour Party in the 1930s, with Dalton in favour of rearmament. However, Dalton was willing to fund Bevan's measures for the NHS, in what he saw as the advance of socialism in action. And when Bevan was in the midst of his battle with Gaitskell, Dalton still maintained contact, even though Gaitskell was very much his protégé. Yet as Bevan gravitated towards Dalton on policy grounds, he was to drift away from Cripps in the later years of the Attlee government for the same reason. Unlike Dalton, whom he replaced as Chancellor of the Exchequer on 13 November 1947, Cripps was an austerity chancellor. This inevitably created problems for Bevan, both on health spending and on his housing programme.

While Harold Wilson supported Bevan in the dispute with Gaitskell in 1951, and resigned with him, Bevan's strong political allies and friends were generally *outside* the Cabinet. Briefly Undersecretary of State for Air, John Strachey was then Minister of Food from 27 May 1946, before eventually reaching Cabinet on 28 February 1950 as Secretary of State for War. George Strauss was a junior minister under Alfred Barnes at Transport before becoming Minister of Supply on 7 October 1947. This all said, the Cabinet minutes for the Attlee government hardly reveal that Bevan was frequently isolated or struggling for allies. He did contribute regularly to Cabinet discussion, as would be expected for a self-confident politician of strong views in such a significant department, but the overwhelming sense is of a loyal Cabinet minister. Bevan was willing to fight his corner on any issue, was fiercely protective of the health service, and unafraid of anyone else. Until the events that led to his resignation, he was disciplined and loyal.

This discipline also extended into his personal life. In order to function effectively as a Cabinet minister, Bevan completely changed his daily habits. He lived a regimented existence. Rather than sitting up until the small hours reading, debating or enjoying listening to music, Bevan ensured he had his full quota of sleep. After all, he had to be at the department every morning; he could not afford to lie in, which he previously enjoyed. Throughout his period in the Attlee government, he and Lee lived in a large flat in London, 23 Cliveden Place. With Lee back in Parliament, a London base was essential, and Lane End Cottage was sold. Bevan and Lee ensured that the flat was large enough to accommodate James and Ma Lee as well. On taking office in 1945, the *Daily Mirror* ran an admiring piece about Bevan's home life.[22] Alongside photographs of Bevan and Lee lunching together and Lee curled up on the sofa next to her husband, the flat was described as a 'handbox Regency home'. Lee declared: 'My husband is my hobby.' Bevan was shown as relaxed: 'Slippery polished floors with mats to trap the uninitiated, pirates-treasure maps of the Empire pinned up on the study walls and "Nye" answering questions about his share of the housework by saying, "Only the aristocrats work – the working man dodges work all he can".' It was 'the kind of house into which people pop without formal invitation'.

Bevan still found time to indulge his interests, particularly the arts. His friendships always included the political *and* non-political. He spent evenings with friends like Graham Sutherland, Henry Moore, John Piper and Francis Bacon. He and Jennie Lee even had their own private artist, a student, Jane Lane ('a rare Rossetti-type of beauty'), who painted a frieze on the walls of the flat.[23] But it was always difficult for Bevan to relax outside the private confines of his home. His wartime parliamentary opposition had brought him great notoriety. Those who wished to bring him down sought to embroil him in scandal. Bevan liked to take an evening walk after a long day at the department, and one night a woman who looked like a prostitute placed her arms around his neck. Bevan was conscious of someone else trying to take a photograph, but managed to free himself. Every morning, Lee had to get up early to pick up the post before she and Bevan's secretary, Betty (whom they shared with George Orwell), opened it. Lee wanted to intercept the hate mail and 'packets of filth' that were regularly sent by members of the public.[24] Bevan's 'vermin' remarks about the Tories in 1948 were to heighten still further his controversial reputation.

Lee supported Bevan throughout all his battles in the Attlee Cabinet, and sacrificed her own career for him. Personally, her support for Bevan was second to none. This is not to say that she constantly sought to influence his policy choices. Rather, Bevan took his own decisions and she reinforced his beliefs. There is no evidence that she was even a 'critical friend'. Politically, she was actually restricted by her marriage to the Minister of Health and Housing. While she faithfully served her constituents, she held back from pushing herself forward. She did not stand for the Labour Party's governing body, the NEC. She never sought to embarrass him with parliamentary questions: 'There was no rivalry between us – if there had been our whole relationship would have gone up in smoke.' She was always nervous listening to Bevan's speeches and was glad when they were safely over. Bevan himself was so protective he disliked being present if Jennie Lee was speaking.[25]

Bevan continued to indulge his taste for the good life. In 2006, the *Western Mail* ran a story: 'Shock corruption claims hit Welsh hero Bevan.' The allegation was a simple one of mutual back-scratching while Bevan served in the Cabinet. Bevan is said to have been improperly assisting Rene de Meo, an Italian nightclub owner, in securing import licences for furniture he wished to bring in from Italy. In return, Bevan dined lavishly on steaks and oysters at de Meo's nightclub, deliberately flouting the wartime food rations. He often brought Lee, and, when they had meals in the club as opposed to in the private flat, they did not pay. Jennie Lee and her mother also allegedly visited the club to collect food. But, despite a police investigation, after a former Ministry of Transport official raised the matter with the police, the Attorney General, Hartley Shawcross, took the matter no further. Lee's version is very different. She confirms that de Meo was a friend, with whom she and Bevan stayed in Italy; de Meo had an older brother there who was a priest. She says she caught her mother accepting meat from de Meo, and put a stop to it: 'I had visions of the blazing front-page headlines if we had been caught black-marketing.' She knew how many enemies Bevan had, and told de Meo that 'Nye above all people must keep strictly to the letter of the law'.[26] Even on Lee's version, if this racket had been going on for some time, what is not explained is the fact that, apparently, neither she nor Bevan noticed the excess amounts of meat at home.

As with all members of the Attlee government, and their senior civil servants, Bevan was under tremendous personal strain, and this may provide an explanation. He was under so much pressure he did not notice. Morrison suffered a thrombosis in early 1947, which put him out of action for a couple of months. Bevin died in office as Lord Privy Seal, on 14 April 1951. Cripps' health declined dramatically in 1951, and he died on 21 April 1952. The driver of Bevan's ministerial car died, and one of his officials suffered a nervous breakdown. Bevan himself had flu, which developed into pneumonia. He was cared for by his friend, Dr Daniel Davies. Given the way his father had died, this was a time of particular concern. However, *if* Bevan was evading food rationing, he should not have been. His behaviour would stand in stark contrast to that of Cripps, whose own Spartan lifestyle, as a vegetarian and teetotaller, set the tone of his austerity chancellorship.

In the photograph of the new 1945 Labour Cabinet, Bevan certainly looks slightly apart, aloof and awkward at the far side of the back row. To a certain extent this was a product of the fact that he had spent most of the previous six years attacking the Labour ministers in the wartime coalition, whom he now had to serve alongside. But it did not come to represent the political reality. Bevan was a strong and decisive Cabinet minister, able to have his own way on key issues, keenly aware of the need to compromise when he had to, and disciplined. He was naturally a *constructive* socialist who was completely at home holding the levers of power. He quickly understood his department, gained the respect of his civil servants and drove forward his positive agenda for change.

Chapter 10

The Creation of the National Health Service

O n 2 May 1946, the National Health Service Bill passed easily through the House of Commons, by 359 votes to 172. Its purpose was set out clearly in Section 1(1), establishing a specific duty upon the Minister of Health to promote the establishment 'of a comprehensive health service designed to secure improvement in the physical and mental health of the people of England and Wales and the prevention, diagnosis and treatment of illness and for that purpose to provide or secure the effect of provision of services'.[1] However, the passage of the National Health Service Bill through Parliament was only the start of the battle to create the service. For Bevan faced two major obstacles. The first was whether he could nationalise the hospitals themselves. The second was whether the doctors would be full-time salaried professionals within the National Health Service. Throughout 1947 and the first part of 1948 Bevan negotiated with the British Medical Association (BMA). If he could not secure the participation of the medical professionals, the service would be strangled at birth.

There was nothing inevitable about the creation of the NHS, as Charles Webster has argued in his authoritative political history.[2] There *had* been a steady growth in health provision before the outbreak of the Second World War, but the services offered were a patchwork. The first part of the 1911 National Insurance Act had provided for a right to consult a general practitioner, treatment for tuberculosis in a sanatorium and maternity benefit. Lloyd George, then the Liberal chancellor, had persuaded private companies already providing such schemes to accept the new proposals by allowing such bodies to become 'approved societies' and manage funds.[3] This scheme had two major weaknesses. First, there were around 7,000 'approved societies' that administered the service, and quality varied considerably. For example, some provided contributions towards dental and ophthalmic treatment; others did not. Second, aside from in the case of tuberculosis treatment (the disease was a great killer in the twentieth century prior to the Second World War), the insured worker's dependants were not covered and were forced to rely on other public health care provision.[4] For example, local authorities were statutorily obliged to provide maternity services under the Maternity and Child Welfare Act 1918 and the Midwives Act 1936. But, by 1935, only 35 per cent of notified births were taking place in hospital, and service coverage varied tremendously across different areas.[5] There were teaching hospitals with great reputations, but the hospitals were in two systems: 3,000 public hospitals run by local authorities and 1,000 self-governing voluntary hospitals.[6] Herbert Morrison's large London County Council ran a good hospital service, but the standard provided depended upon the wealth of the relevant local authority. Poorer local authorities were not in a position to provide the same service as those with more money. There were also some excellent health services provided in the voluntary sector, not least by the Tredegar Medical Aid Society, but the hospitals tended to be small and required financial contributions from people. In his seminal book *The Road to 1945*, Paul Addison has argued that the new centralised state Emergency Medical Service, created early in the Second World War to treat air-raid victims, was crucial.[7] For it employed nurses and doctors directly, and commandeered hospitals, whether in the voluntary or municipal sectors. Not only did it provide a model, unified structure, it had also made the voluntary hospitals dependent on government funding. Something would have to be done when the Emergency Medical Service was wound up at the end of the war, otherwise a large number of hospitals would be left in financial difficulty.

By 1945, there was a consensus across the political parties about a new health service, but not its form. As part of his scheme of reconstruction, Beveridge had included an 'assumption' that there would be a 'national health service for prevention and comprehensive treatment' available to all. Henry Willink, the Churchill coalition's Minister of Health from 1943 until 1945, had published a White Paper in 1944, *A National Health Service*. The Willink White Paper contained the NHS principles of a comprehensive system free of charge and available to all, but there was a crucial aspect that Bevan wanted to change. Willink's plan proposed leaving voluntary and local-authority hospitals with their existing owners. The public organisation would come from setting up advisory planning boards at area and regional levels. There was a logical, practical, political reason for doing this: local government would object strongly to the accretion of powers into the hands of the Minister of Health and away from them. In contrast, the Socialist Medical Association, led by Mr Somerville Hastings MP (a surgeon) and Dr David Stark Murray, pressed a different case through its journal, *Medicine Today and Tomorrow*, seeking a fully nationalised service, with a salaried medical profession, scaling down private practice.

Bevan's vision of a National Health Service was of a truly public service owned by the public. All hospitals would be nationalised, and the only separate class of hospital would be for teaching. Bevan's structure was to be very centralised, with 14 regional boards appointed by the Minister of Health and local management committees. There was an outcry in local government. Sir Harold Webbe, the Conservative leader on London County Council, said of Bevan: 'he is so full of his own importance that he is prepared to pit his knowledge against the accumulated experience of this Council which is to be butchered to make a Welshman's holiday.'[8] While local government might be deeply unhappy about its loss of power, they were clearly weaker than Labour's 1945 Minister of Health, who was carrying out the Attlee government's programme on the back of its landslide victory in the general election of 1945. Yet there was one major complicating factor. Local government had a spokesman in Cabinet: Herbert Morrison. In addition, Morrison's successor as leader on London County Council, Lord Latham, was a close ally of his. Latham held the leadership for a key period at the start of the Attlee government, until July 1947.[9]

Attlee's contribution in Cabinet was very important as Bevan fought out the battle for the nationalisation of the hospitals with Herbert Morrison. His victory over Morrison in Cabinet was quick and decisive. The key clash occurred as early as 18 October 1945. Bevan's proposals for nationalised hospitals had been opposed by Morrison, who had taken it upon himself to circulate his own Cabinet memorandum on 'The Future of the Hospital Services' some six days before.[10] Morrison's arguments were inconsistent. While arguing passionately for his proposals he sought to persuade the Cabinet that his alternative scheme was not much different from Bevan's: 'In the first place, how does the Minister of Health's scheme differ from the alternative of a local-authority service, with joint hospital boards, and with the Ministry of Health as the responsible central Department?' On the one hand, he praised Bevan for the 'order and simplicity of the solution which he offered for a complex and difficult administrative problem'. On the other, he argued that 'we should think seriously before embarking on a project which would still further hold up the completion of the scheme for a National Health Service'. In truth, Morrison had taken a scattergun approach. The final sentence of the memorandum included the kernel of his argument: the consequences to 'local government of slicing off one of its most cherished functions, [and] the antagonism and suspicion which the Government would arouse amongst local authorities throughout the land'.

The issue was the first one on the Cabinet agenda.[11] Morrison set out his case first; while 'he fully appreciated the attractions of a logical and clean-cut scheme of the kind proposed' by Bevan, 'the Cabinet ought to consider fully whether the opposition which they would arouse and the detrimental effect which the loss of hospital functions would have on local government in general, did not outweigh the arguments based on grounds of administrative convenience and technical efficiency'. Bevan was firm in response: 'he still felt that the only way to make the hospital services efficient was to centralise responsibility for them.' Members of the Cabinet then lined up behind Bevan. Arthur Greenwood, as chair of the Cabinet's Social Services Committee, backed him. Minister of Agriculture and Fisheries Tom Williams and Minister of Education Ellen Wilkinson also backed a national scheme. So, crucially, did Leader of the House of Lords Christopher Addison, now Lord Addison, who felt that a centralised system would be of great benefit in health education and nurse-training. Morrison received some support from the Home Secretary, James Chuter Ede, who had a local-government background, having served as a Surrey county councillor. William Jowitt suggested a compromise position of the Minister of Health being able to give directions to hospitals in the first instance, while First Lord of the Admiralty A. V. Alexander argued for a more thorough consideration of the matter. Attlee, however, intervened decisively, seizing on the weaker part of Morrison's argument that, in reality, there was little difference between the two schemes: 'The Prime Minister said that the differences between the proposals made by the Minister of Health and the alternative scheme suggested by the Lord President of the Council were possibly less fundamental than they seemed to be.' He then added: 'Whichever course was adopted, there would inevitably be controversy, and the predominant feeling in the Cabinet seemed to him to be generally in favour of the solution proposed by the Minister of Health.' He sweetened the pill for Morrison: 'While approving this proposal in principle, however, the Cabinet would want to look at the details again when they were more fully worked out.' The Cabinet duly agreed, and Morrison was beaten.

Once this decision was taken in principle, with Attlee's backing, there was no going back. That is not to say that Morrison took it lying down. Far from it; he still sought to throw spokes into Bevan's wheels whenever he could. In the five months between this Cabinet meeting and Bevan finally producing his draft National Health Service Bill on 1 March 1946, Morrison fell back on procedural points.[12] In Cabinet on 3 December 1945, as Bevan sought Cabinet authority for ending the buying and selling of medical practices, Morrison had argued that it was 'unsatisfactory that the Cabinet should be asked to settle particular parts of the scheme for a National Health Service before they had seen the scheme as a whole'.[13] Yet the ground shifted from beneath Morrison's feet, for London County Council itself decided not to take Bevan on. Bevan took delight in reminding Morrison: 'In general the reactions have not been unfavourable. The local authorities are divided in their views. The London County Council accepts the proposals subject to minor points on which I think they can be met.' He added: 'in general I do not anticipate strong opposition from local authorities *particularly in view of the lead given by the L.C.C.* [my emphasis].'[14] It did not stop Morrison making a last-ditch attempt to delay the bill. When Cabinet approved the draft bill on 8 March 1946, Morrison played his final card: parliamentary time. He replied directly to Bevan, saying he felt the bill would arouse contro-versy, and 'it would barely be possible to get them through all their stages in the House of Commons before the end of July.'[15] Attlee again intervened and said some other bills could be carried over into the next session. The Cabinet agreed that 'National Health Service Bills should be introduced as soon as possible'. It was finally over for Morrison.

In contrast to the swift victory over Morrison, Bevan was engaged in a lengthy strategic battle with the BMA for the best part of 18 months. The contemporane-ous minutes kept by the BMA, together with the government documents, reveal a strategy of resolve then compromise that succeeded in bringing the service into existence on 5 July 1948. On 6 January 1947, Bevan wrote to the presidents of the Royal Colleges of Medicine to ask them to enter into discussions on the health service. On 28 January 1947, the Representative Body of the BMA accepted his invitation on the basis that the discussions were comprehensive, that Bevan did not discount the possibility of further legislation and that there was a second plebiscite of the profession at the end of the discussions. On that basis, on 7 February 1947, the Negotiating Committee of the BMA resolved to 'express its willingness to enter into discussions with the Minister'.[16]

While the negotiations with the BMA were gruelling, Bevan's positive relation-ship with the presidents of the Royal Colleges should not be underestimated. The president of the Royal College of Surgeons, Sir Alfred Webb-Johnson, approached Bevan within days of his taking office as Minister of Health. They met in a private room at the Café Royal, and were served a large plate of oysters. Bevan quipped: 'when I was a nipper, we could buy that lot for a few pence; then the price went up when Mayfair thought they were aphrodisiacs.' Dr Eardley Holland, presi-dent of the Royal College of Obstetrics and Gynaecologists, told Bevan, 'you see, Minister, this is a matter of great importance to me for I am responsible for all the pregnant women in this country'. Bevan smiled at him: 'You're boasting!' There was also Lord Moran, the president of the Royal College of Physicians (or 'Corkscrew Charlie' as he was known), who respected Bevan, describing him as 'a rare phenomenon. Always ready for new mental adventures.' Even Dr Roland Cockshut, an aggressive BMA Council member, said that Bevan 'had the finest intellect I ever met'.[17]

Bevan was also deeply appreciative of the work of the nurses. On 8 November 1945 he announced a 'charter for nurses' promising the introduction of a 96-hour fortnight as soon as circumstances allowed. He hoped this would assist the medical-recruitment drive. His Labour Party Conference speech of 1947 also focused on the nurses, rather than the doctors, referring to the improvement of their pay and conditions, and the need for sufficient numbers of them in order to run the NHS.[18]

Bevan first met the Negotiating Committee of the BMA on 28 February 1947, and confirmed that he did not seek to limit the discussions or exclude the idea of amending the legislation. The committee then set up a number of subcommittees, and 31 meetings took place between those bodies and Bevan's representatives.[19] The representations made were then collated for presentation personally to Bevan. As a result, Bevan and the Secretary of State for Scotland, Arthur Woodburn, who had taken over the office on 7 October 1947, met the BMA's Negotiating Committee for a gruelling two-day session on Tuesday, 2 December, and Wednesday, 3 December 1947. On 7 November, prior to the meeting, the committee had produced a 'case document' that made a scathing attack on the National Health Service Act 1946: 'the wording of the Act is in places so obscure that to bring it into force as it stands will create chaotic conditions.'[20] Given this attitude, Bevan opened the meeting very aggressively. The Negotiating Committee had proposed to send out its case document to the wider medical profession. Bevan said he 'was shocked by this and did not see what purpose could be achieved by discussing it'. He added that he 'could not understand the Committee's state of mind. Was it, or was it not, a Negotiating Committee?' His point was that if the committee's argument was that the *whole* Act was unacceptable, there was no room for compromise. Dr H. Guy Dain, chairman of the council, equally determined, replied tartly that the purpose of the meeting was 'to discover from the Minister whether he was satisfied that the profession's points were reasonable' and if so, whether he would amend the Act. Bevan, however, was in no mood to compromise: 'if the points that the profession had put forward were to be embodied in the Act, a new Act, not an amending Act, would be necessary. In this case, he regarded himself as free to inform the profession that, on the Negotiating Committee's own statement, negotiations were barred.'[21]

The negotiations were dominated by four issues: GPs' ownership of the goodwill of their practices; their freedom to practise without being directed as to where; a right of appeal to the regular courts against dismissal; and remuneration (a key issue in terms of whether GPs felt they could retain their independence, or whether they felt they would become akin to full-time, paid civil servants).[22] It was the issue of the distribution of doctors that the meeting initially dealt with. Bevan again put his view strongly. A doctor could not 'establish himself anywhere in the public service and claim remuneration from public funds [...] the profession would be informed where there were vacancies where it was possible for them to enter public practice.'[23] Dr Dain replied that Bevan misunderstood the concept of a *need* for doctors, and areas could not be defined as 'over-doctored or under-doctored'.[24]

Most of the other major issues were discussed. Particular concerns were also raised by Dr Charles Hill, then secretary of the BMA, as to partnership agreements. Hill, who was later to serve as a Cabinet minister in the Conservative government of Harold Macmillan, made life difficult for Bevan. The ownership of practices, and compensation for their nationalisation, was to be a consistent problem over the next few months. Hill put technical points to Bevan. If a deadline date were set to qualify for compensation, what would be the position as regards compensating those doctors who entered into partnership agreements prior to the deadline, but who sold and/or purchased shares afterwards? For the moment, Bevan provided reassurance on this point, and fell back on the compensation package to persuade the profession, stating that he had £66 million to distribute and wished to have the help of the profession in doing so.[25]

On the Wednesday, the second day, Bevan's tone had altered. He was now handling the meeting in a very different way. His themes were reassurance and conciliation, the aggressive tone gone. He was a great tactician. He said that while voluntary hospitals would be taken over, private nursing homes would not.[26] He also tried to calm fears of a full-time salaried medical profession. There would not be one single salary as such. There would still be the opportunity for private income. He set out the four types of hospital accommodation which would be available: that which was free; that in which patients could pay for some 'additional amenities'; wards where surgeons, radiologists and pathologists could charge up to a maximum; and wards where there could be unlimited charging. He accepted that GPs had to refer patients to specialists save in certain cases such as venereal disease.[27] As regards pay specifically, he reiterated the effect of a calculation he had outlined on the Tuesday: there would be a fixed element of £300, and then a further 'capitation fee', a proportional element based on the number of patients on the GP's list. Basing the £300 on a mathematical equation using 95 per cent of the general population, he agreed to reconsider this percentage after two years. There would also be mileage payments.[28]

These apparent concessions did not give Bevan an easier ride. He had an uncomfortable moment over a right of appeal to the courts. The BMA was arguing that a doctor struck off, or deemed unfit to practise in the NHS by a statutory tribunal, should have a right of appeal to the regular courts against the decision. It was put to Bevan that miners had such a right. Bevan managed to find a distinction: a miner could not appeal on the ground that his 'dismissal was not justified on the facts'.[29] He was correct in saying that there would have to be other grounds of appeal in the case of the miners. However, there was a better answer: that if the correct statutory procedure was not followed, there was a recourse to the regular courts for the doctors in any event – a point *The Times* was to illuminate some weeks later, and that Bevan would probably have been better to deploy here.

In the meeting, the newly appointed Woodburn certainly took a junior role to Bevan. But he supported Bevan's strong line, and the proposition that since the NHS was the will of Parliament, it should be implemented.[30] Bevan, however, at the end of two obviously tiring days, seemed to be pleading with the profession in his closing remarks. The contrast to his opening remarks could not be greater: 'I beg and pray that you will consider whether now it is advisable to make a recommendation to the profession to give the whole scheme a trial.' Bevan became frustrated with the BMA, which fuelled his desire to appeal over their heads to the individual doctors.

Doctors were furnished with some substantial documents in December 1947 from the BMA and Bevan. The extent to which they read them in detail over the festive season is unclear. But Bevan's concern regarding what the BMA would say to the individual doctors was well founded. Take the BMA's statement dated 18 December 1947: 'It would be useless to disguise that on this subject the differences between the Minister and the profession are deep. On no single major issue has the Minister responded to the reasoned arguments of the profession.'[31] Bevan had anticipated this, and tried to counter the statement with a 34-page document of reassurance. In stark contrast to his initial belligerence at the meeting with the Negotiation Committee earlier that month, Bevan again asked the profession to give the NHS a chance. There would be 'lessons of trial and error'. There would be 'amending Acts, without any doubt'. But the differences between the Minister and the doctors were 'never insurmountable'; and the central aim of concern for the welfare of the people was shared by both.[32]

By early 1948 problems for Bevan were mounting. At a 'special representative meeting' of the BMA on 8 January 1948, a motion was passed that 'this Meeting expresses great dissatisfaction with the results of the attempted negotiations with the Minister of Health and with his unswerving attitude and lack of understanding of the profession's ideals. The Meeting wishes also to express its complete lack of confidence in, and mistrust of, the Minister of Health.'[33] On the face of it, Bevan was in significant difficulty. One way or another he was going to have to persuade many within the medical profession to accept the service. Both carrot and stick were available to Bevan; the stick was most certainly what he termed the 'constitutional point': that the BMA, as an interest group, could not prevent a piece of legislation passed by an elected Parliament from being implemented. The BMA could not be, and would not *want* to be, the sole reason why the people could not have their health service. The carrot was the concessions that Bevan could or should make. That was the question to which his mind now turned. And he was helped by the fact that the special representative meeting of the BMA on 8 January set 13,000 (out of 20,500) votes in the forthcoming plebiscite of GPs as the level that would justify non-cooperation with the health service, a high requirement.[34] Bevan would not need to convince a majority of GPs to accept the service. He would also have to hope that the BMA Negotiating Committee he had met was not representative of the medical profession as a whole.

On 16 January 1948, Attlee asked Bevan to report to Cabinet on developments 'in view of the publicity given to the difficulties which appear to have arisen in your discussions with the B.M.A.'[35] Bevan therefore produced a memorandum for Cabinet consideration. In it, he attacked the BMA secretary, Dr Hill, for his negativity and his desire to 'sabotage' the Act. He then concentrated on three areas of dispute: the position of partnerships, for which he now proposed, as a concession, to appoint a legal committee to consider the options; the right of appeal to the ordinary courts from a tribunal decision on dismissal; and the issue of the fixed salary – no compromise was proposed on the last two points. 'Nothing, I believe, could prevent the doctors – as an organisation – from voting against the Act this month. That does not mean that they will not, as individuals, take part in it.' That was because Bevan thought that if the government stuck firmly to a set date for the introduction of the health service, those GPs who did not participate would lose their present income, their right to a share on the £66 million available as compensation for partnerships, and their right to take private patients in hospital pay beds.[36]

Bevan's decision to retain the implementation date come what may was a calculated gamble. He was relying on his own strategy and the self-interest of the individual doctors to bring cooperation over the next few months. He felt that the BMA's aggressive stance would not be reflected in the behaviour of the doctors, who could make or break the NHS: a judgement that proved to be accurate. On 22 January 1948, the Cabinet considered the memorandum, and agreed to support Bevan's proposed course of no compromise. Bevan said that the

Negotiating Committee was 'dominated by a reactionary and vocal group who, partly for political reasons, were seeking to prevent the Act from coming into operation'. The Cabinet did, however, think that more should be done to 'explain the Government's case'. It therefore resolved to approve Bevan's proposal of establishing a committee on partnership agreements, and the bringing of the service into operation on the intended date of 5 July. Bevan agreed to consult Morrison 'on the further measures which might be taken to ensure that full information [...] was made available both to the general public and the medical profession'.[37] The Cabinet anticipated that, as the 5 July deadline approached, and as 'doctors had to decide as individuals whether they would come into the national service, the British Medical Association were likely to modify their attitude.'[38]

On 29 January 1948, anticipating a significant vote against the service in the BMA plebiscite, Bevan sought permission from No. 10 to give an oral answer in the House of Commons regarding the way the ballot was conducted.[39] He attacked the BMA: 'the Association conducting the ballot is itself engaged in a campaign to induce the doctor to vote one way [...] it is bound to cast doubt on the validity of the result.' Bevan also noted that it was not a secret ballot: 'It was because open votes of this sort were removed from our constitutional practice that the secret ballot was established.'[40] But trying to split the BMA's position from that of the individual doctor was a risky strategy for Bevan as he was running the risk that the BMA might refuse to work with him as an individual and appeal over his head to the prime minister.

That said, Bevan's position was not generally regarded as totally unreasonable. The issue of allowing a right of appeal to the regular courts against a doctor's dismissal caught the attention of *The Times*, who ran an article in favour of Bevan's position on 31 January 1948, referring to the BMA Council's criticism of Bevan for 'depriving doctors of their "elementary right of appeal to the courts". The Act does nothing of the sort.' *The Times* correctly observed that if the procedures set down were not followed, there would in any event be an appeal to the courts.[41]

On 2 February, the Cabinet agreed on the motion for a parliamentary debate on 9 February, welcoming the service coming into force on 5 July and stating 'that the conditions under which all the professions concerned are invited to participate are generous and fully in accord with their traditional freedoms and dignity'.[42] Bevan again set out a strong position. He 'did not in fact contemplate making any further concessions to the doctors; but it was the view of the Cabinet that the passage of a motion in these terms would not preclude the Government from making changes in the scheme, if they thought fit, before 5th July.'[43] Bevan also asked for Attlee's support: 'He would [...] be glad if the Prime Minister would also speak in the debate.' Attlee said he was in principle willing to speak, and would decide whether to do so in the light of the course of the debate. On 6 February 1948, the Ministry of Health wrote to Laurence Helsby, Attlee's private secretary, enclosing a suggested note for the prime minister's intervention, and both *The Times* article and Bevan's answers to questions put by the *Lancet*. In these answers, Bevan reassured doctors that the idea of a 'basic salary' would not lead to a full-time salaried service, though of course he 'could not read into the mind of any future Minister'. Bevan also set out his decision to appoint a committee of legal experts to obtain a 'collective legal opinion of high standing' on the status of legal partnerships once the service came into being. However, he remained strong on the implementation date of 5 July.[44] The Ministry of Health also provided Attlee with 'Suggested notes for [...] intervention in the health service debate'. There were essentially two points for Attlee to make: firstly, he should offer an assurance that the Cabinet was behind Bevan; secondly, from a constitutional perspective, he should reject the notion that 'Governments can be forced to do other than they and Parliament intend by a campaign of deliberately organised sabotage'.[45] Bevan clearly needed Attlee to intervene if he was to pursue a tough line in the coming months. This would have shown the stiffness of the government's resolve that the service should come into operation and that the BMA should not be able to block it. It would also have protected Bevan from being isolated from his colleagues and taken away the possibility of the BMA approaching Attlee with a view to negotiating with Bevan himself as a potential casualty.

This was the crucial moment for Attlee to shape the negotiations. However, the prime minister declined to intervene, providing a short note on the day of the debate indicating that he had decided not to speak.[46] Bevan could not have felt anything but frustration at this. It locked him and the BMA into a game in which one of Bevan's hands had been tied. However, the Cabinet *had* agreed that the implementation date of the service should remain unchanged. Bevan's strategy therefore had to be one of compromise as opposed to belligerence; but he knew that the extent of that compromise need not be incompatible with the fundamental principles upon which the NHS was based.

In his speech in the House of Commons on 9 February 1948, Bevan could not resist criticising the BMA as 'politically poisoned people'. He wanted to show that he *was* willing to listen to the individual doctors: the problem was the BMA. He began: 'it can hardly be suggested that conflict between the British Medical Association and the Minister of the day is a consequence of any deficiencies that I possess, because we have never been able yet to appoint a Minister of Health with whom the B.M.A. agreed.'[47]

Bevan concluded with a flourish: 'I [...] deplore the fact that the best elements in the profession have been thrust on one side by the medical politicians, who are not really concerned about the welfare of the people or of their own profession, but are seeking to fish in these troubled waters.'[48] Bevan still trusted his belief in what individual doctors would do.

He remained concerned about a direct appeal to Attlee over his head. He was willing to consider a further minor change, such as increasing the amount of basic salary, but felt it would be

> bad tactics to take up this point soon after the result of the plebiscite is published – a month or two of delay would let the matter settle down, and would also give time for individual doctors to turn over in their minds what the future would hold for them personally if they persisted in refusing to join the scheme.[49]

In fact, the 21 February plebiscite brought the results Bevan expected. On an 84 per cent turnout, 4,735 voted for the service from a total of 45,549.[50] Of GPs specifically, 17,037 voted against the service, well in excess of the 13,000 threshold set.[51] But Bevan knew that the BMA would find it difficult to stand against the tide of public opinion. And if he could persuade the BMA to hold a further plebiscite, he only had to change the views of around 4,000 doctors in order to meet the BMA criterion.

Things were looking up. At a special representative meeting of the BMA on 17 March 1948, a motion was rejected that the prime minister be asked to reopen negotiations.[52] Bevan's calculations regarding the BMA were proving accurate. The BMA could not be seen as the lone voice against the will of the people, and negotiating with Bevan was the only way out of the impasse. In the same month, Bevan also brought in five sets of regulations in order to make the service operational.[53] These reminded the BMA of the minister's power to legislate by this method, and, in a sense, dangled the carrot of an amending Act: if the BMA could persuade Bevan to promise an amending Act, they could portray it as a victory, even if the contents of such an Act did not include any great concession.

Given his relationship with the presidents of the Royal Colleges, it was, appropriately, Lord Moran of the Royal College of Physicians who wrote to Bevan on 24 March 1948: 'the co-operation of the general practitioners could be won if the Minister made it crystal clear that no whole-time salaried medical service would be brought in ever, either by legislation or by departmental regulation.'[54] On 6 April 1948, *The Times* ran the story of this move by the Royal College of Physicians, which it saw as 'a real prospect of a peaceful solution to the controversy'.[55] Bevan was already alive to this, and the previous day had asked for a meeting with the prime minister and Addison, the Lord Privy Seal.[56]

The stage was now set. Bevan made a statement in the House of Commons on 7 April 1948. It was one of the most important speeches of his career. The rewards of a well-judged speech were great: the possibility of a compromise in the long-running feud with the BMA was within his grasp, and, better still, he did not have to hold out his hand too far or make too many grand gestures. Moran's request was one he could easily deal with, primarily because it was an illusory compromise: Bevan had never said anything different. He did, though, make two further concessions: there would be the amending Act and also some changes on the capitation fee, something the Cabinet Secretary Norman Brook had previously identified to Attlee as a possible area for compromise. Carefully delivering his draft statement virtually word-for-word, Bevan observed:

> The Royal College of Physicians has made the useful suggestion, with which the other Royal Colleges associate themselves, that I should now make it statutorily clear that a whole-time service will not be brought in by regulation, but would require further legislation to make it possible. My colleagues and I accept that, most cordially.[57]

Bevan went on to give a further assurance that a full-time salaried profession was not the final purpose of introducing a fixed element of £300 in doctors' pay:

> I for my part have always conceived it rather as an assurance for the young beginner and for the older practitioner wishing to ease up in old age, and as a peg on which to hang additional assured payments for doubtful areas or other risks – and these are all worthy objects.

However, if it was causing concern:

> Let all new entrants to practice have the advantage of this assured element of £300 for a period of, say, three years. Then let each decide for himself whether he will forgo it and pass to a system of plain capitation fees, or stay as he is with his fixed £300 plus a lower proportionate rate of capitation.

He added:

> Similarly, let any doctor in established practice be able to elect for himself at any time to go on the system of £300 fixed payment, plus

the lower capitation rate, if and when he wants to – for example, in old age – instead of the higher rate with no fixed payments at all.[58]

On the point as regards the appeal to the ordinary courts, Bevan gave assurance that the 'Chairman of the Tribunal under the Act will be a lawyer of high professional standing appointed by the Lord Chancellor'.[59] But a statutory right of appeal was not conceded, and neither were the central principles of the service.

Bevan had not achieved the Socialist Medical Association's goal of a wholly salaried service. He had not eliminated private medical work. But he had done what he had promised the Cabinet he would do as far back as 8 January 1946, when he had said that he 'wished to enter into his discussions with the main interests concerned on the basis that no concessions should be made on the *main principles* of his scheme [my emphasis]. Within these principles, however, there would be scope for adjustment.'[60] Bevan had nationalised the hospitals and introduced a comprehensive health care service free at the point of delivery.

With the BMA holding a further plebiscite in May 1948, Bevan was confident that he could bring the NHS into operation on 5 July even though that plebiscite was likely to be lost. He reported to the Cabinet on 29 April 1948:

> In Scotland there was likely to be a large majority in favour of participation. In England and Wales substantial numbers might vote against participation in the scheme; but the Minister was confident that sufficient support would be forthcoming to enable him to bring the Service into operation on the appointed day.[61]

Bevan was vindicated. The BMA Council made a statement on 8 May 1948 indicating the result of the April plebiscite. Of 54,724 practitioners, 40,622 voted (a turnout of just over 74 per cent). The overall vote against the National Health Service Acts was 25,842 to 14,620. As regards the question addressed specifically to consultants, GPs and full-time voluntary hospital staff, 13,981 were against the Acts, 9,588 of whom were GPs. Nearly 44 per cent of the GPs who voted against the Acts in the February plebiscite had not opposed it this time: some 7,449 doctors. Bevan's judgement about the individual doctors was correct: the reality was that of the original 20,500 GPs who could vote, fewer than half had opposed the service. Bevan had not needed to reduce opposition among GPs to a minority in order to meet the BMA criterion, but he had done so. His strategy of limited compromise had succeeded.

Overall, of course, Bevan did not have a majority of professionals in favour of the NHS. But his work had, as he predicted, brought enough professionals to cooperate with the NHS to meet the 5 July deadline. The BMA Council was able to take the view that 'on some fundamental issues the profession has gained a substantial victory'. Its recommendation to the Representative Body was that it was 'prepared to advise the profession to cooperate in the new service on the understanding the Minister will continue negotiations on outstanding matters'.[62] This recommendation held through the meeting of the Negotiation Committee on 20 May 1948, and the special representative meeting of 28 May 1948.[63] By June 1948, 26 per cent of GPs in England had already joined the NHS; in Scotland the figure was 36 per cent, and in Wales, 37 per cent.[64]

Harry Eckstein's study of the BMA's tactics concentrates on Bevan's change from a strong stance to a conciliatory one, and offers two explanations: Bevan's desire to see the NHS implemented and his greater power over the implementation of the Act as opposed to its drafting. Other influence is ascribed to Addison, and Arthur Greenwood, who until 1947 was directing the Cabinet committee with broad coordination on social services.[65] Bevan's natural attitude was undoubtedly the one displayed at the start of the meeting with the Negotiating Committee in December 1947. He wanted to be aggressive; he wanted to make it clear that the doctors could not frustrate the will of Parliament. But Attlee's failure to intervene in the NHS debate in February 1948 took away this option. In one sense, this was not so much casting Bevan adrift as reining in some of the more pugnacious aspects of his attitude to the BMA. In another, it restricted Bevan's freedom of manoeuvre. But Bevan had already ensured that he had Cabinet backing for keeping the date of 5 July to bring the service into operation. This placed an end date to the strategic game he and the BMA played out in the spring of 1948. He feared losing his authority if the BMA went over his head, and the prospect that the service would fail at the outset if the doctors did not cooperate; the BMA feared both public opposition if it stood in the way of the service, and the prospect of losing its own authority if individual doctors decided to cooperate.

From his speech of 9 February 1948 in the House of Commons, Bevan sought to isolate the BMA from the doctors it represented, and the question that remained was to what extent he should offer compromise. The reality is that Bevan did not backtrack in a major way: he did not need to, and he knew it. He only had to do enough to turn the tide of opinion among GPs to a limited extent. He had already offered pay beds in hospitals for specialists, and had allowed GPs to do private work. He offered a legal committee to look into partnerships in January 1948, but that was a complex question in any event. His final compromises on pay in his speech of 7 April 1948 did not concede the basic principle of the capitation payment, and the promised amending Act would simply contain an assurance about a full-time salaried service that he had been suggesting throughout.

Bevan was therefore able to implement the National Health Service Act without compromising its essential elements. That he was able to do so is a testament to his strategy during 1947 and 1948. His ability to read the interests of the individual doctor and BMA alongside his commitment to the date of 5 July meant that Bevan was in effect dictating the terms of the game. Attlee's decision not to intervene significantly helped Bevan. It was an example of the styles of the prime minister and departmental minister complementing each other. On the NHS, Attlee and Bevan were a perfect combination. Attlee tempered the freedom with which Bevan could express his views towards doctors, and reined in some of his more aggressive pronouncements. What the result would have been had Bevan adopted the stronger line from February 1948 is unknown. What is certain is that the strategy he *did* adopt was an effective one. He had the tenacity, the drive, the commitment to the NHS and the skills to see it into existence. It was not so much that the doctors had their mouths stuffed with gold, though undoubtedly finance was part of the bargain. The reality was that they were slowly manoeuvred into position by a determined navigator working under the watchful eye of his cautious captain. The scale of Bevan's achievement in establishing the NHS should not be underestimated. This was not only the state taking responsibility for providing a service, it was a cultural shift in attitudes to health in the UK. Health care free at the point of delivery was now a right, an expectation, not a luxury.[66]

Despite Attlee's backing, Bevan remained concerned that the prime minister had not been sufficiently partisan in public on the issue, and he wrote to him on 2 July 1948: 'Our people all over the country will be making speeches this week-end claiming credit for the Labour Party for these great Acts. They will be made to look foolish if their leader attributes their parentage to all-Party inspiration.'[67] By this time, Bevan's concern was not whether he could bring the service into operation, but that the prime minister should claim full credit on behalf of the Labour Party for its creation. In any event, the set-piece speech preceding the service coming into effect was given by Bevan himself on 4 July 1948 at a party rally in Manchester.

The moment marked the apex of Bevan's career as a minister, yet the speech has been better remembered not for its claim that the rest of the world would learn from Britain's great social achievement in creating the NHS, but for his remarks about the Tories, which are worth quoting in full. Bevan saw poverty as avoidable; for him it was a consequence of poor social organisation. Recalling having to live off his sister's earnings, and being told to emigrate, he went on:

> That is why no amount of cajolery, and no attempts at ethical or social seduction, can eradicate from my heart a deep burning hatred for the

Tory Party that inflicted those bitter experiences upon me. So far as I am concerned they are lower than vermin. They condemned millions of first-class people to semi-starvation. Now the Tories are pouring out money in propaganda of all sorts and are hoping by this organised sustained mass suggestion to eradicate from our minds all memory of what we went through. But, I warn you young men and women, do not listen to what they are saying now. Do not listen to the seductions of Lord Woolton [the Conservative Party chairman]. If you are selling shoddy stuff you have to be a good salesman. But I warn you they have not changed, or if they have they are slightly worse than they were.[68]

After the speech, and the outraged response from the Tories, Attlee wrote privately to Bevan urging him to be more careful, 'in his own interests'. But this was not a mere outburst in a fit of temper. While Bevan often spoke without prepared written texts, he *did* practise his speeches, often on his friends, striding back and forth, going through the themes and ideas. As a Cabinet minister, he studiously compiled notes and statistics for use in his speeches in a specific file, categorising information into key areas: 'Employment'; 'Housing'; 'NHS'; 'Vital Statistics'.[69]

There is a view that Bevan linked ideas to the people who espoused them. Lush put it like this: while people accused Bevan of being hard and vicious with people, he 'always argued that individuals [...] epitomised ideas, and if they had the wrong ideas, in killing the idea you were killing the person'.[70] Thus, here, Bevan was linking the idea of creating mass poverty with the Tory Party that was responsible for it. On the other hand, in *Why Not Trust the Tories?*, Bevan *does* make a clear distinction between the person and the politics: 'Human beings are complex creatures, and most generalisations about them give little light [...] I don't think a Tory, considered as a person, is any worse or better than anyone else.' He added: 'The private morals of many of our leading Tories are beyond reproach, whereas their public morals are execrable.' He gave an example: 'In their personal circle they would hesitate to tell lies, yet in public, deception is accepted as part of their technique of government.'[71] Indeed, what Bevan did not do in the 'vermin' speech was name any individual as being responsible for the welfare policies of the 1920s to which he was referring. Lord Woolton was mentioned in a different context, as the effective modern-day Tory seeking to promote an amnesia about what had gone before. Bevan *could* have named an individual. The obvious candidate was Neville Chamberlain, given that he was Minister of Health three times, twice in the 1920s and once, briefly, in 1931, and then Chancellor of the Exchequer from 5 November 1931 until becoming prime minister on 28 May 1937. By 1948, his reputation tarnished by his advocacy of a policy of appeasement in the late 1930s, Chamberlain was not a difficult target either. But Bevan resisted doing so, sticking to the principle of separating person and politics. Yet even this argument only goes so far. For Bevan had, in fact, cited the *whole* Tory Party, and not even made a distinction between parliamentarians and ordinary Tory voters and members. It was that which gave great impetus to the creation of Tory 'Vermin Clubs' all over the country and which galvanised the Tory rank and file.

Despite this, Bevan's words do not represent a venting of the spleen that was quickly regretted afterwards. The only real conclusion is this: Bevan said it because he meant it. That is what makes the speech so controversial. For it offends against a very British notion of fairness: that although the players on the pitch can do their best to win, and a hard tackle can still be a good tackle, after the match they shake hands and respect each other. Bevan's remarks, while most certainly made in the context of political competition, represented an unfair tackle, such that respect off the pitch became impossible for some Tories. It made it difficult for Tories to say that, while they disagreed with Bevan's ideas, they respected Bevan the man.

Yet Bevan's own words, in this same speech, captured the significance of the moment: 'The eyes of the world are turning to Great Britain. We now have the moral leadership of the world and before many years we shall have people coming here as to a modern Mecca.' Bevan had made health care a permanent Labour issue: time and again, Conservative leaders have had to persuade the public that they can be trusted with the NHS. But the achievement was not only political. Just before the NHS came into existence, British households received a leaflet about the new service. One phrase in it summed up the impact of the NHS: 'it will relieve your money worries in time of illness.' Bevan had removed one of the shadows from the lives of British people. His own political philosophy, emphasising collective action but respecting the importance of the individual, was made real. The NHS became part of the fabric of British society. It was fitting that, in Danny Boyle's London 2012 Olympics opening ceremony, the NHS was a centrepiece celebrating *British* achievement.

Chapter 11

Bevan's Record on Housing, 1945–51

The creation of the NHS was an incontestable achievement which, even putting aside the rest of his political career, makes Bevan one of the greatest twentieth-century government ministers. On housing, the achievement has been the subject of more debate. Housing was a difficult issue for Labour in the 1950 and 1951 general elections, and Harold Macmillan, as housing minister in the second Churchill government from its return to office in 1951, built a formidable reputation on achieving a target of building 300,000 houses per year. Attlee should have split health and housing into two departments in 1945. Bevan did not disagree with the obvious link between standards of housing and public health that led the prime minister to give him responsibility for both issues. However, having the same Cabinet minister responsible for both the creation of the NHS *and* housing the nation after the destruction of the Second World War was more than an overload. It left Bevan having to deal with the intricacies of both sides of his department when either half in itself would have been too much for a single minister.

Bevan deserves great credit for his running of this gargantuan department, but the workload in itself is more a point in mitigation than an absolute defence. Bevan must still be judged on his progress in both fields. Indeed, when Attlee did try to take the responsibility for housing away from him, Bevan sought to keep it. After Labour narrowly won the 1950 general election, Attlee wanted a 'big drive on housing' and sought to move responsibility to Hugh Dalton, combining it – quite sensibly – with town and country planning. However, Bevan was unwilling to be solely health minister without his housing responsibilities.[1] Eventually, the department was broken up in January 1951, when the housing responsibility finally passed to Hugh Dalton, as the minister of the new Local Government and Planning department. Hilary Marquand took Health, and Bevan the Ministry of Labour, with fateful consequences. Until then, responsibility for housing issues was spread over at least seven ministries. Aside from Health itself, there was Town and Country Planning, Works, and Supply; the Board of Trade was the key on imports, and the availability of workers depended on the Ministry of Labour and National Service. In addition, the Secretary of State for Scotland had responsibility for housing north of the border.

Bevan devoted a chapter of *Why Not Trust the Tories?* to the issue of housing.[2] His principal argument against the Tories was that they put the profit motive above all else: 'If you vote Tory at the next election you are, in fact, voting against your chances of obtaining the home you want in the place you want it, and at reasonable cost. Do remember that the next time you and your family talk of your dream home.'[3] As ever with Bevan, there is myth and reality, and the two are often difficult to distinguish. There are two major criticisms of Bevan's stewardship of housing: firstly, that he was too inflexible, even a snob, about the type of houses that should be built, and that his insistence on greater luxury was at the expense of speed; and, secondly, that he chose to neglect housing because he concentrated so much on health.

These charges are based principally on Dalton's assessment of the position when he took over the housing programme:

> I tried to loosen up some of the regulations and leave the local authorities more freedom. I left them free, for instance, to include either one or two w.c.'s in a three-bedroomed council house. On this point Bevan had been a tremendous Tory. Always, he had said, there must be two.

Dalton also claimed that Bevan had told him: 'I never spent more than an hour a week on housing. Housing runs itself.' For Dalton:

> it must be honestly confessed that, when the Tories came in, they built many more houses than we had done, though some of which they had built had lower standards than most of ours. But this, I am afraid, was only a secondary debating point. It was the totals of new houses which counted with public opinion and public comfort.[4]

Unsurprisingly, Jennie Lee is Bevan's most passionate defender against this onslaught. 'Why did Hugh Dalton [...] deride Nye's insistence on having two lavatories in the three-bedroomed type of council house designed for mixed families?' She adds: 'Did he not know that with father coming home from work and the children coming home from school, how much it helped mother if they did not always have to climb upstairs, father maybe with work-soiled clothes and the children with muddy boots?' The problem was that Dalton, an old Etonian whose father, John Neale Dalton, had tutored the future George V and was a canon of St George's Chapel, Windsor, 'by birth and upbringing belonged to a privileged world. He had not sympathy nor imagination enough to bridge the gap. A reduction in housing standards would mean more houses for the same amount of cash, and that would win approval.'[5]

Bevan had a vision of the type of housing he wanted built, focusing on the needs of the working class. Based on his Tredegar upbringing, and his service in local government, Bevan's housing programme was based on the assumption that local authorities were best placed to deliver on local housing. Conscious of the poor housing into which the working families of Tredegar had been cramped, Bevan's emphasis was on good-quality, lasting council houses built for rent. He was not willing to build swathes of temporary housing that would only succeed in providing the postwar working classes with more miserable accommodation. He was willing to provide temporary accommodation as a necessity, and to repair homes damaged during the war, but, by early 1946, he concluded, 'the time was rapidly approaching when labour could be most usefully employed on new building.'[6] He was certainly willing to focus on erecting prefabricated homes, but they should be permanent. The 'prefabs', as they became known, were to be produced by firms involved in constructing the temporary harbours used on the Normandy coast after the D-Day landings in June 1944. Bevan approved the 'large-scale production of certain approved types of permanent prefabricated houses by a group of large firms associated with the construction of the Mulberry harbours'.[7]

In order to start the enormous house-building programme needed, Bevan had to introduce a battery of six pieces of legislation.[8] This provoked the concern of the Lord Privy Seal, Arthur Greenwood, who urged Bevan to make as much progress as he could before Christmas 1945.[9] There is a 'compliments' slip in the government papers which is stamped 'Lord Privy Seal' and written by hand: 'M/H [presumably 'Ministry of Health] do not appear to be good legislators.'

There was an early skirmish between Morrison and Bevan on local-authority freedom. An initial government proposal was to set a statutory maximum value of houses eligible for monetary advances under the Small Dwellings Acquisition Act and the Housing Act. Instead, Morrison thought the new Act should give the government power to vary it by order. Bevan thought that having a maximum *already* fixed within which local authorities could exercise discretion was preferable, since having the formal power to increase the figure in the legislation 'would imply that we were losing the battle on [keeping down] building costs'.[10] In his view, if house prices fell moderately, local authorities could use their discretion to advance money for better houses, and the government could extend the scope of the Acts by new statutes. If they fell significantly, the figure could be reduced by informing local authorities that the minister would not sanction advances for houses above a certain value. Bevan wanted a statutory maximum (£200 million) that he did not wish to see 'exceeded in any circumstances'. Morrison wrote, ominously, 'Accept, but – If he comes along for another Bill I shall be cross'.[11]

There were two major obstacles to faster progress with house-building: the first was the scarcity of raw materials, particularly timber, in the aftermath of the Second World War; the second was the economic situation after the currency crisis of 1947. Originally, on taking office, Attlee had merely appointed a stand-ard Cabinet committee to deal with housing with Arthur Greenwood as chair. But growing problems with the number of houses being completed led Attlee to abolish this committee in December 1945 and create, instead, a stronger Cabinet standing committee on housing which he himself chaired.[12] Attlee, listening to the suggestion of the economist Douglas Jay, who served as Attlee's private secretary before becoming MP for Battersea North in July 1946, then created a Housing Production Executive in April 1946 in order to coordinate the various elements of the house-building programme, including raw materials and labour.[13]

Bevan was very concerned about the lack of timber, and set out the problem at the first meeting of Attlee's new Cabinet standing committee on 23 January 1946: 'whereas optimistic forecasts had been made some months ago, there was a serious shortage of timber for housing. Swedish timber had not come forward in the quantities expected, partly on account of a shortage of coal in Sweden.' Bevan added: 'so far as he was aware, no timber had yet been imported from Germany, although a mission sent to Germany several months ago had reported favourably on the prospect of obtaining supplies from that country.'[14]

Jay, however, disagreed that timber was an immediate problem. In a note to Attlee on 31 January 1946, Jay assessed the position for the first quarter of the year: 'All the timber is already available for this allocation, and no difficulties can therefore arise before April.'[15] This may well have been correct, but it hardly added to the sense of urgency Bevan was seeking to create. Nonetheless, Jay did suggest four steps forward. First, since the supply of Swedish timber depended on the supply of British coal, more coal exports should be made available. Second, there needed to be an agreement with Russia to increase supplies from Russia itself and Finland. Third, pressure on the British Zone in Germany to increase the level of timber exports needed to be maintained. Finally, economies needed to be made in the amount of timber required for each house.

Cripps, still President of the Board of Trade, produced a memorandum on 4 February 1946 that included a thorough statistical analysis of timber needs and

1. *Nye's parents David and Phoebe with his sister Arianwen.*

2. *Nye looking at Ebbw Vale Steelworks.*

3. *The 1945 Labour Cabinet: Nye stands slightly apart at the end of the back row.*

4. *Nye as Minister of Health and Housing.*

5. *Nye and Jennie relaxing at home.*

6. *Nye strides along Downing Street towards No. 10 for a Cabinet meeting.*

7. *Nye before a poster publicising the National Health Service.*

8. *Nye and Jennie at a hospital bed in the newly created National Health Service.*

9. *Nye giving his infamous 'Vermin' speech, 4 July 1948.*

10. *Nye with the first Indian prime minister, Nehru.*

11. *Nye with his great rival Hugh Gaitskell, and Barbara Castle.*

12. *Nye denouncing the Suez invasion in Trafalgar Square.*

sources for that year. Using revised figures, he estimated only a small shortfall: 1,305,000 timber standards were required and it was thought that 1,280,000 would be available (98 per cent). However, only a very small proportion could be sourced from home: 30,000 standards could be produced with 100,000 from stocks. The entire remainder would have to be imported, principally from Canada (450,000), Sweden (200,000) and Germany (250,000). Cripps gave an assurance that the North German Timber Control Commission in the British Zone in Germany was being strengthened under Sir Gerald Lenanton, the current director of the Home Timber Production Department of the Ministry of Supply. He argued that the crucial issue was whether enough coal could be provided to Sweden to enable the wood cut by the Swedes to be exported to Britain rather than be used as domestic fuel.

The ramifications of the housing problem across the government were neatly illustrated by the immediate response of Tom Williams, the Minister of Agriculture and Fisheries, and Joseph Westwood, the Secretary of State for Scotland, who were responsible for the nation's forests: 'Any additional fellings in this country, must have very serious effects on the home forests [...] If we continue to cut immature timber suitable for pit props we shall be damaging our future home supply of timber beyond repair for many years to come.'[16] Jay briefed Attlee before the Cabinet meeting of 7 February 1946 that the question for discussion was whether there should be an increase in the coal made available to Sweden.[17]

The Cabinet discussion itself was not productive. Cripps dominated it, setting out the arguments in his memorandum. Bevin waded in and advised Cripps to talk to Edvard Kardelj, the vice prime minister of Yugoslavia, since he 'had heard that one of our firms might be willing to establish sawmills in Yugoslavia'. There was also a suggestion of possible supplies from Romania, but it was agreed that for 'improvement in the long-term prospects we must rely mainly on re-opening our pre-war sources of supply from Russia and Finland'.[18] Progress remained slow, as Bevan set out in a report to Cabinet on 6 May 1946. Up to 31 March of that year, local authorities had only provided 741 permanent new houses; 2,570 new houses had been constructed and 791 had been built under licence. Furthermore, 19,482 temporary houses and 3,200 temporary huts had been installed; 12,573 existing premises had been adapted; 78,224 unoccupied war-damaged houses had been repaired; and 18,370 had been requisitioned for residential use.[19]

It became clear that it was foolish to pin hopes on imports from the British Zone of Germany. The North German Timber Control Commission faced numerous challenges, including the need to use timber for firewood due to a lack of coal, inadequate transport facilities, damaged ports (particularly Hamburg, which was built on wooden piles needing underwater repair before it could be dredged), slow recovery of German trade operations due to uncertainty about British intentions and de-Nazification, wastage, and labourers not being as productive as their British counterparts due to lack of food.[20] John Hynd, Chancellor of the Duchy of Lancaster, pointed out that the British Zone was the least forested of the German occupation zones in any event.[21] The only option Cabinet Secretary Norman Brook could offer was for Attlee to ask Hynd to look into the diversion of the timber used in vegetable boxes for Denmark and Holland.[22]

Bevan's patience ran out, and he produced his own memorandum for Cabinet on 17 July 1946.[23] His tone was almost despairing: 'I ask that the inclusion of arrangements for the importation of adequate supplies of timber suitable for house building should be recognised as an urgent necessity, and the Government should take all possible action to this end.' He pointed out that, even after taking the Treasury's timber subsidy into account, the cost of timber was 198 per cent above the 1939 figure whereas the increase in cost of other materials over the same period was only 76 per cent. Bevan bemoaned the 'serious difficulties in supply' and said that there was no practical substitute for timber. Even steel was more expensive and not readily available. He was exasperated with the failure to increase dramatically supplies from Germany. Bevan urged his colleagues to 'agree that in discussions with Russia the inclusion of arrangements for the import of softwood building timber should be treated as an urgent necessity'. He also emphasised the need to increase coal supplies to Sweden.

Rather than provide an impetus to government action, Bevan's memorandum prompted two other Cabinet members to produce their own. Cripps was quick to reply, and defended his own previous estimate that there was little difference between supply and demand. He argued that the situation had deteriorated due to price demands and then a timber operators' strike in British Columbia, and to German output falling below estimates. Cripps was also very pessimistic about imports. On Russia, noting that there had been a refusal to supply timber so far, all he could say was that negotiations were ongoing; on Germany he was seeking an 'early discussion' with the Control Office and the North German Timber Control. With Sweden and Finland, Cripps noted that the shortage of British exports, particularly of coal, was restricting timber supplies, though he felt more supplies could be obtained from Finland in return for British supplies of iron for shipbuilding and electrical sheets. Cripps doubted that any increase could be obtained from Canada, where 35 per cent of the output was already being supplied to Britain. He expected that there probably would be a 'timber gap' by the end of the year, but that little could be done to prevent this.[24]

Hynd, a pragmatic former NUR clerk, offered a more positive, common-sense outlook. While dismissing the possibility of any increased supplies from Austria, since the Austrian government was controlling its own exports and could obtain better prices elsewhere, Hynd was more upbeat about the situation in Germany: 'the only remaining bottlenecks in Germany are shortage of skilled labour, food, and transport from forest to railhead.' He offered some additional ideas, including whether there were any further suitable vehicles that could be sent from Britain to assist in transportation from the forest to the railway.[25]

Christopher Eastwood, then principal assistant secretary at the Cabinet Office, tried to make sense of the various submissions with a forensic analysis of the position in a note to Attlee: 'The three papers before the Cabinet are a little confusing.'[26] He commended Cripps' paper as the one to base the Cabinet discussion upon, since it dealt with 'the whole softwood position'. He saw Bevan as dealing with the demand issues and John Hynd the supply. He was mildly critical of Bevan, who had raised the issue of high timber costs: 'No proposals are, however, made as to how these costs could be reduced.' Eastwood ended on a very pessimistic note: 'It may well be that it will not be possible to supply quite the full quantity that the Minister of Health requires for housing.' Bevan was up against a brick wall.

When Cabinet met on 25 July 1946, Bevan again opened strongly on the need for 'drastic action' on timber supplies.[27] However, the discussion became bogged down: even in respect of Hynd's suggestion that more vehicles be taken to Germany, it was pointed out that, domestically, there were competing claims for vehicles for open-cast coal mining and for other building and civil-engineering work. Rather, the services should make available their surplus vehicles already in Germany. All the Cabinet could conclude was for the Overseas Reconstruction Committee to give 'further consideration' to the issue of increasing imports from Germany, and it took note that Cripps would 'take all possible steps to increase timber imports from countries other than Germany'.

Not deterred, Bevan continued to seek a way forward, and produced another memorandum for the Cabinet on 8 November 1946, arguing that timber supply was 'the one matter which is entirely outside my control and which on present indications will go far to wreck our housing programme'.[28] His options were limited. Reluctantly, he compromised on design to reduce the amount of timber required for each house: 'from two standards to 1.6 standards per house: this means a number of economies which are tolerable but regrettable, e.g. the elimination of timber joists and boarding throughout the ground floor and the substitution of solid floors.' As he correctly realised, however, this was a 'palliative and not a cure', since there would still be difficulties in sourcing alternative materials. Nonetheless, Bevan estimated that this change would enable the annual number of permanent houses being constructed to increase from 180,000 to 225,000. The only other measures Bevan could take were to argue for a greater proportion of existing timber supplies to be allocated to housing, and to increase timber imports. Bevan's eye focused on Canada, which he thought had plentiful supplies of softwood. He also – again – emphasised the need to increase timber supplies from occupied Germany and to consider looking for supplies from Yugoslavia, in addition to seeking to increase supplies from the usual Baltic suppliers. The problem was that the argument for increased imports had been put so many times that it was difficult to see what the way forward was.

Bevan asked Attlee on 8 November 1946 if he could bring the matter before Cabinet. Attlee, however, saw no merit in this: 'The principle of getting as much as possible is agreed. You should now get in touch with your colleagues on particular problems as they arise.'[29] Attlee had a point. The prime minister never believed in wasting time on pointless discussion, and he was correct that all concerned agreed that as much timber as possible should be obtained for the house-building programme. Bevan accepted this, but still put the point to Attlee that, while he was satisfied that the position was understood at the political level, he was keen that the civil services should understand too.[30] Bevan did not give up. He proposed a target of 240,000 houses for 1947, and persisted in drawing the issue to the attention of the Cabinet in yet another memorandum of 10 December 1946: 'The most serious difficulty is with regard to timber.'[31]

By the time more timber became available, Bevan faced a ferocious squeeze on his housing programme from the need to divert labour away from constructing homes to producing products for export, to deal with the balance-of-payments deficit. The problem was the 'convertibility clause' in the American loan agreement: the commitment to convert sterling that was due to come into effect on 15 June 1947.[32] In the event, due to a drain on dollars, the government suspended convertibility on 20 August 1947. With the American loan running out, the government introduced austerity measures, tightening rations. The specific problem for Bevan, however, was that, facing a balance-of-payments deficit, the government needed to turn its domestic labour to producing more material for exports, not building housing in Britain.[33] By early 1948, Bevan had been repeatedly offered the option of importing prefabricated timber homes from Austria. A full investigation in late 1946 had ruled this out on the grounds that a wholly timber property would cost so much more than a brick equivalent; with far less money available two years later, Bevan did not even think the proposal worth discussing.[34] After a peak of 251,000 new homes being completed in 1948, the total fell back to 205,000 in 1949.[35] Troubled by this, Bevan scored a notable victory in 1950 when he was able to persuade the Cabinet to accept a substantial increase in the target number of houses to be built. Bevan argued that there had been 'alarming repercussions' as a result of the reductions that occurred as a consequence of the

1949 and 1950 target figures (170,000 and 148,000, respectively, though they had been exceeded), and that the reduction to 120,000 for 1951 (which had been agreed in November 1949) was unsustainable.[36] Bevan thought that it was better to increase this by 140,000 immediately rather than bow to the inevitable political pressure further down the line. In the event, Cabinet agreed a target of 200,000 per year for three years: not as many as Bevan wanted, but a substantial increase nonetheless.[37] As it turned out, 205,000 were completed in 1950 and 202,000 in 1951.[38] Ever the pragmatist, Bevan increased the target for private-sector house construction to one-fifth of new houses per district, from nine-tenths having to be council houses. He also agreed, as minister, to consider applications to go above one-fifth in exceptional circumstances.[39]

One of Bevan's earliest critics was the economist Douglas Jay, who served as Attlee's private secretary before becoming MP for Battersea North on 25 July 1946. Jay wanted to take a stick to the local authorities that he saw as inefficient. He wanted the Ministry of Works to sideline them with more building of its own, and to set up a new housing corporation to act where local authorities were failing. He accused Bevan of putting ideology before practical politics, and of being 'very doctrinal' in his adherence to local-authority house-building.[40] Bevan, on the other hand, justified his position in terms of outcome. He quite simply could not see that the creation of another government body would help with the labour or raw-materials shortages.[41] Jay's criticisms were given real weight by the backing of Christopher Addison, a great authority on the subject of housing. After all, Addison had been appointed president of the Local Government Board in the aftermath of the First World War, in January 1919, and later that year had changed the board into the Ministry of Health. Addison then passed the Housing and Town Planning Act 1919, the first such act, which gave rise to the building of council houses in the twentieth century. Addison's criticism was undoubtedly well founded, based as it was on his early experience of local authorities faced with the prospect of having to translate the principles of his housing act into reality. In addition, a national coordinating body would also have been better able to match the available labour to the number of planned new houses in any given region. Bevan had himself argued for *national* planning of house-building at the 1945 general election. His position became more nuanced when he was in power. Bevan appreciated that local authorities not only had experience of house-building, but were also the planning authorities with unrivalled local knowledge. To have created a National Building Corporation was one thing, but to equip it with the political clout to bypass local-authority opposition was another. More likely would have been the situation where a national corporation found itself in conflict with local authorities that would still have had knowledge of specific sites, not simply in terms of their development potential, but also local feeling and, crucially, control over the planning apparatus that existed. A National Building Corporation would have posed questions as well as answered them. Even the formal concept of comprehensive planning permission, introduced in the Town and Country Planning Act 1947, would not have prevented such a rivalry, though the idea of 'new towns' in designated areas under the New Towns Act 1946 did put something of a national overview into practice in any event.

A more valid criticism of Bevan was that he offered little in the way of local-government reform until it was too late. If local authorities were ineffective house-builders, and there was to be no National Building Corporation either, Bevan did not offer an alternative option. Ministry of Health officials bemoaned the vague information given to the department by some local authorities, which further slowed the progress of house-building: 'The description of materials covered by demands from Local Authorities is not always precise enough to determine whether or not the materials are essential to enable a house to be occupied.'[42] Bevan had an attachment to local-authority structures being clearly identified with communities that he thought best for involving local people. In 1945, the wartime coalition had appointed the barrister Sir Malcolm Trustram Eve to chair a commission considering the structure of local government. In 1947, Eve's Local Government Boundary Commission had recommended the creation of a 'new county borough' authority covering up to 200,000 people, limiting the role of existing county councils.[43] Bevan was unimpressed, and concerned about regional local-government units that ceased to be truly *local*: 'These would not be local government units in any proper sense of the term.'[44] For him, the purpose of local government was to be 'near to the people as to ignite and keep their interest'.[45] In the spring of 1949, Bevan sought agreement in Cabinet to appoint a Royal Commission on local-government reform, but the idea was squashed by Morrison, who said such an idea 'may prove embarrassing to the government [...] we may be told that once again we have taken the course favoured by Governments which shirk difficult decisions and be criticised for falling back on the delaying device of setting up a Royal Commission.'[46] The commission was then dismissed by the Local Government Commission (Dissolution) Act 1949, and Bevan eventually produced his own plan for local government in the October of that same year. Sticking to a model of smaller local-government units, he proposed around 300 single-tier authorities for England and Wales that could range widely in size from serving 50,000 people to a million, depending on the communities they served. This was, however, vehemently opposed by James Chuter Ede. Ede did not think it feasible to replace England's historic two-tier local-authority structure of county and parish; the population was attached to it and change would reduce participation in local government.[47] By this point, the 1945 Parliament was in its fifth and final year; soon afterwards, the government had a single-figure majority following the general election of February 1950. Any chance of carrying through such a radical reform was gone.

When the Conservatives returned to power in 1951, they had the advantage of positive balance-of-payments figures for 1952, 1953 and 1954.[48] With the postwar raw-materials shortage having eased, the average time taken for local authorities to build a house was short. To build a house from the damp course level to roofing was less than four months.[49] This enabled Macmillan to complete increasing numbers of houses, from 248,000 in 1952 to a peak of 354,000 in 1954, which included 262,000 built by the public sector.[50] This said, there is a positive case to put for Bevan's housing record, given the constraints he was working within. The only realistic comparator was the progress after the First World War. Between April 1945 and March 1948, 396,000 houses were built: 227,000 new, 23,000 rebuilt and 146,000 temporary. Thus, Bevan had succeeded in producing an annual rate of 132,000 whereas the post-First World War average from January 1919 to September 1922 was 56,000.[51] There are, however, two problems with this analysis: the first is that First World War figures may not be reliable. Another estimate for the three years from 1919 is that around 183,000 houses were completed, 56,000 of which were by the private sector. This would give an annual average of 61,000.[52] Secondly, the voters were not satisfied with the rate of progress: in 1950 and 1951, their verdict was far more important than the verdict of history.

Chapter 12

Bevan as a Cabinet Minister

U ntil the events that led to his resignation, Aneurin Bevan was a vocal but loyal member of the Attlee Cabinet. Jennie Lee argues that 'From first to last Nye tried unceasingly to prevent the Labour Government from making a number of mistakes that he earnestly believed were fatal, both for our country's future welfare and for the contribution we at that time could have made to the easing of world tensions'.[1] But this remark more accurately reflects the frustration of Lee's political position in the 1945–51 period than it does the reality of Bevan's performance as a Cabinet minister. Perhaps Lee liked to think Bevan was in Cabinet fighting manfully against all the policies she had doubts about. But Bevan was not a serial dissenter within the government. He *did* often put an alternative case, but it was always within reasonable bounds. He would argue something strongly, but was willing to accept compromise and the collective decision. Until the final two years of the Attlee government, with the great clash on the introduction of charges into the NHS and the programme of defence rearmament brought about by the Korean War, Bevan was a strong Cabinet minister. Well informed, his interventions ranged over a number of areas. He spoke with authority because he was willing to master the detail of Cabinet memoranda circulated to ministers prior to formal meetings.

In the period 1945–8, Bevan was an enthusiastic supporter of the government's policies in any event. However, in Cabinet, he initially opposed the American loan of November 1945. Bevan was unhappy that Britain was going cap in hand to the Americans for help.[2] He feared that Britain would become an obedient child of American capitalism. His view was short-sighted in one sense since it is difficult to see how the National Heath Service could have been funded without it, but Bevan was not alone in having doubts. Even Dalton, who later put his full weight behind the loan agreement, was horrified at the initial American position. A proposal by the British for a $2.5 billion credit at 2.5 per cent interest, and a further $2 billion interest free was rejected. The economist John Maynard

Keynes, who was negotiating on behalf of the government in Washington, was sent a strong telegram by Dalton in which Dalton said that he 'could not stomach' much of the American position.[3] There remained in British circles some hope that the Americans might provide money as a gift, particularly as Britain had stood alone in the Second World War in the key period of 1940 after the fall of France. Eventually, the loan consisted of a line of credit of $3.75 billion until 31 December 1951, when the money would be repaid in 50 annual instalments with a yearly interest of 2 per cent.[4] Only Shinwell and Bevan continued to oppose the loan in Cabinet (Shinwell feared that a planned economy in Britain would be impossible as a result). In the Commons division lobbies on 13 December 1945, Jennie Lee and Michael Foot were among the 23 Labour MPs who rebelled and voted against the loan. The problem with this position was that it ignored the financial realities Britain faced in 1945. When the US abruptly ended Lend-Lease on 21 August 1945, it meant that Britain faced a yawning balance-of-trade gap. Keynes famously said that Britain faced a 'financial Dunkirk'. Without money, most of the Attlee government's plans would be impossible to carry through. Bevan did then accept the inevitable. Later, he was in favour of Britain receiving Marshall Aid. The US Secretary of State, George Marshall, had concluded, in April 1947, after the failure of the foreign-ministers council meeting in Moscow, that Stalin was counting on the economic collapse of Western Europe.[5] Marshall argued that America must 'finish the task of assisting those countries to adjust themselves to the changed demands of the new age' or straitened economic conditions would see them fall prey to Communism.[6] The Marshall Plan was born; Bevan did not oppose a measure that would alleviate economic distress.

The Attlee government set about the creation of the modern welfare state with the National Insurance Act of 1946. Bevan warmly approved of the National Insurance (Industrial Injuries) Act of the same year, which made insurance compulsory for workplace injury. The wartime coalition had already passed the Family Allowances Act 1945, which introduced the payment of child benefit from August 1946. But Bevan did contribute in Cabinet to the major debates on National Insurance over the 1945–6 winter. On 1 December 1945, Arthur Greenwood, as chair of the Cabinet's Social Services Committee, drafted a report to full Cabinet that supported the Beveridge model of sickness and unemployment benefit without a limited period during which the benefits could be claimed. It was also suggested that pensions be made available to all on retirement, and widows' pensions were introduced. Hugh Dalton set the terms of the Cabinet debate with a response four days later that objected to three aspects: failing to limit the period for claiming unemployment benefit, paying a single pensioner over half of the weekly entitlement for a married couple, and paying pensions even where the person concerned had not retired.[7] Dalton conceded on the pensions rate, and in the event James Griffiths, the Minister for National Insurance, introduced a bill with rates of 42s. for a married couple and 26s. for a single pensioner, with retirement ages of 60 for women and 65 for men. It was accepted that pensioners could not work *and* draw pensions. At Cabinet on 13 December 1945, Bevan was highly critical of the idea of a fixed period for claiming unemployment benefit, since he argued that the state would still be obliged to maintain the person in some way after that time even if work had not been found. He argued, looking back on his interwar experience, that it was a question of semantics: whether the subsequent payments were by way of 'benefit' or 'assistance', the person could not be left without any payment at all.[8] In the event, a 30-week limit was agreed 'but with extensions for contributors with good employment records'.[9] What Bevan did not do was argue strongly against the very principle of National Insurance. Save for married women, who could opt out of paying contributions, the compulsory National Insurance payment was the not insignificant sum of 4s. 11d. per week.[10] In the 1930s, he had objected to workers contributing at all. Yet this debate on National Insurance showed Bevan at his pragmatic best. The principle of National Insurance had wide support in Cabinet. There was no purpose in fighting a losing battle, and he had targeted his fire effectively. In any event, the National Assistance Act 1948, which Bevan introduced, plugged the remaining gaps. A 'National Assistance Board' would provide payments to anyone not covered by the reforms already enacted, leaving local authorities responsible for remaining residential care needs. The Attlee government had provided true 'cradle to grave' provision and finally taken away the shadow of the workhouse from the lives of working people.

The government also set about a programme of nationalisation. Under the auspices of Morrison's Lord President's Committee, the structure of the publicly owned industries was modelled on the London Transport Board, for which Morrison had set out his ideas in his 1933 book *Socialisation and Transport*. Each was to be run by a board; however, rather than have workers as members of these committees, the government appointed members. First, the government nationalised the Bank of England; bank stock was substituted by government stock. Proceeds then went to the Treasury rather than dividends to private investors. The government would now appoint the court of directors, including the governor. The Conservatives did not even oppose the measure in the Commons. The coal nationalisation – a particular passion for Bevan – provided a model for the operation of Morrison's committee, which agreed on a nine-member National Coal Board appointed by the Minister of Fuel and Power. Members of the board were given salaries pegged to civil-service levels. Alongside the Coal

Industry (Nationalisation) Act 1946, two other measures that year also caused little debate. Cable and Wireless Ltd was bought fully by the government; the nationalisation of civil aviation brought together smaller private aviation companies into three corporations. The following year, the Electricity Act 1947 created a Central Electricity Authority, to be chaired by Walter Citrine, which would be given control over more than 14 area boards. The Gas Act 1948 was the last of the uncontroversial nationalisation measures. Based on the Electricity Act, there would be 12 area boards under a central gas council, which would, 'in effect, act as a central financing body for the industry'.[11]

While these nationalisations aroused little debate, and Bevan was in favour of them, one thing he did not do in Cabinet at the time was pursue the idea of the workers themselves playing a part in their management, something he was to regret in later life. In postwar West Germany, under Konrad Adenauer of the Christian Democratic Union, the first postwar German chancellor, 'dual boards' were used in corporate governance: the executive board controlling day-to-day matters and a controlling supervisory board. Employees were well represented on the latter. Cripps, speaking in 1946, had rather loftily commented that there were 'not as yet a very large number of workers in Britain capable of taking over large enterprises'.[12] Bevan fundamentally disagreed with this. Whether he made that point privately to Cripps is unknown. However, this was not something Bevan pursued strongly in Cabinet. Whether he would have been successful in such a line of argument is a moot point, though the wider issue of the effective working of the nationalised boards was something the Attlee government itself started to discuss in its final two years. Morrison himself produced a memorandum, 'Efficiency and public accountability of socialised industries' on 31 March 1950, arguing: 'There is a widespread feeling that the Boards are not operating as efficiently as might be expected; in particular, the Boards seem to suffer from some of the vices of large bureaucracies and the interests of the consumers seems to be given second place.' Morrison felt that an efficiency check was necessary.[13]

The first controversy over the principle of nationalisation itself arose over transport in 1947. Rail nationalisation was easy enough: the network was war-damaged and there were only four large private companies to take into public ownership: Great Western; Southern; London and North Eastern; and London, Midland and Scottish. It was the road-haulage part of the Transport Act 1947 that provoked some criticism of the state, which was perceived as restricting individual freedom. Vehicle licences were graded A, B and C. The holder of an 'A licence' could carry goods for hire or reward; the holder of a 'B licence' could carry their own goods, and, if certain requirements were met, the goods of others; holders of 'C licences' could carry only their own goods. To nationalise the sector, the government proposed to purchase A and B licences. But it was the plans for C licences that provoked opposition. To assert a measure of public control, the government found itself in the position of having to tell traders they could only carry their *own goods* certain distances. A 40-mile radius was initially proposed.[14] Eventually, the government dropped its restrictions on C licences.[15] However, this would allow private companies to purchase vehicles and apply for a C licence to maintain their freedom. There was a mass move to C licences to avoid the restrictions of nationalisation, an increase from 350,000 in 1946 to 766,578 in June 1951, making the measure a practical failure.[16]

The year 1947 was very difficult for the Attlee government. Through the various crises, Dalton wrote, 'our self-confidence weakened, individually and collectively.'[17] The first problem was presented by the winter 'deep freeze'. Snow fell somewhere in the UK every day from 22 January to 17 March 1947.[18] Shinwell, as Minister of Fuel and Power, had anticipated a problem with coal supplies that winter in November 1946, when he had warned Attlee of the 'likelihood that total supplies this winter shall fall short of total requirements by something like 2 and 5 million tons'.[19] The weather was unpredictably bad, but Attlee and Shinwell had ruled out a compulsory scheme to limit coal consumption to keep stocks higher in the event of worse weather than expected. At Cabinet on 19 November 1946, a public announcement about cuts in coal allocations was avoided. Rather, cuts in actual deliveries *against* allocation would be made. Average weekly consumption for that month would be set as a maximum for use during each week over the winter. Coal deliveries to hotels, clubs and 'places of amusement' were then cut by 10 per cent.[20] The measures were insufficient. By 5 February 1947, Shinwell had to tell Attlee that, in the bad weather, coal movement was such that there was a 'grave risk' of power stations having to close down.[21] Indeed, many did run out of coal and close down. Until the weather improved in March, thousands of people were left freezing in their homes. Factories closed and unemployment temporarily soared. The Conservatives coined their election slogan, 'Shiver with Shinwell'.

Britain was also importing far more than it was exporting. Provided the American loan was in place, the gap could be bridged. However, by April 1947 Treasury civil servants were warning that half of the American loan would be exhausted by the June. The concern was the operation of the sterling convertibility clause in the loan agreement due to come into operation on 15 July.[22] Organisations would become able to demand payment in dollars rather than pounds, and dollars could then be spent outside Britain. Britain would be spending far more dollars than it was earning. In anticipation of the July deadline, the government agreed cuts in imports. A general £200 million reduction was agreed upon, save that the Cabinet decided not to include canned meat and fish at a cost of £19 million.[23] It was not enough. The deadline itself passed, but, after a brief lull, with echoes of the financial crisis of 1931, the rate of selling of shares on the London stock market began to rise dramatically. With government gilt-edged stock particularly affected, Britain started to draw on what remained of the American loan. By the end of July, Dalton estimated that 'at the present rate of drawing, the Credit will not last beyond November and will probably be exhausted in October, or even possibly in September.'[24] Britain's dollar reserves were falling rapidly. When Cabinet met on 13 August, Dalton proposed the suspension of convertibility, to put a stop to the drain on dollar reserves.[25] Three days later, British officials, led by Joint Second Treasury Secretary Sir Wilfred Eady, left for Washington to negotiate with the Americans. On 19 August, the Cabinet agreed the suspension in principle.[26]

Attlee's position was now under threat. The charge that he had offered no firm direction in a crisis stuck because that was his 'chairmanship' model of leadership, allowing consensus to emerge, and speaking for the majority view. A number of ministers – Morrison, Bevin, Dalton and Bevan – had returned to London during the crisis. Though Attlee had returned to London from his holiday in North Wales to take charge, he had quickly rejoined his family on their summer break. By 20 August, journalists openly asked about his retirement.[27] That same day, with Attlee gone, Morrison presided over Cabinet to agree the exchange of letters with the American government that had been negotiated by Eady.[28] Ministers were left to agree the details of the more unpalatable measures required, including a ban on foreign travel. It was Dalton who then wrote to US Treasury Secretary John W. Snyder: 'This action is of an emergency and temporary nature.'[29] Eventually on 27 August, the formal announcement was made suspending convertibility, with accompanying austerity measures, including a freezing of the tea ration and a cut in the meat ration on 7 September to 1s. per week. Other measures included a ban on foreign currency being made available for pleasure trips abroad from October.

In early September, the plotting against Attlee began in earnest. During the crisis, on 17 August, Dalton and Cripps had sounded out Bevin about replacing Attlee, but he refused. Cripps' plan was that he, Dalton and Morrison should go together to ask Attlee to resign in favour of Bevin. Morrison was not in favour. For a start he thought he would make the best prime minister, and, secondly, he would not serve under Bevin.[30] Cripps and his wife invited Bevan and Jennie Lee to tea to talk over the possibility of replacing Attlee with Bevin. Cripps even mooted being prime minister himself. Bevan was dismissive of the idea, declaring: 'he did not believe in palace revolutions' and kept out of it.[31] Cripps did eventually visit Attlee on 9 September, alone. He told Attlee he wanted Bevin as prime minister and Minister of Production. Attlee would then be chancellor, and Dalton

Foreign Secretary. Attlee said Bevin did not want to leave the Foreign Office. He also pointed out the rivalry between Morrison and Bevin – his strongest argument against Bevin taking over.[32] Attlee rang Bevin and asked if he wanted to change jobs; Bevin, with Attlee's fate momentarily in his hands, loyally confirmed that he did not.[33] Attlee then bought off Cripps by offering him the job of being the minister in charge of economic affairs.

Throughout the summer of 1947, the debate on the government's most contested nationalisation, iron and steel, also rumbled on. The measure was difficult to justify in anything other than ideological terms. The relationship between management and unions was not particularly strained. Even when the Labour Party had moved to the left in the 1931–5 parliament, a policy of state ownership of iron and steel had been rejected.[34] In November 1945, John Wilmot, as Minister of Supply and Aircraft Production, set out three options for the industry. The industry could be regulated, as it had been before the Second World War, with the government controlling prices, affecting development and imports. A public body could oversee a reconstruction plan. Or there could be outright nationalisation. The problem with the final option was defining what actually formed part of the iron and steel industry, since it was so broad: 'from ore and coal mining to the production of many important semi-manufactured and finished goods, including chemicals, fertilisers, plant and machinery and steel furniture'.[35] In December 1945, the British Iron and Steel Federation presented a report to Wilmot offering a compromise position of 'modernisation', including the building of 24 new blast furnaces.[36]

Bevan was not interested in any option other than nationalisation. In this first major Cabinet debate on the principle of nationalisation itself, Bevan stuck firmly to the argument that the government should not waver. For him this was more than a question of intellectual consistency on the benefits of nationalisation for British industries. This was the first time the government's commitment to public ownership had come into serious question. There was also the fact that Bevan's home area, now his parliamentary constituency, contained a steelworks. Bevan knew the hardship that had been caused in the period when work had ceased at Ebbw Vale; he knew the difficulties of negotiating with the governments of the day and private owners to see that local people were gainfully employed. For him, iron and steel nationalisation was not only ideologically sound, it would also have tangible practical effects by providing far greater certainty about the future of Ebbw Vale than would continued private ownership.

With the parliamentary session for 1946–7 already very crowded, the matter was delayed until 1947–8. Wilmot committed the government to a 'large measure of public ownership' in the Commons on 17 April 1946 and, in the interim, a

Central Board would direct the industry.[37] A year after this Commons announcement, on 14 April 1947, Wilmot produced a plan to nationalise the 'central core of the iron and steel industry – i.e. the production of iron ore, pig iron and steel, together with certain closely allied processes in the re-rolling sections of the industry, including the production of plates, sheet steel and tinplate.'[38] There would be a central authority directing companies rather than the area boards used for electricity and gas. After a stormy meeting between Sir Andrew Duncan and Ellis Hunter of the Iron and Steel Federation and Wilmot, Morrison and Attlee for the government in May 1947, the government started to consider a possible compromise.[39] On 26 June 1947, the Cabinet authorised 'confidential discussions' with the Iron and Steel Federation about an alternative scheme.[40] Morrison and Wilmot were given the task of negotiating, and on 21 July 1947 they put forward their compromise: a government 'power of acquisition of iron and steel undertakings' on the 'tacit understanding' that there would not be immediate nationalisation. That matter was kicked into the long grass, to be considered in the next parliament.[41]

Bevan remained strongly opposed to a compromise, and even threatened to resign if there were no legislation in the 1947–8 parliamentary session.[42] The Cabinet formally considered the issue on 31 July. Bevan argued that Labour supporters in the country would be deeply disappointed if the compromise were accepted. After all, public ownership of iron and steel had been a 1945 general-election manifesto pledge: 'Only if public ownership replaces private monopoly can the industry become efficient.' Dalton backed him. With the Cabinet divided, Bevin intervened and proposed delaying matters until the autumn, ostensibly on the basis of consulting the unions.[43] Attlee, to Morrison's disappointment, was not in favour of compromise, either. In October, the prime minister announced a nationalisation of 'the relevant portions of the iron and steel industry'.[44] However, with the currency crisis of July and August the iron and steel issue had fallen down the order of priorities, and was left to the 1948–9 parliamentary session.

It was the ongoing debate on iron and steel that had influenced Attlee in his discussion with Bevan about moving from the Ministry of Health in the government reshuffle of autumn 1947. Younger politicians were promoted. Attlee replaced Cripps at the Board of Trade with the 31-year-old Harold Wilson, while, fatefully for Bevan, the 41-year-old Hugh Gaitskell became Minister of Fuel and Power in place of Shinwell, who was demoted. Arthur Greenwood, by then Minister without Portfolio, and a heavy drinker, was sacked. Dalton also lost his job as chancellor. When he arrived at the House of Commons to deliver his budget on 12 November 1947, just before 3 p.m., he gave John Carvel, a lobby correspondent for the *Star*, some details, which were published at 3.45 p.m. in a newspaper scoop. Dalton resigned because of the leak, and Cripps, after only six weeks as Minister for Economic Affairs, became chancellor in his place. Dalton did not return to government until 31 May 1948 as Chancellor of the Duchy of Lancaster.

Attlee had suggested that Bevan move to the Ministry of Supply, though remaining as a Cabinet member. This would have allowed him to drive through iron and steel nationalisation, and was an indication of Attlee's preferred outcome on the nationalisation debate. Morrison disagreed, and suggested Strauss instead: 'I am not sure this job is up his [Bevan's] street, able + brilliant as in many ways he is.' Morrison urged Attlee to be firm about the iron and steel nationalisation going ahead in the next parliamentary session, but felt Bevan was the wrong man to take it forward, since 'the iron + steel people have to be handled with […] care'. Attlee replied that Bevan might be more suited to the Board of Trade, but that in any event 'he needs a change of office'. Attlee said he was seeing Bevan that day, 23 September, to get a firm position from him about the iron and steel nationalisa-tion.[45] Both Attlee and Morrison were coy in this correspondence. Attlee already knew Bevan's position. A 'top secret' memorandum had been prepared for him by a civil servant, W. S. Murrie, the previous month, in which Bevan was listed, along with George Tomlinson and John Strachey, as the ministers in favour of immediate nationalisation.[46] Similarly, Morrison did not want Attlee to be too firm, nor did he want Bevan to have control of the negotiations, since he wanted to find a compromise position short of outright nationalisation if possible. As it turned out, Attlee offered Bevan either the Ministry of Supply or the Board of Trade, both of which Bevan turned down.[47] He had no wish to move from Health at such a delicate stage of his negotiations with the BMA.

In the summer of 1947, India gained its independence. Bevan was naturally in favour, but it was Attlee himself and Cripps, with his previous experience and contacts with the INC, who dominated government policy towards the subcon-tinent. It was notable that the Cabinet minister responsible for India, Frederick Pethick-Lawrence, was in the Lords, not the Commons, where he could have played more of a part. India was one of the few issues Attlee took an active role in as prime minister, rather than seeking to find agreement among his ministers. He had attended Haileybury College, a public school with origins in a training college for civil servants for the Raj. He was one of seven MPs who had served on the Indian Statutory Commission, appointed in 1927 under the chairmanship of Sir John Simon to consider India's constitutional future, and had a personal com-mitment to the subcontinent. The challenge was to produce a solution acceptable to Hindus and Muslims. Attlee initially sent a 'Cabinet Mission' led by Cripps to India in March 1946, but this reached a stalemate, as the Muslim League refused to cooperate with a proposed interim government to be set up prior to independence. The viceroy, Lord Wavell, put forward a 'Breakdown Plan' of a phased British withdrawal on 31 March 1948 in the absence of Hindu–Muslim agreement on the way forward. Attlee did not see that as an exit from India with honour for Britain, and replaced Wavell as viceroy with Lord Mountbatten, who was sworn in on 24 March 1947. Eventually, Mountbatten negotiated what became known the 'Mountbatten Plan', with a vote in each province posing a choice of joining India or a separate Muslim state, Pakistan. British India would be partitioned. On 27 May, Cabinet approved the plan, and India gained its independence on 15 August.

Bevan was realistic about the negotiations over Indian independence, and the need for compromise, but he was troubled by the government's policy on Palestine. He was deeply sympathetic to the Jewish cause. He had significant Jewish friends. He developed a particularly close relationship with Israel Sieff and his wife Becky. Israel Sieff was very well connected in the Jewish community, a business partner of Simon Marks for the majority of his life in Marks & Spencer, and a close friend of the Zionist leader Chaim Weizmann. Sieff said of Bevan: 'Nye belongs in that gallery of the dwelling-place of my mind in which I keep my private collection of great men.'[48] Sieff and Bevan often spent time together reading or playing bowls. It was to Sieff that Bevan revealed a secret that he hid from his other friends: he wrote poetry. He even read his poems to Sieff, but told him that he could never publish them: 'I'm too shy. What would my friends say? There's hardly anybody I'd dare read the stuff to.'[49] There always was a part of Bevan that he wanted for himself, hidden from public view. Indeed, so hidden are the poems that they do not seem to have survived in any archive. This is despite the fact that Bevan always preserved the works of others that he was given. He kept a number of manuscript poems and a short story from another Jewish lady, Eva Metzger, among his private papers. When he visited Israel with Jennie Lee in January 1954, he was treated as well as any foreign leader.

To appreciate Bevan's position on Palestine politically, it is worth sketching out the background. The British Foreign Secretary, Arthur Balfour, had declared British support for a Jewish homeland with his eponymous declaration of 1917. In 1922, the League of Nations had approved the British Mandate for Palestine, and Britain sought to strike a balance between facilitating Jewish immigration and protecting the rights of the Arab inhabitants. As Nazi Germany stepped up its oppression of the Jews in the 1930s, more and more moved to Palestine. This, together with an Arab uprising from 1936 to 1939, led the then Colonial Secretary, Malcolm MacDonald, to publish a White Paper on 17 May 1939. This restricted Jewish immigration to 75,000 per annum for four years; afterwards the

Arabs would have to sanction further admissions. The American president, Harry S. Truman, wrote first to Churchill on 24 July 1945, and then to Attlee weeks later on 31 August, to demand that Britain allow 100,000 Jews to enter Palestine immediately. That would have cleared the existing camps in Europe. Attlee was unwilling to accede to the demand: 'the only practicable course is to maintain the present arrangement for immigration.'[50] At that time, it was 1,500 people per month. The problem for Attlee was that the world's moral opinion was against him, as the horrors of the 6 million Jews murdered in the Holocaust emerged.

The main charge against Attlee and Bevin on Palestine is that they simply abandoned it to civil war when they handed the problem over to the UN. On 29 November 1947, the UN General Assembly passed Resolution 181 to end the British Mandate by 1 August 1948 and introduce a 'two-state' solution. Britain announced that it would withdraw on 15 May 1948. The day before, 14 May, the State of Israel was declared. Within 24 hours, Egypt, Syria, Jordan, Lebanon and Iraq all invaded Palestine, starting the Arab–Israeli War of 1948–9. By the time of the armistice agreements of 1949, Israel had taken nearly four-fifths of the old British Mandate territory, with the Palestinians restricted to the West Bank (then controlled by Jordan) and the Gaza Strip (then controlled by Egypt). Hundreds of thousands of Palestinians became refugees.

Bevan's position was a straightforward one. He argued that the rate of Jewish immigration into Palestine should be increased: 'If some concession were made, the Jewish Agency would find it easier to give effective co-operation in checking both terrorism and illegal immigration.'[51] He also wanted to partition Palestine. His argument did not constitute an extreme or unrealistic position. To find an agreed position between Britain and America on the way forward, 'experts' had met from both sides. The Cabinet Secretary Norman Brook chaired for the British; the diplomat Henry F. Grady led for the US. The proposals, announced by Morrison as chair of the Cabinet's Palestine Committee, became known as the Morrison–Grady Plan, and involved a form of partition: a government to have overall control of Jerusalem and Bethlehem with an Arab and a Jewish state within a federal structure.[52] Truman refused to approve this proposal, but Attlee and Bevin hoped to maintain Britain's influence in the Middle East, and take an even-handed approach without unduly antagonising the Arabs. But, given that Britain had issued the Balfour Declaration in the first place, and in any event ceased cooperation with Egypt after Nasser nationalised the Suez Canal in July 1956, Bevan's analysis was prescient. He also had a better reading of American domestic politics than either the prime minister or the Foreign Secretary. Truman was always going to stay committed to the Jewish people, and could not engage constructively in talks for a solution until the request for 100,000 Jewish immigration certificates had been granted. Neither Attlee nor Bevin understood the key role of the Jewish vote in American politics. British policy had not prevented the establishment of the State of Israel and had not prevented the displacement of hundreds of thousands of Palestinians, a refugee problem that remains central to the Middle East question in the twenty-first century.

Bevan can, therefore, take great credit from his advocacy of the Jewish cause in Cabinet. Yet, even on this question that he felt so passionately about, he was still willing to compromise. Dalton recorded the discussion in Cabinet on 20 September 1947: 'Decide that Creech Jones shall stay at U.N.; that we will, as recommended, give up the Mandate; that we will implement any plan on which Arabs and Jews agree; but that we won't use force to impose on either any plan to which the other objects.' Bevan did not oppose this.[53]

He was also in favour of Britain's decision to develop its own atomic bomb. This was taken in secret: not even the whole Cabinet knew about the decision at the time; a Cabinet committee on 'Atomic Energy' dealt with such matters. The crucial meeting was on 25 October 1946. Bevan was not a member of the committee: Attlee, Bevin, Dalton, Cripps, Addison and Wilmot were the Cabinet members present. Sir Michael Perrin, a Ministry of Supply official who attended, later told the BBC's *Timewatch* that the crucial contribution to the meeting was from Bevin, who staggered into the meeting late, having fallen asleep after lunch. He did not like the idea of a British Foreign Secretary being dictated to by a US Secretary of State. He did not appreciate the way he had been spoken to by the current incumbent, James F. Byrnes, and declared that Britain had to have its own independent nuclear deterrent: 'We've got to have the bloody Union Jack on top of it.'[54] Whether Bevan found out or suspected what was going on is a moot point. Given the confidentiality of the business of the committee, Bevan made no comments at the time. But he supported the decision.[55] He thought it gave Britain status and a measure of foreign-policy independence from the US.

Bevan retained a deep antipathy to American capitalism, following his hero José Enrique Rodó in his critique of its garish materialism and stultifying effect on spiritual well-being. But he was a realist who accepted the Atlantic alliance was a necessity. He abhorred Stalin's totalitarianism. He could also see that there was a military imperative in protection from the Soviet Union's belligerence. In February 1948, in the so-called 'Czech coup', the Communists took control of Czechoslovakia, thus placing it under Soviet control. There was also the break between Stalin and Tito's Yugoslavia. Yugoslavia had sent two army divisions into Albania in late 1947 without consulting Stalin. The disagreement escalated over the issue of the Soviet Union's recruitment of Yugoslav agents for intelligence work directly over the heads of Tito's government. In June 1948, Yugoslavia was excommunicated by the Cominform, an organisation formed by Stalin in an attempt to revive the 'Communist International'.[56] When the Russians blockaded West Berlin from 24 June 1948, Bevan was in favour of using tanks as backup to the airlift actually within the Soviet zone.[57] On 4 April 1949, in Washington, the North Atlantic Treaty Organisation (NATO) was created, committing the US to the defence of Western Europe. Western Europe would not need to wait for America's entry into a third world war. Bevan saw this as essential, and *Tribune* was in favour, too. Fewer than ten Labour MPs voted against the formation of NATO. Konni Zilliacus did, and Bevan supported his expulsion (following due process) from the Labour Party, along with D. N. Pritt, Lester Hutchinson and Leslie Solley.

Bevan was very careful to keep his distance from the government's left-wing critics. But backbench criticism of the government was, on the whole, muted. Michael Foot, having won Plymouth Devonport in 1945, was on the back benches throughout Attlee's premiership. He was of course a natural admirer of Bevan's work at the Ministry of Health. Yet his criticism of other ministers was hardly pointed. For example, Foot's biographer, Kenneth O. Morgan, writes: 'On domestic issues, Foot's Commons speeches followed a fairly unremarkable course in their calls for more socialism.' The Labour left actually concentrated on the government's foreign policy, and specifically Ernest Bevin's Atlanticism.

Opposition to the Attlee government was disparate and unorganised. On 29 October 1946, 21 Labour backbenchers put their names to a letter to Attlee seeking a different foreign policy that would be a middle way between America's unbridled capitalism and the totalitarianism of the Soviet Union. The signatories included Foot and Richard Crossman, who had entered the Commons in 1945 for Coventry East, together with James Callaghan and Woodrow Wyatt, hardly known as rebellious left-wingers. The letter was a precursor to a curious episode a month later concerning an amendment to the King's Speech. Drafted by Crossman, the motion sought 'a democratic and constructive socialist alternative' to 'the otherwise inevitable conflict between American capitalism and Soviet communism'. Forty-three Labour MPs were willing to support it, including Jennie Lee, who was unlikely to have done so without Bevan being in favour, not because she was not a woman with her own independent views, but because she was conscious of causing him embarrassment as Minister of Health.[58] Oddly, Crossman moved the amendment on 18 November 1946, but then did not call for a division. Two ILP members did so, but the government won the vote by 353 to none, though there were abstentions, including Foot.[59] The episode showed that the Attlee government had no coherent internal party opposition. In April 1947, 72 Labour MPs did vote against peacetime conscription. The *New Statesman* then published *Keep Left*, a pamphlet arguing for a 'third force' foreign policy independent of the US and the Soviet Union in the Cold War. It had been written over Easter weekend by Foot, Richard Crossman and Ian Mikardo, who had entered the Commons in 1945 for Reading. Bevin was furious. In his party conference speech in May 1947, at Margate, he angrily declared that he had been stabbed in the back. Events overtook that debate in any event, with Britain being offered Marshall Aid. Foot sided with Bevin on this, taking the view that if the Soviet Union did not wish to be part of the Marshall Plan, 'then they alone will be the architects of a divided Europe.'[60]

At times, Bevan became the archetypal poacher turned gamekeeper. In June 1948, during the dockers' strike, Attlee used troops and declared a state of national emergency. He was out of sympathy with the strikers since he felt that their conditions had improved and that their guaranteed minimum wage was a step forward. Together with the National Dock Labour Board, which had curtailed the old casual employment regime, Attlee felt that the dockers had had a good deal from his government. The same Bevan who had excoriated Bevin for his trade union restrictions in 1944 argued for 'wide powers' in Cabinet on 28 June 1948: 'to deal with any trouble that might arise if relations between troops and strikers become strained'.[61]

In office, Bevan proved to be brilliant in high politics. Perhaps the ultimate demonstration of his loyalty to the Attlee government came during the further economic crisis it faced over the devaluation of the pound in 1949. Initially, it was Gaitskell, still at that time Minister of Fuel and Power, who took the initiative. It cemented his reputation as having expertise on economics, certainly with Attlee. In January 1949, he penned a paper setting out the problem facing the government, and possible solutions. An expected £300 million gap in the dollar account had widened to between £500 and £600 million. Dollar expenditure had to be scaled back and dollar earnings increased. There were two means of achieving this. The first was deflation, to reduce imports by reducing incomes and increasing exports by cutting money costs (and, therefore, prices); the second was devaluation. Gaitskell's argument for the latter course resonated with Bevan. Gaitskell saw deflation as a conscious policy of creating unemployment and that those who would pay the price were the unemployed and those who suffered wage reductions since they would actually '*pay* for the high exports, whereas with devaluation it is people with fixed incomes who do the real paying – in the form of higher import prices'.[62] Bevan had no trouble accepting this argument, and saw devaluation as a painful necessity. Harold Wilson and Douglas Jay, who, together with Gaitskell, were christened the 'Young Economists' by Dalton, advanced the policy of devaluation, and Cabinet ministers accepted the logic.[63] Attlee accepted the emerging view, and at Cabinet on 29 August 1949 confirmed that '[o]pinion had hardened in favour of devaluation' before dispatching Bevin and Cripps to Washington to negotiate on the extent and timing of the devaluation.[64] The disadvantage of the policy was the increase in the cost of food and raw materials bought from the dollar area. On 18 September 1949, Cripps announced the devaluation from $4.03 to $2.80, with a penny increase on the price of bread.

On 29 September 1949, at Attlee's request, Bevan made a barnstorming speech in the House of Commons defending the government. He argued that the government had achieved a great deal considering the near-bankrupt economy it had inherited in 1945, and blamed international circumstances for the devaluation: 'owing to the pattern of international trade having been so badly ruptured by the war, we find ourselves unable to purchase from the dollar areas the raw material and the food we require without [...] this painful expedient of devaluation.'[65] His opponent in the debate was Churchill, as leader of the opposition. Churchill challenged Bevan to a historical review. Bevan said Churchill 'sub-edits history, and if there is any disagreeable fact, overboard it goes'.[66] As events turned out, the devaluation succeeded in its aims, with the gold reserves recovering and, by 1950, Britain no longer needed Marshall Aid. But, by then, Bevan's disagreements with the Attlee government had become fundamental and far-reaching.

Chapter 13

Principles and Personalities

The Conservatives sought to make Aneurin Bevan the anti-hero of the 1950 general election. Held in winter, on 23 February, the Attlee government was narrowly re-elected to office with an overall majority of only five seats. His Ebbw Vale position secure, Bevan embarked on what was now his customary speaking tour of the country, though he often met with personal hostility. His 'vermin' speech had made him a natural target for Conservative activists, who packed meetings to give him a hard time. Churchill set the tone for the Conservative attack with a sarcastic reference to Bevan in a tribute to the dead Lloyd George: 'There can be no greater insult to his memory than to suggest that to-day Wales has a second Lloyd George.'[1] Some local Conservative associations would 'design a "float", and tour the town exhibiting a house of the kind Mr. Bevan wouldn't build but the Conservatives would'.[2] Speaking in Bristol on 10 February, Bevan had 'considerable difficulty in [even] obtaining a hearing'.[3] Fortified by his belief in a Labour victory, and relishing the contest, Bevan fought on, seizing on Churchill's remark that 'it may soon be all right' to increase the petrol ration, by calling the Tory leader 'a short-term merchant' who was 'trying to bribe the British people'.[4]

Churchill was denied his return to Downing Street – for the time being. With Labour returned to office, Bevan's major concern was that, despite the tiny working majority in Parliament, the iron and steel nationalisation should be implemented. The level of controversy was such that the whole parliamentary timetable had been dictated by efforts for it to reach the statute book. The Conservative-dominated House of Lords was always going to reject the bill. The government's 1949 Parliament Act had reduced the delaying power of the Lords, now meaning that any bill passed by the Commons in two sessions within one year would become law. The Iron and Steel Bill had been introduced in a first session in 1948–9, and a short session of Parliament held from January 1950 to create the second session necessary.[5] Churchill savaged the government as 'the handmaids and heralds of Communism'.[6] At Cabinet the week after the general election, on 2 March, Bevan argued that if the government 'showed any signs of hesitancy', the 'confidence of [...its...] supporters would be undermined' and the Tories would be emboldened to seek a promise of no further action until after another general election.[7] But the government pressed on, and, finally, in February 1951, the nationalisation took place.

By 1950, it was clear that Stafford Cripps' tough economic measures had succeeded. The £381 million deficit in the balance of payments in 1947 had been transformed into a healthy surplus of £307 million by 1950.[8] National income rose from £8.5 billion in 1947 to just under £9.7 billion in 1948, and over £10.2 billion in 1949.[9] With the exception of the winter of 1947, when the fuel crisis caused a short-lived spike in the unemployment figures, the jobless total was kept below half a million. Cripps took a strong moralistic line, and this was even a factor in the decision to hold the general election that winter; he allegedly did not want to present a budget prior to a general election with political considerations unduly influencing his thinking. However, when Attlee called together Morrison, Cripps, Addison, Dalton and chief whip William Whiteley on 7 December 1949, only Morrison had been opposed to a winter poll, principally because he felt that the weather would affect turnout at Labour's expense.[10]

Cripps' policies had already had profound consequences for Bevan's housing programme, and the relationship between the two men was becoming increasingly strained. As Cripps' biographer, Peter Clarke, puts it in his consideration of the Attlee government: 'during its first term of only five years, if Cripps was thought to have a protégé or favourite son among the rising generation of ministers, it was Bevan who was naturally cast in this role.'[11] In his usual succinct way, Attlee saw this as highly significant: 'He [Bevan] cut loose after Stafford went [in October 1950, Cripps resigned as chancellor due to ill health].'[12] In fact, the Bevan–Cripps relationship had been deteriorating throughout the previous year. In October 1949, discussing the charge against Cripps that he had misled the public over the need for devaluation, Bevan had dismissed the chancellor as suffering from 'persecution mania' and criticised him as lacking what men in public life needed, 'thick skins or an aristocratic temperament'.[13]

As Cripps looked around for savings in departmental budgets, it was inevitable that the NHS would once again come into view. As Morrison put it:

Nye is getting away with murder was the general feeling of my colleagues. It was not so much a selfish attitude to the problems of his
fellow ministers, it was Bevan's unquestioning regard for dogma. The

original plan was that the medical services should provide everybody with everything needed for nothing and nothing must alter that.[14]

Bevan regularly sought increased funding for the NHS, presenting Cripps with supplementary estimates for new money. In 1948–9, Bevan had sought an extra £53 million over and above his initial estimate.[15] In 1949–50, he estimated spending at £228 million, and a vastly increased £365 million for 1950–1. Bevan did not see this as financial mismanagement; rather, he saw it as ensuring that the NHS had sufficient funds to meet the health needs of the people. Eventually, in October 1949, after devaluation, Bevan pragmatically accepted prescription charges *in principle*, but did not implement them. With the election out of the way, the issue of NHS spending was considered again. At Cabinet on 13 March 1950, the day before a debate on supplementary estimates for NHS costs for 1950–1, it was agreed that Cripps would announce a ceiling on spending.[16] The logic for this was a simple one: the NHS was 'already making an unfairly large claim on our resources' and, as a consequence, the government should be prepared to impose charges. There should be effective spending controls over the expenditure of Regional Hospital Boards and Hospital Management Committees. Overall expenditure was to be capped at £392 million, and, with new charges to raise £42 million, the cost to the Exchequer would be £350 million. Specifically, prescription charges would be imposed as part of a new scheme, but not in isolation – the £6 million anticipated yield was already taken into account in setting the £392 million figure.

Emboldened, Morrison went even further and suggested that any future development in the NHS should come to Cabinet or Cabinet committee; Cripps agreed to this on the basis that the precise setting of the spending ceiling should be excluded from consideration by the committee.[17] On 30 March 1950, Bevan had had to defend the NHS against Cripps' proposal.[18] His arguments were measured and pragmatic. He accepted that the NHS would develop, but did not accept that all changes involved increased maintenance costs. Bevan floated the idea of making savings elsewhere, and argued that it was unfair that hospitals had to account for the annual cost of capital works for which they could not borrow. For him, this provided a 'misleading picture'. Bevan argued that there was no substantial economic benefit to be gained from imposing charges, and he was concerned about the confusion regarding withholding sickness benefit or pensions during hospital stays. He added that he had deliberately not gone into detail on the proposed recovery of one-third of costs for chemists (£26 million), dentists (£39.5 million) and opticians (£90 million), since he wished to set out the matter of principle.[19]

Bevan's tactic of not discussing detail was an astute one. He was deliberately avoiding seeing out the specifics in Cabinet, so that its members lacked the information needed to consider the proposals properly. In the short term, it worked. Cripps did not impose any charges in his budget of 18 April 1950. However, it proved a pyrrhic victory, as, on 6 April 1950, the Cabinet decided to set up a committee to fix total NHS spending for 1951–2 and succeeding years, and to keep NHS expenditure under review on a monthly basis. This effectively diluted Bevan's influence over any future decisions on imposing charges. The dispute was serious enough for Attlee to intervene directly and set the committee membership on 21 April. Attlee took the chairmanship, and the other seven members included not only Bevan but Woodburn, Morrison, Addison, Gaitskell and Marquand.

Gaitskell was appointed in Cripps' place to represent the Treasury view. After the general election, Gaitskell had been moved from the Ministry of Fuel and Power to become Cripps' number two at the Treasury. At the same time, Attlee briefly considered Bevan for the post of Colonial Secretary, but instead decided on Jim Griffiths as a safer pair of hands. Having himself held the Dominions portfolio for a period during the Second World War, Attlee knew the sensitivities of the Commonwealth leaders. He was particularly concerned about how the white minorities in South Africa and Rhodesia would be handled by Bevan. Indeed, when Bevan took over the Shadow Colonies brief in opposition February 1956, he confessed to knowing little about them.[20] Bevan remained at Health.

Gaitskell supplanted Bevan's position with Cripps. He grew closer to the chancellor politically and personally. A wartime civil servant, Gaitskell had an eye for detail and, having been central to the decision to devalue the pound the previous year, a growing reputation in economics. While Bevan pressurised Cripps for more money for the NHS, Gaitskell supported Cripps in carrying out his austerity policies. Bevan and Gaitskell formed a triangular relationship with Cripps. The disagreement between Bevan and Gaitskell went beyond the clash in high politics. It was also deeply personal. For a period, certainly up to the end of June 1950, Bevan had been attending Thursday-night dinners with Gaitskell hosted by Cripps for those ministers most associated with economic portfolios. Another attendee, Harold Wilson, told Michael Foot that, over these dinners, Gaitskell kept raising the issue of the health service charges: 'It became a mission or an obsession with him.' According to another guest, John Strachey, Bevan would lash out at Gaitskell and be met with silence or 'a dry, factual contradiction'. On the way home one night, Strachey took Bevan to task, asking why he was deliberately making 'a rift between yourself and one of the really considerable men of the Government?' Bevan took issue with the word 'considerable' and replied, 'But he's nothing, nothing, nothing.' Strachey continued:

I tried to explain to Bevan that the quiet, rather slight man who sat opposite him had 'a will like a dividing spear'. I might have saved my breath for all the effect I had on Bevan. I talked the thing over with Stafford Cripps, and with that curious fatalism about personal relations which he often exhibited, Stafford shrugged his shoulders and said there was nothing to be done.[21]

On 29 June 1950 Bevan wrote to Cripps to say that he would no longer be meeting him on a weekly basis on Thursday nights for dinner. This note is lost, but Cripps' reply and Bevan's subsequent letter are both reprinted in the second volume of Foot's biography of Bevan. Cripps sent Bevan a curt three-sentence reply and stated: 'Would it not have been friendly to have stated your real reason for giving up our weekly meetings at dinner?' Bevan, clearly stung by the response, set out his feelings in more detail: 'I am not such a hypocrite that I can pretend to have amiable discourses with people who are entirely indifferent to my most strongly held opinions.'[22]

There is an argument, put by Archie Lush, that one of the reasons for Bevan's antipathy towards Gaitskell was his background: Winchester School and New College, Oxford, in contrast to Bevan's upbringing in Tredegar. Similarly, commenting on the early 1950s, Lush also observed that there were not many Bevanites among the miners' group of MPs.[23] Lush explains that while Bevan did mix with people from different backgrounds, he justified this by saying that this was how he found things out; he was not going to gain knowledge from those with the same background as him. Bevan undoubtedly saw conversation itself – with a variety of different people – as an intellectual experience. But none of this explains his issue with Gaitskell. Lord Healey, recalling Bevan's famous 1954 remark about the ideal Labour leader being 'a desiccated calculating machine', said that this could not apply to Gaitskell, as 'he was not desiccated and he was not calculating'.[24] It may have been unfair to have called Gaitskell emotionally dry but the word 'desiccated' is very revealing. For there was a fundamental personality difference between Bevan and Gaitskell. Bevan saw Gaitskell's cool analysis of situations as unemotional and uncaring. For him, Labour politicians should of course be rational and thoughtful in their approach – he was a man of great intellectual curiosity himself – but he saw Gaitskell as cold and lacking empathy. Had Bevan lived to hear Gaitskell's powerful 1960 Labour conference speech in which, anticipating a defeat in a floor vote on unilateral nuclear disarmament, he vowed to 'fight, and fight, and fight again to save the party we love', he might have taken a different view.

On 5 June 1950, with Soviet military equipment, North Korean troops crossed the 38th parallel, the line of latitude dividing North and South Korea, starting the Korean War, the first proxy conflict of the Cold War between the US and the Soviet Union. The North Koreans advanced rapidly. By September, only Pusan, on the south of the Korean peninsula, remained unconquered. The UN (in Resolution 85 of 31 July 1950) gave the US command of the military operation to repel the invasion by the North. American and South Korean forces held Pusan. The first British troops arrived on 28 August. Bevan, along with the other members of the Attlee government, supported this, seeing it as essential militarily.

Embroiled in the conflict, with fears of a third world war, the US government pressurised Britain to vastly expand its defence spending. The government had been united in recognising the new Chinese republic created by the Communist revolution of 1949, while the US still supported the former regime of Chiang Kai-shek. Now Bevan began to disagree with his colleagues. Cripps circulated a memorandum to Cabinet on 1 August 1950 on the 'additional effort which might be made by the United Kingdom to increase the defence preparedness of the North Atlantic Powers, in response to President Truman's recent appeal and his offer of financial assistance'. The Ministry of Supply had estimated what additional expenditure was physically possible in the next three years, and calculated a total of £814 million. Cripps proposed committing the government to a net defence expenditure of £950 million a year for the next three years. Bevan was immediately critical, and expressed 'grave misgivings'.

Bevan was never blind to military imperatives. He could see the need to drive back the North Korean invaders. It was the *overall* direction of American foreign policy that he now objected to. He said that foreign policy had been 'based on the view that the best method of defence against Russian imperialism was to improve the social and economic conditions of the countries threatened by Russian encroachment'. He believed that the US was abandoning this to focus on military defence, and Britain would be 'ill-advised' to follow it. He also raised the issue of affordability, and – knowingly – predicted great difficulties for the budgets of the social-services departments.[25] In the event, after the US Eighth Army took the North Korean capital, Pyongyang, on 19 October, Mao Zedong, chairman of the Chinese Communist Party, took action, with some Soviet air support, and drove the American troops back. With Bevin ill, Attlee visited President Truman in December 1950 and received an assurance that the US would not use nuclear weapons without consulting Britain and Canada.[26]

Meanwhile, Gaitskell's move to shadow Cripps was proving a great one for him. Cripps' health was failing and he eventually resigned on 16 October 1950. Gaitskell was duly appointed in his place. Dalton's opinion was that 'no one (ruling myself out) could face this job who was senior to the Young

Economists and that, of these, Hugh [Gaitskell] was incomparably the best, far ahead of either Harold Wilson or Douglas Jay'.[27] Bevan may not have been on Dalton's radar, but Gaitskell himself was keenly aware of the threat Bevan posed. He spoke to Dalton a month before Cripps stepped aside; Dalton wrote in his diaries: 'Nye is absolutely fed up with the Ministry of Health. They have had the most frightful wrangles on the Cabinet Committee on finance of Health Service. Gaitskell is sure he ought to be moved. What about Ministry of Labour?'[28] Bevan was incensed by Gaitskell's promotion, and wrote to Attlee to express his displeasure. Attlee responded by offering him the Ministry of Labour. Bevan, correctly fearing an attack by Gaitskell on the health budget, delayed making a decision. Only when he received assurances on wider issues beyond his departmental remit – the actual content of which became controversial later on – did he relent, and he was appointed on 17 January 1951. Jennie Lee records that Bevan's 'understanding with the Prime Minister was that no health charges would be imposed'.[29] It seems unlikely that Attlee ever said anything this explicit. But he did say to Bevan, the day before he became Minister of Labour, that he would be happy to tell the press that, in addition to his departmental duties, Bevan would be 'one of the Ministers intimately concerned with economic and production problems'.[30]

Bevan only remained at the Ministry of Labour for three months. Understandably, his political energies were to be diverted onto his battle with Gaitskell over the imposition of charges in the NHS. However, he did make an impact at this new department. Bevan was immediately faced with the problem of increasing the number of men called up for National Service to meet the new demands of the armed forces in light of the rearmament programme. He endorsed the position of his predecessor, George Isaacs, on lowering the call-up age to 18 and reducing the number of deferments for apprentices. Specifically, he endorsed Isaacs' position of maintaining indefinite deferment for coal miners but taking it away from agricultural workers, on the basis that there was no shortage of farm labour.[31] Bevan also took up the cause of the NUR with some enthusiasm. A few weeks after his arrival at the Ministry of Labour, in February 1951, the NUR sought a wage increase of 7.5 per cent in default of which there would be a national strike. The matter came to Cabinet on 22 February 1951. The transport minister, George Barnes, wanted to stand firm on an offer of 5 per cent made by the British Railway Executive. Bevan, however, pushed through a proposal for the NUR to have its full 7.5 per cent. Ministers were very concerned about the effect of a national rail strike.[32]

Bevan was far less comfortable dealing with the consequences of the Conditions of Employment and National Arbitration Order ('Order 1305'). Originally introduced during the Second World War, the order prohibited strikes and required cases to be brought to an arbitration panel. Under this provision, the Attorney General, Hartley Shawcross, prosecuted seven London dockers, who received fines in February 1951. Bevan was savaged at a meeting of the PLP as a consequence.[33] Bevan did have strong views on the loyalty to be shown by the unions to Labour governments. But he must have pinched himself as he realised that he had come full circle since his battles with Bevin as wartime Minister of Labour. He was now the Minister of Labour bringing down the might of the law on working people.

In the meantime, at Cabinet on 25 January 1951, Gaitskell set out his spending plans, including the vastly expanded defence programme.[34] There would be an additional £500 million spent on defence in the first year, £880 million extra in the second year, and £1 billion in the third year, all excluding the costs of the new productive capacity that would be required to carry the programme through. Gaitskell stressed that the terms of trade were turning adversely in 1951, that there was a shortage of raw materials and that the spending was on the basis of there being no US help. There would be a 'double diversion' of industry, from civilian to defence work, and from manufacturing for the home market to exports. Reservists would be called up to the forces. On 15 February 1951 Bevan spoke in the Commons:

> if we turn over the complicated machinery of modern industry to war preparation too quickly, or try to do it too quickly, we shall do so in a campaign of hate, in a campaign of hysteria, which may make it very difficult to control that machine when it has been created.[35]

Attention now focused on Gaitskell's forthcoming budget. So intense was the Bevan–Gaitskell battle over the next six weeks that the Cabinet Secretary Norman Brook did not initially include the discussions on the health service charges in the Cabinet minutes. Rather he wrote to Attlee after the crisis on 28 May that he felt that the events leading to the resignation should be included but that his descriptions should be 'moderate in tone'.[36]

At Cabinet on 22 March 1951, Gaitskell outlined his proposals.[37] He stated that there was a strong case for an increase in old-age pensions. He proposed an increase in increments for those working beyond retirement age and four shillings per week increase for men over 70 and women over the age of 65. The chancellor also proposed increases in other benefits, including the allowances for widowed mothers with children and for the children of persons receiving sickness and unemployment benefit. The cost would be met by savings elsewhere and on social services. The practicable way that Gaitskell said he could see was to cut NHS spending. He said that an estimate of £423 million had been put forward for 1951–2 when the spending in the current year was £393 million, and confirmed that the NHS Cabinet committee, which had met a week earlier, had (despite Bevan's objections) proposed a £10 million reduction in hospital expenditure, a charge of half the scaled fee for false teeth and a £1 charge for spectacles, together with a shilling charge for prescriptions. Bevin suggested, as a compromise, a £400 million ceiling that would obviate the need for prescription charges, but the charges would still be required on teeth and spectacles. Marquand put his view that charging for teeth and spectacles was not a 'serious infringement' of the principle of a free health service, since those who needed them were usually in good health. He felt it would be a different matter to introduce charges for the sick, and that prescription charges were a further issue altogether.[38] Morrison reported that Attlee was in favour of the charges.

Bevan was strong in his response. He said that he regretted the introduction of a ceiling at a time of rising prices, which was bound to have the effect of reducing the standard of service. It was 'deplorable' to abandon the principle of a free service for a mere £23 million (£10 million in efficiency savings and £13 million to be raised from the charges) and, further, it was wrong to say (as Gaitskell had) that the money was needed for pensions. The real cause was the defence programme, and he added that, with the raw-material shortage – something Bevan had all too much knowledge of in his housing brief – it was impossible to spend the money on defence very wisely. Dalton, now Minister of Local Government, entered the discussion and backed Gaitskell, on the basis that there was a 'balance of national advantage' in helping pensioners. Morrison and Alexander concurred, and Griffiths, as Colonial Secretary, but, perhaps more pertinently, a former Minister of National Insurance, accepted 'some encroachment' on the principle of a free health service 'with reluctance'. He said, however, that he did not wish to maintain the spending ceiling for many years. Edith Summerskill, who had been appointed Minister of National Insurance after the election on 28 February 1950, said that, while she had always opposed prescription charges, she had less of a problem with charging for teeth and spectacles. She added that she found it difficult to reconcile the objection being raised with the National Health Service (Amendment) Act 1949. This was, of course, a jibe at Bevan for accepting the principle of prescription charges. Wilson entered the fray at this point and said that he would prefer a cut in defence spending, since it would be difficult to spend the allocated monies. Shinwell, restored to the Cabinet as Minister of Defence, said that health had never been free and comprehensive in practice, and that the physical resources were not available to secure this. George

Isaacs, now Minister of Pensions, took the discussion in a different direction by arguing for an increase in war pensions, though he accepted that the current proposals provided some relief in cases of special hardship. Gaitskell accepted the dropping of prescription charges on the basis Bevin put forward, but stuck to his guns on teeth and spectacles.

Bevan spoke at length to Hugh Dalton on 6 April. He was savage about Gaitskell: 'He had no standing in the party, now he was trying to be a second Snowden, an iron Chancellor trying to please his friends in the Treasury [...] Hugh had blindly accepted an impossible re-armament programme.'[39] Dalton's impression was that Bevan felt an effort was being made to drive him out. He felt he had been double crossed by Attlee. He had refused to become Minister of Labour for some time and had only agreed on the promise of no cut to social services. Dalton wrote to him the next day, and urged him: 'Don't do it now!' in consideration of an election later that year. Bevan did not respond.[40]

The division was set. Bevan and Gaitskell directly confronted each other at the Cabinet meeting on the morning of 9 April.[41] Bevan stated: 'In a Budget totalling over £4,000 million there must be tolerances which would allow the Chancellor if he wished to forego his insistence on a saving of only £13 million on the health service.'[42] He suggested two ways forward: increasing the contribution to the NHS by the National Insurance Fund or reducing the £13 million surplus at which the Budget was aimed. Gaitskell was clear in response:

> he was not prepared to adopt either of the courses suggested by the Minister of Labour. They would both be inflationary in effect. Moreover if he had such a sum at his disposal he would certainly wish to consider to what purpose it could most usefully be applied. He was by no means satisfied that even within the social services, the health service had the first claims on any additional money that might be available.

There was a further Cabinet meeting that evening, held at 6.30 p.m. Attlee was in hospital with a duodenal ulcer, and Morrison took the chance to visit him. Gaitskell recalled that Morrison read 'a message from the PM which in effect gave his vote to me and urged the Cabinet to stand by me'.[43] Bevan was characteristically blunt:

> He had given five years to building up the Health Service; he had proclaimed it on many public platforms as one of the most outstanding achievements of the Labour Party in office; he had, in particular, upheld the conception of a free Service as the embodiment of Socialist

principles. It was too much to ask him now to go into the division lobby in support of a measure authorising the imposition of charges for dentures and spectacles provided under this Service.[44]

Bevan added that he believed that he could influence the government more from without than within. Once a minister had reached that position, he believed it was time to go.

Harold Wilson added that if the decision were maintained, he would also feel compelled to resign. There was then a melancholy discussion, ranging over issues such as a possible general election and weakening electoral prospects for many years to come if the resignations occurred. There was even a claim that it would be a 'tragedy' if the inspirational leadership in world affairs gained by the Attlee government with all its achievements was cast away. Bevan responded: 'It was not he who had taken the initiative in proposing charges under the Health Service. The potential crisis, if one developed, would have been provoked by those who made this proposal.' He added: 'Besides these grave consequences, the issue which now divided the Cabinet seemed relatively small.' Bevan suggested a number of possible compromises. Firstly, the matter could be postponed for six months, by which time Attlee would be back. Alternatively, a £400 million ceiling could be set for NHS spending and an announcement made that the government was considering steps to ensure that their spending level was not exceeded. He was also willing to concede prescription charges, but not charging for teeth and spectacles. Bevan had, after all, already conceded in 1949 that prescription charges did not involve a breach of the principle of a free service. Given his views on a free health service, this was an indication of how far Bevan was willing to go to find compromise.

Gaitskell was immovable: 'none of these alternative courses would give him a sufficient assurance that the necessary savings would in fact be secured.' He fell back on the findings of the Cabinet committee set up at Morrison's suggestion 12 months previously, where he said that all other methods of reducing expenditure had been considered but none was effective in keeping expenditure within the £400 million limit. Bevan changed tack, and warned the Cabinet that if he resigned he would make clear that the differences he had with his colleagues went further than the NHS. He would express the view that too much was being spent on defence too quickly as a consequence of US pressure. George Tomlinson, by now Minister of Education after Ellen Wilkinson had died tragically of an overdose on 6 February 1947, ruefully observed that £13 million was too high a price to pay for the resignations. Morrison wound up the debate with only Bevan, Wilson and Tomlinson dissenting from the Cabinet line that the charges be introduced.

As the dispute reached its conclusion, it was Gaitskell, rather than Bevan, who refused to compromise. In his final, unhappy, weeks at the Ministry of Labour, and under a great deal of stress, Bevan addressed London dockers at Bermondsey on 3 April 1951.[45] Under pressure from hecklers during his speech, Bevan unwisely declared: 'I will never be a member of a government which makes charges on the National Health Service for the patient.' That meant that, if Gaitskell could ensure that he delivered his budget as drafted, Bevan would leave the Cabinet. Bevan was not the type of person to back down, and, once he had made such a public statement, he could not credibly do so in any event. The political prize on offer for Gaitskell was a glittering one: he and Bevan were the leading Labour figures in the next generation. Bevan's resignation would damage irrevocably his prospects in a future leadership contest. As events were to show, given his premature death in 1960, the day Bevan resigned turned out to be the day he lost the leadership of the Labour Party forever.

Bevan's resignation has the 'what if' element to it. If Attlee, with his revered consensus-finding skills, had not been in hospital, things might have been different, but, that said, Attlee still saw the key participants in the drama at his bedside on 10 April. He saw Bevan and Wilson at 10.30 a.m., and Gaitskell at 11.15 a.m. Attlee agreed a form of words with Bevan and Wilson and put them to Gaitskell: 'to the effect of a ceiling of £400 million and if charges were necessary then they would have to be passed.' Gaitskell refused to accept this way out, and offered his resignation unless he could immediately announce the introduction of the charges. Attlee accepted that, in that case, Bevan and Wilson would have to be the ones to leave the government.[46] That same day, James Callaghan and a number of other junior ministers, including Alfred Robens, Arthur Blenkinsop and Fred Lee, all wrote to Bevan to ask him to delay his resignation. On receipt of the letter Bevan asked to see Callaghan and criticised Gaitskell: 'Hugh is a Tory. Why do they put me up against it? They have known my position for weeks.' As Callaghan put it: 'I certainly did not go away from that conversation believing, as others have said, that Nye was looking for an excuse to resign. On the contrary, I felt he was tormented as to whether he was taking the right course.'[47] When Callaghan saw Bevan later that day, he was talking of postponing the charges as a method of compromise.

A key question is whether it was the element of principle or that of personality that was dominant in Bevan's later decision to resign. With Bevin's illness imping-ing upon his ability to carry out the role of Foreign Secretary, Attlee consulted widely in February 1951 about his possible successor. The prime minister was not keen to appoint Bevan as he felt it would send a bad signal to the US regard-ing support for the Korean War. Bevan's known position was that he opposed increased spending on rearmament at the expense of the NHS. Gaitskell, upon whom Attlee was increasingly relying for advice, thought Morrison 'the only person with the capacity to do it and be acceptable to the Party and the country'.[48] On 10 March 1951, Morrison duly became Foreign Secretary. Dalton records a story John Freeman recounted to him about Bevan when he was consulted in early 1951 about Bevin's successor at the Foreign Office. Attlee asked Bevan for his view. Bevan said he would like the job. Attlee said: 'I've been looking up the records and I find that the Foreign Office has never led on to the premiership.' Bevan then responded: 'Oh then give it to Herbert.'[49] There is a historical inaccuracy here. For example, the Earl of Rosebery had succeeded to the premiership from the Foreign Office in 1894, but this is an indication that Bevan's resignation *did* contain a strong personal element.[50] Bevan had now been passed over for promotion on three specific occasions since the general election of February 1950. But the dominant element was one of principle. The issues of rearmament and NHS charges were related. The defence programme obviously affected the affordability of a free health service, which Bevan saw as an ideal to protect. Bevan opposed the defence programme on both foreign policy and economic grounds. It was not only the American emphasis on militarism; it was also his conviction that a defence programme on that scale was wholly unrealistic. The amount of money allocated would not be spent in the time allocated. In this, as will be seen, he was proved entirely correct.

On 18 April 1951, Attlee wrote to Bevan. He was shaken by Bevin's death only days before (on 14 April) and said he hoped that everyone would 'forget' their differences. Attlee then sent a handwritten letter to Bevan two days later. Attlee had read the Cabinet minutes, and sought clarification: 'I must, therefore, ask you to let me know how you stand on this matter.' Bevan's resignation letter was timed at 2.30 p.m. on 21 April 1951:

> The Budget, in my view, is wrongly conceived in that it fails to apportion fairly the burdens of expenditure as between different social classes. It is wrong because it is based upon a scale of military expenditure, in the coming year, which is physically unattainable, without grave extravagance, in its spending.

Attlee replied that day:

> I note that you have extended the area of disagreement with your colleagues a long way beyond the specific matter to which I understood you have taken objection. I had certainly gathered that if the proposal

for imposing charges on dentures and spectacles were dropped, you would have been satisfied.[51]

This was not accurate. Bevan's opposition to the defence programme was long-standing and that, together with the NHS charges, was to be central to his resignation speech.

Chapter 14

Resignation

Aneurin Bevan, Harold Wilson and the left-wing Minister of Supply, John Freeman, resigned from the government on 24 April 1951. The resignation that did not happen was that of John Strachey, who was by then Minister of War. He had been involved in discussions but was always reluctant. At Bevan's home, Jennie Lee remembers Strachey sitting 'squirming by our sitting-room fireside enjoying exquisite thrills, but he had no intention of resigning.'[1] Strachey had, of course, only recently been promoted to the Cabinet. Bevan was under great pressure; he cared deeply for Lee's father, whose health was by now declining rapidly. Yet, amidst the tragedy of these heady days, there was still a touch of comedy. The porter in this particular Macbeth was none other than Archie Lush. Bevan's friend, Dr Daniel Davies, had arranged for Lush to see an outstanding rectal-cancer surgeon in London, Mr Lloyd Davies. On the train on the way up, Lush travelled with a number of Welsh MPs. He teased them: 'On behalf of the Ebbw Vale Division, he has got to resign, no question at all.' As Lush was being examined, he told the surgeon to telephone the Beaverbrook newspapers: 'tell them Archie Lush has come to have his bloody bottom examined and to tell Bevan not to resign.'[2]

'Good' resignation speeches are rare in British politics. There is the example of Robin Cook who resigned as Leader of the House of Commons in protest at the failure to obtain a further UN resolution before the conflict in Iraq. Cook's resignation speech of 17 March 2003 was greeted with a standing ovation from fellow parliamentarians, though Cook noticeably made clear that he had no designs on the leadership of his party. Other speeches have dripped with poison. The classic example is that of Geoffrey Howe, who resigned as Leader of the House of Commons and deputy prime minister. In his highly effective speech of 13th November 1990, Howe laid bare his own 'conflict of loyalty', providing an open invitation for Michael Heseltine to stand against Margaret Thatcher for the leadership of the Conservative Party. Similarly, former chancellor Norman

Lamont's withering description of John Major's government as 'in office but not in power' in his resignation speech of 9 June 1993 became a defining phrase.

Bevan's resignation speech has always been in a league of its own in terms of controversy and impact. The worst section contained a mixture of savagery and sarcasm towards Gaitskell, whom Bevan portrayed as a closet Tory, a man in favour of the propertied class: 'Everybody possessing property gets richer. Property is appreciating all the time, and it is well known there are large numbers of British citizens living normally out of the appreciated values of their own property. The fiscal measures of the Chancellor of the Exchequer do not touch them at all.'[3] The speech also provoked a debate over its immediate electoral impact. The Labour government was defeated in the general election of 25 October 1951. Many Labour MPs felt that the political crisis was a major factor. As Tony Benn put it: 'Without Gaitskell's Budget and the resignations I doubt we would have lost the general election of that year.'[4] In fact, the month after Bevan's resignation, Labour's Gallup opinion poll rating increased by 2 per cent, and Attlee's approval rating shot up by 8 per cent.[5] What MPs *thought* about the contribution of Bevan's resignation to the 1951 election defeat is far less important than the actual long-term impact.

Bevan's resignation speech was so significant because it was the first official, public marker of Labour division in the postwar era. The Labour Party had been very united under Attlee's premiership. Days prior to the resignation, Crossman had prepared a paper for the Keep Left group in which he made a number of sensible suggestions for compromise between Bevan and Gaitskell, including delaying the operation of the charges on teeth and spectacles and keeping them in place for one year only. Crossman labelled the situation the 'Cold War in the Cabinet' and prophesied that a split would only serve to bring in a Tory government, as Labour would go to the polls a split party.[6] The problem – ironically – was that Labour had achieved so many long-cherished goals. The 'completion of Labour's mission' (to use Crossman's later words) in the first three years of the Attlee government was a seminal achievement, but it was at the price of having implemented the policies the Labour Party largely agreed upon, opening up the potential for disagreement.[7]

The question was: what now? Bevan's resignation statement heralded the public beginning of postwar Labour division on this question. For example, having nationalised vast swathes of British industry, there were few candidates left to be taken over by the state. In the general election of February 1950, the only definite Labour promises on nationalisation were the beet sugar manufacture and sugar-refining industry, and the cement industry. This was indicative of the paucity of its options. The problem for Labour was that it had argued for nationalisation as a solution to the country's economic ills for so many years before it won a parliamentary majority in 1945. Once it had achieved nationalisation of so many industries, it faced a new dilemma. This debate has often been characterised as 'consolidation versus advance': between those who believed that Labour should turn its attentions to private consumer affluence and those who thought that the nationalisation programme needed to be driven further forward. In the short term, there was a public perception problem, aptly described by George Orwell: 'nationalisation would not of itself make the laundries more efficient [...] Nationalisation is a long-term measure [...] great numbers of people may lose all enthusiasm [...] having looked forward to it as a sort of panacea, and then found it makes no immediate difference.'[8]

Bevan's resignation crystallised division in the later days of the Attlee government, but it was not a clear division. He is not easily placed on the side of 'advance' rather than 'consolidation'. Tate & Lyle's 'Mr Cube' campaign in the 1950 general-election campaign objecting to the Labour nationalisation proposals on the sugar industry symbolised the difficulties with public perceptions of further nationalisation. Hence the Labour Party discussed further nationalisation at Dorking in June 1950, and Bevan argued for consolidation. Bevan *had* threatened to resign from the government over nationalisation, but it was on the specific case of iron and steel, which the government carried through. As the controversy over iron and steel nationalisation rumbled on, *Keeping Left*, a pamphlet published in January 1950 by the *New Statesman* as a successor to *Keep Left*, said this: 'In the last few years we have learned to distinguish the means of socialism from its ends, and the tools of social revolution from their uses.' It added that nationalisation should be used 'flexibly'. It reflected: 'In coal and transport, nationalisation stopped the rot. In gas, electricity and steel it provides the only basis for maximum technical advance. But the next steps are not so obvious or so simple.'[9] In fact, on domestic policy, Bevan and Gaitskell were more united than it seemed; the arguments in the 1951–5 parliament concentrated on foreign policy. The debate over the advance of socialism in Britain – exemplified in Bevan's own *In Place of Fear* on the Labour left and Tony Crosland's 1956 work *The Future of Socialism* on the Labour right – was to prove more theoretical than practical.

At the time, Bevan's resignation statement met with a storm of criticism. The most cruel remark came from Beaverbrook's *Daily Express*, which said that Bevan 'made all the impact of a bust and broken bulldozer'.[10] As Dalton put it: 'Nye flopped in the House today on his resignation speech. No cheer when he entered, in the middle of questions, nor when he rose, at the end of questions, hardly any cheers while he was speaking, nor when he sat down.'[11] Bevan was 'nervously exhausted', drained from the Cabinet battles.[12] He questioned whether he would stay in politics at all. He even considered leaving Parliament altogether and to stand for the leadership of the NUM. As Lee puts it: 'Will Lawther, then President, was due to retire. If Nye stood he would win. After careful thought he decided to keep his power base in his constituency, where his hold was secure, and stand for the Treasurership of the party.'[13]

One major problem with the Bevan speech was its length. It took around 45 minutes to deliver, and if a speech is to be received badly, which Bevan knew it would inevitably be, then a shorter, more pointed speech would have been better.[14] Allied to this was the toxic mixture of issues that the speech raised. The most powerful section in his speech, upon which he was proved correct, namely the defence programme, was lost among everything else. He castigated it as dead in the water since the programme could not be carried out without raw materials and non-ferrous metals, which Britain was dependent upon importing:

> I say therefore with the full solemnity and the seriousness of what I am saying that the £4,700 million arms programme is already dead. It cannot be achieved without irreparable damage to the economy of Great Britain and the world, and that therefore the arms programme [...] is already invalidated.[15]

Bevan as constructive statesman still shines through this speech. He felt – and he was certainly not the first or the last in the postwar era to advocate this – that economic planning should be separated from the Treasury. 'They know nothing about it. The great difficulty with the Treasury is that they think they move men about when they move pieces of paper about.' Bevan did not wholly repudiate the record of the Attlee government. In any event, he could hardly do so: 'By the end of 1950 we had as I said in my letter to the Prime Minister, assumed the moral leadership of the world.'[16] He struck at Gaitskell:

> I listened to the Chancellor of the Exchequer with great admiration. It was one of the cleverest Budget speeches I had ever heard in my life. There was a passage towards the end in which he said that he was now coming to a complicated and technical matter and if members wished to they could go to sleep. They did. While they were sleeping he stole £100 million a year from the National Insurance Fund.[17]

Bevan put the argument on the NHS on the basis of a slippery slope towards more and more charging:

He has taken £13 million out of the Budget total of £4,000 million. If he finds it necessary to mutilate, or begin to mutilate, the health services for £13 million out of £4,000 million, what will he do next year? Or are you next year going to take your stand on the upper denture? The lower half apparently does not matter, but the top half is sacrosanct. Is that right? If my honourable friends are asked questions at meetings about what they will do next year, what will they say?[18]

In a reference to Shakespeare's bloody *Titus Andronicus*, he rounded on Gaitskell with a vivid image: 'The health service will be like Lavinia – all the limbs cut off and eventually her tongue cut out too.'[19]

Bevan also had to deal with one major inconsistency in his own position, which was that he himself had accepted legislative provision for prescription charges to go up to a shilling in December 1949. He justified it on the basis that he had thought it would never be introduced due to its impracticability.

I will tell my honourable friend something else too. There was another policy – there was a proposed reduction of 25,000 [units] on the housing programme was there not? It was never made. It was necessary for me at that time to use what everybody said were bad tactics on my part – I had to manoeuvre, and I did manoeuvre and save the 25,000 houses and the prescription charge.[20]

On the day after Bevan's resignation, Tuesday, 24 April, there was a meeting of the PLP in Westminster Hall at 9.30 a.m. It was a tempestuous and poisonous two-hour meeting. Harold Wilson and John Freeman both made statements pledging not to bring the government down. Gaitskell then defended his budget and took the line that even if the arms programme were not implemented that would still not ease the situation. Gaitskell 'wanted this to be a popular budget that would win votes and it would have been a popular budget if it had not been attacked, as it had been, in some quarters'. Gaitskell was followed by applause that Dalton provocatively helped to prolong. In response, Bevan dared Gaitskell to publish the Cabinet papers, and then attacked Gaitskell directly: 'But for my Health Service he would never have been Chancellor of the Exchequer […] I have served more years in the Labour Party than he.' Bevan compared Gaitskell to Philip Snowden, saying that it was in that same room that he had been shouted down when he warned the party about the direction it was taking before the crisis of 1931.[21] Dalton remembers Bevan as 'sweating and screeching', seemingly 'on the edge of a nervous breakdown'. Bevan even said at one stage: 'I think I had better sit down.' The real insult to Bevan, however, was the comparison of him with Oswald Mosley. Dalton himself had initially whispered the comparison to Herbert Morrison, who was sitting alongside him. It was not a favourable one. Not only was Mosley at this time the pariah leader of the British Union of Fascists, but this was a direct reference to a meeting of the PLP on 20th November 1930 when Mosley himself had been out of control.[22] Had the comment remained *sotto voce*, it might not have caused the trouble that it did. But James Chuter Ede, who was chairing the debate, inflamed the situation further by saying that one of the speeches had reminded him of Mosley. 'Now you've said it,' shouted Bevan. This tempestuous meeting was followed by a more sober occasion, a memorial service for Ernest Bevin at Westminster Abbey. The next day, Wednesday, 25 April, the Labour Party's NEC backed the budget with only four dissensions: aside from Bevan, Tom Driberg, Ian Mikardo and Barbara Castle. Politically, the game was over. It was a low moment. Ironically, it was Churchill who said something positive in the House of Commons smoking room when he saw Bevan and Lee. He ignored Bevan himself, but told Lee not to underestimate her husband.[23]

Jennie Lee thought Bevan was fully justified in resigning from the government. John Freeman told Hugh Dalton that she was 'Opposition minded and doesn't like Nye being in the Government'; she also had 'a guilt-complex about a Cabinet Minister's salary'.[24] Given Bevan and Lee's taste for the good life, the final argument can be dismissed. It is also unfair to say that she *disliked* him being in government. She was very proud of his achievements in office, particularly the NHS. What is fair to say is that she was a natural dissident. But she should not be seen as a negative influence continuously tempting Bevan into the political wilderness, and eventually succeeding. Bevan had remained a Cabinet minister for the best part of six years. When he resigned, she – and Michael Foot – fortified him in his belief that he had taken the right course. But the decision to resign was Bevan's. Thus, politically, resignation brought Bevan closer to Lee: both were now cast in the role of rebel. But, as Bevan's discomfort in opposition during the 1951–5 parliament was to show, he continued to long for the levers of power.

On 29 April 1951, the *Observer* published a full-page profile of Bevan, which made a series of stinging criticisms: 'One of the most serious weaknesses of this able and lonely man is a lack of objectivity, of the ability to look and listen dispassionately.' Comparing him to one of the twentieth century's other great Welsh politicians, it added: 'Where Lloyd George could sum up others precisely, Bevan can tell you little more than how *he* feels about them. Correspondingly, he lacks self-criticism.' These are serious charges, and should not be dismissed lightly. On this basis, Bevan was incapable of impartial thinking, too prone to emotional outbursts and responses, and unconsciously self-absorbed. His background was, on this argument, a handicap that had caused him to think far too highly of himself. This final criticism was also made by Attlee. He was convinced that Bevan would cause trouble after his resignation: 'We are in for a good deal of bother with Nye Bevan – too much ego in his cosmos.'[25] Attlee's assessment was based on personal observation. Bevan could not even resist the temptation to stand out from the crowd at the wedding of Attlee's daughter, Felicity, by refusing to wear morning dress as all other guests did.[26]

That Bevan had an extraordinary self-belief is obvious. No public figure could have acted as he did during the Second World War and withstood the barrage of criticism without that. He could also, at times, let his temper and emotions get the better of him. But, on the whole, he was able to play the political game as well as anybody else of his generation. He certainly *did* have the capacity to see logic in the arguments of others. He enjoyed deconstructing opposing positions and setting up his own arguments in response. But his speeches could easily give one a different impression. He did use powerful language, and his approach was shaped by his experiences in local politics. He often took unmitigated, strong positions in public. In the raucous environment of the meetings he attended in the 1920s, the key was to get on your feet and make your point clearly and quickly. Subordinate clauses or qualifications to an argument could be difficult to maintain without being shouted down. Bevan always remembered the jibe of 'Tennyson's Babbling Brook'. He *was* also self-aware, and could be self-deprecatory. Barbara Castle recalls a story about when he addressed an annual conference of Young Socialists (after his resignation) when a speaker was nearly reduced to tears by a temperamental loudspeaker. When Bevan spoke he immediately referred to the problem: 'I would say to my young friend, do not worry that the loudspeaker failed. If it had only failed more often when I was speaking, I would not be in the difficulties I am in now.'[27]

While the Attlee government remained in office, Bevan was not an active backbencher, and, on the whole, avoided further controversy. There was an awkward exchange in the Commons on 2 May between Bevan and his successor at Health, Hilary Marquand. Bevan argued that foreigners should not be charged for using the NHS, and a Tory MP, Major Tufton Beamish, playfully raised the issue of teeth and spectacles. Marquand jibed at Bevan: 'I took the liberty of assuming that my right hon. Friend, when he asked for powers to impose charges, had in mind that he might impose charges.'[28] Five days later, on May Day, Bevan spoke in Glasgow on famine in India in terms that resonate today: 'People are dying inside the British Commonwealth for lack of food. Nehru has warned them that they may die by millions – all because mankind has got its priorities wrong.'[29] In July, he co-wrote (with Harold Wilson and John Freeman) the introduction to a *Tribune* pamphlet, *One Way Only*, in which he set out his argument for 'fair shares' between the rich and poor nations of the world. He defined international socialist policy as bearing down on poverty and injustice.[30]

Freed from the burdens of office by his resignation, he and Lee spent August on holiday in Yugoslavia. There he met Marshal Tito and the poet Milovan Djilas, who was then Tito's deputy. He also met Vladimir Dedijer, another writer–politician who was later Tito's official biographer. Bevan immediately bonded with Djilas and Dedijer, who became his firm friends. With them he could again enjoy 'star-tapping' in conversation about intellectual Marxism. He also admired Tito's insistence on an independent foreign policy from Stalin's Soviet Union. He used his free time to draw together themes he had written about in *Tribune* in the 1930s, and thought about for many years, and, helped by Lee, he completed most of the manuscript of what was to be his only real book, *In Place of Fear*, which was to be published in 1952.

Meanwhile, Morrison had a tough few months as Foreign Secretary. The Persian government nationalised the oil wells at Abadan in May 1951. Morrison wanted to take military action, but could not persuade Attlee or the Cabinet. In May 1951, two Cambridge spies, Donald Maclean and Guy Burgess, defected to the Soviet Union. There was also Egypt. Under the Anglo-Egyptian Treaty of 1936, Britain was allowed to station troops in Egypt to defend the Suez Canal. Bevin had sought renegotiation of the treaty in October 1946, but talks had broken down over Egypt seeking sovereignty over the Sudan, to which the Sudanese were opposed. Morrison sought to renew negotiations with Egypt when he became Foreign Secretary. British troops could still be stationed in the zone around the Suez Canal until 1955 under the 1936 treaty, but Morrison did not want Britain to have to leave Egypt entirely. He sought to establish a 'Middle Eastern Command' managed principally by the US, France, Turkey and the UK, with Egyptian participation, on the basis of troops from the other countries still being able to use the canal zone. The Egyptians were hostile to the continued British presence, and, on 8 October, during the general-election campaign, announced the abrogation of the 1936 treaty and its predecessor Sudan Condominium treaties of 1899. Again, Morrison's instinct was to use force, but he could not persuade Attlee. Bevan avoided confronting Morrison in the Commons on these issues. In his introduction to *One Way Only* he had pressed the issue of the inequity between the rich and poor nations of the world. He thought Britain had to think more carefully about the social implications of exploiting the natural resources of less developed countries, including Persia. He saw a link between social change and political freedom. He was in favour of withdrawing troops from Egypt as he saw no purpose in having a base in another country unless it was with the consent of the local population.[31]

In September 1951, having survived 17 months with a wafer-thin parliamentary majority, Attlee decided to call the general election for 25 October. The key factor was the king's proposed trip to Australia: Attlee wanted the parliamentary situation resolved before his departure. As it turned out the king was too ill to travel, but Attlee had made his decision, despite Morrison's protestations to delay via telegram from the Cunard ocean liner *Queen Mary* (he had been to San Francisco for the signing of the Japanese peace treaty). As a member of the NEC, Bevan played his part in drafting the election manifesto. The subcommittee consisted of Bevan, Dalton, Sam Watson, secretary of the Durham Miners' Association, and Morgan Phillips. On nationalisation, the debate over which additional industries should come under public control was fudged, and a vague pledge was inserted: 'We shall take over concerns which fail the nation and start new public enterprises wherever this will serve the national interest'; the debate over rearmament was glossed over: 'peace cannot be preserved by arms alone.'

The campaign started with the Labour Party's annual conference in Scarborough on the first three days of October. There the grassroots party members' views on rearmament were made plain as Shinwell, defence minister since the February 1950 election, lost his place on the constituency-elected section of the NEC. Bevan came top of the poll, and his declared supporter Barbara Castle was newly elected in second place. Two other Bevanites, Tom Driberg and Ian Mikardo, increased their votes. Dalton, Griffiths and Morrison saw their votes drop but held on to their places. This was the fifth consecutive time that Bevan had been elected in first place. He was highly popular with party members. As a minister, his NHS was a symbol of socialism in action, and his creative statesmanship had been combined with brilliant attacks on the opposition. Bevan showed party members what difference a Labour government could make, and why the Conservative Party should be kept out of office. He reminded them of their greater purpose in campaigning on their local streets at election time.

Prior to the conference, another *Tribune* pamphlet, *Going Our Way*, had criticised trade union leaders on the NEC for not reflecting the views of their members in their voting. Allegedly, it was at Scarborough that a decision was made to stop Bevan ever becoming party leader: Arthur Deakin, Bevin's successor as general secretary of the TGWU, Will Lawther, president of the NUM, and Tom Williamson, general secretary of the General and Municipal Workers union, met in the St Nicholas Hotel.[32] Aside from his long-standing rivalry with Bevin (and his relationship with Deakin was no better), Bevan saw these trade union leaders as 'by his standards, politically unimaginative and negative'. He disliked what he saw as their *conservatism*, their tendency to be reactive to the movements within the capitalist system, rather than to think proactively beyond its confines.[33] In response, Deakin, Lawther and Williamson supported the leading Labour politicians on the right of the PLP: Bevin, of course, but also, later, Morrison and – with particular consequences for Bevan – Gaitskell. This dynamic only changed when Frank Cousins took over as general secretary of the TGWU in May 1956, after the brief eight-month tenure of the ill Arthur Tiffin. That moment marked a change in Bevan's relationship with leading trade union leaders. Cousins and Bevan did not agree on everything. Cousins was suspicious of *any* government – including a Labour one – regulating the unions; Bevan thought this incompatible with his own belief in *parliamentary* socialism. However, with their shared mining backgrounds, and having both come of age in the high-unemployment interwar period (Cousins was only seven years younger than Bevan), the two men shared a desire to *change* society for the better.[34] For Bevan, this radicalism was a welcome change from what he saw as the cautious thinking of trade union leaders.

In the conference debate on the manifesto, Bevan urged unity in the face of the enemy.[35] The Conservatives seized on the division in the Labour Party, denouncing Bevan as a Communist who was preparing to overthrow Attlee and seize the premiership himself if Labour won the election. Bevan's old BMA adversary Charles Hill, who had been elected the National Liberal and Conservative MP for Luton in 1950, took the opportunity to exact a measure of revenge. Already famous as the BBC's 'Radio Doctor', Hill applied his broadcasting skills to campaigning. He twisted the knife: 'The thought of Nye Bevan as Prime Minister of this country fairly turns the tummy over. As one wag had put it – "The end is Nye".' Churchill sought to bundle together the foreign-policy issues of Persian oil and Egypt with Bevan's resignation, mocking Attlee about Abad-*anne*, Sud-*anne* and Bev-*anne*. Attlee dealt with the issue in his own radio broadcast in his usual direct, laconic style, saying that he fully intended to remain as party leader after the election and that Bevan was not a Communist. While Bevan went on his usual nationwide speaking tour, the Labour campaign sought – to the extent it could – to keep him out of the limelight: in addition to Attlee, the party's radio broadcasts were by Morrison, Gaitskell and Jim Griffiths. David Butler's authoritative study of the 1951 general election concluded: 'On the whole the Labour tactics seem to have been successful in damping down the issue as far as it could be damped down.'[36]

The Labour Party was duly defeated in the general election, despite winning more votes than the Conservatives. The problem was that the tiny Liberal Party could only afford to run 109 candidates, rather than the 475 they had run in 1950. In the absence of a Liberal candidate, Liberal voters tended to favour the Conservatives; Attlee estimated that they 'tended in most areas to give two or three votes to the Conservatives for every one they gave to Labour'.[37] Thus, Winston Churchill returned to Downing Street for his second spell as prime minister with a government majority of 17. Labour was back in opposition.

Part V

In Opposition, 1951–60

Chapter 15

The Bevanites, 1951–5

Aneurin Bevan was a man of power. His period as a Cabinet minister had brought the best out in him. The early 1950s were to demonstrate that opposition could bring out the worst in him. For Bevan had all the credentials to be Labour Party leader. By 1951, he was not only experienced in high office, but he had achieved great things in government. He had a vision of society – to be given expression in his book *In Place of Fear* – in which human spirit meant more than material wealth. With his seat on the NEC, he had influence within the Labour Party machinery, and a passionate following among party members. He had personal charisma and was a magnetic speaker. Even Gaitskell's wife, Dora, thought that Bevan, rather than Gaitskell, should have been party leader.[1] Speaking to Richard Crossman, Attlee said that Bevan 'had the leadership on a plate'. He wanted Bevan to succeed him, but: 'he wants to be two things simultaneously, a rebel and an official leader, and you can't be both.'[2]

Bevan was a very reluctant rebel, and whether he was actively a rebel *leader* is a moot point. In any event, in the 1950s his leadership prospects depended entirely on his fellow MPs. Thus, Bevan was fighting a losing battle from the start. For the right of the PLP, in particular Gaitskell, was supported by its strong backers in the trade union movement, Deakin, Lawther and Williamson. Young, Oxford-educated MPs surrounded Gaitskell, including Tony Crosland and Roy Jenkins, and became known as the 'Hampstead Set': Gaitskell lived there, in the Frognal area. Ian Mikardo noted wryly that a 'somewhat incongruous alliance developed between these horny-handed sons of toil and the delicately nurtured aristos of the Hampstead Set who surrounded Gaitskell'.[3] Bevan's support in the so-called 'Bevanite' group, as it was to become known, was to prove too small to give him sufficient backing in the House of Commons to win a leadership election.

On 26 April 1951, three days after his resignation, together with Wilson and Freeman, Bevan attended a hastily arranged meeting that marked the start of the 'Bevanites'. Bevan now provided a new focal point for left-wing MPs. As Foot put it, 'once Bevan resigned, all other Left-wing activities were swamped by it'.[4] The question for the meeting was the form the left-wing activities would now take in the light of Bevan's resignation. Fifteen people attended. Seven were members of the old Keep Left group, and included Barbara Castle, Richard Crossman, Foot and Ian Mikardo. In addition to the three ex-ministers, the remaining eight included Jennie Lee and Tom Driberg. The Keep Left label was dropped; Jo Richardson, who had been secretary of the Keep Left group since Ian Mikardo had been elected to the NEC in October 1950, became the new secretary of the Bevanites. Richardson meticulously kept records, including a 'membership list', which, by 1952, contained 51 names, including 47 MPs.[5] Gaitskell, naturally, suspected the Bevanites of being organised primarily to win the party leadership for Bevan.[6] They were a highly talented bunch, containing two future party leaders (Wilson and Foot), and 14 future government ministers. They were articulate; a number were journalists. Foot, Jennie Lee and J. P. W. Mallalieu, an Oxford graduate and MP for Huddersfield East, formed the *Tribune* editorial board. Crossman, once an Oxford don, was a true intellectual in politics, and the deputy editor of the *New Statesman*. Another Oxford alumnus, Tom Driberg (though he left without a degree), had a column in *Reynold's News*. Gaitskell felt the Labour right was 'handicapped [...] vis-à-vis the Bevanites because of the *New Statesman* and *Tribune*'.[7] The Bevanites met on a weekly basis, producing papers for discussion. In addition, they encouraged debates among the Labour rank and file. 'Brains trusts' had begun in the summer of 1950. Advertised in *Tribune* and the *New Statesman*, they were named after the BBC wartime radio show to which listeners sent in wide-ranging questions to a panel. The Bevanites took on the idea with gusto. The conspiratorial Mikardo usually chaired the panels, and they toured the constituency parties, already saturated with copies of *Tribune*. Labour Party members attended in their droves. Individual party membership soared to its highest ever level: over 1 million in 1952 and 1953.[8]

Yet, for all this, the Bevanites did not produce a detailed set of policies on welfare or nationalisation. Mark Jenkins has argued: 'If, in the main, Bevanite pamphlets exhibit a lack of concrete proposals for domestic reform it is due solely to their commitment to the party programme, which they believed could not be implemented without a major shift in the emphasis of Labour's foreign policy.'[9] This is not a convincing argument. After all, the Atlantic alliance *had* produced the money – in the form of the American loan and Marshall Aid – for the Attlee governments to carry out their programmes. Had Labour policy abroad changed, it is not clear how this would have changed matters at home. There is, in fact, a deeper explanation that neither Gaitskellites nor Bevanites would care to admit: Gaitskell and Bevan were not that far apart on domestic policy. Both identified themselves as socialists. While their adherence to the main political actors, Bevan and Gaitskell, divided their followers, beyond that it was not so easy to identify Bevanites as 'left' and Gaitskellites as 'right'. Take Crossman's description of the Bevanites:

> The Group really is extraordinarily heterogeneous. What a mysterious thing 'the Left' is. Why is this person Left and that person Right? What binds the Group together? In our case, there is the old Keep Left Group, which did work out a certain homogeneity, with superimposed on it Nye Bevan and Harold Wilson, who have virtually nothing in common, and a number of their personal supporters, such as Will Griffiths and Hugh Delargy, who, as far as I can see, have no coherent political attitude. However, I suppose most Cabinets look much the same.[10]

The deeper division was on foreign policy, on which all the major Bevanite controversies flared up in Parliament. Until the summer of 1950, Bevan had been a supporter – albeit an unenthusiastic one – of the Atlantic alliance, seeing it as a financial and military necessity. When, as a consequence of the Korean War, he saw American foreign policy as driven more by ideological antagonism towards Communism, he started to look for alternative British foreign policy in the cold-war era. The first major division in the PLP in the new parliament was on the Japanese peace treaty, which was opposed by the Soviet Union. Labour policy was in favour, but over 30 Labour MPs voted against, including Bevan, and a hundred abstained, on 26 November 1951.

On the issue of the defence programme itself, Bevan was entirely vindicated. On 6 December 1951, fortified by civil-service advice from Ian Bancroft, later Head of the Home Civil Service, and others, Churchill told the House of Commons that the government would be unable to spend all the money Gaitskell had allocated to rearmament and sarcastically congratulated Bevan, saying, 'it appears by accident, perhaps not for the best of motives [he] happened to be right'.[11] Crossman recorded Churchill's speech as 'quite remarkably conciliatory and non-controversial, with several admissions that he found our defence preparations far better than he expected'. For Crossman the reference to Bevan was the 'only dramatic moment'.[12] That same night Crossman extracted Michael and Jill Foot from drinks with Randolph Churchill and Christopher Soames, the prime minister's son and son-in-law, respectively. Jill, Jennie and Nye dined at The Ivy before returning to Bevan's house to celebrate 'the conversion of Churchill to Bevanism and the conclusion of Nye's book'. Bevan completed the evening's celebration by reading aloud from Havelock Ellis' introduction to Rodó's *The Motives of Proteus*.

Bevan frequently read aloud from the book, often challenging American visitors with its views of North American civilisation.[13]

Crossman's view is that Bevan was 'almost exclusively concerned to be Leader of the Party rather than to formulate left-wing policy'.[14] Bevan veered between a deep resentment of Gaitskell and his own instinctive understanding of the concept of power, which led him to the conclusion that being part of a team of plotters would not bring him back to the centre of politics. The balance between these two conflicting feelings determined Bevan's behaviour throughout the 1951–5 parliament. Barbara Castle recalls his mood in the period after his resignation as 'curiously ambivalent' – he was capable of lashing out, much to the frustration of his friends: 'It seemed to us that he wanted Bevanism without the Bevanites.'[15] The problem was that, while Bevan raged about what he saw as the unfair treatment that led to his resignation – the Cabinet majority siding with Gaitskell over his paltry £13 million – he also knew that becoming a rebel leader of the small group around him was no way to get his hands back on the levers of power. There are moments when Bevan's impulsive behaviour lends itself to easy criticism. The more significant point, however, is that resignation left Bevan with very few options. He did eventually stand again for the Parliamentary Committee, but most of his time was spent reflecting on events.

Bevan was deeply uncomfortable if asked to exercise leadership over the Bevanites. For example, the Arms Estimates were to be presented to Parliament on 25 February 1952. His attitude to the position of the Bevanite group, as described by Crossman, is very revealing:

> His reply was typical. 'Oh, I dare say the best thing would be to leave each person to decide for himself.' [...] So far from being a great strategist or organizer of cabals, Nye is an individualist [...] He dominates its discussions simply because he is fertile in ideas, but leadership and organisation are things he instinctively shrinks away from.[16]

Archie Lush had it right when he observed that Bevan was 'a lone wolf in many ways' and 'not an easy mixer'.[17] He also had human weaknesses that should not be shied away from. He could be intolerant, and did not suffer fools gladly. As a consequence of his 1920s battles in Tredegar, Bevan was quick to anger, and if he did not find a particular question interesting, could be very dismissive even in discussions with his friends. He would openly tell them that their questions were totally ridiculous and, at times, he was not the easiest person to get on with. He sometimes found it difficult to work closely with others. This was in stark contrast to the position he found himself in as a government minister, where his clear sense of direction and purpose was an asset in terms of his control over the civil-service machine. But the Bevanites were not an established machine with designated jobs looking to the top for strong leadership. Rather, they were a collection of individuals bound together by their association with Bevan himself. Geoffrey Goodman even goes as far as to say that, at times, Bevan found his 'Bevanite group' something of an embarrassment.[18] Unable to exercise substantial power, Bevan was also often absent from the lunches for the 'Bevanite MPs' that Crossman organised each week at his house in Vincent Square, which was close to Westminster. He preferred to spend his time at his flat with his older friends like Foot.

In Place of Fear was published in April 1952. It sold well, no doubt helped by the fact that Bevan was a well-known, controversial figure whose actions attracted attention. Published simultaneously in hardback and paperback, 37,000 copies were quickly off the shelves.[19] Reviews were less favourable. *The Times* snobbishly remarked: 'The close relationship between thought and experience, which an academic education seeks to break down, is obviously important, for it is the symbols of Mr Bevan's past experience which still remain the formative influence in his thought.'[20] Actually, Bevan's background gives *In Place of Fear* true authenticity. That he was self-educated is hardly a valid criticism. But that is not to say that *In Place of Fear* is flawless. For all Bevan's wide reading, one notable gap, Marx aside, was his knowledge of intellectual debates in economics. For example, he was never seriously interested in classical economics; he was inspired by Rodó's critique of American capitalism, but the likes of Adam Smith and David Ricardo did not feature among the authors he read and reread. Such texts were to him dry and uninspiring. This shows in places. He makes a strong case for the advancement of *democratic* socialism through Parliament, the institution he saw as 'a weapon, and the most formidable weapon of all, in the struggle'. Yet, at the end of his discussion on the role of the legislature, he devotes only three short paragraphs to arguing that Britain was not 'exposed to world trade movements to an extent that limits the application of Socialist policies to her own economy'. In criticising international finance for the currency crises under the Attlee government, there is no mention of the American loan or Marshall Aid.[21]

In Place of Fear has suffered from unfavourable comparisons with Tony Crosland's 1956 *The Future of Socialism*. Attlee, tongue-in-cheek, placed his copy of *In Place of Fear* on his bookcase next to Aesop's *Fables*.[22] Crosland felt that the ascendancy of private-property rights in British society had already been dealt with, and that the Attlee government's achievements had made it possible to pursue a goal of equality without needing to stymie wealth creation. Rather, wealth creation was in the interests of socialists, since wealth needed to be generated in order to be redistributed. Bevan did not believe that the ascendancy of private-property rights had been effectively dealt with. Throughout the 1950s, until his death, he continued to believe in public ownership. For him, if the government could not take control of the economy's 'commanding heights' it could not properly direct and plan the economic affairs of the nation. The key to *The Future of Socialism* is that it separated means and ends: state ownership should not be an end in itself.

Nonetheless, *In Place of Fear* is a classic socialist tract. Its brilliance lies not in a thorough, academic approach to different issues, but in its emphasis on *individual* freedom and fulfilment. With poverty and unemployment a product of the organisation of society, neither could be eliminated unless you could change the way society was organised. Bevan took as his starting point that private property, poverty and democracy were society's main conflicting forces. Private-property owners possessed the bulk of the country's wealth and thus dominated its politics and policies. Thus, the 'function of parliamentary democracy, under universal franchise, historically considered, is to expose wealth-privilege to the attack of the people'. Bevan believed that socialists had to use Parliament to bring the 'main streams of economic activity', including major industries, under public direction: 'The emergence of modern industry, with its danger of depersonalisation of the worker, challenges the vitality of democratic principles. In the societies of the West, industrial democracy is the counterpart of political freedom.' This was not a Marxist position that *all* property was theft; rather, 'You can make your home the base for your adventures, but it is absurd to make the base itself an adventure.'[23] The desire to own one's own living space was one thing, but the privileged few accumulating ever vaster swathes of the country's wealth was another. An Englishman's home could be his castle, but *economic power* should not be concentrated in a few private hands. Once the whole community had power over the economic affairs of the nation, expressed through Parliament, its challenge was to shape policy to the *needs of the individual*: 'If the policies of statesmen […] do not have for their object the enlargement and cultivation of the individual life, they do not deserve to be called civilized.' Bevan saw the purpose of his NHS as the alleviation of individual suffering: 'A free Health Service is a triumphant example of the superiority of collective action and public initiative applied to a segment of society where commercial principles are seen at their worst.'

This same concern runs through the section on international politics. Bevan was critical of the Soviet Union: 'The existence of huge forced labour camps, the ruthless punishment meted out to political opponents, the disappearance without trace of people who offend against the ruling clique, the appalling doctrine of "associative crime"; all these are deeply offensive.' He then challenged the US: 'So far the history of the United States shows that it is her habit to arm for war and disarm for peace. The question now arises, can she arm for peace?'[24] His criticism of the US was that it defined itself not in terms of what it was for, but what it was against: Communism. He concludes with a passage on the goal of international relations. It was not 'the defeat of Communism, or of Socialism, or the preservation of this or that way of life. It is not even the conquest of poverty, for that term is capable of so many different and contradictory definitions.' For Bevan, it was 'the defeat of hunger in the most literal physical sense. Until hunger has been left behind as a racial memory, it will not be possible to say that man has won a decisive victory in his long struggle with his physical environment.'[25]

In Place of Fear was not systematic. Bevan's mind roved across different topics. For example, he could not resist a swipe at the press: 'Of all monopolies, monopoly of opinion is the worst [...] The British people have never been less informed about what is happening in the rest of the world.' Bevan offered a remedy: 'There is only one corrective for this and it is the one denied us: cheap and plentiful supplies of newsprint so that it is comparatively easy to start new journals and to seek out a readership now rendered inarticulate by the mass circulations.'[26] Elsewhere, he criticised modern education for failing to teach children to question the assumptions upon which society was based, but did not develop this into a positive argument for educational change.

The emotional power of *In Place of Fear* is exemplified in its poignant final chapter, entitled 'Democratic socialism'. Bevan quoted the final line of Dylan Thomas' famous poem, 'A refusal to mourn the death, by fire, of a child in London': 'After the first death, there is no other.' Every human being is unique, irrespective of race, religion, class or nationality: 'The capacity for emotional concern for individual life is the most significant quality of a civilized human being.' He was deeply troubled by group mentality and cruelty to outsiders. How could the ruling classes in centuries past not be moved by the tears of boys sent to be executed on the gallows? How could the Nazis 'put the Jews outside the walls of their personalities' in the Holocaust? One sentence sums it up: 'There is no test for progress other than its impact on the individual.' J. P. Mallalieu said this in his review of *In Place of Fear*: '*in the end* it becomes the fight of "I", the ordinary man who longs to live his life fully and at peace. There, I think, is the essence of *In Place of Fear*. There too, I feel, is the essence of Nye Bevan.'[27] In that judgement, he was entirely correct.

In Parliament, the Bevanite controversy really began in the same month, in a debate on 5 March 1952. Churchill's government had produced a Defence White Paper setting out its expenditure. The Bevanites were not in favour of carrying out the rearmament programme. Attlee, ever trying to seek a compromise position, decided to set the party line that the White Paper should be approved in principle in line with the previous government's policy of following rearmament, but with no confidence expressed in the Churchill government to carry it out. That meant that the party would put down an amendment to the government motion to approve the White Paper and abstain on the motion itself. The Labour amendment was defeated by 314 votes to 219. The Conservative majority, usually around 20, had significantly increased, so many Labour MPs had not voted for the amendment. On the motion itself, rather than abstaining, 57 Labour MPs voted against, over one-sixth of the PLP.

Alf Robens and James Callaghan (who, along with others such as Strauss and Strachey, formed the 'Keep Calm' group in 1952, ostensibly to moderate between the Gaitskellites and Bevanites) wanted to take away the Labour whip from the rebels. Gaitskell felt there was a potential advantage in being able to attack Bevan if he left the party.[28] The day after the defence debate the Parliamentary Committee came up with the approach of criticising the 57 rebels and reintroducing standing orders, which had been suspended in 1945 as a goodwill gesture to encourage rather than impose loyalty to the party line. Also, all MPs would now have to sign to say they accepted standing orders. While Attlee proposed this at a full meeting of the PLP, he disappointed Gaitskell as he 'made a fairly strong speech to start with but did not attempt to explain our resolution'.[29] Instead, George Strauss proposed merely to reintroduce standing orders, and this was carried by a majority of 162 to 72.

The bad feeling continued into the 1952 party conference, which opened on 29 September in Morecambe. Dalton called it 'the worst Labour Party Conference, for bad temper and general hatred, since 1926, the year of the General Strike'.[30] There was a swell of support for the Bevanites from the Constituency Labour Parties. For the constituency section of the NEC, Bevan topped the poll and other Bevanites, Barbara Castle, Richard Crossman, Tom Driver, Ian Mikardo and Harold Wilson, were all elected. Morrison, Dalton, Gaitskell and Callaghan all failed to get elected. On the third day of the conference the hostility was open, with both Will Lawther and Arthur Deakin being 'very provocative' in the face of the Bevanites' 'continuous booing'.[31] 'Shut yer gob,' was Lawther's firm – if inelegant – response. After the conference, Gaitskell gave a speech at Stalybridge that stirred the pot. He cited 'the number of resolutions and speeches which were Communist-inspired' and added: 'It is time to end the attempt at mob rule by a group of frustrated journalists.'[32] Foot was incensed. Putting aside the jibe about the number of scribblers in the Bevanite ranks, the reference to Communism had a particular resonance. 'McCarthyism' was taking hold in the US, as Senator Joseph McCarthy listed, and subsequently investigated, alleged Communist infiltrators in the American government, causing a witch-hunt of alleged Communists in public life. Not even McCarthy, said Foot, 'had ever attempted a vaguer, more unprovable, and therefore more despicable smear'.[33] Foot had already compared Gaitskell to the reviled traitor, Philip Snowden, chancellor in both prewar Labour governments, after his 1951 budget, and this merely heightened Foot's ill will towards him. Attacks on Bevan himself continued apace, the *Manchester Guardian*'s editor, A. P. Wadsworth, having taken a personal dislike to Bevan as a result of the 'vermin' speech.[34] Bevan abhorred McCarthyism, and what he saw as the persecution of Paul Robeson, for a time denied a passport for failing to sign an affidavit confirming he was not a Communist.

There was now a serious disciplinary issue in the party. In October 1952, the Parliamentary Committee recommended to the PLP that groups within the party be disbanded, which was passed by 188 votes to 51. Bevan stood against Morrison for the deputy leadership the following month, but – with very little support beyond the Bevanite group – lost by 194 votes to 82. In December 1952, the Bevanites complied with the decision of the PLP, and formally disbanded. On 28 January 1953 the NEC ordered that the 'Tribune Brains Trust' be investigated by subcommittee to see if it too constituted a party within a party. On 18 February 1953, while the subcommittee did criticise them as against the spirit of recent PLP decisions, no ban was imposed.

Bevan was becoming increasingly disillusioned and frustrated with domestic politics, and before the end of the month set off on a trip to Israel, India, Burma and Pakistan. In a speech in Delhi on 28 February 1953 to the Indian Council of World Affairs, Bevan set out his conception of foreign policy. He made a key distinction between a 'third force' (which he advocated) and a 'third bloc', which he saw as dangerous. The US and the Soviet Union were intransigent; what 'India and other nations wanted to do was to prevent other nations from lining up with either *bloc* or getting sucked into the cauldron'. Bevan's vision of the world was not tri-polar; rather, it was multi-polar. The emergence of a third 'group' of countries in addition to the two superpowers would only reinforce the existing problem, which he saw as a 'kind of demonology'. The world had its gods and devils: the debate was which was which.[35] In August, he and Jennie Lee visited Yugoslavia, and in December they went to Egypt. Bevan's reputation abroad was growing. In June, Crossman visited the Italian Socialist leader, Pietro Nenni. Nenni held Bevan in high regard, and came to stay with him and Lee.[36]

At the start of the 1953–4 parliamentary session, for the second year in a row Bevan stood against Morrison for the deputy leadership of the party. Morrison won by a similar margin of 181 votes to 76, with both candidates' votes slightly down. When Bevan secured a ninth-placed finish in the elections for the Parliamentary Committee, there was a palpable sense that the infighting was at an end. Bevan was now back in the fold. That hope was shattered on 13 April 1954 when Bevan took the despatch box in a parliamentary debate and in doing so totally undermined Attlee. The Foreign Secretary, Anthony Eden, had made a statement on the containment of Communism in the Far East. The US Secretary of State, John Foster Dulles, was coming to London to argue for the setting up of a South East Asia NATO as a counterweight to Chinese influence. Of particular concern was the recent success of Communist insurgents in French Indochina. Attlee, conscious of the twin problems of containing Communism but also maintaining party unity, took no firm position in the debate, thus enraging Bevan, for whom the virulently anti-Communist Foster Dulles personified America's ideological crusade against Communism. After Eden thanked Attlee for his contribution, Bevan rose: 'Is the right hon. Gentleman aware that the statement which he has made today will be deeply resented by the majority of people in Great Britain? Is he further aware that it will be universally regarded as a surrender to American pressure?'[37] The next day, Bevan resigned from the Parliamentary Committee on the issue of South East Asia policy, which meant that a vacancy was created. Under the standing orders of the PLP, the position would be offered to the recipient of the highest vote in the previous Parliamentary Committee elections who had not been successful in securing a place.

As luck would have it, that person was Harold Wilson. Despite his support for Bevan on South East Asia, Wilson *did* decide to take Bevan's place, and, when he announced his decision to the other Bevanites, it was clear that he had previously discussed the matter with Crossman. Mikardo felt that from that moment on Bevan never fully trusted Crossman.[38] Crossman rather brutally told Bevan that it was now more likely that Wilson would be prime minister than that he would be.[39] Bevan's instincts on Crossman were sound. The two men had discussed Bevan's behaviour in the debate against Attlee. Crossman was unhappy with Bevan's failure to consult beforehand. He told Bevan that attacking Attlee openly was a poor tactic. Surely building Attlee up for his stand on the hydrogen bomb was a better policy, since strengthening Attlee would weaken Gaitskell and Morrison, thus moving the party to the left? Bevan disagreed: 'We have to expose the futility and weakness of the little man.' There was, however, more than an element of Bevan trying to justify himself *ex post facto* after a loss of temper. Crossman remembers him looking sheepish when discussing the matter. In any event, Crossman reported the whole conversation with Bevan to Wilson: 'I also said (I think I had better tell you this) that what he had done was to weaken his own position and strengthen yours enormously.'[40] It was obvious that Wilson was making moves on the political chessboard. According to Wilson's biographer Ben Pimlott, Bevan had taken 'a friendly, avuncular interest in Wilson, and became one of the few politicians (as well as one of the first) to cross the Wilsons' doorstep in Southway'.[41] However, the political reality was that Wilson needed to emerge from Bevan's shadow to pursue his own ambitions. Later in the year, Crossman married his third wife, Anne McDougall. Wilson deliberately absented himself from the wedding on account of the presence of Bevan and Lee.[42] Dalton's jibe that he was 'Nye's Little Dog' carried weight.

Further Bevanite controversy erupted over the issue of German rearmament. In Europe the main Anglo-American concern in 1954 was to achieve the twin aims of West German independence and the inclusion of that country into the Western defence organisation. The French had proposed a 'European Defence Community' (EDC) as early as 1950, principally to dilute the effect of German rearmament. The agreed NATO policy was for an EDC with a European army at its disposal that would include a West German element. However, the French attraction to their own proposal declined, as they wanted neither German rearmament nor a lack of control over their own military as part of the EDC. The matter was continually put off by the French, until Pierre Mendès-France, prime minister of France from June 1954, finally put the matter to the National Assembly on 30 August 1954. This killed off the proposal, since the assembly voted to postpone discussion of the issue indefinitely.[43] Entreaties from Henri Hauck, a Labour attaché at the French embassy, to Barbara Castle for the British left to drop its opposition to the EDC to save Mendès-France fell on deaf ears. While Mendès-France was not a socialist, the alternative, Hauck argued, was a more pro-American French leader. Mendès-France was a friend of Bevan's, and had visited him at his home. Castle pointed out that Mendès-France favoured bringing Germany into the Western alliance, which the Bevanites did not.[44] As Barbara Castle put it: 'it is the growing nationalistic fervour in the Federal Republic under Chancellor Adenauer's leadership which alarmed most of us.'[45] Adenauer had initially proposed a West German paramilitary police force in August 1950, and argued for a German military contribution to a European army.[46]

Tribune published a pamphlet, *It Need Not Happen: The Alternative to German Rearmament*. Bevan took the lead in producing the pamphlet, which argued that Germany could be reunited, but that it would need the agreement of the Soviet Union. Arming West Germany not only had the potential to threaten the Soviet Union, which was not conducive to providing an international environment in which the German problem could be debated and resolved, but also the newly armed country might seek to unite itself with the east with a new war. Matters came to a head at the 1954 party conference, held from 27 September in Scarborough. The issue provoked great debate in the hall. Bevan paced up and down in his hotel room developing his speech. He was concerned about the dangers of open competition with the right of the party, but he saw the issue of German rearmament as one of fundamental principle. He knew only too well that Gaitskell, Morrison and their allies in the unions had great capacity to cause problems for him. But Lee urged him not to be restricted in what he was saying by a fear about how Morrison would react.[47] The NEC proposed an emergency resolution, which Attlee recommended on 28 September: 'It means that we should be asking the National Executive Committee to meet the European Socialists to try and find if we can agree on a common policy for controlling German rearmament and making sure that if Germany is rearmed she will be rearmed under control on our side.'[48] The resolution was carried by 3,270,300 votes to 3,022,000. The rival resolution from the Amalgamated Union of Foundry Workers, agreeing about the need for a democratic and united Germany but opposing German rearmament, was narrowly defeated 3,281,000 to 2,910,000.

It was not a good conference for Bevan. Having lost twice to Morrison in elections for the deputy leadership, he now took on Gaitskell in an election for party treasurer, giving up his constituency seat on the NEC. He knew he was fighting a losing battle. Gaitskell had the big union bosses, with their bloc votes, lined up behind him. Bevan's frustrations found an outlet at a *Tribune* rally on 29 September 1954, when he made his remark about the 'right kind' of leader of the Labour Party being a 'desiccated calculating machine'. Bevan duly lost the treasurership to Gaitskell by 4,338,000 to 2,032,000 votes.

For all these political setbacks, Bevan did have some cheer in his personal life. In the summer of 1954, Bevan and Lee purchased Asheridge Farm in Buckinghamshire for £15,000. Bevan hankered for space after his nine years living in London. With its heavy entrance door and wide oak staircase, the house, set in 54 acres, was the ideal country retreat. Bevan insisted on trying to farm the land. It was not a large holding, but nonetheless he upgraded the cowsheds, built up a Guernsey herd of cows, and added pigs. At the time of his death in 1960, the *Western Mail* reported that he had 1,200 chickens, a number of pigs and a herd of beef cattle.[49] This was a welcome distraction, providing him with a haven of peace away from political controversies. Sometimes he simply preferred staying there to attending lunches with Crossman and other Bevanites.[50] Bevan and Lee were not short of money, either. Bevan was able to make money from penning newspaper articles, and friends such as Sir Charles Trevelyan provided funding. Jack Hylton, the famous 1920s and 1930s band leader who went on to form the light entertainment-company Jack Hylton Television Productions Ltd in 1955, also provided cash, though Bevan did share this money with political colleagues to help with election expenses.[51] Lee kept money in an account to spend on treats for Bevan, who could continue to indulge his taste for fine wine.

The Bevanite controversy climaxed in an attempt to expel Bevan from the party in the early part of 1955. Expulsion would have been of great advantage to Gaitskell, since Bevan would not even be eligible to stand against him in a future leadership contest, let alone threaten to beat him. Gaitskell forensically set out the case on three grounds in a paper to Attlee.[52] The first was Bevan's intervention in the Commons on the proposed South East Asia NATO. The second was that, in a special party meeting on 9 February 1955, Bevan moved a motion seeking to reconfirm Attlee's Commons statement of 18 November 1954 that talks with Russia on Germany should take place and that he wished to move such a motion in the Commons Chamber. However, there was no agreement in the Parliamentary Committee that placing such a motion on the order paper was a desirable method. More detail was sought on a Soviet promise of elections, and Bevan's proposal was defeated by 93 to 70. This did not stop Bevan putting down a motion on 15 February 1955. On 24 February, Attlee moved in a party meeting to condemn Bevan, with the vote carried by 132 to 72. The third arose from the government debate on the hydrogen bomb in March 1955. A Labour amendment recognised the value of nuclear weapons as a deterrent. Attlee's view was that the American testing of the hydrogen bomb (H-bomb) – a far more powerful nuclear weapon than the atomic bomb (A-bomb) – changed the nature of warfare completely.[53] Conventional armies were obsolete; there were only two viable options: peacemaking and deterrence. The PLP had voted to support the government's plans to build a British hydrogen bomb. Bevan openly confronted Attlee in the debate, asking whether the use of nuclear weapons was favoured in circumstances where the opponent was only using conventional weapons. He was one of 62 MPs who abstained rather than vote in favour of the Labour Party amendment. Nonetheless, Attlee reacted to Gaitskell's paper with caution. He did not want to see Bevan expelled from the party.

Bevan's clash with Attlee marked a break between Bevan and Bevanites such as Crossman, Wilson and Freeman. Crossman supported Attlee's line in the debate, since he wanted Britain to be 'independent of America and using its power to mediate between East and West'. He saw no other way of doing this.[54] Bevan's argument was that there was no moral difference between the atomic bomb and the hydrogen bomb, since both would produce 'indiscriminate slaughter of human beings'. Bevan's criticism of Churchill was for his failure to put forward a constructive strategy of negotiation with the Soviet Union. He mocked Churchill's promise to 'meet the Soviet leaders and talk tough and then have supper. The last supper, I presume.' Bevan said he could meet the Soviets *immediately*, and that a failure to do this was reckless. Attlee was aligning Labour with this, so he could not support his party's amendment.[55] This was hardly Bevan's finest hour. After all, he had supported Britain having an atomic bomb on the same basis that Crossman supported the hydrogen bomb: keeping British foreign policy independent of the US. Crossman believed that it was another example of Bevan's poor decision making. He berated Bevan for his behaviour since his resignation from the Parliamentary Committee, labelling it 'wild and harmful'; he was cutting, telling Bevan that he was now 'further from effective power and nearer to the danger you mentioned of becoming a Jimmy Maxton.'[56] The memory of the disaffiliation of the ILP in 1932 was still fresh in Bevan's mind. He dreaded becoming a peripheral figure of little influence.

Bevan was in despair. He knew that the Bevanite group did not present him with a viable route to power. The controversies had taken their physical toll. In the summer of 1955, Dalton observed: 'His hair has suddenly gone quite white, and his bushy eyebrows too. And his face the colour of beetroot. This may be the fresh air of the farm, or it may be drink.'[57] An incident in his private life illustrates the personal strain he was under. On the late evening of Saturday, 3 April 1954, at around 9.50 p.m., Bevan collided with a coach on the London–Oxford road. He fled the scene, which is hardly creditable behaviour. At Beaconsfield Magistrates Court on 7 May, he was fined £20 for dangerous driving and £5 for failing to stop after an accident. He was also disqualified from driving for three months. Bevan was defended by the Labour MP Sydney Silverman, a qualified solicitor. Controversy that Bevan had received special treatment was generated by his 'secret letter', which was handed in to the chairman of the bench, Sir Norman Kendal, and which outlined special mitigating circumstances that led to a substantial reduction in the fine for failing to stop. Sir Frank Newsam, the permanent secretary at the Home Office, noting the large volumes of comment on the matter, suggested writing to Kendal himself, who duly responded: 'we did not do anything for Bevan which we should not have done for any accused person.' Bevan's explanation for failing to stop was that 'he knew that if he did his name would be flashed to London and his mother-in-law was not well and alone in her house and would be pestered out of her life by every journalist in London before he could get home to protect her'.[58] Bevan certainly adored Lee's mother, who was ill with cancer during this period. The alternative explanation is that Bevan was accompanied by a famous titled woman whom he did not want to expose to scandal.[59] The strain also affected Jennie Lee, who found herself before the magistrates in Chesham, Buckinghamshire, a year later. On 4 April 1955, she had pulled out late from a pub car park onto a main road, in front of a van that had to brake violently to avoid colliding with her. She drove across the street, onto a pavement, causing two pedestrians to jump out of her way and pinning another against the door of a house. Lee pleaded guilty to driving without due care, was fined, and accepted 'an error of judgement'.[60]

On 7 March 1955, the Parliamentary Committee met to consider how best to deal with Bevan. With only Jim Griffiths, Harold Wilson, Hugh Dalton and Alf Robens against, the recommendation was to withdraw the whip. Two days later, the committee went further and decided that when the matter came before the PLP, the committee would consider it a vote of confidence. Bevan was ill, so the PLP did not meet until 16 March. Fred Lee, the MP for Newton in Lancashire, put forward an alternative motion of censure, but that was defeated by 138 votes to 124, and the whip was withdrawn from Bevan by 141 votes to 112. The theatre of battle now moved to the NEC, which would have to consider whether to expel Bevan from the party. There was a flurry of correspondence from local parties and trades councils to representatives on the NEC against the expulsion. Bevan still, however, had implacable enemies in the trade unions. One private letter to Gaitskell, possibly written by TUC general secretary Sir Vincent Tewson, is particularly damning; 'Somewhere along the road [...] Nye ceased to be of use to democratic socialism and became a rogue elephant – a menace to the movement.'[61]

It was Attlee who intervened decisively in the meeting of 23 March 1955: 'Bevan should be asked to prepare a statement for the NEC, and submit to questioning on it by a subcommittee of the Executive, which would report back to the full body.'[62] This was approved by the tight margin of 14 voted to 13. Attlee quickly took control of the situation. He met Bevan, who agreed a statement of apology. By the time the subcommittee met on 29 March, events were already in train, and the NEC met the next day and accepted Bevan's apology by 20 votes to six. The party whip was restored on 21 April and the matter was concluded. In his study of Labour Party disciplinary issues, Eric Shaw sets out a variety of reasons for the failure to expel Bevan: Ian Mikardo's daughter changed her wedding date so that her father was available; Jean Mann, a right-wing opponent of Bevan, did not vote to expel him; and the coming general election, together with boundary changes, meant that those searching for seats were wary of incurring the wrath of party members by voting to expel Bevan. But Shaw ultimately cites Attlee's position as the key: 'Another decisive factor – which, alone, probably turned the table – was Attlee's opposition to expulsion.'[63] In this assessment, Shaw was entirely correct. Attlee – ever the seeker of consensus – had once again promoted party unity above other considerations. He saw keeping Bevan inside the party as the preferable option.

With the Labour Party in turmoil, Anthony Eden, who had replaced Winston Churchill as prime minister on 7 April 1955, called the general election just eight days later, on 15 April, with polling day set for 26 May. Bevan did all he could do to promote internal party unity in the face of the external threat, and sought to make a virtue of the fact that Labour MPs had been able to debate major issues facing the nation during its period in opposition, contrasting this with the slavish, blind loyalty of Conservative MPs. The point itself was probably the best that Bevan could do in the circumstances, but the image he chose to describe the Conservative MPs caused great controversy, as he compared them to Gadarene swine in the Gospel of Matthew who rushed into the sea and died. As David Butler put it, in his study of the election: 'It was only an innocent biblical metaphor, but it was eagerly seized on by Conservative speakers and journalists as evidence that the man who had once called them vermin was now calling them swine.'[64] Winston Churchill, recently retired as prime minister, spoke in his Woodford constituency on 16 May 1955, and savaged Bevan as:

> The politician who causes most anxiety to every friend and ally of Britain all over the world. Undoubtedly his influence in the Socialist Party is great and growing. This is the man, this voluble careerist, who has called at least half his countrymen all sorts of names which have been helpful on our party platform.[65]

Bevan was mentioned by name in 10 per cent of the Conservative candidates' election addresses.[66]

The Conservatives won a comfortable victory, taking 49.7 per cent of the popular vote against Labour's 46.4 per cent, and winning 344 seats to Labour's 277. Michael Foot lost Plymouth Devonport to the Conservative Joan Vickers by just 100 votes. Bevan was singled out for blame for Labour's defeat. As the Tory *Sunday Dispatch* put it: 'Apart from their own impressive record as a government, the Conservative Party's greatest asset was undoubtedly Mr Aneurin Bevan.' On the left, the *News Chronicle* cited the internal Bevanite conflict: 'The Labour Party has assuredly got what was coming to it [...] A party which offers itself as the Nation's only alternative government cannot afford the confusion of civil warfare.' No serious commentator could escape the fact that the internecine conflict in the Labour Party was a key factor. Even the more measured approach of the *Sunday Times* cited division:

> The Labour Party has reaped the fruits of its divisions; but, more than that, it has patently failed to inspire even its own supporters with faith in a dynamic programme. Its old policies have been exhausted or discredited and there is nothing to take their place, except the snares of

neutralism and the exercises of the Left intellectuals, which are deeply distrusted by trade unionists.[67]

The *Daily Mirror* offered two other reasons: the old, tired, weak leadership and the inferior Labour Party organisation. None of these explanations, however, can hide the underlying reason for the defeat: this was, after all, the 'age of affluence' and consumerism to which the Conservatives were far more attuned than Labour. Bevan's argument that the Tories were 'merely picking the fruit of the trees that Labour had planted' could not persuade swing voters.[68] Bevan knew that if he was to exercise greater influence over the political and electoral destiny of the Labour Party he could not afford to have another parliament like 1951–5.

Chapter 16

The Pragmatic Bevan, 1955–7

A ttlee finally announced his intention to retire on Wednesday, 7 December 1955. After 20 years in the post, the election to succeed him was to be conducted remarkably swiftly. Nominations for the new leader had to be in within 48 hours, with the election itself the following Wednesday, 14 December. The identity of the three nominated candidates was entirely predictable. Morrison, by now 67, faced the two leaders of the next generation. Gaitskell was 49, and Bevan 58. Age was undoubtedly a crucial issue between Morrison and Gaitskell. When Gaitskell won the leadership, the first thing he told Morrison was: 'Herbert, there is nothing but the years between us.'[1] By electing Gaitskell, the PLP was settling the leadership issue for a considerable period, rather than electing the ageing Morrison with the possibility of a further leadership election not too far down the road. Hugh Dalton had run Morrison's leadership campaign in 1935, but now organised for his protégé and friend Gaitskell. In a none-too-subtle speech during Labour Party Conference week in Margate in October 1955, he said that, if Attlee resigned, 'we must have a younger man, not a caretaker Leader, approaching seventy years of age'.[2] Attlee never really forgave Morrison for his manoeuvrings against him, and by hanging on to the leadership himself he had effectively denied him the top job.

The final numbers cast in the ballot were a disappointment to both Bevan and Morrison. Gaitskell won an absolute majority on the first vote, taking 157 votes to 70 for Bevan and 40 for Morrison. Bevan's vote was entirely in line with the 'Bevanite' following in the PLP. He had been unable to push his vote far beyond the 57 whose rebellion in March 1952 had marked the start of the 'Bevanite' controversy. He had actually done slightly better when he had stood against Morrison for the deputy leadership in November 1951, when he had attracted 82 votes. This is not, however, to suggest that the so-called 'Bevanites' voted en bloc for Bevan. Harold Wilson, sensing the momentum behind Gaitskell, had promised him his support as early as October 1955.[3] In return Gaitskell appointed him Shadow Chancellor of the Exchequer. John Freeman's view is that Bevan and Wilson 'both saw Gaitskell as the real enemy to their intentions'.[4] In reaching an accommodation with Gaitskell, Wilson was avoiding open confrontation. The age difference between Bevan and Wilson was the same as that between Morrison and Gaitskell. At 39, ten years junior to Gaitskell, Wilson could compromise and bide his time to pursue his leadership ambitions.

Bevan's options during this contest were very limited. He understood power innately and appreciated the strength of Gaitskell's support. In January 1981, at a conference at Wembley Stadium, the Labour Party, to the consternation of those who were shortly to leave to form the Social Democratic Party (SDP), adopted the 'electoral college' method of electing the party leader. Rather than it being a matter only for MPs, the electoral college was now split between MPs, party members and the trade unions. For Bevan, this change was 30 years too late. That is not to say that before 1981 party members' views were irrelevant. They could lobby their MPs at local party meetings, and could not be ignored entirely. But this was no substitute for having a section in an electoral college in which Bevan would have been dominant. This said, it would not have been a panacea. Bevan's unpopularity with certain trade union bosses would have balanced his strong position among party members. But an electoral college would have changed the dynamics of the Bevan–Gaitskell competition for the party leadership.

As it was, Bevan had only had one realistic option, and he exercised it. He met Herbert Morrison for dinner and discussed how, together, they could halt the Gaitskell bandwagon.[5] Ten Labour MPs subsequently signed a letter to Bevan asking him to withdraw in favour of Morrison provided Gaitskell did so too. Bevan was agreeable. Gaitskell, however, had no incentive to vacate his position of strength, and sailed to victory. The contest for the deputy leadership was postponed until after the Christmas recess. It was a two-horse race between left and right, though this time Bevan faced Jim Griffiths. In the ballot on 2 February 1956, Bevan lost by 141 votes to 111. One new MP, Will Stones, who sat for Consett, told Dalton that, while he had voted for Gaitskell for the leadership on the basis of his wide electoral appeal, he had supported Bevan as his deputy: 'his roots are in the working class.'[6] The problem was that not enough MPs agreed.

Disappointment was following disappointment. In October 1955, Gaitskell had won an even more resounding victory over Bevan for the post of party treasurer than in the previous year, taking over 5 million votes. That, together with the leadership and deputy leadership election defeats, starkly demonstrated that Bevan was banging his head against a brick wall. Constructed by the right of the PLP, with their supportive union bosses, Bevan could neither climb it nor smash it down. In his 1955 campaign for the treasurership, he openly attacked the trade union bloc votes: 'Because of their structure this means in reality that it is the leaders of the general unions who are in effective control of the Labour Party.'[7] Deeply frustrated, he did not behave magnanimously in his latest defeat. The loss to Jim Griffiths was the final straw. After Griffiths had spoken, Gaitskell asked if Bevan had anything to say. Dalton remembered that Bevan responded with a 'contemptuous, scowling gesture, seen by all, and remained seated'.[8] Some 48 hours later, on Saturday, 4 February, Bevan addressed a *Tribune* rally in Manchester. It was Bevan at his most ill-tempered. He said that whether he was a team player depended very much on the game he was being asked to play. Without naming Gaitskell, he savaged his Hampstead Set, who asked for new thinking: 'You would have thought the history of the socialist movement began when they came into it.' He asked if the party should 'burn the books' and cast William Morris and Karl Marx aside. He said he was not interested in the Labour Party unless it aimed to transform the dominance of the propertied classes in society.[9]

The speech proved to be cathartic. Bevan could do nothing about the new dynamics of power at the top of the PLP. Gaitskell was well established in post. Unless Bevan wanted to continue as a rebel accused of being unable to cooperate with others for the greater good, he had to work with Gaitskell. Sensing this, after the weekend, Gaitskell called Bevan in to see him and offered him the post of Shadow Colonial Secretary. While Bevan would unquestionably have preferred the role of Shadow Foreign Secretary, he knew he had little option but to accept the offer. In public, Bevan asserted his views on 'free speech' in the Labour Party for only a few more weeks, attacking the 'secret meetings and caucuses' of the parliamentary Labour Party and Labour groups on local councils, which led to members being disciplined by the party when they spoke out against the line agreed by the majority. 'Damn it all,' he lamented, reflecting on his own position, 'you can't have the crown of thorns *and* the thirty pieces of silver.'[10]

As it turned out, Bevan was the Shadow Colonial Secretary for less than ten months. Bevan hated what he considered to be the old-style colonialism displayed on the Tory benches. He believed that Britain should treat people around the world as equals, not subordinates. On one occasion his passion got the better of him, and he told the Movement for Colonial Freedom on 8 June that they should give the British government 'as much trouble as possible'.[11] On the whole, though, he was a very competent Shadow Colonial Secretary who quickly got to grips with the issues. He disliked the way the Colonial Office invariably backed the acts of its governors, not least in Cyprus. Only weeks after Bevan took on the portfolio, a Cypriot leader, Archbishop Makarios, was deported from the island. Alan Lennox-Boyd, the Secretary of State for the Colonies, announced this to the Commons on 12 March 1956. Two days later, in the Commons, Bevan effectively savaged Lennox-Boyd's fait accompli: 'The question of not having a debate beforehand is very serious indeed, because we have grave responsibilities to our Colonies and dependencies.'[12] In the event, Cyprus eventually gained its independence in 1960, but was partitioned in 1974 after the Turkish invasion.

It was the start of a good year for Bevan. In April 1956, Khrushchev and the Russian premier, Nikolai Bulganin, visited London. The NEC invited them to a dinner in the House of Commons on 23 April. The event itself became a farce, as the visitors were taken to task on the repression of political opponents at home. George Brown harangued Bulganin and Khrushchev during their speeches, frequently interrupting. Gaitskell presented Khrushchev with a list of social democrats who were imprisoned in Soviet satellite states. Bevan backed him up: 'There are Social Democrats in prison in countries under the immediate control of the Communist Party.' Khrushchev tried to argue that they were 'enemies of our country', but Bevan attacked him: 'We have not the same interpretation of the enemies of the working class as Comrade Khrushchev has.'[13] Khrushchev was furious, but Gaitskell and Bevan had offered a united front.

When the Egyptian president, Nasser, nationalised the Suez Canal in July 1956, Bevan made a considerable impact on the issue, far greater than that of the actual Labour Shadow Foreign Secretary, Alf Robens, whose position inevitably came under threat as a consequence. Bevan set out his position in *Tribune* on 3 and 10 August. He was considered and thoughtful. He saw the argument for Nasser nationalising the Suez Canal since he had no truck with the canal being treated as an imperial possession; however, he argued that waterways that were vital to world commerce should be internationalised, and administered by a supranational body. Bevan's pro-Israeli sympathies were also at play here. Nasser sought to portray himself as the legitimate leader of Arab nationalism; Bevan criticised Nasser for elevating Egyptian nationalism above all other priorities, including economic and social reform of Egypt. While Nasser's actions may have put the issue of the Suez Canal onto the international agenda, Bevan's view was that he had actually damaged the reputation of underdeveloped countries with his aggression. What Bevan did not condone was the use of force by the British and French governments to recover the canal. On 30 October, Eden announced to the Commons that Israeli troops had invaded Egypt, and urged Israel and Egypt to cease conflict. He gave a 12-hour ultimatum to Nasser to agree to British and French troops being stationed in Port Said, Ismaïlia and Suez. None was forthcoming, so Britain and France took military action. On 1 November, Bevan spoke in the Commons. While he was consistent in his condemnation of the use of military force, he expressed some sympathy for the strategic problem the government faced: 'It would be a very great mistake for us, even on this side of the House, to indict the existing Government as though they bore the exclusive responsibility for the existing state of affairs.' He argued:

> mankind is faced with an entirely novel situation [...] The advent of the hydrogen bomb has stalemated power among the great Powers. The use of the threat of war, which formerly helped to solve many international difficulties – and when the threat could not do it war tried to do it – is no longer available to statesmen. The great Powers are stalemated by their own power.[14]

This contrasted with Gaitskell's less compromising stance. Broadcasting to the nation on 4 November, he said: 'We have violated the Charter of the United Nations. In doing so, we have betrayed all that Great Britain has stood for in world affairs.'[15] Gaitskell called for Eden to be replaced as prime minister. As a consequence, Gaitskell, rather than Bevan, was singled out as being unpatriotic. Henry Fairlie, writing in the *Daily Mail* in May 1957, said: 'When the Suez Canal was flowing through Sir Anthony Eden's drawing-room – so the accusation goes – Mr Gaitskell was playing political ducks and drakes in its muddy waters.'[16] Bevan and Gaitskell's approaches may have been an effective combination of outright condemnation and measured reflection, but it was the US that reined in Eden on Suez. For the US had a sharp financial weapon to use on Britain. The Americans could block a British drawing on the IMF, without which the run on the pound seemed likely to drain Britain's foreign-exchange reserves. Eden took this threat seriously, and announced a ceasefire on 6 November. Meanwhile, the Tories seized on Bevan's performance and used it to discomfit Gaitskell. Adapting the musical *Annie Get Your Gun*, R. A. Butler, then the Leader of the House of Commons, teased: 'Anything Hugh can do, Nye can do better.'[17] It emerged that Britain and France had actually colluded with Israel in creating a pretext for an invasion; Bevan was quick to see this:

> We believed at first, and it subsequently transpired to be the case, that going in to separate the forces of Egypt and Israel was a mask and behind that mask the real intention was to achieve the objectives which the prime minister has had in mind ever since last August – the seizure of the Canal and, of course, the downfall of Colonel Nasser.[18]

On 4 November, in the midst of the Suez crisis, the Soviet Union invaded Hungary, to suppress the revolt that had started on 23 October when a rally on the streets of Budapest turned into a mass demonstration demanding a reinstatement of the deposed prime minister, Imre Nagy, and an end to Soviet rule. Bevan's view was that Eden's invasion of Egypt took away any claims by Britain to be on the moral high ground in international affairs in so far as aggression against other countries was concerned: 'I do not believe that it is possible to separate the events in Hungary from the events in Egypt.'[19]

Bevan's good year became an excellent one. He also won the post of party treasurer at the third attempt. The 1956 party conference took place over the first five days of October in Blackpool. With Bevan finally on board, Gaitskell retired from the post, leaving Bevan in a straight fight against George Brown. The Belper MP was another standard-bearer of the party right, but this time, Bevan prevailed by 3,029,000 to 2,755,000 votes. Bevan now had three large unions on his side: the NUM, the NUR and the Union of Shop, Distributive and Allied Workers (USDAW). On 5 October, *Tribune* celebrated with a front-page headline: 'Oh! What a Beautiful Morning!' This was overdone. It was not that the party had suddenly become Bevanite. Rather, with Bevan now at least formally back in the fold, the opposition to him had lessened. Frank Cousins had replaced Deakin at the TGWU, and, in the words of his biographer, Geoffrey Goodman, 'stuck his neck out and invited Bevan and the Bevanites to forget the old differences and work together for a united Party'.[20] When the new parliamentary session opened on 6 November, there was political momentum behind Bevan. Gaitskell duly acknowledged it by promoting him to Shadow Foreign Secretary in place of Robens; Bevan took third place in the Parliamentary Committee elections later that month.

For all this political success, the personal strain of the 1950s was becoming more intense. When Bevan was in Scotland in June 1957, Jennie Lee drafted a letter to him that she never, in the event, sent. However, she published part of the letter in *My Life with Nye*, and her biographer, Patricia Hollis, published the letter in full. There was one heartfelt paragraph, the welling up of emotion from her many years of supporting him. Lee was going through a very tough patch. She had lost her father and Ma Lee had cancer. She was afraid her brother's heroin addiction would become public knowledge. She was considering standing for the women's section on the NEC as part of a slate of five candidates that also included Jo Richardson, Lena Jeger and Judith Hart.[21] In despair, she now wrote: 'Many people sustain you by believing in you, and no human being can go on without some encouragement [...] Why don't you give me a little self-confidence?' She continued: 'Or is it your real and unshakeable conviction that nothing I do matters a damn, is it just me, my personal stupidities and inadequacies, or is this your personal conviction about all socialist activity?'[22] Of course, Bevan did think that what Lee did mattered. But, with his journey back towards the centre of political influence within the party, Bevan was becoming more and more focused on regaining political power for Labour. He wanted to leave his time of powerless opposition behind him.

Bevan's speech at the Labour Party Conference in Brighton on 4 October 1957 has often been seen as the apogee of his accommodation with Gaitskell. It created not only a political divide, but also a great emotional rupture on the left of the Labour Party. Seen not only as mere repudiation of previously held beliefs, the speech produced an intense experience both in the conference hall itself and in his friends, as reflected in their response to him afterwards. In reality Bevan's position on the hydrogen bomb was entirely consistent with the position he had taken on the Attlee government's decision to manufacture an atom bomb. Emotionally and intellectually, he did not wish to tie Britain too tightly to America. José Enrique Rodó was far more influential than Marx in Bevan's critique of capitalist society. Bevan thought American capitalism vulgar and materialistic at the expense of human spiritual fulfilment. Take this quotation from Rodó's *Ariel*, with which Bevan enthusiastically concurred:

> North American prosperity is as great as its inability to satisfy even an average concept of human destiny. In spite of its titanic accomplishments and the great force of will that those accomplishments represent, and in spite of its incomparable triumphs in all spheres of material success, it is nevertheless true that as an entity this civilization creates a singular impression of insufficiency and emptiness.[23]

Bevan did not believe that the void should be filled by religious faith; rather, he saw human expression in artistic, as well as materialistic, terms. He was very pleased when, as Minister of Health, he had persuaded the Cabinet to legislate to permit local authorities to spend money on 'cultural activities'.[24]

Bevan was never blind to the problems of the Soviet Union either. He did of course seek to use Nikita Khrushchev's conception of national planning to support his argument that a planned economy was superior to unchecked free markets. He lauded the launch of Sputnik into space in October 1957 as evidence of Soviet technological superiority over the US. Khrushchev certainly wanted to out-compete the West. In his book, *The Cold War*, John Dunbabin characterises the Soviet leader's strategy thus: 'Here Khrushchev looked partly to what he hoped would prove the manifest attractiveness of the communist system.'[25] Bevan saw those attractions and often included them in his articles in *Tribune*. But Bevan also expressed deep concerns about the Soviet Union. Geoffrey Goodman recalls seeing

Bevan at a party conference in the 1950s on his return from the Soviet Union, and asking him how he saw it.[26] Bevan gave a thorough assessment. He never did see socialism as an end point; rather, he felt society would be in a continuous state of development. This was not in the sense of a Trotskyite 'continuous revolution', but a sense that the community would constantly evolve. This is not to suggest that Bevan foresaw the wholesale collapse of the Soviet Union in 1991, but he did feel that the Soviet system would have to transform fundamentally to survive. Bevan had a naturally critical mind. While his friends on the international stage included Nehru and Tito, he still saw the problems in the 'non-aligned' countries as well. Bevan took Tito to task about the fate of socialist politicians victimised in Yugoslavia because they disputed the leader's power: 'Milovan [Djilas], I gather has been stripped of all his public offices and has now retired into private life [he had been placed under house arrest]; whilst apparently the same thing has happened to Vlado [Vladimir Dedijer].'[27] Bevan would not turn a blind eye to events simply because it suited his argument. Besides, both men were his friends.

Bevan's position on the hydrogen bomb in October 1957 was unsurprising; what had been more surprising was his earlier opposition to it. On 2 December 1955, he had been questioned on the inconsistency of his then support for the atomic bomb and his opposition to the hydrogen bomb. Bevan's comparison, 'drowning in a bath with drowning in an ocean', certainly pointed up the fact that the H-bomb was by far the more powerful nuclear weapon, but it was hardly a convincing answer.[28] He *had* disliked what he saw as ideology dominating American foreign policy. He had put the case on different issues in the 1951–5 parliament for Britain to be less tied to the foreign policy of the US. But he had to accept the nature of geopolitics. From November 1945, when Britain had accepted the American loan, the Atlantic alliance was a reality, with Britain as the junior partner. Without its own nuclear deterrent, Britain would be completely subservient to the US: that, after all, was the argument that had previously convinced him. While the H-bomb had superseded the A-bomb (Britain exploded an H-bomb in April 1957), that had not changed. If anything, Suez had reinforced Britain's junior position. To have a measure of independence from American foreign policy, and standing on the world stage, Britain needed its own H-bomb. Without it, Bevan could not even *try* to set about his idea of using non-aligned countries to break the deadlock of the Cold War.

On Wednesday, 25 September 1957, Bevan attended the NEC's Home Policy Committee meeting having returned from Russia where he had had discussions with Khrushchev. Crossman dismissively recorded: 'No doubt he has come back from Russia, sold by Khrushchev on his role as peacemaker in the nuclear age.'[29] In the meeting itself Bevan drew a distinction between the international socialist position and the position of the party. Bevan reported that Khrushchev had given an assurance that if Britain ceased H-bomb *testing* Russia would follow, meaning that America must follow too. Then Bevan also set out that a decision to stop H-bomb testing would have the consequence of a decision to stop UK production of all nuclear weapons. Indeed, Bevan had attended the Fifth Congress of the Socialist International in Vienna from 2 to 6 July 1957 and their resolution proposed 'that the cessation of H-bomb tests should not be made dependent on first obtaining agreement on the remainder of a disarmament programme or on the sort of political settlements upon which the Western Powers were insisting'.[30] Bevan's position was now in favour of multilateral nuclear disarmament, not a British decision to cease nuclear testing as a matter of principle. It was Sydney Silverman and Barbara Castle who pressed Bevan on the specific position of British unilateral ending of tests. They asked if Bevan was evading this. One obvious line that Bevan *could* have taken is a commitment to unilateral nuclear disarmament in the event that negotiations with other countries failed. This was not a choice he was willing to make: 'Nye said that he had thought about this matter more than any other political problem in his whole life and had come to the conclusion that this [renouncing unilateralism] was what he meant.'[31]

By the time of the NEC meeting of Monday, 30 September 1957, the tension was building. Crossman recalled: 'I suppose we were all feeling terribly ratty as a result of not knowing whether Nye was going to blow up the party this week.'[32] The nuclear-disarmament debate revolved around three resolutions, numbers 23, 24 and 25. Number 23 called for an international disarmament agreement and was uncontroversial. Number 24 demanded rejection of British nuclear weapons. Number 25 demanded that Britain immediately stop H-bomb testing. The NEC agreed that the 23rd and 25th resolutions should be accepted on the basis that number 25 meant suspension, and that number 24 should be rejected. Crossman put forward a compromise position where number 24 was remitted on the basis that the party should consider the case for a non-nuclear defence policy.

It was at this point that Bevan weighed in against the case for unilateralism. He asked the NEC how the repudiation of nuclear weapons could be done without consulting the Commonwealth, without ending the alliance with the US and without jeopardising the Baghdad Pact (which sought to curtain Soviet influence in the Middle East).[33] Russia 'would be appalled if we suddenly abdicated'. Bevan's emphasis was practicality: 'Surely it would be a mistake to take all the cards out of the hand of Labour's next Foreign Secretary.'[34] Crossman was stunned: 'I think this was the first occasion on which the majority of those present had heard one of Nye's intellectual emotional somersaults. I lent across to Sydney [Silverman] and said, "You are the only honest man here."' Silverman lacerated Bevan: 'He, Sydney, could not see anything else in this speech but a complete and utter repudiation of everything for which Nye had stood three days before. He, Sydney, was going to stand where he had stood.' Sam Watson told Crossman afterwards that he delivered to Bevan a bottle of whisky and ten accompanying little bottles, five of tonic water and five of soda water. By the end of the evening Bevan could not tell the difference. They had spoken for two nights: 'Sam had gradually got Nye round to the mood of the next Foreign Secretary and the representative of the world's mineworkers.'[35]

One interpretation from Crossman is that this was a victory for Gaitskell:

> every member of the executive has watched this test of strength between Hugh and Nye, and knows from inside the qualities which each man showed – Hugh firm, obstinate, not very adroit but keeping his eyes fixed on the long-term objectives; yet immensely more powerful personally, practically more skilful but completely failing to achieve his long-term objectives because of the pendulum swing of his emotions.[36]

Naturally, it was difficult for those close to Bevan to explain his behaviour. Some indulged in wishful thinking. Tom Driberg's view was:

> When the full truth is known of the three days of agonising private argument that proceeded that conference I believe it will be found that Bevan sacrificed his personal convictions for the sake of the unity of the party which he cared for more than he cared for himself, and because it was put to him overwhelmingly that there was no hope of electoral victory and of a socialist cabinet unless he did so.[37]

Michael Foot was another who could never accept that Bevan could really get along with Gaitskell, demonstrating that the teams around politicians often generate far more bad feeling than the main protagonists.

Bevan did not speak as he did out of a forced compromise with Gaitskell. Rather, he thought carefully about what he was going so say, and said it for a simple reason: he believed in it. Having spoken to Khrushchev immediately before the conference, Bevan had concluded that unilateral disarmament would be futile. Over the days before the speech he practised as he always did, pacing up and down, throwing lines at people, testing their reactions. He walked the promenade with Geoffrey Goodman, at the conference as industrial reporter for the *News Chronicle*. However, the phrase 'naked into the conference chamber' may have actually come from the Durham miners' leader whom Bevan had known since the 1930s, Sam Watson.[38]

The atmosphere in the conference hall was electric.[39] There was a swirl of emotions among Bevan's friends and admirers. A combination of hurt and anger spilled out from the conference floor back to Bevan, leading him to declare: 'If you carry this resolution and follow out all its implications and do not run away from it you will send a British Foreign Secretary, whoever he was, naked into the conference chamber.' He added: 'You can always, if the influence you have upon your allies and upon your opponents is not yielding any fruits, take unilateral action of that sort.' When speakers are under most pressure they tend to fall back on their most central beliefs, and as members shouted from the floor at Bevan to disarm now his response was framed in terms of power: '"Do it now," you say, "Do it now." But it is not in your hands to do it now. All you can do is pass a resolution.' He pressed on: 'What you are saying is that a British Foreign Secretary gets up in the United Nations, without consultation – mark this; this is a responsible attitude! – without telling any members of the Commonwealth – without consultation at all. And you call that statesmanship? I call it an emotional spasm.'

Bevan had a strong practical case for the position he took:

> If war broke out between the USA and the Soviet Union, this country would be poisoned with the rest of mankind. What we have, therefore, to consider is how far the policies we are considering can exert an influence [...] over the policies of the USA and of the Soviet Union.

Bevan made the case for multilateral disarmament:

> if resolution 24 is read with its implications it means that as decent folk you must immediately repudiate all the protection and all the alliances and all the entanglements you have with anybody who uses or possesses or manufactures hydrogen bombs. That is our dilemma. I find it a very, very serious dilemma.

Bevan accepted the moral case against the hydrogen bomb: 'No nation is entitled to exterminate an evil by invoking a greater evil than the one it is trying to get rid of. The hydrogen bomb is, of course, a greater evil than any evil it is intended to meet.' But he countered it with a plea for negotiating strength: 'What I would like to have is the opportunity of exerting influence upon the policies of those countries [the US and the USSR], but this is not the way to do it.' The final section of the speech was directed squarely at his comrades who supported resolution 24:

'You have not realised that the consequence of passing that resolution would be to drive Great Britain into a diplomatic purdah.' The resolution was backed overwhelmingly: by 5,836,000 votes to 781,000.

Bevan's friends and supporters were devastated. The left-wing political cartoonist Victor Weisz, known as Vicky, mournfully sketched a cartoon of Gandhi: 'I went naked into the conference chamber.' Jimmy Cameron of the *News Chronicle* was stunned.[40] Crossman thought the speech 'ghastly'; he watched 'this vast, blue-suited figure and bright red face with the iron grey hair – angry (and he's terrific when he is angry), mortally offended and repudiating with violent indignation the suggestion that he was grooming himself as foreign secretary. It was this suggestion which really brought out his best replies.'[41] For Foot, even recalling Bevan's words was an intense experience; for him, it was the most 'heartbroken audience he [Bevan] had ever addressed in his life, and he would not relent.'[42]

Bevan and Gaitskell's closeness on policy was further demonstrated by the document on nationalisation, *Industry and Society*, which was overwhelmingly endorsed at the same party conference. An amendment moved against *Industry and Society* by the NUR was defeated by 5,383,000 votes to 1,442,000. His supporters again saw this document as an example of Bevan compromising with Gaitskell to maintain party unity. On 11 October 1957, Jennie Lee argued that 'We *can still win* the fight for more nationalization [my emphasis]'. Having been with Bevan for his pre-conference meeting with Khrushchev, she sympathised more with his renunciation of unilateralism, and supported him in making his speech. She had more reservations on nationalisation. Specific proposals on nationalisation were limited to the two industries that had been put back into private hands by the 1951–5 Churchill government: iron and steel; and road haulage. Bevan certainly took a pragmatic view that the unity of the party was vital in securing a general-election victory over the Conservatives. But – as with his speech at Dorking in 1950 – Bevan was not arguing for a long list of industries to be taken into public ownership. He knew the political dangers of this from experience. The real issue for Bevan with *Industry and Society* was that he again missed the chance to set out a vision of an industrial management structure in which workers could play a full part. Instead, it was Tony Crosland who took the opportunity to move the debate on nationalisation forward. The Morrisonian nationalisation model involved industries being taken over by the government, run by appointed boards, and compensation paid. Crosland's idea was that the government should purchase shares in the 200 or so largest companies in Britain. Hence profit could be shared between private shareholders and the public realm. Bevan was circumspect in his comments, making one light criticism in the *News of the World* that increasing government share ownership would not be 'even the main way in which public ownership will be increased'.[43] What Bevan did not say was what the main way would be. If he had reservations about the Morrison model, and the Crosland model, what was the Bevan model? Here, the Bevanites' lack of attention to domestic policy was also exposed as a problem. Belief in public ownership was an abstract principle without practical proposals for implementation. Thus, it was the revisionists who provided a practical policy to show that public ownership should be seen as a means with which to achieve greater equality, rather than an end in itself. As Peter Shore later wrote: 'Gaitskell had himself claimed that "socialism is about equality" [...] the sooner private ownership was contracted and public ownership extended, the sooner would Gaitskell's own goal of greater equality be reached.'[44]

After the conference, Foot and Bevan continued their argument on the pages of *Tribune*. Bevan and Foot's names appear on the banner of the issue of 11 October 1957. Bevan asserted his continuing left-wing credentials with an article on the space race: 'nevertheless it must be credited to the Russian system, that like the rocket mechanism itself, it retains the capacity for successive explosions, proving that the original thrust of the October 1917 revolution is by no means exhausted.'[45] Foot's response to Bevan was sharp. The number of concessions to Bevan's position were few. Foot did concede that Bevan hated nuclear weapons as much as anybody else, but Foot's purpose was clear: 'I tried to explain why I remain entirely unconvinced by Aneurin Bevan's argument.' Foot struck at the heart of Bevan's case, namely that Nikita Khrushchev's position was central to his change of mind:

> indeed it is suggested in some quarters that the Soviet government may not be altogether opposed to the stand Aneurin Bevan took at Brighton. That may well be true but it would be strange indeed if Mr Khrushchev backed Britain having the bomb because he wanted Britain to be suitably equipped to deter Mr Khrushchev. We live in a comic-opera world but it is not quite as comic as that.

Foot also repudiated the argument that without a nuclear bomb Britain could not exercise influence in the world. He pointed out that both Communist China and Tito's Yugoslavia were exerting influence without a nuclear-weapons capability: 'Similarly Britain without the bomb could still exercise immense influence on the United States.' Foot insisted that the position of the unilateral disarmers was not simply to destroy the weapons and then have nothing further to do with negotiation:

of course that is one answer to Aneurin Bevan but if it were the only answer then there would be justice in his further charge that those who are stopping the manufacture of the bomb are more concerned with satisfying their own consciences than in taking effective measures to secure world peace; that they prefer the ivory tower to the conference table where alone peace can be secured; that they would be quite ready to put Britain in 'diplomatic purdah'.

Foot's attack was sustained: 'how long and in what condition is Aneurin Bevan, or anyone else for that matter, prepared to accept our present military dependence on the United States? Forever and on any condition? Of course not.' Foot was almost derisory, setting out that Bevan conceded that if negotiations failed then unilateralism would be the answer. The breach was a significant one, leading Foot to become part of the Campaign for Nuclear Disarmament (CND), which became a dominant cause for the rest of his life, and he spoke passionately at its launch in Central Hall, Westminster, on 17 February 1958.[46]

The rupture between Bevan and Foot is skirted over in the second volume of Foot's biography of Bevan. This is not, however, to suggest that Foot ever hid anything about the extent of his falling out with Bevan. He told his biographer Kenneth O. Morgan about one incident that occurred at some point during 1958, after a reception at the Polish embassy at which both men had been drinking. Bevan and Jennie Lee returned to the Foots' house in St John's Wood afterwards. Foot and Bevan argued about the issue of nuclear weapons and it came close to violence. Neither man struck the other, but Bevan did smash one of Jill Foot's antique Sheraton chairs on the floor before storming out. Only the intervention of the wives – Jill Foot rang Jennie Lee the next day – effected a sort of personal truce.[47] In June 1958 Gaitskell went so far as to suggest to Hugh Dalton that Foot was encouraging Beaverbrook to attack Bevan; and indeed Dalton claimed to have seen references to Bevan in the *Daily Express* and *Sunday Express* suggesting that he was not on Beaverbrook's approved 'White List'.[48] Jennie Lee became unhappy with Foot's writings in *Tribune*, which she saw as unfair to Bevan. In April 1959, Foot penned an editorial praising Yugoslavia: 'The Yugoslavs think they have done pretty well these last ten years in forging a new society by their own unaided efforts.' He was sharply rebuked by Lee, who accused him of writing the sort of untrue material that press relations officers in Yugoslavia would put out to support Tito. She reminded him of the fate of Tito's enemies, Dedijer and Djilas. Lee also pointed out that Foot had omitted that Yugoslavia had been protected from Soviet aggression by the West's making it known that such Soviet action would be treated as an act of war involving NATO. She remarked acidly:

'I know you will remember that Nye was the first to give this firm promise.'[49] There also is a revealing entry in Crossman's diary in June 1959, the best part of two years after Bevan's Brighton speech:

> When I suggested we might recreate an informal group with Nye to discuss nuclear weapons, Michael told me he had no kind of relations with Nye. Only once this year had he seen him. He had been over to the farm just after Aldermaston [Foot attended the marches on the Atomic Weapons Research Establishment in the West Berkshire village]. He had a pleasant afternoon but only because each side had carefully avoided discussing anything serious at all. In fact, Michael and Nye have had no political contact for over a year.[50]

Geoffrey Goodman, who saw both Bevan and Foot during this period, remembered one particular comment from Bevan about Foot, when he dismissed Foot's political credo on the basis that, deep down, Foot remained a Liberal.[51] This was undoubtedly a criticism, aimed squarely at the heart of Foot's fidelity to the socialist cause. For Bevan's socialism was never fixed in time; it evolved and changed, and one of his gifts as a politician was that he was able to react and respond to the changing environment that he found around him. Bevan did not simply see a need to evolve his tactics in order to reach his ultimate socialist goal. Rather, for him, that flexibility was a central tenet of his socialism. It was more than a question of tactics. As he had argued in *In Place of Fear*, the socialist had to deal with the world *as it was*, not how he ideally wanted it to be. Barbara Castle's view is that Bevan and Foot were both rare people, able to 'pass through the temptations of the fleshpots, enjoy them, learn from them and emerge unscathed'.[52] Both Bevan and Foot, despite their forays into party rebellion, retained absolute personal integrity. The issue with nuclear weapons was such that neither was willing disingenuously to finesse his sincerely held view. Neither could sympathise with the position of the other. Both were unquestionably objective enough to *understand* the arguments of the other, but neither could appreciate *why* the other took the view he did. The problem was that the bomb, and what to do about it, laid bare the differences between Bevan and Foot.

An accommodation with Gaitskell was something Bevan understood as necessary in order for the Labour Party – and him personally – to hold power again. Crossman characterised it as a 'tacit agreement by the Left and the Right that we should stop a futile argument about abstract principles and concentrate on reaching practical agreements on working policies.'[53] But Bevan did not simply concede issues to Gaitskell. The two men had never been that far apart on nationalisation;

both believed in the principle of public ownership; the questions were its extent and form. On the latter point, Bevan certainly failed to grasp an opportunity to move the debate forward, but he did not sacrifice the ultimate goal of nationalisation. On foreign policy, Bevan's 1957 repudiation of unilateral disarmament was not wholly inconsistent with his previous views. It was consistent with the view he took of the necessity for Britain to have its own independent deterrent when a Cabinet minister. In fact – and this was a problem for his relationship with Foot – the inconsistent period was when he was a Bevanite. Foot found it far more difficult than Bevan to set aside his personal animosity towards Gaitskell. He could not even bear to sit in a television studio alongside Gaitskell.[54]

Bevan was far more of a pragmatist than Foot. He could not understand why Foot could not see, as he had set out in his Brighton speech, that unilateral nuclear disarmament was something that a country could *always* do, but why would you do it if you could at least try to use the weapons you held as bargaining chips on the negotiating table to bring about the simultaneous disarmament of other countries first? Foot, on the other hand, could not understand why Bevan would not see that the possession of the H-bomb was futile since a nuclear war would inevitably bring about universal destruction. There is also a deeper point here. Bevan saw the hydrogen bomb from the point of view of the statesman, the British Cabinet minister who would be faced with the issue in practice. Foot saw it from the point of view of the protester, the marcher on Aldermaston, the dissenter who shouted loudly at the politician to change his mind and see sense. That, in a nutshell, was the difference between Bevan and Foot. Bevan was most comfortable as a man of power. Foot was most comfortable as a man of dissent. This period is an important one in the Bevan–Foot story, for what it reveals about their relationship as much as anything else. But too much can be read into the negativity of the two men towards each other. They did what close friends often do during a disagreement, and lashed out at each other. It is a saving grace that they reconciled before Bevan's death.

Chapter 17

The Final Years, 1958–60

A s it turned out, Aneurin Bevan's Brighton speech did not mark the beginning of the end of the Labour Party debate on nuclear weapons. Far from it. Some five months later, Crossman was despairing of the way the issue seemed to pervade all political discussions: 'We now seem to have got into one of those dialectical clinches in this country when there is only one subject of political conversation.'[1] Bevan had had his say on the issue. Now, as Shadow Foreign Secretary, he set about preparing for the position in government.

Some issues were straightforward. He was in favour of allowing China into the UN, and excoriated the Americans for preventing it: 'the vision of the leaders of the United States falls so lamentably short of the material power they command.'[2] The US still did not diplomatically recognise Mao's China, only Chiang Kai-shek's Formosa. For Bevan, China could be part of a new world order in international affairs, and was a country outside the bipolar cold-war division. On Cyprus, an issue upon which he had made an impact as Shadow Colonial Secretary, Bevan continued to offer support to the Greek Cypriots. In this he was entirely in tune with his former allies. Jo Richardson, for example, took to the stage at the 1958 Labour Party Conference in Scarborough to express her solidarity with the Greek Cypriots. Bevan wrote in *Tribune* on 10 October 1958 that Turkey (whose minority Turkish population on the island sought partition) and Britain had to make concessions in the way that the Greeks themselves had: 'The Greek Government and the leaders of the Greek Cypriots have given up their demand for Enosis; that is, for union with Greece. Up until quite recently this was the main stumbling block to a settlement.' He argued that the time had come for 'a constitutional settlement offering peaceful progress towards eventual independence'. An agreement was initially reached between Turkey, Greece, the Turkish and Greek Cypriots and the UK in February 1959 ('the Zurich and London Agreements'), and Cyprus became independent in 1960.

Bevan also managed to unite the Labour Party on the issue of the East and West both disengaging from Germany. Bevan had already expressed concern about Adenauer's West Germany and whether the 'military revival of Germany once more makes her the arbiter of European destinies'.[3] On 2 October 1957, at the UN, the Polish foreign minister, Adam Rapacki, proposed that, if East and West Germany agreed that there would be no production or storage of atomic weapons on their territory, the Polish government would give a similar undertaking. Czechoslovakia also supported the proposal; thus there would be a nuclear-free zone in central Europe. Bevan supported this, as he saw this as an opportunity for areas of the world to be independent of the two superpowers. He thought the Russians had seriously underestimated the extent to which their prestige had been undermined by their invasion of Hungary, and felt it worth exploring whether the Soviet Union would agree to something along the lines of the plan and contribute to world peace.[4] After visits to Bonn and Berlin, Bevan further argued in the House of Commons on 20 December 1957 that the demilitarisation of East and West Germany was a price the German people would be willing to pay for reunification: 'I spoke to very large numbers of Germans and I put the proposition forward in the frankest possible way and had a very great measure of support, especially in Berlin.'[5] But Khrushchev was not going to concede East Germany. His view of East–West relations was resolutely adversarial.[6]

Despite the failure of the European Defence Community, the six member states of the European Coal and Steel Community (France, West Germany, Italy, Belgium, the Netherlands and Luxembourg), established in July 1952, signed the Treaties of Rome in March 1957, creating a common market and an atomic-energy community, bringing the European Economic Community (EEC) into existence from January 1958. Bevan was strongly opposed to the idea, for two reasons. First, he saw a contradiction between arguing for economic planning and the very concept of a free-trade area. But, more importantly, he opposed the EEC because of its threat to the sovereignty of national parliaments. Bevan believed in the British Parliament as the vehicle for the advance of socialism. He thought the EEC would undermine its authority. The whole idea was 'the result of a political malaise following upon the failure of Socialists to use the sovereign power of Parliaments to plan their economic life'. If all went well with the EEC, national parliaments would end up doing nothing; in bad times it would be considered an offence for national parliaments to interfere, thus they would become irrelevant.[7]

Bevan's travelling was a feature of his period as Shadow Foreign Secretary. In April 1957 alone, he visited India and Pakistan, Iraq, Israel, Malta and Turkey. Nehru welcomed him with open arms in India, where he addressed both houses of the Indian parliament, and argued for an ideal of the Commonwealth at a time when India was considering leaving. The most controversial trip, however, was to Italy in February 1957, with Crossman and Morgan Phillips, to the Italian Socialist Party conference in Venice. Crossman records that Bevan was 'ebullient, impeccably dressed in his beautiful new suit, fresh white linen, with his handkerchief falling out of his breast pocket, pretentiously discussing the qualities of Italian wine, pretending to knowledge of Venetian architecture'.[8] On 1 March 1957, the *Spectator* ran an article attacking Bevan, Crossman and Phillips for drunkenness during the conference.[9] All three successfully sued for libel, though the *Spectator* later claimed (after all three men were dead) that Crossman had boasted some 15 years later that he and Bevan were 'pissed as newts'.[10]

In late October, Bevan left for only the second visit of his lifetime to the US, on Cunard's *Queen Mary*. He was not particularly impressed by his three-week tour, and criticised the young Americans he had met for their 'distressing conformism – a tendency to think in headlines'. Yet the trip was an important pointer to the kind of Foreign Secretary Bevan would have been had Labour won the 1959 general election. He gave eight lectures to largely academic audiences, met Foster Dulles at the State Department, and the Supreme Court Justice Felix Frankfurter. On 12 November, he met President Eisenhower in the White House. He met with some hostility, particularly at the Economic Club in New York, where he rather unwisely compared the Chinese revolution with the American War of Independence. Nonetheless, he relied on his natural charm to win over those he met. At the *Washington Post*, the editorial staff presented him with a book and a box of cigars. He emphasised his hostility to Communism; on 5 November, he told students at Dartmouth College in New Hampshire: 'I am not a Communist, and I find many features of Soviet society utterly repugnant.' Bevan knew that Eisenhower had a negative attitude towards renewed negotiations with the Soviet Union, but put his own case clearly. He argued that Russia's launching of Sputnik satellites into space the previous month had proven right their claim that they could send ballistic missiles to American cities. His message to Eisenhower was that World War III would be on the American doorstep. The two superpowers were 'now capable of mutual mass destruction' and an East–West summit was desirable. Bevan arrived back at Southampton on 19 November having not only delivered his message, but also displayed his personal magnetism. *The Times* lauded Bevan's way of 'softening his barbs by a beguiling if not puckish bonhomie'.[11]

In December 1957, he visited Adenauer in Bonn, and again relied on his personal charisma to deliver an unpopular message. On 12 December, he spoke at the Council of International Affairs in Bad Godesberg and argued for German 'detachment', by which he meant that Germany could be unified but 'no German Government could choose sides or weapons'.[12] This limited national sovereignty was a difficult message for a German audience, so the following evening, speaking in West Berlin, he struck a lighter note. *The Times* described Bevan's speech as 'witty […and…] often interrupted by spontaneous applause and laughter'. He warned that the Soviet launch of Sputnik was a warning about Russian technological advances, and again argued for an area of disengagement in central Europe.[13]

On other issues, Bevan was accused of shifting position. Crossman charged him with directly contradicting himself. One example occurred in March 1958. On 6 March, there had been a joint meeting of the TUC and the NEC, considering a joint draft statement of policy. Frank Cousins, supported by Bevan, had proposed including a commitment not to employ nuclear weapons pre-emptively. Rather, they would only be used in retaliation if used on Britain first. The debate moved on to the issue of using nuclear weapons in response to a Russian attack using conventional weapons. Crossman continues: 'Nye then made a powerful speech, saying that he himself would rather see a Russian conventional army occupy Britain than make the world a charnel house by using nuclear weapons first.'[14] On 17 March, there were talks held on defence on an ad hoc basis in Gaitskell's office. Gaitskell and Bevan were joined by Jim Griffiths, George Brown, John Strachey, Denis Healey, Lynn Ungoed-Thomas and Crossman.[15] With Ungoed-Thomas 'a rather uneasy ally', Crossman formed the view that the others 'had all got Nye completely convinced that the proper sharp division is no longer between conventional and nuclear weapons but between controllable weapons, including conventional and atomic tactical on the one hand, and uncontrollable thermo-nuclear on the other.' Bevan later added: 'We've got to get it across to the Russians that, if they attack us, we shall create a belt of destruction behind the Russian armies right across the satellite countries.' Crossman noted: 'This from the man who, only ten days ago, was saying that he would rather see Britain occupied by Russia than use a nuclear weapon!' He added:

> I came to the conclusion that Nye had been squared by an agreement under which, if he will become a supporter of nuclear tactical weapons, the others might agree to a declaration against the use of thermo-nuclear weapons first. This kind of deal seems to me absolutely odious but I suppose it's practical politics.[16]

It was not actually odious for Bevan to seek a consensus position. He was never a man to be pushed into anything unwillingly. Bevan probably had gone too far with his language in the meeting on 6 March. It was hardly the first time he had allowed his mouth to run away with him. The underlying issue, however, was complex. Once Bevan had set aside the doctrinal purity of unilateralism, he was inevitably faced with the messy compromises of seeking multilateralism in an ever-changing world situation.

This was not a comfortable period for Bevan. He worried about the prospect of Gaitskell as prime minister. When he dined with Crossman: 'Straightaway he began to discuss the hopelessness of Gaitskell's leadership, his lack of instinct, his tendency to look over his shoulder and to hold up his finger to see which way the wind was blowing.' Bevan was frustrated with Gaitskell's stubbornness: 'If he disagrees with you, that's that, and you can't influence him. He isn't a man who is impressed or influenced. He is just scared or runs away. Gaitskell's piddling all the time for fear of losing the election and every principle is sacrificed.'[17]

Harold Macmillan, who had succeeded Eden as prime minister in January 1957 following the latter's resignation over the Suez crisis, called the general election on 8 September 1959, with polling day set for 8 October. The general expectation was that the Conservatives would win.[18] As it happened, when Macmillan made his announcement, the new unity of Bevan and Gaitskell was aptly symbolised as they were together in Moscow for conversations with Khrushchev. Bevan had even covered up for Gaitskell, standing in for him at a press conference when the Labour leader had got drunk on vodka and could not be woken.[19] They flew back to the UK the next day. There was, however, a marked difference in the dominant themes in their speeches throughout the election campaign. Gaitskell made 53 major speeches, in comparison to the 37 Attlee had made during the 1955 campaign. Gaitskell focused on economics, and argued that the inequalities in wealth were unnecessary. Aside from his line that the Conservatives would 'almost completely destroy the Health Service', Bevan sought to keep the Suez issue alive: 'In the eyes of the world the guilt was the guilt of Macmillan and his friends. But if, on October 8, you vote for the Tories once more, then the guilt will be yours.' Bevan also savaged the Conservatives' fitness to govern:

> I think Mr Macmillan and Mr Selwyn Lloyd [then Foreign Secretary] will be regarded by the rest of the world as men with blood on their hands and guilt in their hearts, because I know there are hundreds of millions of people all over the world who say that we ought not to make them the ambassadors in the Conferences that are to come.[20]

Bevan's contribution to the campaign was again through traditional campaign speeches. The 1959 general election was the first covered by television, and Macmillan made a well-received eve-of-poll broadcast. Bevan's death in 1960 meant that he never had the chance to master the art of the new media for campaigning purposes. With his rhetorical style, his forte was addressing large crowds. How well that would have adapted itself to television is a moot point. He had not been a regular radio performer. It was said that Bevan had been kept off the airwaves during the 1950 general-election campaign, 'due in part at least to his discomfort at the microphone'.[21] While he was the master of the oratorical barb, he was also unquestionably capable of charming his audiences. However, Bevan's method of *developing* argument in a speech was less suited to the television studio. In 1959, he was best used on the stump. The reaction to Bevan was less hostile than in previous elections; Frank Cousins had now replaced him as 'the [left-wing] bogey of the Conservative press'.[22]

On Monday, 28 September, speaking in Newcastle, Gaitskell promised that there would be no increase in standard or other income tax rates 'so long as normal peacetime conditions continue'. Macmillan gleefully used Bevan's words against the Labour leader, criticising him for building a 'false reputation' on an 'addiction to figures' which 'led Mr Bevan to describe him as a desiccated calculating machine. That is now only a half-truth. I think he is still rather desiccated but his reputation as a calculator has gone with the wind.'[23] Bevan thought that Gaitskell had committed a major error, since he felt that the promise was wholly unrealistic and unlikely to be believed by the electorate. The fight did not leave Bevan; he still fought on to win, but he knew how difficult it was going to be for Labour to win a majority.

Bevan was accompanied on his campaign tour by his close friend, the journalist Geoffrey Goodman. They often spoke until late into the night over whisky. Goodman had first met Bevan at a conference in St Pancras Town Hall just after the launch of the NHS in July 1948. Bevan demanded to know which newspaper Goodman was from. When Goodman told him it was the *News Chronicle*, Bevan grinned: 'Ah, well boy, it's not a bad paper as bad papers go.'[24] Goodman was also a friend of Michael Foot, and often wrote anonymously in *Tribune*. He was a man of staunch integrity, and entirely trustworthy. Bevan knew this, and, as a consequence, opened up to him in a way he did with only a few people. He even trusted Goodman to draft newspaper articles for him. Just before the election campaign of 1959, Goodman had joined the *Daily Herald*, and his first assignment was to report from Bevan's campaign. Two themes ran through Bevan's speeches: foreign policy and the domestic economy. He felt the Conservatives were failing to appreciate that the zenith of the British Empire had long passed, and – choosing his words carefully to avoid a newspaper splash on a split with Gaitskell – pressed for the use of the public sector to influence the level of employment.

His private mood was one of depression. His discussions with Goodman roved far and wide. He worried that, as British Foreign Secretary, he might not have the wholehearted backing of Prime Minister Gaitskell, given their past rivalry. Bevan had a very strong sense that '[w]e are moving into a world in which smaller and smaller men are strutting across narrower and narrower stages'.[25] What exactly Bevan meant by this needs to be considered carefully. He worried about political leaders around the world failing to grasp the scale of change. He was concerned about Khrushchev in the Soviet Union. In particular, Bevan could not accept the certainty of Communism. His argument was that for socialism to flourish it had to grow like a plant. The problem was that you did not start with a set of gardener's instructions describing exactly how the plant would grow. Using a different metaphor, Bevan saw the whole process of historical development as a moving stage. He spoke about technological advances, the development of instant communications, how leaders would cope with the social and political change that would bring. He scoffed at attempts to decide what the 'end point' of society might be; for him that was absurd and self-defeating. Society would evolve and continue to evolve. However, that did not mean that you should put aside your own vision of how society should be. Bevan still thought that politicians needed a vision of the kind of society they were seeking to create.

Goodman had a distinct sense that, while Bevan was unaware of the stomach cancer that was to kill him nine months later, he intuitively felt that he had very limited time left. Jennie Lee was worried about Bevan's health throughout the campaign, during which he fell ill with flu. He spoke for Lee in Cannock, and then, at her insistence, he retreated to Asheridge, where he was laid up for a few days on doctor's orders. Much to his disappointment, the speaking engagement he then had to cancel was for Foot, who was seeking to regain Plymouth Devonport. Goodman worried that there was a more serious problem with Bevan's health.[26]

The Conservatives won a comfortable victory, taking 49.4 per cent of the popular vote against Labour's 43.8 per cent, and winning 365 seats to Labour's 258. In the aftermath of the defeat, on the suggestion of Gaitskell, Bevan agreed to take on the role of deputy party leader, with Jim Griffiths standing aside. However, he was never well enough to make a great impact. The party conference had been moved to the weekend of 28–29 November, for a general-election post-mortem. There he made his final great speech. On the opening day, Barbara Castle was voted into the chair, and had spoken passionately: 'It simply won't do to say that nationalisation is out of date.' Gaitskell 'gave a wintry frown'.[27] Gaitskell himself then argued that – on balance – nationalisation had cost the party votes. Labour had to make clear that nationalisation was not an end in itself, but a means to a more equal society. Foot took to the platform and attacked Gaitskell for his 'uncertainties'. The *Sunday Pictorial* speculated: 'Bevan's speech today could mark a break between Labour's two top personalities and could start a new struggle for power within the party.'[28]

Bevan actually made a brilliant play for ideological unity. For both Castle and Gaitskell had cited Bevan's dictum on conquering the economy's commanding heights: 'So Barbara and Hugh quoted me. I used to be a boy, taught as a boy [...] one of Euclid's deductions: if two things are equal to a third thing, they are equal to one another.' He went on: 'If Euclid's deduction is correct, Barbara and Hugh are both equal to me, and therefore must be equal to one another.' He argued that the differences of opinion in the party were not so as to cause permanent division. His peroration was one of his finest:

> I have enough faith in my fellow creatures in Great Britain to believe that when they have got over the delirium of the television, when they realize that their new homes that they have been put into are mortgaged to the hilt, when they realize that the moneylender has been elevated to the highest position in the land, when they realize that the refinements for which they should look are not there, that it is a vulgar society of which no decent person could be proud, when they realize all those things, when the years go by and they see the challenge of modern society not being met by the Tories who can consolidate their political powers only on the basis of national mediocrity, who are unable to exploit the resources of their scientists because they are prevented by the greed of their capitalism from doing so, when they realize that the flower of our youth goes abroad today because they are not being given opportunities of using their skill and their knowledge properly at home, when they realize that all the tides of history are flowing in our direction, that we are not beaten, that we represent the future: then, when we say it and mean it, then we shall lead our people to where they deserve to be led.[29]

Bevan, who felt increasingly tired after the election campaign, went into the Royal Free Hospital on Gray's Inn Road on 27 December, ostensibly for an operation on a stomach ulcer.

The most poignant of the final Bevan–Foot meetings is the one that took place just before Bevan's operation. Lee asked Foot to take in some books and have a 'rough argument' with Bevan to make things seem normal. Bevan berated Foot for his 'quixotry' in standing again in Plymouth Devonport, which he had failed to regain. Bevan said he could not win the seat. Foot quickly scotched the suggestion that Ebbw Vale might soon be available, and Bevan gently laughed at Foot's suggestion that his forthcoming operation was for the best, remembering that that was what his whip, Charles Edwards, MP for Bedwellty, used to say during internal party struggles. Bevan, not that he needed to, reaffirmed his commitment to the Labour Party: 'never underestimate the passion for unity and don't forget it's the decent instinct of people who want to do something.' After such a profound statement of what it meant to belong to the Labour Party, Bevan and Foot then idly chatted about the two books Bevan had at his bedside, J. B. Priestley's *Literature and Western Man* and H. L. Mencken's *Treatise on the Gods*. Reflecting on the discussion, Foot felt: 'I hadn't argued but everything else was back to normal between us.' When Foot next saw Bevan, two days after his operation, 'he had all the tubes and paraphernalia stuck in his sides and could not speak or give any real sign of recognition.'[30] But at least the two men had reconciled. Bevan eventually returned home from the Royal Free Hospital on 14 February 1960.[31]

Just over a month later, he gave his final major interview, to the *Guardian* at Asheridge. He was on fine form, and mocked Macmillan for reading political biographies: 'My experience of public life has taught me to know that most of them are entirely unreliable. I would rather take my fiction straight.' He also derided those who wrote political memoirs while still active in public life: 'They do nothing but mischief. If they tell the truth it is hurtful, but usually they don't tell the truth.' He confirmed he had been 'reading newspapers avidly' since they were his 'one form of continuous fiction'. With an eye still on returning to the political front line, he confirmed that he was not seeking re-election as party treasurer now that he was deputy leader.[32] Lee, who had been told by Bevan's friend Dr Daniel Davies that he had terminal stomach cancer, kept the fact from him. When she spoke at his memorial service, she told the gathering: 'Nye was a fighter. He gave blows and took them and did not whine.' She added on a personal note: 'in the six months of his illness Nye never saw a tear.'[33] One of his final visitors was Nehru, who called in having attended a Commonwealth conference.[34]

Death came very quickly, on 6 July 1960. The *Daily Express* reported his final hours in precise detail. Dr Tom Wise apparently arrived at Asheridge in a black Morris car at 11.17 a.m., remaining with Bevan at the house for 33 minutes until 11.50 a.m. Bevan died at 4.10 p.m., and Dr Wise returned at 4.35 p.m. Lee began the telephone calls to let people know at 5.10 p.m.[35] Also present at Asheridge Farm was Bevan's brother-in-law Jack Norris, Arianwen's husband, and John Machen, a physiotherapist and a friend and Mrs McGhee, the housekeeper and secretary. Jack Norris telephoned Arianwen, who in turn told Bevan's sister Blodwen and brothers William and Iorwerth. He telephoned Myfanwy directly. Archie Lush, by then chief county inspector of schools for Monmouthshire, left South Wales for Asheridge on the morning after Bevan's death.[36] Lee received a telegram at Asheridge from Macmillan: 'Please accept my deepest sympathy in your great loss.'[37]

Bevan's memorial service took place at Westminster Abbey. This was unusual for a politician who had never even been a party leader, but the Labour Party requested the abbey on the basis that Bevan was a national figure, rather than the House of Commons Church at St Margaret's Westminster, which would be usual for a parliamentarian. There was a debate in government as to whether the exception for Bevan should be made, but Bevan's old friend, the Bishop of Southwark, Mervyn Stockwood, intervened, and gave a strong case for holding the ceremony at Westminster Abbey. As 'an old and close friend' of Bevan who was comforting Jennie Lee, he said the request came from her, that she did not want the service to be seen as a 'Labour Party stunt', and that Bevan would see it as appropriate, not hypocritical.[38] This was accepted, and the service took place on 15 July 1960 at 6.00 p.m., officiated by the Reverend Donald O. Soper. Hymns included 'Guide Me O Thou Great Redeemer' and 'Jerusalem'. Bevan's actual funeral was a cremation at the Greater Gwent Crematorium, Croesyceiliog, Cwmbran, in South Wales' Eastern Valley. Some years later, on 14 October 1972, another Bevan memorial service took place on Waunpound, a plain on the hill between Tredegar and Ebbw Vale, to mark the unveiling of four stones commemorating him. The stones are in a spot where Bevan held outside meetings to speak to his constituents. There is a central stone that symbolises Bevan himself and three others that point towards the three major towns in his constituency, Ebbw Vale, Rhymney and Tredegar. They are a fitting tribute on the hills upon which he found his magnificent voice.

Conclusion

Greatness may be a difficult concept to define. But there is no doubt that Aneurin Bevan was a great man. On 21 March 1949 *Time* magazine reported that Bevan had stood 'amid the tall black blocks of Bolton's cotton mills in Lancashire and told the assembled workers: "homes, health, education and social services – these are your birth-right."' *Time* noted that these were not the values of life, liberty and prosperity that John Locke had held dear, and took the view that more Britons now agreed with Bevan than with Locke.[1] This is very significant. For it is evidence that in creating the NHS, Bevan had not just created a lasting institution, he had changed the whole British attitude to social services. Health care became a *right*. In the US, the controversy over President Barack Obama's Patient Protection and Affordable Care Act 2010, which introduced a 'penalty' for those who had not taken out medical insurance, was about freedom. The question was about individuals being forced to take out insurance, and freedom for the states in not having to participate in the federal programme. In other words, the American debate still centres on the values of Locke, whereas in Britain the principle of a universal health system free at the point of delivery based on need is so entrenched that the question in British politics is not whether there should be a such a system, but how best to improve the quality of the health care it provides.

Like all great men, Bevan had his unattractive side. He could be stubborn, bloody-minded and irascible. Even to his friends, he could be intolerant and insensitive. At times, Jennie Lee felt unsupported. His unpredictability, particularly in the early 1950s, brought problems. But to appreciate why Bevan felt so angry about injustice it is necessary to understand his background. While Bevan was shaped by the common industrial struggles across the South Wales coalfield, he was a distinctively 'Monmouthshire' figure, a representative of the English-speaking

Welsh Valleys, and a proud Welshman. He was less affected by the Communism of other valleys such as the Rhondda. It is instructive to compare him with the other Welsh miners' leaders of the interwar period. Unlike Bryn Roberts, he did not go on to become a union official, and, unlike Arthur Horner, he did not join the Communist party. Like so many of his contemporaries, his education was a combination of self-teaching and attendance at the Central Labour College.

The political environment in the South Wales coalfield when Bevan was most active locally throughout the 1920s was tough. Bevan's accusatory oratorical stance, in which he stood slightly bent forward, finger pointing, was a product of a political theatre in which the audience was often baying at the speaker. He knew that to sustain an argument orally, quick thinking and a willingness to slap down opponents was essential. It also honed Bevan's greatest oratorical skill, invective. Whether used offensively, or defensively, against hecklers, Bevan was the master of the put-down.

Bevan's burning sense of injustice also had a simple cause. He saw poverty, and its effects on his friends and family, including his father who died of pneumoconiosis. His rage was against a *political and economic system* that could organise the country's resources in such a way as to cause this misery. Poverty and unemployment were not the fault of the individual, but a product of the structure of society. This belief defined his politics. Alongside this great crusade, it is fair to say he was well acquainted with the dark political arts, and was both victim and beneficiary of them. He struggled in SWMF elections against his old tutor, Sidney Jones, as his supporters were less adept at rigging ballots. However, he was the winner in what is perhaps one of the great *coups d'état* of twentieth-century Welsh Labour politics, the unseating of a sitting MP, Evan Davies.

This is not to suggest that the local politics of Wales in the 1920s were especially brutal or savage. Rather, this was the time in which Bevan and his generation came of political age. After the extension of the franchise to include all men over 21 in the Fourth Reform Act of 1918, the Labour Party asserted itself in South Wales local politics in the interwar period, and became the dominant force in parliamentary terms as well. There is a deeper point here. Bevan's rise from Tredegar to the Ministry of Health was representative of political changes in the South Wales coalfield in the first half of the twentieth century. The idea that William Abraham, 'Mabon', had expressed to the miners when Bevan was a boy was to create a coalition of interests between the workers and the employers. Politically, this was expressed in the dominance of the Liberal Party across the coalfield, built on the solid pillar of Nonconformity. However, the society in which Bevan grew up was changing. The union meeting rivalled the chapel as a centre of social life. Bevan may have risen higher, in political terms at least, than his Tredegar contemporaries. But his career exemplifies the increasing self-confidence of the society he grew up in.

Once he entered Parliament, he was often pilloried for living the high life. The 'Bollinger Bolshevik' barb was used to suggest that Bevan had betrayed the very people he had grown up among and represented. Bevan was at home debating issues around Beaverbrook's dinner table. He, quite rightly, considered anybody his equal, from whatever background. He saw nothing wrong with enjoying fine wine or food at the Café Royal. If the criticism that Bevan was a hypocrite for this is accepted, the logical conclusion must be that left-wing politicians should wrap themselves in sackcloth for fear of criticism. Perhaps fittingly, it was at the Café Royal that he proposed to Jennie Lee. Their marriage in 1934 marked a step change in Bevan's personal and political life. It was only then that he broke his final formal ties to Tredegar by giving up his seat on Monmouthshire County Council. He still cared deeply about his constituency, and local people responded by electing him again and again. However, the focus of his life shifted permanently to the national stage. Jennie Lee may have been an unorthodox wife, but she provided stoical emotional and political support to Bevan throughout all the great battles of his career.

Bevan was often subject to personal attacks, which intensified once he came to national prominence as Churchill's arch-critic during the Second World War. Lee even had to intercept hate mail and excrement posted to him. Bevan's at times one-man opposition during the war may have pushed him to the front of the political stage, but it was at a heavy personal cost. In July 1945, credit must go to Clement Attlee for appointing Bevan to the Ministry of Health. It brought out the best in him. At the meeting of the Conservative Party at the Carlton Club on 19 October 1922, Stanley Baldwin called Lloyd George 'a dynamic force' that could be a 'terrible thing'. The same phrase could be applied to Bevan. Unharnessed, as was demonstrated in the early 1950s, Bevan could be destructive. But until his resignation from the Attlee government in April 1951, Bevan channelled his energies into becoming one of the outstanding Cabinet ministers of the twentieth century. For Bevan, political leaders had to be not just in touch with the people, but of them: 'The first function of a political leader is advocacy. It is he who must articulate the wants, the frustration, and the aspiration of the masses. Their hearts must be moved by his words, and so his words must be attuned to their realities.'[2] Judged by this standard, his own, Bevan excelled at the top table of British government, often putting forward the views of working-class Labour voters. Even on housing, where his record is less impressive than on health, he fought manfully in Cabinet to find a way to solve the raw-materials shortage. His aim of building quality housing for the working classes rather than compromising on design was hardly ignoble, even if the electorate ultimately did punish Labour for its record.

It would be an overstatement – and unnecessary – to say he totally lacked personal ambition. Rather, it is fair to say that he could put other considerations above pure personal ambition. This is what he did with his resignation from the government in April 1951. In the final weeks before he left the government, he was incredulous that he was being driven out of government for a paltry sum of £13 million in a total budget of over £4,000 million. There is an element of 'what if' here. Had he stayed in the government in 1951, and not pushed the issues of NHS charges and the defence programme to the limit, he would have had an 'insider' position to make a strike on the leadership. Yet such analysis is fruitless. As it happened, Bevan did not flounce out of the Attlee Cabinet: he resigned because of matters of principle and personality, though the former were dominant. He was willing to compromise to remain in the government, but what he did not do was elevate political calculation about his own personal fortunes above other issues that he saw as important. To criticise Bevan for resigning amounts to saying that he should have been more self-interested.

On policy grounds, the apparently parsimonious Gaitskell is more open to criticism. Gaitskell certainly had a point about health spending not being allowed to spiral out of control. However, he had his £13 million from the health budget to fund a defence programme so large that all the monies allocated to it could never realistically be spent in the proposed timescale. After the resignation, that Bevan was later proved correct that the defence budget was too large to be spent so quickly was, however, scant consolation for the years he spent in uneasy rebellion in the 1951–5 Parliament. Above all, Bevan understood the concept of power, and he knew that the so-called Bevanites did not provide him with a platform from which to obtain the Labour leadership. This is not to say that Bevan was not bloody-minded. He had a capacity to self-destruct. This was shown time and again, whether it was his 'vermin' speech or his resignation from the Parliamentary Committee in 1954. Bevin and Morrison may have been his great political enemies within the Labour Party, but Bevin's much-quoted assessment was wrong. Bevan *was* his own worst enemy.

Another form of counterfactual argument is more productive. Geoffrey Goodman has argued that if Bevan had lived he would have been a British version of Charles de Gaulle. This analysis is prescient. De Gaulle's vision of a 'Europe, from the Atlantic to the Urals' was an expression of a 'third force' foreign policy. De Gaulle saw in Europe an alternative centre of power to the US and the Soviet Union. France would have a foreign policy in contrast to Britain's Atlanticism. Bevan also disliked the division of the world's countries into two rival camps, and worried that the emphasis on arms was at the expense of tackling world poverty. Where he parted company with De Gaulle was on what a 'third force' should be. He saw the EEC as a threat to British national sovereignty. Bevan was a patriot. He believed that, as British Foreign Secretary, he could make a difference: 'I do not take the view that Great Britain is a second-class Power. On the contrary, I take the view that this country is a depository of probably more experience and skill than any other country in the world.'[3] He saw his own contacts with non-aligned countries, such as Yugoslavia and India, as key to his strategy. That he – perhaps alone among leading British politicians of his day – had a high reputation with the leaders of these countries is undeniable. Bevan was not the only British politician to seek some sort of breakthrough in cold-war diplomacy, either. Churchill wanted to hold a 'Big Three' summit between the leaders of Britain, the US and the Soviet Union, and tried to use Stalin's death in March 1953 as the catalyst to bring such talks about. But he could not persuade Eisenhower. Gaitskell's biographer, Brian Brivati, points out: 'Bevanism represented a road for British democratic socialism which advocated an alternative to an alliance with either of the superpowers. It was Gaitskell more than any single individual who ensured that the British labour movement did not take the Bevanite road.'[4] Perhaps; but Bevan never had the chance to be Foreign Secretary. Clement Attlee – on the whole an excellent chooser of Cabinets – would have made Bevan Foreign Secretary had Labour won the general election of 1955.[5] Had Gaitskell won in 1959, Bevan would also have been Foreign Secretary. Consequently, Bevan's 'third force' foreign policy was never more than a laudable aim to break the deadlock of the Cold War.

In office, the likelihood is that he would have had to compromise. Detaching Britain from America was always going to be extremely difficult. Bevan himself had pointed out the problem of the 1945 American loan in Cabinet. Britain's financial dependency on the US was always going to have an impact on its foreign policy. When Britain did act independently of America, in the Suez crisis, it was quickly brought back into line. Certainly Bevan's trip to America in 1957 showed that he could charm them if necessary. His renunciation of unilateralism at Brighton in 1957 was consistent with his pragmatic approach to the Atlantic alliance during his period as a Cabinet minister. Without an independent nuclear deterrent, Britain would be even more subservient to the US in world affairs. That logic applied as much to the H-bomb as to the A-bomb. Bevan may have been repelled by America's ideological aggression – exemplified in McCarthyism – in the early 1950s, but his Brighton speech was practical and realistic: hallmarks of his career. As it turned out, Bevan and Gaitskell never had the chance to settle their disputes in government again. Both were dead by the time Harold Wilson won the keys to No. 10 in October 1964. Crossman's analysis of Wilson's prospects of occupying the nation's top political job when he took Bevan's place in the Parliamentary Committee in 1954 proved far-sighted.

Bevan's reputation as an 'old-fashioned socialist' rests principally on his attitude to domestic economic policy. During the 1959 general-election campaign, Bevan told Geoffrey Goodman one night that history had passed the working class by.[6] There is an argument that the Labour and Trade Union movement had missed a great opportunity in 1945–51. There is no shortage of critics who claim that the Attlee government was not left-wing enough. The Marxist historian Ralph Miliband argued: 'From the beginning the nationalization proposals of the Government were designed to achieve the sole purpose of improving the efficiency of a capitalist economy.'[7] The argument is that the working class was mobilised for the war effort, and the NHS was the foundation stone of socialist development and the creation of new socialist Britain. The difference between critics such as Miliband and Bevan is that Bevan was actually a member of the Attlee government. In making the criticism he is vulnerable to a charge that he himself did not do more while he was in government.

Yet what Bevan actually meant was something slightly different. He believed that the key to power was in the working classes having command of the economy's 'commanding heights'. In the context of nationalisation, this meant working people having a role in management. Bevan had legitimate concerns about the Morrisonian structure of the industries that had been nationalised under Attlee. Bevan thought it a mistake not to have the workers take a greater responsibility for the success of the nationalised industries. As he wrote: 'The advance from state ownership to full Socialism is in direct proportion to the extent the workers in the nationalised sector are made aware of a changed relationship between themselves and the management.'[8] On this issue, Bevan had previously clashed with Will Lawther. Lawther's view was that he did not want to run the coal industry; he wanted to defend his NUM members against the employer.[9] Bevan felt that the working class needed to move to a more positive role in running the economy. This is hardly an extreme position, even if some of his colleagues disagreed. Indeed, in the last two years of the Attlee governments, even Morrison became concerned about the inefficiencies of the models he had himself created. If there is a criticism of Bevan on this issue, it is that he did not offer a coherent 'workers' democracy' alternative to the Morrisonian model, or, indeed, to the Crosland model of government share ownership which was agreed upon in 1957.

Bevan had a point when he said that the Attlee government had not introduced a planned economy. There is some debate about what is meant by 'economic planning'. Evan Durbin distinguished between government intervention and a 'general supersession of individual enterprise'.[10] The Attlee government had certainly not achieved the latter aim. Richard Toye argues that, in respect of nationalisation superseding the private sector, 'the leadership group [of the Attlee government] had largely abandoned Labour's pre-1945 conception of the planned economy'.[11] What the consequences would have been had the Attlee government sought to implement such a level of economic planning is a moot point. Had they, for example, sought to fix wage levels in advance across industry (or introduced some sort of 1970s-style 'incomes policy'), they would have met vehement trade union opposition. Toye argues that, while the 'balanced budget' orthodoxy of the interwar Treasury was in need of reform, 'Labour's conception of a socialist planned economy to replace capitalism was [...] an overblown response to a genuine problem.'[12] There was also the model France developed – the setting of targets by the 'Commissariat général du Plan', the identification of the probable constraints on meeting them, and the encouragement of private enterprise and nationalised industry to gear up to meet them. This was partly by generating the conviction that what was planned would actually come about, and partly by providing access to capital. Introducing such a strategy in the UK would have been more difficult. Cripps had briefly served as Minister for Economic Affairs for six weeks prior to becoming chancellor in November 1947. Harold Wilson did then introduce a formal Department of Economic Affairs to deal with long-term economic planning in 1964, but the Treasury gradually clawed back influence, particularly after his deputy leader, George Brown, left the post in 1966.

The debate between 'socialist' and 'social democratic' schools of thought in Labour history has not enhanced Bevan's reputation. The historian Steven Fielding characterised the distinction as follows: the 'socialist' school historically committed to a radical transformation of the capitalist economy, while the 'social democratic' view saw the Labour Party as unable to widen its electoral appeal beyond the working classes to win parliamentary majorities more regularly.[13] In his 1959 party conference speech, Bevan playfully used the term himself: 'I am not a communist, I am a social democrat.'[14] But Bevan, wedded to the principle of public ownership, with his history of standing up for the jobless, seemed part of what Crosland defined as the outmoded socialist literature of the past, concerned with unemployment when inflation would be the main issue of the future.[15] On the one hand, there was the unrealistic 'socialist' assumption of a future economic collapse, which Crosland's *Future of Socialism* openly challenged: 'alas, the mischievous enemy has retreated, and gone into disguise as well; and the simple orders for a backs-to-the-wall defence must be countermanded, and replaced by a more elaborate but less exciting plan.'[16] On the other, the 'social democratic' critique seemed to strike at the heart of Bevan's political mission to win power. When Tony Blair rewrote Clause IV in 1995, he called the Labour Party 'a democratic socialist party', but dropped the commitment to nationalisation. It looked as if Gaitskell and the 1950s revisionists were right. Bevan, wedded to public ownership, was out of date.

This analysis is misleading. For, like all politicians, Bevan was a product of his time. The social conditions he saw and experienced in his native Tredegar convinced him that there was something deeply wrong with the organisation of British society. There was an established propertied class, protected in Parliament by the Conservative Party. The capitalist economy, with its inevitable reliance on private enterprise, produced unemployment. He saw public ownership as part of the solution. It was more democratic, it could circumvent existing vested interests, and it could facilitate a planned economy in which employment could be kept at a high level. Conventional wisdom in the 1950s and 1960s relied on Keynesian stimuli and demand management to keep employment high. But Bevan thought – correctly – that Keynesianism was about reforming capitalism, not a means to a socialist society. Yet he never argued for the total elimination of private enterprise. And in his belief in the existing Clause IV he was joined by Clement Attlee, who believed in it until the end of his days, and who was not surprised when Gaitskell's attempt at reform failed. In fact, all the members of the Attlee Cabinet believed in the principle of nationalisation. They differed on specific cases such as iron and steel, but no member of the Cabinet ever seriously argued that the postwar direction of the government away from 1930s private enterprise to state ownership was wrong. Even the Conservatives, when they returned to power in October 1951, only returned two industries to private ownership, over which there had been the most political controversy: road haulage, and iron and steel (though Richard Thomas & Baldwins Ltd, owner of Ebbw Vale Steelworks, remained in public ownership).

No serious Labour politician of the 1950s argued that the Labour nationalisations should be reversed. Tony Crosland himself warned Gaitskell against his attempt to change Clause IV of the Labour Party constitution.[17] The criticism of Bevan's advocacy of public ownership ultimately comes down to the fact that he was the one most committed to the principle of nationalisation. His passion for it was born of his experience of what he saw as the worst effects of the free market in the interwar period. His background meant his belief in public ownership was intellectual *and* emotional. In the last months of his life, he set out his opposition to Gaitskell's attempt to reform Clause IV, and argued that, if it succeeded, Labour would not 'differ in any important respect' from the Conservatives and that the political system would return to how it was when the Liberals and Conservatives were Britain's two main parties. Labour would have no distinct purpose.[18]

Bevan certainly did think that further public ownership was crucial to increasing equality. But both Bevan and Gaitskell believed in a measure of public ownership. As Bevan put it in *In Place of Fear*: 'If the public domain of industry were *large enough to influence the conduct of the rest* [my emphasis], most [...] direct and indirect controls would not be needed, and the men and women running them could be released for productive work.'[19] Bevan thought a large nationalised sector was an advantage to private industry: 'The facilities given to national planning when industries are publicly owned are obvious. Control and direction of investment is easier, and a more secure market is provided for the private industries.'[20] Gaitskell thought it unwise to draw up a lengthy new 'shopping list' for nationalisation while he was party leader. But he did not believe in mass privatisation. Neither was Bevan blindly arguing for *more* nationalisation at all costs. Kenneth O. Morgan puts his finger on Bevan's realistic approach: 'For all his rhetoric, Bevan, like Herbert Morrison, was, from 1948, an advocate of consolidation, making the foundations more secure before pushing on to the next phase of the socialist advance.'[21] Public ownership was a central plank of the postwar consensus, and it was an accepted principle for over 30 years after the end of the Second World War. The Wilson government renationalised the steel industry in 1967, and Edward Heath found himself having to nationalise Rolls-Royce and Upper Clyde Shipbuilders when unemployment spiralled in 1972.

As regards the personal Bevan–Gaitskell division, what both men accepted in the late 1950s was that a working arrangement between them was essential for Labour to become a contender for government again. Bevan and Gaitskell were undoubtedly different in background and temperament. Yet another major difference was the point at which they entered Parliament. Gaitskell did not win a seat, Leeds South, until 1945, whereas Bevan won Ebbw Vale in 1929. At least partly as a consequence, Bevan was a quintessentially interwar politician, who underestimated the consumerism of the 1950s. The defining domestic political issue of 1918–39 was unemployment, and Bevan saw politics as a fight against poverty. The 1950s was the first decade of the postwar pre-election 'giveaway budgets'. Tory chancellors, R. A. Butler in 1955 and David Heathcoat-Amory in 1959, offered tax cuts to the electorate prior to the national polls. Such largesse was not a central part of interwar politics. Bevan did not begrudge the televisions and cars that the new consumer society sought. Rather, he questioned the hierarchy of values. He did not like to focus exclusively on material wealth: 'The accumulation of material possessions is no compensation for the rupture between the individual and society that is characteristic of competitive society. Those who succeed in the struggle equally with those who fail are invaded by the universal restlessness.' Bevan went further: 'The virtues of contemplation and of reflection are at a discount. Aesthetic values attend upon the caprice of the financially successful. The price ticket is displayed upon the Titian and the Renoir, and they are bought more for their prospective appreciation in capital value than for their intrinsic merit.'[22] In this view he was out of touch with a section of the electorate. Dominic Sandbrook captures it: 'If anything, for middle-class Britons it was the austerity of the war years that had been anomalous, not the affluence of the following decade. Consumerism and advertising had long been dynamic forces in British society.'[23]

When Labour did regain power in 1964, it was fitting that the new prime minister was the man who had resigned with Bevan in April 1951 before moving towards Gaitskell in 1955 to become Shadow Chancellor of the Exchequer. Harold Wilson put down a marker when he stood unsuccessfully against Gaitskell in November 1960. When Gaitskell died in January 1963, Wilson beat George Brown and Jim Callaghan to the leadership. Symbolically, before his victory, Wilson, gathered with his supporters, drank to Bevan: 'There is one toast we must drink, to the man who is not here, the man who should have done it, Nye Bevan.'[24] Michael Foot, having published the first volume of his biography of Bevan the previous year, was an enthusiast for Wilson. He also 'had this wonderful sense that the incredible has happened and that all kinds of things which had been impossible before Gaitskell's illness are now possible again'.[25] Wilson abolished NHS prescription charges in 1965. He drew on his Bevanite past, balancing Bevanites and Gaitskellites in his Cabinet. Crossman was appointed Minister of Housing and Local Government in 1964, before becoming Leader of the House of Commons in 1966, then took over at Health and Social Services in 1968. Castle was appointed the first Minister of Overseas Development in 1964, before taking over as Minister of Transport in 1965, then taking the title of 'First Secretary of State' when she became Secretary of State for Employment and Productivity in 1968. She openly adapted Bevan's book title when she introduced her *In Place of Strife* White Paper in 1969. This sought to regulate industrial relations, including an enforced 'pause' for negotiations, and the option of imposing a strike ballot. Vehemently opposed by the unions because of the interference with free collective bargaining, Callaghan led the opposition in Cabinet and the proposals were dropped. Jennie Lee served in the government, but not at Cabinet level. She was responsible for the arts, first as a parliamentary undersecretary and then at ministerial level from 1967. Bevan would have thoroughly approved of the Open University, which she introduced, with solid backing from Wilson, in 1968. Balanced against the Bevanite personnel were the Gaitskellites. Jenkins was a radical Home Secretary from 1965, before swapping jobs with Callaghan after the devaluation crisis of 1967 and becoming chancellor. In June 1968, prescription charges were reintroduced as part of Jenkins' efforts to deal with the balance-of-payments deficit. Crosland was a radical Secretary of State for Education and Science from 1965 to 1967, driving forward the abolition of many grammar schools, before taking over at Trade, then becoming Secretary of State for Local Government and Regional Planning in 1969.

Michael Foot succeeded Bevan as MP for Ebbw Vale in 1960. He remained on the back benches during the first Wilson governments of 1964–70, then served under Wilson when he returned to power in 1974 as Secretary of State for Employment. When Wilson retired in 1976, Callaghan defeated Foot for the leadership. Foot became Leader of the House of Commons, keeping what was then a minority government in office by dealing with the Liberals and nationalist parties in Parliament. After Labour lost office in 1979, Foot finally became party leader in 1980. It was a very difficult period, which ended in a landslide electoral defeat to Margaret Thatcher's Conservatives in 1983. Yet, for all the party divisions during Foot's tenure, including the creation of the breakaway Social Democratic Party (SDP), one factor would have been a great positive for Bevan. The 'New Left' came to prominence in the 1970s, and the Campaign for Labour Party Democracy, founded in 1973, argued for new 'electoral colleges' to elect the leader and deputy leader of the party, with three sections for the unions, party members and MPs, rather than the choice being left to MPs alone. Finally, this change was made in 1981. Such an arrangement would undoubtedly have enhanced Bevan's prospects of becoming party leader had it been introduced in Attlee's time.

That said, Bevan's failure to win the leadership does not affect his continuing relevance. Bevan remained optimistic that his vision of a society organised to eliminate poverty and with power in the hands of the individual could still be realised. He believed in people reaching their full potential. As a statesman, he combined vision with practical action. One of his greatest oratorical gifts was the ability to take his listeners on a journey to a more humane and equal world. That conception of a more meritocratic, less divided society is not an anachronism. Bevan remains an inspiration to the British left. In life, Bevan had an aura about him. Two of his Tredegar 1920s contemporaries sum this up. Take Dai Price: 'I could never fathom him [...] there was something extraordinary about him.' Another, Jack Thomas, said: 'You could always feel his presence.'[26] Over half a century after his death, millions of people still benefit from his life's greatest achievement. There are so few politicians about whom that can be said. Two of the great lines in W. B. Yeats' poem, 'The Second Coming', are: 'The best lack all conviction, while the worst / Are full of passionate intensity.' In Aneurin Bevan's case, this was not true. He was of the best, yet he was a man of conviction *and* passionate intensity.

Further Reading

Michael Foot's two-volume biography of Bevan is well worth reading. There is also an abridged one-volume edition edited by Brian Brivati. John Campbell's *Nye Bevan and the Mirage of British Socialism* gives a critical view. Bevan was the subject of one interim biography: Vincent Brome's *Aneurin Bevan*. Mark M. Krug's *Aneurin Bevan: Cautious Rebel* provides an American perspective. Clare Beckett and Francis Beckett's *Bevan* provides a good introduction to his life. There is an excellent, short essay on Bevan in Kenneth O. Morgan's *Labour People: Leaders and Lieutenants, Hardie to Kinnock*. Morgan also provides another fine piece on Bevan in *Resurgent Adventures with Britannia: Personalities, Politics and Culture in Britain*, edited by Wm Roger Louis. *The State of the Nation: The Political Legacy of Aneurin Bevan*, edited by Geoffrey Goodman, contains an interesting set of essays on different aspects of Bevan's life. There is also Mark Hayhurst's essay 'Duty bound', published in full in the *Guardian* on 28 May 2005, and available online (see reference below). Bevan's own speeches and writings have been collected by Charles Webster in *Aneurin Bevan on the National Health Service*. Vernon Bogdanor's Gresham College Lecture of 16 October 2012, 'Aneurin Bevan and the socialist ideal', is excellent. It is available online (see reference below). Jennie Lee's *My Life with Nye* is an invaluable resource. Patricia Hollis' *Jennie Lee* is superb.

Notes

Preface

1   E-mails to the author 14 November 2014, 16 November 2014, 19 November 2014, 23 November 2014 and 28 November 2014.
2   E-mail to the author, 28 November 2014.
3   Born in Edinburgh.
4   E-mail to the author, 19 November 2014.
5   *The Times*, 28 June 1958.
6   E-mail to the author, 19 November 2014.
7   Review in *London Review of Books*, 7 May 2015.
8   E-mail to the author dated 19 November 2014.
9   E-mails to the author dated 12 June 2015, 14 June 2015 and 15 June 2015.
10   Hansard, HC (series 5), vol. 444, col. 1603, 24 November 1947.
11   Hansard, HC (series 5), vol. 444, col. 1604, 24 November 1947.
12   E-mail from Michael Hill to the author dated 13 June 2015.
13   Aneurin Bevan, *In Place of Fear* (1952; London: Quartet Books, 1978), p. 26.
14   Aneurin Bevan, *In Place of Fear* (1952; London: Quartet Books, 1978), p. 35.

Introduction

1   *The Times*, 5 November 1956.
2   Ibid.
3   The speech can be heard on YouTube. See http://www.youtube.com/watch?v=XZmw8XIoZeY (accessed 15 May 2014).
4   *Daily Herald*, 7 July 1960.
5   William Barklay, *Daily Express*, 7 July 1960.
6   *Tribune*, 8 July 1960.
7   The other three who made the list were Tony Benn (97th), David Lloyd George (79th) and Tony Blair (67th).
8   'Bevan is ultimate Welsh hero', *BBC News* [website], 1 March 2004. Available at http://news.bbc.co.uk/1/hi/wales/3523363.stm (accessed 15 May 2014). The poll was organised by Culturenet Cymru.

9   *The Times*, 26 May 2011.

10   *The Times Magazine*, 5 November 2011.

11   The author was a delegate at the conference, held 18–19 February 2012, and was sitting in the conference hall.

12   'The NHS in England', *NHS* [website]. Available at http://www.nhs.uk/NHSEngland/thenhs/about/Pages/overview.aspx (accessed 15 May 2014).

13   Bevan seems to have first used the words in late 1955 or January 1956. See Charles Webster (ed.), *Aneurin Bevan on the National Health Service* (Oxford: University of Oxford Wellcome Unit for the History of Medicine, 1991), pp. 219–22.

14   Under the 1964–70 Labour governments, the abolition of capital punishment and prison birching, together with the liberalisation of laws regarding divorce, censorship, abortion and homosexuality, changed British society for ever. A number of these changes reached the statute book whilst Jenkins was Home Secretary. He shares credit with the backbenchers who promoted measures as private members' bills: for example, David Steel's Abortion Bill, and Leo Abse's Sexual Offences Bill, both of which became law in 1967.

15   Aneurin Bevan, *In Place of Fear* (1952; London: Quartet Books, 1978), p. 21.

16   Herbert Morrison, Baron Morrison, *Herbert Morrison: An Autobiography* (London: Odhams Press, 1960), pp. 263–4.

17   Author's interview with Geoffrey Goodman, 21 November 2011.

18   As quoted in *The Times*, 5 July 1948.

19   Morrison, *An Autobiography*, pp. 265–6.

20   Jennie Lee papers, JL/6/3/4/1, postcard received by Bevan on 12 December 1955 from an anonymous correspondent.

21   *Daily Sketch*, 24 May 1955.

22   Bevan told Brome firmly on 24 August 1953: 'I hold myself free to express any opinion or take any action that I feel may be open to me when the book is published.' Letters are in the Jennie Lee papers, JL/6/3/2/1.

23   See Brome's obituary in the *Daily Telegraph*, 30 October 2004.

24   Michael Foot, *Aneurin Bevan*, vol. 2: *1945 to 1960* (London: Davis-Poynter, 1973), p. 655.

25   Michael Foot, *Aneurin Bevan*, vol. 1: *1897 to 1945* (London: MacGibbon & Kee, 1962), p. 13.

26   John Campbell, *Nye Bevan and the Mirage of British Socialism* (London: Weidenfeld & Nicholson, 1987), p. xii.

27   John Campbell, *Roy Jenkins: A Biography* (London: Weidenfeld & Nicolson, 1983). Campbell later wrote a full biography: *Roy Jenkins: A Well-rounded Life* (London: Jonathan Cape, 2014).

28   *New Statesman*, 9 July 1960.

29   It appears that Zhou actually thought that he was being asked about the 1968 student protests in Paris, but President Nixon's interpreter decided not to correct him. As Daniel Finkelstein put it: 'The misunderstanding enriches the quote rather than undermines it.' *The Times*, 17 July 2013.

30   Terry Eagleton, *Why Marx Was Right* (New Haven and London: Yale University Press, 2011), p. 239.

31   Ibid., pp. 238–9.

32   Author's interview with Geoffrey Goodman, 21 November 2011.

33   Labour Party, *Report of the 58th Annual Conference* (London: Labour Party, 1959), pp. 107–9.

34   Bevan, *In Place of Fear*, p. 128.

35   Ibid., p. 127.

36   Labour Party, *Report of the 58th Annual Conference*, p. 152.

37   Ibid., p. 153.

38 Labour Party, *Report of the 48th Annual Conference* (London: Labour Party, 1949), p. 134.
39 Labour Party Archive, General Secretary's papers, LP/GS/Dork/ADD/2ii.
40 Labour Party Archive, General Secretary's papers, LP/GS/Dork/ADD/2vii.
41 Labour Party Archive, General Secretary's papers, LP/GS/Dork/ADD/2ii.
42 Labour Party, *Report of the 48th Annual Conference*, p. 172.
43 Ibid., p. 171.
44 Labour Party, *Report of the 58th Annual Conference*, p. 153.
45 'He sensed a year ago his career was near the end', *Daily Express*, 7 July 1960.
46 Labour Party, *Report of the 58th Annual Conference*, p. 154.
47 Barbara Castle, 'A passionate defence', in Geoffrey Goodman (ed.), *The State of the Nation: The Political Legacy of Aneurin Bevan* (London: Victor Gollancz, 1997), p. 39.
48 Labour Party, *Report of the 58th Annual Conference*, p. 154.
49 Kenneth O. Morgan, *Labour People: Leaders and Lieutenants, Hardie to Kinnock* (1987; rev. edn, Oxford: Oxford University Press, 1992), p. 205.
50 Dai Smith, *Aneurin Bevan and the World of South Wales* (Cardiff: University of Wales Press, 1993), p. 258.
51 Kenneth O. Morgan, 'Nye Bevan', in Wm Roger Louis (ed.), *Resurgent Adventures with Britannia: Personalities, Politics and Culture in Britain* (London: I.B.Tauris, 2011), p. 194.
52 Campbell, *Nye Bevan and the Mirage of British Socialism*, p. 29.

Chapter 1: The Welsh Valleys Childhood, 1897–1911

1   As quoted in Michael Foot, *Aneurin Bevan*, vol. 2: *1945 to 1960* (London: Davis-Poynter, 1973), p. 239.
2   Dai Smith, *Aneurin Bevan and the World of South Wales* (Cardiff: University of Wales Press, 1993), p. 92.
3   For example, Dr Charles Hill, secretary of the BMA during the negotiations with Bevan, used the phrase during his election broadcast on 16 October 1951, by which time he had entered politics. See *The Times*, 17 October 1951.
4   David Brooks, *The Social Animal* (New York, NY: Random House, 2011), p. 300.
5   Aneurin Bevan, *In Place of Fear* (1952; London: Quartet Books, 1978), p. 45.
6   Smith, *Aneurin Bevan and the World of South Wales*, p. 15.
7   As quoted ibid., pp. 182–3.
8   'Democratic values', Fabian lecture, September 1950.
9   The author's great-grandfather Henry James Edwards was born exactly a year before Bevan on 15 November 1896 in the Eastern Valley of the South Wales coalfield, and was one of 22 children, of whom only eight survived into adulthood.
10 See Kenneth O. Morgan, *Rebirth of a Nation: Wales 1880–1980* (1981; Oxford: Oxford University Press, 1982), pp. 79–80.
11 Smith, *Aneurin Bevan and the World of South Wales*, p. 46.
12 Michael Foot, *Aneurin Bevan*, vol. 1: *1897 to 1945* (London: MacGibbon & Kee, 1962), p. 14.
13 Author's interview with Lord Kinnock, 29 March 2011.
14 Foot, *Aneurin Bevan*, vol. 1, p. 14.
15 Ibid., p. 17.
16 John Campbell, *Nye Bevan and the Mirage of British Socialism* (London: Weidenfeld & Nicolson, 1987), p. 6.
17 Foot, *Aneurin Bevan*, vol. 1, p. 16.

18 Ibid., pp. 16–17.
19 Author's interview with Lord Kinnock, 29 April 2011.
20 Foot, *Aneurin Bevan*, vol. 1, p. 19.
21 Author's interview with Lord Kinnock, 29 March 2011.
22 As quoted in Foot, *Aneurin Bevan*, vol. 1, pp. 17–18.
23 Section 132 of the Local Government Act 1948. See Bevan, *In Place of Fear*, pp. 74–5, n. 12.
24 As quoted in Foot, *Aneurin Bevan*, vol. 1, p. 19.
25 Ibid., p. 20.
26 George Orwell, *Essays* (London: Penguin and Secker & Warburg, 2000), p. 88.
27 Bevan, *In Place of Fear*, p. 38.
28 Stephen Coleman, *Daniel De Leon* (Manchester: Manchester University Press, 1990), p. 76.

Chapter 2: The South Wales Coalfield, 1911–19

1   Hywel Francis and Dai Smith, *The Fed: A History of the South Wales Miners in the Twentieth Century* (1980; 2nd edn, Cardiff: University of Wales Press, 1998), appendix IV.
2   He was MP for the newly created Rhondda West from 1918 to 1920.
3   Unofficial Reform Committee, *The Miners' Next Step: Being a Suggested Scheme for the Reorganisation of the Federation* (1912; repr., London: Germinal & Phoenix Press, 1991).
4   Kenneth O. Morgan, *Rebirth of a Nation: Wales 1880–1980* (1981; Oxford: Oxford University Press, 1982), p. 149.
5   Ibid., pp. 146, 151–2.
6   Unofficial Reform Committee, *Miners' Next Step*, p. 17.
7   Ibid.
8   As quoted in Dai Smith, *Aneurin Bevan and the World of South Wales* (Cardiff: University of Wales Press, 1993), p. 83.
9   Unofficial Reform Committee, *Miners' Next Step*, p. 31.
10 Robin Page Arnot, *A History of the South Wales Miners' Federation 1898–1914* (London: Allen & Unwin, 1967), p. 327.
11 Aneurin Bevan, *In Place of Fear* (1952; London: Quartet Books, 1978), p. 40.
12 Ibid.
13 Francis and Smith, *The Fed*, p. 4.
14 As quoted in Michael Foot, *Aneurin Bevan*, vol. 1: *1897 to 1945* (London: MacGibbon & Kee, 1962), p. 24.
15 Article in the *Daily Express* in 1932, as quoted ibid., p. 23.
16 Hansard, HC (series 5), vol. 322, col. 252, 7 April 1937.
17 Ibid.
18 This happened with the author's maternal grandmother's dog 'Lady', a pet she was extremely fond of as a child. During a tough period her father was forced to drown the dog in a pond on the hills above Blaenavon.
19 Hansard, HC (series 5), vol. 322, col. 252, 7 April 1937.
20 Hansard, HC (series 5), vol. 461, col. 1459, 17 February 1949. The line in Gray's poem, which Bevan quoted, is: 'How jocund did they drive their team afield!'
21 Foot, *Aneurin Bevan*, vol. 1, pp. 34–7.
22 Harold Finch, *Memoirs of a Bedwellty MP* (Risca: Starling Press, 1972), p. 22.
23 As quoted in Smith, *Aneurin Bevan and the World of South Wales*, p. 202.
24 Aneurin Bevan, 'The best advice I ever had', *Reader's Digest* lxiii/378 (October 1953).

25 *Time*, 21 March 1949, p. 30.

26 Foot, *Aneurin Bevan*, vol. 1, pp. 27–8.

27 Gwyn Thomas, *The Alone to the Alone*, Library of Wales (1947; Cardigan: Parthian, 2008), p. 9.

28 Jack London, *The Iron Heel* (Stilwell, KS: Digireads.com, 2007), p. 106.

29 Labour Party, *Report of the 48th Annual Conference* (London: Labour Party, 1949), p. 169.

30 Bevan, *In Place of Fear*, pp. 21–2.

31 Martin Ceadel, *Thinking about Peace and War* (1987; Oxford: Oxford University Press, 1989), pp. 114–9. Ceadel notes the importance of the 'democratic-control movement', whose aim was 'to bring the selfishly bellicose under democratic control'. The first-established 'peace society' in the First World War was the Union of Democratic Control.

Chapter 3: Local Politics, 1919–28

1   Aneurin Bevan, 'Foreword', in W. W. Craik, *Bryn Roberts and the National Union of Public Employees* (London: Allen & Unwin, 1955), [no page numbers].

2   *Daily Herald*, 25 May 1945.

3   Oliver Powell, interviewed by Hywel Francis, 29 November 1973, in the material collected by Professor Dai Smith, Richard Burton Archives, Swansea University, SWCC/MND/13.

4   Letter written by Lush to Foot after the publication of the second volume of Foot's biography, as quoted in Dai Smith, *Aneurin Bevan and the World of South Wales* (Cardiff: University of Wales Press, 1993), p. 227.

5   See Harold Finch, *Memoirs of a Bedwellty MP* (Risca: Starling Press, 1972), p. 40.

6   Ibid.

7   W. W. Craik, *The Central Labour College, 1909–29* (London: Lawrence & Wishart, 1964), pp. 123–4.

8   Michael Foot, *Aneurin Bevan*, vol. 1: *1897 to 1945* (London: MacGibbon & Kee, 1962), pp. 39–41.

9   Finch, *Memoirs of a Bedwellty MP*, p. 22.

10 This final book was given to Bevan by Ted Gill, an Abertillery man who was on the executive of the Plebs' League, on 14 October 1919. This list is to be found in Smith, *Aneurin Bevan and the World of South Wales*, p. 205, and is based on Smith's examination of the books on the bookshelves of Bevan's sister, Arianwen, in the 1980s.

11 J. Beverley Smith, et al., *James Griffiths and His Times* (Ferndale, Rhondda: Labour Party Wales and the Llanelli Constituency Labour Party, 1979), p. 77.

12 As quoted in Smith, *Aneurin Bevan and the World of South Wales*, pp. 206–7.

13 *Plebs*, January 1921, pp. 19–21.

14 Aneurin Bevan, *In Place of Fear* (1952; London: Quartet Books, 1978), p. 41.

15 Ibid.

16 Hywel Francis and Dai Smith, *The Fed: A History of the South Wales Miners in the Twentieth Century* (1980; 2nd edn, Cardiff: University of Wales Press, 1998), p. 28.

17 A National Wages Board was created, 'though only with limited powers for interpreting district decisions'. See C. L. Mowat, *Britain between the Wars, 1918–1940* (London: Methuen, 1968), pp. 123–4.

18 *Merthyr Express*, 16 April 1921.

19 Sir Archie Lush, interviewed by Hywel Francis, 11 May 1973, in the material collected by Professor Dai Smith, Richard Burton Archives, Swansea University, SWCC/MND/13.

20 This account is set out in Susan E. Demont, 'Tredegar and Aneurin Bevan: A society and its political articulation 1890–1929', DPhil thesis, University of Wales, March 1990, pp. 279–80.

21 Oliver Powell, interviewed by Hywel Francis, 29 November 1973.

22 Hansard, HC (series 5), vol. 270, col. 404, 9 November 1932.

23 *Tredegar Valley District Monthly Report*, 15 July 1921.

24 Oliver Powell, interviewed by Hywel Francis, 29 November 1973. Sue Demont covers this issue in 'Tredegar and Aneurin Bevan' but draws no firm conclusion about the reason for Bevan's unemployment.

25 D. J. Davies, interviewed by David Egan, 3 November 1972, in South Wales Miners' Library, Swansea University, SWCC/AUD/173. Michael Foot's account is that the payment was not received until 1926. See Foot, *Aneurin Bevan*, vol. 1, p. 50.

26 Foot, *Aneurin Bevan*, vol. 1, p. 48.

27 Finch, *Memoirs of a Bedwellty MP*, p. 60.

28 Bevan, *In Place of Fear*, pp. 44–5. There is some doubt about the date of this incident. Archie Lush told Foot that Bevan was away at a conference in Stoke-on-Trent when the march took place on 27 January 1923. See Foot, *Aneurin Bevan*, vol. 1, pp. 68–9, n. 12. Sue Demont, in 'Tredegar and Aneurin Bevan', explains that there was another march on the workhouse in 1921, which Bevan must have confused with 1923. This would fit, as Bevan was unemployed in 1921 when he returned from the Central Labour College.

29 Oliver Powell, interviewed by Hywel Francis, 29 November 1973.

30 Sir Archie Lush, interviewed by Hywel Francis, 11 May 1973.

31 Though another Query Club member, Oliver Jones, identifies it as 1926, not long after the strike ended. See interview with Oliver Jones, in the material collected by Professor Dai Smith, Richard Burton Archives, Swansea University, SWCC/MND/13.

32 The date of 1924 comes from Sir Archie Lush, interviewed by Hywel Francis, 11 May 1973.

33 By 1930, the library had 70,000 books, according to the *Daily News*, 19 March 1930.

34 See Foot, *Aneurin Bevan*, vol. 1, pp. 58–62, for an account of the Bevan–Lush relationship in the 1920s, and the quotes from Lush about Bevan's involvement with girls.

35 Sir Archie Lush, interviewed by Hywel Francis, 11 May 1973.

36 Councillor W. S. Davies was elected chairman and R. Jones vice chairman.

37 *Merthyr Express*, 6 December 1924.

38 *Western Mail*, 4 October 1924, and *Merthyr Express*, 25 June 1927.

39 Oliver Powell, interviewed by Hywel Francis, 29 November 1973.

40 Tredegar Urban District Council Minutes, 4 April 1923–24 March 1925, Piece Number 32.

41 Demont, 'Tredegar and Aneurin Bevan', p. 367.

42 Medical Officer of Health Annual Report, Tredegar, 1928.

43 See Kenneth O. Morgan, *Rebirth of a Nation: Wales 1880–1980* (1981; Oxford: Oxford University Press, 1982), p. 188.

44 *Merthyr Express*, 5 September 1925.

45 *Merthyr Express*, 6 October 1928.

46 Tredegar Urban District Council Minutes, 16 April 1929–14 April 1930, Piece Number 37.

47 *Merthyr Express*, 11 May 1929.

48 *Western Mail*, 7 April 1925.

49 Tredegar Urban District Council Minutes, 20 April 1926–12 April 1927, Piece Number 34.

50 *Merthyr Express*, 26 June 1926.

51 *Western Mail*, 1 November 1926.

52 Oliver Powell, interviewed by Hywel Francis, 29 November 1973.

53 *Merthyr Express*, 13 November 1926.

54 Minutes of the Miners' Federation of Great Britain Special Conference, London, 4 and 5 November 1926, p. 27, in South Wales Coalfield Collection, Swansea University, SWCC/MNA/NUM/1/1/26, p. 27.

55 Arthur Horner, *Incorrigible Rebel* (London: MacGibbon & Kee, 1960), p. 87.

56 Ibid., p. 67.

57 Interview with Len Jeffreys (Cross Keys), 11 October 1972, in South Wales Miners' Library, Swansea University, SWCC/AUD/272.

58 Ness Edwards, *History of the South Wales Miners' Federation*, vol. 1 (London: Lawrence & Wishart, 1938), pp. 139–40.

59 Taken from University College, Swansea, SWMF bound circulars, 13 December 1926, and quoted in Francis and Smith, *The Fed*, appendix III.

60 Tredegar Combine Committee Notebook [author unclear], Richard Burton Archives, Swansea University, SWCC/MNA/NUM/3/8/26.

61 Bevan, *In Place of Fear*, p. 46.

62 Interview with Oliver Jones, in the material collected by Professor Dai Smith, Richard Burton Archives, Swansea University, SWCC/MND/13.

63 Sir Archie Lush, interviewed by Hywel Francis, 11 May 1973.

64 Foot, *Aneurin Bevan*, vol. 1, p. 95.

65 Hansard records contributions from Evan Davies MP on the following dates: 15 February 1921; 17 March 1921; 20 April 1921; 28 October 1921; 16 December 1925; 4 March 1926; 30 June 1926; 27 April 1927; 20 November 1927; and 29 November 1927.

66 Sir Archie Lush, interviewed by Hywel Francis, 11 May 1973.

67 Smith, *Aneurin Bevan and the World of South Wales*, p. 226.

68 Bull did serve on Monmouthshire County Council for Ebbw Vale South Central.

69 Michael Foot, *Aneurin Bevan*, vol. 2: *1945 to 1960* (London: Davis-Poynter, 1973), p. 97.

70 As quoted in Smith, *Aneurin Bevan and the World of South Wales*, p. 227.

71 *Western Mail*, 8, 25 March 1929, 8–11 May 1929.

72 Richards had previously been the MP for the predecessor West Monmouthshire constituency, first elected in a by-election in 1904 as a Liberal–Labour candidate, then elected as a Labour candidate in both the January and December elections in 1910.

73 *Western Mail*, 31 May 1929.

74 John Campbell, *Nye Bevan and the Mirage of British Socialism* (London: Weidenfeld & Nicolson, 1987), p. 4.

75 See, for example, J. Beverley Smith, 'An appreciation', in Smith et al., *James Griffiths and His Times*, p. 116.

76 Hansard, HC (series 5), vol. 403, cols 2311–12, 17 October 1944.

77 *The Times*, 28 June 1958.

78 Fred J. Hando, *The Pleasant Land of Gwent* (1944; Newport: R. H. Johns, 1949). By 'Monmouthshire', what is meant here is what is now known as the preserved county of 'Gwent', rather than the Monmouthshire County Borough Council created in 1996.

79 Kenneth O. Morgan, *The Red Dragon and the Red Flag: The Cases of James Griffiths and Aneurin Bevan: The Welsh Political Archive Lecture 1988: 4th November 1988* (Aberystwyth: National Library of Wales Press, 1989), p. 14.

80 Harold Hutchinson, *Daily Herald*, 25 June 1958, as quoted in Nina Fishman, *Arthur Horner: A Political Biography*, vol. 1: *1894–1944* (London: Lawrence & Wishart, 2010), p. 20.

81 Walter Citrine, *Men and Work: The Autobiography of Lord Citrine* (London: Hutchinson, 1964), p. 210.

82 Sir Archie Lush, interviewed by Hywel Francis, 11 May 1973.

83 Author's interview with Geoffrey Goodman, 21 November 2011.
84 For the membership figures, see Darron Dupre, 'Bryn Roberts: A forgotten trade union hero'. Available at http://www.bevanfoundation.org/blog/bryn-roberts-a-forgotten-trade-union-hero-part-one/ (accessed 17 May 2014) and http://www.bevanfoundation.org/blog/bryn-roberts-a-forgotton-trade-union-hero-part-2/ (accessed 17 May 2014). NUPE merged with the Confederation of Health Service Employees (COHSE) and the National Association of Local Government Officers (NALGO) to form UNISON in 1993.
85 Aneurin Bevan, 'Foreword', in Craik, *Bryn Roberts*, [no page numbers].
86 Sir Archie Lush, interviewed by Hywel Francis, 11 May 1973.
87 *Merthyr Express*, 8 June 1929.

Chapter 4: Monmouthshire County Council and Parliament, 1928–34

1   *Western Mail*, 6 March 1928.
2   Susan E. Demont, 'Tredegar and Aneurin Bevan: A society and its political articulation 1890–1929', DPhil thesis, University of Wales, March 1990. Appendix IV carries a table of representatives for Tredegar on Monmouthshire County Council.
3   *South Wales Argus*, 23 February 1932.
4   Monmouthshire County Council Minute Books No. 7, July 1926–July 1928, C/M/7; No. 8, August 1928–February 1930, C/M/8; No. 9, February 1930–March 1931, C/M/9.
5   There had to be statutory quarterly meetings under the County Councils (Elections) Act 1891.
6   This said, it is difficult to gauge his contribution from the third minute book onwards due to a change in the style of the minutes, from handwritten to typed, with less recording of discussions.
7   By the County Councils (Elections) Act 1891.
8   *Western Mail*, 4 March 1931.
9   *Western Mail*, 3 March 1931.
10 It was found that 1,476 children were on 3.6 per cent below what was considered 'normal' in industrial areas and 190 children were on 2 per cent below 'normal' in rural areas.
11 See, for example, *Western Mail*, 1 March 1934.
12 Monmouthshire County Council Minute Books No. 10, April 1931–March 1933, C/M/10; No. 11, April 1933–March 1935, C/M/11.
13 Bevan family papers, 'Report on financial situation: South Wales & Monmouthshire necessitous areas conference', by P. H. Stafford (county accountant) and F. J. Alban, 31 May 1932.
14 Monmouthshire County Council, 'Financial estimate for year ending 31 March 1933, R357', in Monmouthshire County Council Minute Books No. 10, April 1931–March 1933, C/M/10.
15 HO 45/25453, 'Memorandum: Note of interview by Bevan with the Home Secretary's private secretary', 2 September 1929, and letter from Clynes to Bevan, 6 September 1929.
16 See Bevan family papers, Bevan to Morrison, 20 April 1931, 'Depressed areas file'.
17 Hansard, HC (series 5), vol. 264, cols 84–5, 5 April 1932.
18 In June 1929, the number unemployed stood at 1.164 million, which increased to 1.52 million by January 1930. See David Butler and Gareth Butler, *Twentieth-century British Political Facts 1900–2000* (London: Macmillan, 2000), p. 400.

19 Robert Skidelsky, *Politicians and the Slump: The Labour Government of 1929–1931* (1967; London: Papermac, 1994), p. 51.

20 Ross McKibbin, 'The economic policy of the second Labour government', in Ross McKibbin, *The Ideologies of Class: Social Relations in Britain, 1880–1950* (Oxford: Clarendon Press, 1994), pp. 197–227.

21 *The Times*, 13 April 1929.

22 Ben Pimlott, *Labour and the Left in the 1930s* (Cambridge: Cambridge University Press, 1977), p. 39.

23 McKibbin, 'The economic policy of the second Labour government', pp. 197–8.

24 Hansard, HC (series 5), vol. 230, cols 338–9, 16 July 1929.

25 Ibid., col. 341.

26 Ibid., col. 342.

27 Ibid., col. 343.

28 Hansard, HC (series 5), vol. 230, col. 1192, 23 July 1929.

29 Ibid., cols 1193–4.

30 Hansard, HC (series 5), vol. 235, col. 2466, 27 February 1930.

31 Ibid., col. 2468.

32 Ibid., col. 2469.

33 Hansard, HC (series 5), vol. 244, cols 758–9, 4 November 1930.

34 Ben Pimlott (ed.), *The Political Diary of Hugh Dalton 1918–40, 1945–60* (London: Jonathan Cape, 1986), p. 112.

35 Ibid., p. 113.

36 Ibid., p. 114.

37 Young stood unsuccessfully for the New Party in the Ashton-under-Lyne by-election of 30 April 1931.

38 Matthew Worley, *Oswald Mosley and the New Party* (Basingstoke: Palgrave Macmillan, 2010), pp. 36–7.

39 *Western Mail*, 27 February 1931.

40 *Western Mail*, 27 April 1931.

41 *South Wales Argus*, 4 May 1931.

42 Sir Archie Lush, interviewed by Hywel Francis, 11 May 1973, in the material collected by Professor Dai Smith, Richard Burton Archives, Swansea University, SWCC/MND/13.

43 The 17 were, in alphabetical order: O. Baldwin, J. Batey, Bevan, W. J. Brown, W. G. Cove, R. Forgan, J. F. Horrabin, J. Lovat-Fraser, S. F. Markham, J. McGovern, J. J. McShane, Lady Cynthia and Sir Oswald Mosley, H. T. Muggeridge, M. Phillips Price, C. J. Simmons and Strachey.

44 Hansard, HC (series 5), vol. 245, col. 628, 3 November 1930.

45 It is not clear precisely when this was. Jennie Lee, in *My Life with Nye* (London: Jonathan Cape, 1980), p. 83, states it was 'after his [Bevan's] much publicized savaging of Lloyd George in his *maiden* speech'; however, the attack on Lloyd George which Foot states left him 'visibly shaken' was the one on the Coal Mines Bill on 27 February 1930. See Michael Foot, *Aneurin Bevan*, vol. 1: *1897 to 1945* (London: MacGibbon & Kee, 1962), p. 118.

46 Lee, *My Life with Nye*, pp. 82–3.

47 *The Times*, 15 February 1933.

48 McKibbin, 'The economic policy of the second Labour government', p. 218.

49 As set out in Labour Party, *Report of the 31st Annual Conference* (London: Labour Party, 1931), p. 5.

50 Hansard, HC (series 5), vol. 269, col. 1220, 27 October 1932.

51 Philip Williamson, *National Crisis and National Government: British Politics, the Economy and Empire, 1926–1932* (1992; Cambridge: Cambridge University Press, 2003), p. 495.
52 Hansard, HC (series 5), vol. 256, col. 1217, 18 September 1931.
53 Hansard, HC (series 5), vol. 260, col. 632, 26 November 1931.
54 Hansard, HC (series 5), vol. 260, col. 2157, 10 December 1931.
55 Hansard, HC (series 5), vol. 270, col. 839, 14 November 1932.
56 Bevan family papers, letter from Ministry of Labour to Bevan, 6 June 1933. Bevan had also forwarded a letter from the SWMF on the issue.
57 *South Wales Argus*, 30 April 1931.
58 *South Wales Argus*, 21 April 1931.
59 Jennie Lee, *This Great Journey: A Volume of Autobiography 1904–45* (London: MacGibbon & Kee, 1963), p. 116. In referring to Lee as 'Casabianca' Bevan was comparing her to the young son of the French naval commander Louis de Casabianca, who, during the Battle of the Nile in 1798, remained at his post and died as the ship burned. The story is commemorated in the poem 'Casabianca' by Felicia Hemans (1793–1835), which begins with the famous lines: 'The boy stood on the burning deck / Whence all but he had fled.'
60 Gidon Cohen, *The Failure of a Dream: The Independent Labour Party from Disaffiliation to World War II* (London: I.B.Tauris, 2007), pp. 32–4. Cardiff and Mid Glamorgan were the ILP's strongest areas in Wales pre-disaffiliation, and by the end of the 1930s the only 'effective presence' in South Wales was in Merthyr Tydfil.
61 Lee, *This Great Journey*, p. 135.
62 Strachey describes Bevan as 'one of the most gifted of their [Labour's] young supporters'. The passage is quoted in Foot, *Aneurin Bevan*, vol. 1, pp. 152–5.
63 *Western Mail*, 25 February 1932.
64 Letter to Arthur Horner from Aneurin Bevan arranging a meeting to discuss a proposal for cooperation with the Communist Party, 30 April 1933, Richard Burton Archives, Swansea University, SWCC/MNA/PP/46/13.
65 Oliver Powell, interviewed by Hywel Francis, 29 November 1973, in the material collected by Professor Dai Smith, Richard Burton Archives, Swansea University, SWCC/MND/13.
66 *Western Mail*, 25 May 1933.
67 Lee, *My Life with Nye*, pp. 137–8.

Chapter 5: London and Jennie Lee

1 Jennie Lee, *My Life with Nye* (London: Jonathan Cape, 1980), p. 81.
2 Patricia Hollis, *Jennie Lee: A Life* (Oxford: Oxford University Press, 1997), p. 84.
3 Fenner Brockway, *Inside the Left* (Leicester: Blackfriars Press, 1942), p. 225.
4 Walter Citrine, *Men and Work: The Autobiography of Lord Citrine* (London: Hutchinson, 1964), p. 345.
5 As quoted in A. J. P. Taylor, *Beaverbrook* (New York, NY: Simon & Schuster, 1972), p. 335.
6 Ibid., p. 198.
7 Robert Crowcroft, *Attlee's War: World War II and the Making of a Labour Leader* (London: I.B.Tauris, 2011), appendix ('The adventurers'), p. 241.
8 Michael Foot, *Debts of Honour* (1980; London: Pan Books, 1981), pp. 71–2.
9 Taylor, *Beaverbrook*, p. 335.
10 Foot, in contrast, did accept the offer of a Cherkley cottage in 1951. Beaverbrook also funded *Tribune*, giving it £3,000 in 1951 when it was particularly short of money. See

Michael Foot, *Debts of Honour* (1980; London: Pan Books, 1981), p. 103. Foot, however, revealed the source of the money only to his wife, Jill.

11 Foot, *Debts of Honour*, p. 73. This is not to say they did not fall out. Foot resigned from the *Evening Standard* in June 1944, unable to reconcile his own left-wing views with Beaverbrook's desire to support the Conservatives when party politics resumed. However, Foot always reconciled with Beaverbrook.

12 Obituary of Michael Foot in the *Independent*, 4 March 2010.

13 Oliver Powell, interviewed by Hywel Francis, 29 November 1973, in the material collected by Professor Dai Smith, Richard Burton Archives, Swansea University, SWCC/MND/13.

14 Bevan had briefly met Lee's parents during the 1931 general-election campaign in North Lanark. See Hollis, *Jennie Lee*, p. 201.

15 Lee, *My Life with Nye*, pp. 81–2; Hollis, *Jennie Lee*, pp. 70–1.

16 Bevan family papers, 'Note of Russia visit'.

17 Aneurin Bevan with John Strachey and George Strauss, *What We Saw in Russia* (London: Hogarth Press, 1931).

18 Bevan family papers, 'Note of Russia visit'.

19 Hansard, HC (series 5), vol. 272, col. 1969, 9 December 1932.

20 In the Bevan family papers there is the official Moscow State Law published account of the trial of 18 men charged with 'wrecking activities' at power stations held in April 1933 at the Supreme Court of the USSR in Moscow.

21 Lee, *My Life with Nye*, pp. 120–1.

22 *The Times*, 14 November 1957.

23 For an account of the engagement and wedding, see Hollis, *Jennie Lee*, pp. 82–3. The information that Jennie Lee did wear rings is from Lord Lauderdale (note at p. 83).

24 Author's interview with Jaselle, Jane and David Williams and Margaret Bevan, 26 October 2013.

25 Author's interview with Lord Touhig, 2 November 2013. The newly elected Gwent County Council 'shadowed' the old Monmouthshire County Council prior to its formal introduction in 1974.

26 Margaret Foster, *Good Wives? Mary, Fanny, Jennie and Me, 1845–2001* (London: Vintage, 2002), p. 231.

27 Ibid., p. 239.

28 As quoted in Hollis, *Jennie Lee*, p. 215.

29 Barbara Castle, *Fighting All the Way* (London: Macmillan, 1994), p. 109.

30 Lisa Martineau, *Politics & Power: Barbara Castle: A Biography* (2000; London: Andre Deutsch, 2011), pp. 54–5.

31 *Daily Herald*, 10 March 1961.

32 As quoted in Hollis, *Jennie Lee*, p. 214.

33 Francis Wheen, *Tom Driberg, His Life and Indiscretions* (London: Chatto & Windus, 1990), p. 13.

34 Hollis, *Jennie Lee*, p. 213.

35 As quoted ibid., p. 207. The various incidents appear at pp. 207–11.

36 See Lee, *My Life with Nye*, pp. 130–2.

37 Hollis, *Jennie Lee*, pp. 201–2.

38 As quoted ibid., pp. 209–10.

Chapter 6: Working-class Unity, 1935–9

1 This is not to say that Ebbw Vale was totally insulated from national factors. In the Labour landslide of 1945, Bevan took 27,209 votes, 80.1 per cent of the vote, an improvement

on 1935. In 1950 and 1951, his vote increased to 80.7 per cent (28,245 in 1950 and 28,283 in 1951) on high turnouts of 86.7 per cent and 87 per cent respectively. In 1955, his vote fell to 79.3 per cent (26,058), as the Conservatives increased their parliamentary majority. In 1959, somewhat against the national trend of another increased Conservative majority, Bevan won 81 per cent of the vote (27,326), but the turnout was higher than in 1955: 85.8 per cent to 83.7 per cent. See: F. W. S. Craig (ed.), *British Parliamentary Election Results 1918–1949* (Chichester: Political Reference Publications, 1969); F. W. S. Craig (ed.), *British Parliamentary Election Results 1950–1970* (Chichester: Political Reference Publications, 1971).

2 As quoted in Jennie Lee, *My Life with Nye* (London: Jonathan Cape, 1980), p. 196.

3 For example, some letters survive in the Jennie Lee papers.

4 *The Times*, 8 February 1932.

5 The correspondence on Ebbw Vale steelworks in the early 1930s is in the Jennie Lee papers, JL/6/1/1/1. That on the coaling station is in JL/6/1/1/2.

6 The material on the colliery closures is in the Jennie Lee papers, JL/6/1/1/3.

7 See Bevan family papers, Bevan to Oliver Stanley, then Minister of Transport, 20 October 1933, 'Depressed areas file'.

8 The letter is in the papers deposited by Professor Dai Smith, Richard Burton Archives, Swansea University. As regards the Ebbw Vale iron- and steelworks, Bevan seems to have been unaware of the efforts made by Stanley Baldwin to persuade Firth, the chairman of Richard, Thomas & Co., to make the purchase. Baldwin convinced Firth to turn to Ebbw Vale, despite the alternative, at Redbourne, Lincolnshire, being a lower-cost option. Perhaps the reason for Baldwin's role not being widely known was that he 'helped quietly and out of the limelight'. See Keith Middlemas and John Barnes, *Baldwin: A Biography* (London: Weidenfeld & Nicolson, 1969), p. 932.

9 These figures are from Clement Attlee, *As It Happened* (London: Heinemann, 1954), p. 81. Morrison, in his autobiography, records Greenwood as having 33 votes in the first ballot and then, on the second ballot, 'all but four of Greenwood's supporters voted for Attlee'. See Herbert Morrison, Baron Morrison, *Herbert Morrison: An Autobiography* (London: Odhams Press, 1960), p. 164.

10 W. Golant, 'The emergence of C. R. Attlee as leader of the Parliamentary Labour Party in 1935', *Historical Journal* xiii/2 (June 1970), p. 313.

11 Kenneth Harris, *Attlee* (London: Weidenfeld & Nicolson, 1984), p. 122.

12 See Hugh Dalton, *The Fateful Years: Memoirs, 1931–1945* (London: Frederick Muller, 1957), p. 82, and Morrison, *An Autobiography*, p. 164.

13 *The Times*, 2 October 1934.

14 See C. L. Mowat, *Britain between the Wars, 1918–1940* (London: Methuen, 1968), pp. 470–3.

15 Hansard, HC (series 5), vol. 313, col. 1533, 22 June 1936.

16 Ibid.

17 Hansard, HC (series 5), vol. 331, cols 1847–8, 15 February 1938. Once the fixed period for which unemployment insurance could be claimed was exhausted the means test then applied.

18 DPP 2/382, Inspector Howell Rees, Glamorgan 'D' Division, to Superintendent William Doolan, County Police Office, 19 June 1936.

19 Ibid.

20 Ibid.

21 Labour Party, *Report of the 37th Annual Conference* (London: Labour Party, 1937), pp. 177–8.

22 *Western Mail*, 28 March 1933.
23 Hywel Francis and Dai Smith, *The Fed: A History of the South Wales Miners in the Twentieth Century* (1980; 2nd edn, Cardiff: University of Wales Press, 1998), p. 194.
24 *Western Mail*, 22 May 1933.
25 *Daily Herald*, 5 August 1936.
26 Richard Crossman archive, MSS.154/3/AU/1/335, Crossman to Bevan, 'Report on Rome visit, June 13 to 15, 1953'.
27 Bevan, writing in *Socialist*, November 1936, as quoted in Ben Pimlott, *Labour and the Left in the 1930s* (Cambridge: Cambridge University Press, 1977), p. 93.
28 Morrison, writing in *Foreward*, 27 June 1936, as quoted in Pimlott, *Labour and the Left in the 1930s*, p. 86.
29 Bernard Donoghue and G. W. Jones, *Herbert Morrison: Portrait of a Politician* (1973; London: Phoenix, 2001), p. 229.
30 It was initially called *The Tribune*.
31 Walter Citrine, *Men and Work: The Autobiography of Lord Citrine* (London: Hutchinson, 1964), p. 293.
32 Ibid., p. 300.
33 Paul Corthorn, *In the Shadow of the Dictators: The British Left in the 1930s* (2006; rev. edn, London: I.B.Tauris, 2013), p. 158.
34 *Tribune*, 7 October 1938.
35 Harris, *Attlee*, pp. 156–7.
36 Barbara Castle, *Fighting All the Way* (London: Macmillan, 1994), p. 81.
37 Michael Foot, *Aneurin Bevan*, vol. 1: *1897 to 1945* (London: MacGibbon & Kee, 1962), p. 289.

Chapter 7: The Second World War, Part I: 1939–42

1 Jennie Lee, *My Life with Nye* (London: Jonathan Cape, 1980), pp. 147–8.
2 Michael Foot, *Aneurin Bevan*, vol. 1: *1897 to 1945* (London: MacGibbon & Kee, 1962), p. 311.
3 *Western Mail*, 5 December 1939.
4 Hansard, HC (series 5), vol. 360, col. 1150, 7 May 1940.
5 Max Hastings, *Finest Years: Churchill as Warlord 1940–45* (London: HarperPress, 2011), pp. 343–4.
6 Foot, *Aneurin Bevan*, vol. 1, pp. 301–2.
7 L. G. Mitchell, *Charles James Fox* (Oxford: Oxford University Press, 1992), p. 264.
8 Robert Crowcroft, *Attlee's War: World War II and the Making of a Labour Leader* (London: I.B.Tauris, 2011), appendix ('The Adventurers'), p. 241.
9 Sir Archie Lush, interviewed by Hywel Francis, 11 May 1973, in the material collected by Professor Dai Smith, Richard Burton Archives, Swansea University, SWCC/MND/13.
10 The author can remember this story being told to him by his grandmother, Olwyn Thomas.
11 Roy Jenkins, *Churchill* (London: Macmillan, 2001), p. 199.
12 Nigel Nicolson (ed.), *The Harold Nicolson Diaries 1907–1963* (London: Weidenfeld & Nicolson, 2004), p. 273.
13 George Orwell, *Essays* (London: Penguin and Secker & Warburg, 2000), p. 137.
14 Ibid., p. 170.
15 Paul Anderson (ed.), *Orwell in Tribune: 'As I Please' and Other Writings 1943–7* (2006; London: Methuen, 2008), p. 75.

16 Jon Kimche, quoted in T. R. Fyvel, 'Orwell at *Tribune*', in Audrey Coppard and Bernard Crick (eds), *Orwell Remembered* (London: Ariel, 1984), p. 214.

17 George Orwell, 'London letter', in *Partisan Review*, summer 1945, in Peter Davidson (ed.), *The Complete Works of George Orwell*, vol. 17: *I Belong to the Left (1945)* (London: Secker & Warburg, 2001), pp. 161–5.

18 Anderson (ed.), *Orwell in Tribune*, pp. 27–8.

19 Jennie Lee, *To-morrow Is a New Day* (London: Cresset Press, 1939), p. 264.

20 *Tribune*, 18 October 1940.

21 *Tribune*, 21 June 1940.

22 Ibid.

23 As quoted in Nigel Nicolson (ed.), *The Harold Nicolson Diaries*, p. 252.

24 Herbert Morrison, Baron Morrison, *Herbert Morrison: An Autobiography* (London: Odhams Press, 1960), p. 265.

25 Jennie Lee, *Our Ally Russia: The Truth* (London: W. H. Allen, 1941), pp. 6–7.

26 *Tribune*, 27 June 1941.

27 Hansard, HC (series 5), vol. 368, col. 467, 28 January 1941.

28 Lee, *My Life with Nye*, pp. 160–1.

29 Hansard, HC (series 5), vol. 378, col. 2249, 26 March 1942.

30 Lee, *My Life with Nye*, p. 152.

31 Hansard, HC (series 5), vol. 376, col. 2222, 18 December 1941.

32 Hansard, HC (series 5), vol. 376, col. 1620, 10 December 1941.

33 Jawaharlal Nehru, *An Autobiography* (New Delhi: Penguin Books India, 2004), pp. 378, 382.

34 Adrian Fort, *Archibald Wavell: The Life and Times of an Imperial Servant* (London: Jonathan Cape, 2009), p. 404.

35 PREM 4/48/8, telegram from viceroy to Secretary of State for India, T. 492/2, 29 March 1942.

36 PREM 4/48/8, prime minister to Sir Stafford Cripps, 2 April 1942.

37 Clarke, *The Cripps Version*, pp. 321–2.

38 *Tribune*, 14 August 1942.

39 Francis Williams, *A Prime Minister Remembers: The War and Post-war Memoirs of The Rt. Hon Earl Attlee KG, PC, OM, CH: Based on His Private Papers, and on a Series of Recorded Conversations* (London: Heinemann, 1961), pp. 205–6.

40 *Tribune*, 21 August 1942.

41 *The Times*, 21 February 1942.

42 Ben Pimlott (ed.), *The Political Diary of Hugh Dalton 1940–45* (London: Jonathan Cape, 1986), p. 362.

43 *Tribune*, 27 November 1942.

44 Hansard, HC (series 5), vol. 409, cols 1385–6, 28 March 1945.

45 Peter Clarke, *The Cripps Version: The Life of Sir Stafford Cripps* (London: Allen Lane, 2002), p. 363.

46 Aneurin Bevan, 'India: Pride and prejudice', *Tribune*, 18 September 1942.

47 *Tribune*, 2 October 1942.

48 Hansard, HC (series 5), vol. 381, cols 527–8, 2 July 1942.

49 Ibid., col. 530.

50 Max Hastings, *All Hell Let Loose: The World at War 1939–45* (London: HarperPress, 2011), p. 82.

51 Ibid., p. 136.

52 John Colville, *The Fringes of Power: Downing Street Diaries, 1939–1955* (London: Phoenix, 2005), p. 526.

53 Hansard, HC (series 5), vol. 381, cols 537–8, 2 July 1942.
54 Ibid., col. 535.
55 Ibid., col. 534.
56 Ibid., col. 534.
57 Ibid., cols 539–40.
58 *Tribune*, 7 August 1942.
59 Hansard, HC (series 5), vol. 383, col. 249, 9 September 1942.
60 Hansard, HC (series 5), vol. 385, col. 134, 12 November 1942.
61 Ibid., cols 134–5.
62 Ibid., cols 134–5.
63 Ibid., col. 132.

Chapter 8: The Second World War, Part II: 1943–5

1 CAB 87/1, RP (41), 16th meeting, 23 July 1941.
2 Sir William Beveridge, *Social Insurance and Allied Services*, Cmd 6404 (London: His Majesty's Stationery Office, 1942).
3 Labour Party, *Report of the 42nd Annual Conference* (London: Labour Party, 1943), p. 20.
4 Ibid., pp. 136–42.
5 Ibid., p. 130.
6 Ibid., p. 139.
7 Hansard, HC (series 5), vol. 385, col. 1399, 3 December 1942.
8 See Nicklaus Thomas-Symonds, *Attlee: A Life in Politics* (London: I.B.Tauris, 2010), p. 103.
9 Paul Addison, 'By-elections of the Second World War', in Chris Cook and John Ramsden (eds), *By-elections in British Politics* (London: UCL Press, 1997), p. 141.
10 Jennie Lee, *My Life with Nye* (London: Jonathan Cape, 1980), p. 169.
11 Paul Addison, 'By-elections of the Second World War', in Chris Cook and John Ramsden (eds), *By-elections in British Politics* (London: UCL Press, 1997), p. 148.
12 Alan Bullock, *The Life and Times of Ernest Bevin*, vol. 2: *Minister of Labour 1940–1945* (London: Heinemann, 1967), p. 305.
13 Hansard, HC (series 5), vol. 399, col. 1069, 28 April 1944.
14 Ibid., col. 1072.
15 Ibid.
16 *The Times*, 3 May 1944.
17 Michael Foot, *Aneurin Bevan*, vol. 1: *1897 to 1945* (London: MacGibbon & Kee, 1962), p. 460.
18 Aneurin Bevan, *Why Not Trust the Tories?* (London: Victor Gollancz, 1944), pp. 4–5.
19 Ibid., p. 30.
20 Ibid., p. 46.
21 Ibid., pp. 49–50.
22 Ibid., p. 51.
23 Ibid., p. 55.
24 While Bevan did not specifically say whether it was for Tredegar Urban District Council or Monmouthshire County Council, it is likely to have been the former, given that he said he carried out the role 'for some years'.
25 Hansard, HC (series 5), vol. 397, cols 2296–7, 9 March 1944.
26 Ibid., col. 2317.
27 Bevan family papers, Bevan to London Co-operative Society, 19 June 1935.

28 Labour Party, *Report of the 44th Annual Conference* (London: Labour Party, 1945), p. 88. Churchill and Attlee's letters appear at pp. 86–8.
29 R. B. McCallum and Alison Readman, *The British General Election of 1945* (London: Frank Cass, 1964), pp. 112–13.
30 As quoted in Foot, *Aneurin Bevan*, vol. 1, pp. 504–5.

Chapter 9: The Labour Governments, 1945–51

1   C. R. Attlee papers, MS Attlee, dep. 18, Correspondence and Papers, 18 May–13 August 1945.
2   Herbert Morrison, Baron Morrison, *Herbert Morrison: An Autobiography* (London: Odhams Press, 1960), p. 245.
3   Bernard Donoghue and G. W. Jones, *Herbert Morrison: Portrait of a Politician* (1973; London: Phoenix, 2001), p. 340, and n. 9.
4   Alan Bullock, *The Life and Times of Ernest Bevin*, vol. 2: *Minister of Labour 1940–1945* (London: Heinemann, 1967), pp. 392–3. Bullock adds in a footnote that both Morgan Phillips and Attlee gave accounts to him of the events of the afternoon.
5   Donoghue and Jones, *Herbert Morrison*, pp. 16–22.
6   Hugh Dalton, *The Fateful Years: Memoirs, 1931–1945* (London: Frederick Muller, 1957), p. 467.
7   See, for example, Dalton, Hugh, *Fateful Years*, p. 468.
8   Sir Archie Lush, interviewed by Hywel Francis, 11 May 1973, in the material collected by Professor Dai Smith, Richard Burton Archives, Swansea University, SWCC/MND/13.
9   C. R. Attlee papers, MS Attlee, dep. 18, Correspondence and Papers, 18 May–13 August 1945.
10 Ibid.
11 She was MP for Middlesbrough East from 1924 to 1931 and for Jarrow from 1935 until her death in 1947.
12 Donoghue and Jones, *Herbert Morrison*, p. 392.
13 On 2 January 1934, at the Education Committee. See Monmouthshire County Council Minute Book No. 11, April 1933–March 1935, C/M/11.
14 Robert Crowcroft, *Attlee's War: World War II and the Making of a Labour Leader* (London: I.B.Tauris, 2011), p. 224.
15 Bullock, Alan, *Ernest Bevin: Foreign Secretary 1945–1951* (London: Heinemann, 1983), p. 77.
16 Ibid., p. 834.
17 Martin and Tawney are quoted in Peter Mandelson, 'Foreword', in Donoghue and Jones, *Herbert Morrison*, p. xix.
18 The draft is found in box 4 of the material collected by Professor Dai Smith, Richard Burton Archives, Swansea University, SWCC/MND/13.
19 *The Times*, 24 June 1947.
20 This memorandum on the organisation of government was reproduced in Kenneth Harris, *Attlee* (London: Weidenfeld & Nicolson, 1984), appendix III, pp. 589–95, along with Attlee's autobiographical notes. Written in the 1930s, it was with a note dated 1948. This quotation is on p. 591.
21 Speech at Oxford, 14 June 1957, as quoted in Antony Jay (ed.), *The Oxford Dictionary of Political Quotations* (Oxford: Oxford University Press, 1996), p. 20.
22 *Daily Mirror*, 14 August 1945.

23 Jennie Lee, *My Life with Nye* (London: Jonathan Cape, 1980), p. 188.
24 Ibid., pp. 188–9.
25 Ibid., pp. 195–7.
26 Ibid., p. 190.

Chapter 10: The Creation of the National Health Service

1   The National Health Service created for Scotland was similarly accountable to the Secretary of State for Scotland pursuant to the National Health Service (Scotland) Act 1947.
2   Charles Webster, *The National Health Service: A Political History* (Oxford: Oxford University Press, 1998), p. 3.
3   John Grigg, *Lloyd George: The People's Champion 1902–1911* (London: Penguin, 2002), pp. 325–6.
4   Charles Webster, *The Health Services since the War*, vol. 1: *Problems of Health Care: The National Health Service before 1957* (London: Her Majesty's Stationery Office, 1988), p. 11.
5   Ibid., p. 7.
6   Ibid., pp. 3, 5.
7   Paul Addison, *The Road to 1945: British Politics and the Second World War* (London: Pimlico, 1994), pp. 179–80.
8   As quoted in Michael Foot, *Aneurin Bevan*, vol. 2: *1945 to 1960* (London: Davis-Poynter, 1973), p. 133.
9   He was succeeded by a Monmouthshire man, Sir Isaac Hayward, who was the son of a Blaenavon miner.
10 CAB 129/3, CP (45) 227, 'National Health Service: The future of the hospital services: Memorandum by the Lord President of the Council', 12 October 1945.
11 CAB 128/1, CM (45) 43rd Conclusions, 18 October 1945.
12 CAB 129/7, CP (46) 86, 'National Health Service Bill: Memorandum by the Minister of Health', 1 March 1946. The draft bill was appended to the memorandum.
13 CAB 128/2, CM (45) 58th Conclusions, 3 December 1945.
14 CAB 129/7, CP (46) 86, 'National Health Service Bill: Memorandum by the Minister of Health', 1 March 1946.
15 CAB 128/5, CM (46) 22nd Conclusions, 8 March 1946.
16 BMA Negotiation Committee Minutes Session 1946–1947, meeting, Friday, 7 February 1947, 12.00 p.m. at BMA House, Tavistock Square, London, para. 160. Dr H. Guy Dain in the chair, with 24 others present.
17 See Foot, *Aneurin Bevan*, vol. 2, pp. 122–4.
18 Aneurin Bevan, 'Speech to Conference', in Labour Party, *Report of the 46th Annual Conference* (London: Labour Party, 1947), p. 197.
19 As quoted in BMA Negotiation Committee Minutes Session 1947–1948, 'The profession and the National Health Service Act, 1946 I. The Negotiating Committee's case', p. 12, para. 2. These subcommittees dealt with 'Hospital and Specialist Services', 'General Practice', 'Public Health Services', 'Mental Health Services', 'Ophthalmic Services' and 'Supperannuation'.
20 Ibid., para. 66.
21 BMA Negotiation Committee Minutes Session 1947–1948, meeting between the Negotiating Committee and the Minister of Health, Tuesday, 2 December 1947, and Wednesday, 3 December 1947, p. 1.
22 BMA Negotiation Committee Minutes Session 1947–1948, 'The profession and the

National Health Service Act, 1946 I. The Negotiating Committee's case'. These were the four issues that remained on the agenda in opposition to the BMA's cooperation line in the Special Representative Meeting of Friday, 28 May 1948, para. 26.

23 BMA Negotiation Committee Minutes Session 1947–1948, meeting between the Negotiating Committee and the Minister of Health, Tuesday, 2 December 1947, and Wednesday, 3 December 1947, p. 2.

24 Ibid.

25 Ibid., pp. 7–8.

26 Ibid., p. 12.

27 Ibid., p. 15.

28 On Bevan's calculation, for 1,000 patients the remuneration would be £300 + £758 = £1,058; for every extra 1,000 patients, another £758 would be added. See ibid., pp. 9, 17.

29 Ibid., p. 9.

30 Ibid., p. 4.

31 BMA Negotiation Committee Minutes Session 1947–1948, 'Statement by the Council of the British Medical Association', 18 December 1947.

32 BMA Negotiation Committee Minutes Session 1947–1948, 'The National Health Service and the Medical Profession: General comments of the Minister, addressed to the individual doctor', p. 34.

33 Minutes of Special Representative Meeting of the BMA, 8 January 1948, para. 39.

34 Ibid., paras 19–21.

35 PREM 8/844, prime minister's minute M.14/48, 16 January 1948.

36 PREM 8/844, CP (48) 23, 19 January 1948.

37 PREM 8/844, CM (48) 6th Conclusions, 22 January 1948.

38 PREM 8/844, CM (48) 8th Conclusions, 29 January 1948.

39 PREM 8/844, note from Ministry of Health to Graham-Harrison at No. 10 Downing Street.

40 Hansard, HC (series 5), vol. 446, cols 1209–10, 29 January 1948.

41 Attlee's private secretary, Laurence Helsby, wrote a note for the prime minister, based on a letter from a member of the public to *The Times*, setting out that the BMA and Bevan had their wires crossed: Bevan *was* proposing an appeal to the High Court from decisions of the General Medical Council. See PREM 8/844, CP (48) 23, 'National Health Service: Attitude of the medical practitioner'.

42 PREM 8/844, CM (48) 9th Conclusions, Minutes 2–3, 2 February 1948.

43 Ibid.

44 PREM 8/844, 'Questions from the *Lancet* and the answers of the Minister of Health'.

45 PREM 8/844, 'Suggested notes for prime minister's intervention in the health service debate'.

46 PREM 8/844, note from the prime minister, 9 February 1948.

47 Hansard, HC (series 5), vol. 447, col. 36, 9 February 1948.

48 Ibid., col. 50.

49 PREM 8/844, note by Attlee's private secretary, Helsby, for the prime minister, 17 February 1948.

50 *Lancet*, 21 February 1948, and *British Medical Journal*, 21 February 1948, as quoted in Kenneth O. Morgan, *Labour in Power 1945–1951* (1984; Oxford: Oxford University Press, 2002), p. 158.

51 BMA Negotiation Committee Minutes Session 1947–1948, Statement by BMA Council: The Plebiscite, 8 May 1948.

52 Minutes of Special Representative Meeting of the BMA, 17 March 1948, para. 53.
53 See BMA Negotiation Committee Minutes Session 1947–1948, minutes of Negotiating Committee, 20 May 1948.
54 As quoted in Morgan, *Labour in Power*, p. 159.
55 *The Times*, 6 April 1948.
56 Note in PREM 8/844.
57 Hansard, HC (series 5), vol. 449, cols 164–5, 7 April 1948. The draft, 'Draft for statement after questions: The Minister of Health', is in PREM 8/844.
58 Ibid., cols 165–6.
59 Ibid., col. 166.
60 CAB 128/5, CM (46) 3rd Conclusions, 8 January 1946.
61 PREM 8/844, CM (48) 30th Conclusions, 29 April 1948.
62 BMA Negotiation Committee Minutes Session 1947–1948, Statement by BMA Council: The Plebiscite, 8 May 1948.
63 Minutes of Special Representative Meeting of the BMA, 28 May 1948, para. 20; BMA Negotiation Committee Minutes Session 1947–1948, minutes of Negotiating Committee, 20 May 1948.
64 As quoted in Morgan, *Labour in Power*, p. 160.
65 Harry Eckstein, *Pressure Group Politics: The Case of the British Medical Association* (London: Allen & Unwin, 1960), p. 104.
66 Hywel Francis and Kim Howells have argued that health, as a human right, was 'being asserted more aggressively and confidently from 1945 onwards'. See Hywel Francis and Kim Howells, 'The politics of coal in South Wales, 1945–48', *Llafur: The Journal of the Society for the Study of Welsh Labour History* iii/3 (1982), pp. 74–85.
67 C. R. Attlee papers, MS Attlee, dep. 72, Bevan to Attlee, 2 July 1948.
68 As quoted in *The Times*, 5 July 1948.
69 Bevan family papers, 'Speech Notes: Rt. Hon. Aneurin Bevan MP'.
70 Sir Archie Lush, interviewed by Hywel Francis, 11 May 1973, in the material collected by Professor Dai Smith, Richard Burton Archives, Swansea University, SWCC/MND/13.
71 Aneurin Bevan, *Why Not Trust the Tories?* (London: Victor Gollancz, 1944), pp. 79–80.

Chapter 11: Bevan's Record on Housing, 1945–51

1 Ben Pimlott (ed.), *The Political Diary of Hugh Dalton 1918–40, 1945–60* (London: Jonathan Cape, 1986), pp. 471–3. Dalton suggested moving Jim Griffiths to Health and Bevan to the Colonies, but Attlee was unwilling to appoint Bevan Colonial Secretary.
2 Aneurin Bevan, *Why Not Trust the Tories?* (London: Victor Gollancz, 1944), ch. 5 ('Will you get that house?'), pp. 65–78.
3 Ibid., p. 78.
4 Hugh Dalton, *High Tide and After: Memoirs 1945–1960* (London: Frederick Muller, 1962), p. 358.
5 Jennie Lee, *My Life with Nye* (London: Jonathan Cape, 1980), p. 187.
6 CAB 134/320, HG (46), 2nd Meeting, 13 February 1946.
7 Ibid.
8 Housing (Miscellaneous Provisions) Bill; Rent Control Bill; Acquisition of Land Bill; Housing (Financial Provisions) Bill; Local Government (Financial Provisions) Bill; Railway Rating Bill; and the Building Restrictions (Wartime Contraventions) Bill.
9 CAB 124/560, Greenwood to Bevan, 20 October 1945.

10 CAB 124/560, Bevan to Morrison, 12 November 1945.
11 CAB 124/560, memorandum to the Lord President, 12 November 1945, with handwritten note by Morrison.
12 The minutes of the Cabinet Housing Committee are in CAB 134/320.
13 PREM 8/232, Attlee to Bevan and others, 11 April 1946.
14 PREM 8/226, HG (46), 1st Meeting, 23 January 1946.
15 PREM 8/226, note for the prime minister by Douglas Jay, 31 January 1946.
16 PREM 8/226, CP (46) 47, 'Timber for housing and for the mines: Joint memorandum by the Secretary of State for Scotland and the Minister of Agriculture and Fisheries', 6 February 1945.
17 PREM 8/226, note to the prime minister, 6 February 1946.
18 PREM 8/226, CM (46) 13th Conclusions, 7 February 1946.
19 PREM 8/231, CP (46) 161, 'Cabinet: Progress report on housing: March 1946: Memorandum by the Minister of Health', 6 May 1946.
20 PREM 8/226, Sir Gerald Lenanton, 'North German timber control: Short summary of present position', 12 June 1946.
21 PREM 8/226, CRC (46) 61, 'German timber: Memorandum by the Chancellor of the Duchy of Lancaster for the Cabinet Overseas Reconstruction Committee', 29 June 1946.
22 PREM 8/226, note from Norman Brook, 6 July 1946.
23 PREM 8/226, CP (46) 277, 'Cabinet: Timber for housing: Memorandum by the Minister of Health', 17 July 1946.
24 PREM 8/226, CP (46) 291, 'Cabinet: Supplies of softwood: Memorandum by the President of the Board of Trade', 22 July 1946.
25 PREM 8/226, CP (46) 294, 'Cabinet: Exports of timber from Germany and Austria to UK: Memorandum by the Chancellor of the Duchy of Lancaster', 23 July 1946.
26 PREM 8/226, note prepared by Christopher Eastwood for the prime minister, 24 July 1946.
27 PREM 8/226, CM (46) 73rd Conclusions, 25 July 1946.
28 PREM 8/226, CP (46) 417, 'Timber for housing: Memorandum by the Minister of Health', 8 November 1946.
29 Ibid.
30 PREM 8/226, Bevan to Attlee, 12 November 1946.
31 PREM 8/226, HG (46) 7, 'Housing: Housing programme for 1947: Memorandum by the Minister of Health', 10 December 1946.
32 PREM 8/489, Part I BP WP (47) 1 (Revise), 25 April 1947.
33 CAB 124/452, Gaitskell to Morrison, 8 August 1947.
34 CAB 124/292, Bevan to Morrison, 5 March 1948.
35 The number of houses built by the public sector had risen steadily from 109,000 in 1946 to 148,000 in 1947, and peaked at 217,000 in 1948. This then fell back to 177,000 in 1949, and 175,000 in 1950, with only a slight increase, to 176,000, in 1951. The private sector was contributing, but not significantly: in 1946, there were 31,000 new privately built houses, and 41,000 in 1947, but there was a corresponding decline: 34,000 in 1948, 28,000 in 1949, a slight recovery to 30,000 in 1950 and a fall to 25,000 in 1951. David Butler and Gareth Butler, *Twentieth-century British Political Facts 1900–2000* (London: Macmillan, 2000), pp. 356–7.
36 CAB 129/39, CP (50) 67, Aneurin Bevan, 'The housing programme (England and Wales)', 13 April 1950.
37 CAB 128/18, CM (50) 71, 6 November 1950.

38 Butler and Butler, *Twentieth-century British Political Facts*, p. 357.
39 CAB 129/39, CP (50) 90, Aneurin Bevan, 'Memorandum: Licences for the erection of new houses', 29 April 1950.
40 PREM 8/228, Jay to Attlee, 15 October 1945.
41 PREM 8/228, Bevan to Tomlinson, 2 August 1946.
42 CAB 139/386, 'Draft report on enquiry into the "Finish the houses campaign" in Scotland', 3 January 1947.
43 Nirmala Rao and Ken Young, *Local Government since 1945*, Making Contemporary Britain (Oxford: Blackwell, 1997), p. 91.
44 Aneurin Bevan, *In Place of Fear* (1952; London: Quartet Books, 1978), p. 121, n. 23.
45 Bevan's article, 'Local government management of the hospitals', published in the *Municipal Journal* on 12 March 1954, is in Charles Webster (ed.), *Aneurin Bevan on the National Health Service* (Oxford: University of Oxford Wellcome Unit for the History of Medicine, 1991), pp. 195–201.
46 CAB 129/34, CP (49) 101, Herbert Morrison, 'Local government', 4 May 1949.
47 See CAB 134/470, Committee on Local Government: Meetings 1–3, Papers 1–9; and Rao and Young, *Local Government since 1945*, pp. 96–101.
48 Butler and Butler, *Twentieth-century British Political Facts*, p. 417.
49 CAB 139/386, Ministry of Housing and Local Government to Central Statistical Office, 'New house construction calculation of average time taken in each stage', 5 November 1952. The total average construction time from foundations to fully completed, including internal plastering, was 9.85 months.
50 Butler and Butler, *Twentieth-century British Political Facts*, p. 357.
51 CAB 139/386, 'House-building before and after the two world wars', signed by B. N. Davies, 27 April 1948. Cripps had asked the Central Statistical Office to research this matter.
52 Butler and Butler, *Twentieth-century British Political Facts*, p. 356.

Chapter 12: Bevan as a Cabinet Minister

1 Jennie Lee, *My Life with Nye* (London: Jonathan Cape, 1980), p. 212.
2 CAB 128/4, CM (45) 57, 29 November 1945.
3 PREM 8/35, cypher from Foreign Office to Washington, 24 November 1945, No. 11789.
4 There was in addition a further $1.25 billion from Canada.
5 Britain received around $3 billion dollars between April 1948 and December 1951.
6 *The Times*, 16 July 1947.
7 PREM 8/290, CP (45) 315, 'Report by the Social Services Committee on the National Insurance scheme', 1 December 1945; and PREM 8/290, CP (45) 323, 'National Insurance scheme: Memorandum by the Chancellor of the Exchequer', 5 December 1945.
8 CAB 128/4, CM (45) 62, 13 December 1945.
9 PREM 8/290, CM (45) 63rd Conclusions, 13 December 1945, 10.00 a.m.
10 This was based on the model that in most households it was the man who worked.
11 PREM 8/1040, CP (48) 14, 'Gas bill: Memorandum by the Minister of Fuel and Power', Part I, 9 January 1948.
12 *The Times*, 28 October 1946.
13 CAB 129/39, CP (50) 60.
14 PREM 8/621, CP (46) 149, 'Nationalisation of transport: Memorandum by the Minister of Transport', 10 April 1946.

15 PREM 8/621, CM (47) 28th Conclusions, 13 March 1947.
16 As cited in Nicklaus Thomas-Symonds, *Attlee: A Life in Politics* (London: I.B.Tauris, 2010), from a quotation in Kenneth O. Morgan, *Labour in Power 1945–1951* (1984; Oxford: Oxford University Press, 2002), p. 108. Morgan uses the minutes of the Socialisation of Industries Committee, 8 March, 9 May 1946 (CAB 134/687) and Proceedings of the Executive Committee of the National Union of Railwaymen, December quarter 1951 (Trades Union Congress papers, Modern Records Centre, University of Warwick, MS 127).
17 Hugh Dalton, *High Tide and After: Memoirs 1945–1960* (London: Frederick Muller, 1962), p. 236.
18 As quoted in Thomas-Symonds, *Attlee*, p. 199.
19 PREM 8/729, CP (46) 423, 15 November 1946.
20 PREM 8/729, CM (46) 98th Conclusions, 19 November 1946.
21 PREM 8/729, note to the prime minister, 5 February 1947.
22 PREM 8/489, Part I, BP WP (47) 1 (Revise), 'Balance of payments working party: Import Programme for 1947–48', 25 April 1947. The document listed a number of causes: a rise in world prices; the fuel shortage affecting exports; 'losses suffered by United Kingdom agriculture'; slow recovery from the ravages of war in Europe and the East, meaning that importation from there was difficult; the price of restructuring Germany; and a dollar shortage.
23 PREM 8/489, Part I, Gen. 179, 'Import programme 1947/48: Note of a meeting with ministers held at 10, Downing Street, S.W.1 on Monday, 19 May, 1947, at 11.0 a.m.'
24 PREM 8/489, Part I, CP (47) 221, 'Cabinet: Balance of payments: Memorandum by the Chancellor of the Exchequer', 30 July 1947.
25 PREM 8/489, Part II, CM (47) 71st Conclusions, Minute 1: Confidential Annex, 17 August 1947, 5 p.m.
26 PREM 8/489, Part II, CM (47) 72nd Conclusions, Minute 1: Confidential Annex, 19 August 1947, 12 p.m.
27 *The Times*, 21 August 1947.
28 Subject to an additional paragraph about the requirement to consult for Article XIV of the International Monetary Fund, without which there would be no further proposals to 'notify any further withdrawals'. PREM 8/489, Part II, CM (47) 73rd Conclusions of a meeting of the Cabinet held at 10 Downing Street, SW1, 20 August 1947, 12.15 p.m.
29 PREM 8/489, Part I, *Exchange of Letters between His Majesty's Government and the United States Government Dated 20th August, 1947* (London: His Majesty's Stationery Office, September 1947).
30 Hugh Dalton, *High Tide and After: Memoirs 1945–1960* (London: Frederick Muller, 1962), pp. 241–2.
31 Lee, *My Life with Nye*, 207.
32 Dalton, *High Tide and After*, p. 245.
33 Kenneth Harris, *Attlee* (London: Weidenfeld & Nicolson, 1984), p. 349.
34 Labour Party, *Report of the 34th Annual Conference* (London: Labour Party, 1934), p. 201.
35 PREM 1489, Part I, LP (45) 228, 'Future of the iron and steel industry: Memorandum by the Minister of Supply and of Aircraft Production', 7 November 1945.
36 PREM 1489, Part I, British Iron and Steel Federation, *Report to the Ministry of Supply on the Iron and Steel Industry* (Fanfare Press: London, 1945), pp. 21–4.
37 Hansard, HC (series 5), vol. 421, col. 2693, 17 April 1946.
38 PREM 1489, Part I, CP (47) 123, 'Proposed scheme for public ownership of sections of the iron and steel industry: Memorandum by the Minister of Supply', 14 April 1947.
39 PREM 1489, Part I, notes of a meeting held on 21 May 1947.

40 PREM 1489, Part I, CM (47) 57th Conclusions, Minute 5, Confidential Annex, 26 June 1947.
41 PREM 1489, Part I, CP (47) 212, 'Reorganisation of the iron and steel industry: Joint memorandum by the Lord President of the Council and the Minister of Supply', 21 July 1947.
42 Dalton, *High Tide and After*, p. 251.
43 PREM 1489, Part I, CM (47) 66th Conclusions, Minute 4, Confidential Annex, 31 July 1947.
44 Hansard, HC (series 5), vol. 443, col. 33, 21 October 1947.
45 Herbert Morrison papers, Letters Box E, 39, Attlee to Morrison, 15 September 1947; Morrison's reply is 40, 19 September 1947; Attlee's subsequent response is 41, 23 September 1947.
46 CAB 21/2243, 'Memorandum by W. S. Murrie for the prime minister', 4 August 1947.
47 Dalton, *High Tide and After*, p. 253, quoting a letter from Cripps.
48 Israel Sieff, *Memoirs* (London: Weidenfeld & Nicolson, 1970), p. 195.
49 As quoted ibid., p. 196.
50 As quoted in Francis Williams, *A Prime Minister Remembers: The War and Post-war Memoirs of The Rt. Hon Earl Attlee KG, PC, OM, CH: Based on His Private Papers, and on a Series of Recorded Conversations* (London: Heinemann, 1961), p. 192.
51 CAB 128/9, CM (47) 23, 18 February 1947.
52 It was also proposed that admission of the further 100,000 Jews should be on the basis of Arab consent.
53 Ben Pimlott (ed.), *The Political Diary of Hugh Dalton 1918–40, 1945–60* (London: Jonathan Cape, 1986), p. 414.
54 As quoted in Peter Hennessy, *Cabinets and the Bomb* (Oxford: Oxford University Press for the British Academy, 2007), pp. 44–8.
55 See, for example, *Daily Sketch*, 3 December 1955.
56 J. P. D. Dunbabin, *The Cold War* (1994; 2nd edn, Harlow: Pearson Education, 2008), pp. 529–31.
57 Kenneth O. Morgan, *Labour in Power 1945–1951* (1984; Oxford: Oxford University Press, 2002), p. 389.
58 Jonathan Schneer, *Labour's Conscience: The Labour Left 1945–51* (London: Unwin Hyman, 1988), p. 58.
59 See account in Kenneth O. Morgan, *Michael Foot: A Life* (London: HarperCollins, 2007), pp. 121–2.
60 *Tribune*, 23 June 1947.
61 CAB 195/6, CM (48) 44, 28 June 1948.
62 Hugh Gaitskell papers, C26, 'Note by HG, January 1949'.
63 For Dalton's 'Young Economists' comment, see Pimlott (ed.), *Political Diary of Hugh Dalton 1918–40, 1945–60*, p. 489.
64 PREM 8/973, CM (49) 53rd Conclusions, 29 August 1949, 11.00 a.m.
65 Hansard, HC (series 5), vol. 468, col. 315, 29 September 1949.
66 Ibid., col. 310.

Chapter 13: Principles and Personalities

1 As quoted in H. G. Nicholas, *The British General Election of 1950* (London: Macmillan, 1951), p. 95.

2   Ibid., p. 242.
3   Ibid., p. 98.
4   Ibid., p. 95.
5   PREM 8/1059, Part I, CP (48) 147, 'Cabinet: Amendment of the Parliament Act, 1911: Memorandum by the Lord President of the Council', 11 June 1948.
6   Hansard, HC (series 5), vol. 458, col. 226, 16 November 1948.
7   CAB 128/17, CM (50) 6th Conclusions, 2 March 1950.
8   David Butler and Gareth Butler, *Twentieth-century British Political Facts 1900–2000* (London: Macmillan, 2000), p. 417.
9   Ibid., p. 411.
10 Ben Pimlott (ed.), *The Political Diary of Hugh Dalton 1918–40, 1945–60* (London: Jonathan Cape, 1986), p. 462.
11 Peter Clarke, *The Cripps Version: The Life of Sir Stafford Cripps* (London: Allen Lane, 2002), p. 524.
12 Francis Williams, *A Prime Minister Remembers: The War and Post-war Memoirs of The Rt. Hon Earl Attlee KG, PC, OM, CH: Based on His Private Papers, and on a Series of Recorded Conversations* (London: Heinemann, 1961), p. 249.
13 Ibid., p. 459.
14 Herbert Morrison, Baron Morrison, *Herbert Morrison: An Autobiography* (London: Odhams Press, 1960), p. 267.
15 CAB 21/2510, memorandum by Norman Brook, 29 March 1950.
16 CAB 129/39, CM (50) 10th Conclusions, Minute 3, 13 March 1950.
17 CAB 195/7: Sir Norman Brook Notebook: Cabinet Minutes, CM (49) 1st Conclusions – CM (50) 26th Conclusions, 16 March 1950.
18 Bevan's memorandum on the National Health Service (CAB 129/39, CP [50] 56) was dated 30 March 1950, and was replying to an earlier Cripps memorandum (CAB 129/39, CP (50) 53, 29 March 1950).
19 CAB 129/39, CP (50) 79, note by the prime minister, 'Committee on the National Health Service', 21 April 1950.
20 P. M. Williams (ed.), *The Diary of Hugh Gaitskell 1945–1956* (London: Jonathan Cape, 1983), p. 438.
21 Both Wilson and Strachey are quoted in Michael Foot, *Aneurin Bevan*, vol. 2: *1945 to 1960* (London: Davis-Poynter, 1973), p. 292. Foot states: 'The words here attributed to Bevan may be accurate, but they should not be taken as his final word on Gaitskell.'
22 The letters are printed ibid., pp. 293–4, but it seems that this is their only source since Cripps' biographer Peter Clarke has been unable to locate the papers in the Cripps archive. See Clarke, *The Cripps Version*, p. 525, n. 184.
23 Sir Archie Lush, interviewed by Hywel Francis, 11 May 1973, in the material collected by Professor Dai Smith, Richard Burton Archives, Swansea University, SWCC/MND/13.
24 Author's interview with Lord Healey, 9 February 2011.
25 CAB 128/18, CM 52 (50), 1 August 1950.
26 PREM 8/1560, 'Top secret – Record of Washington talks – Atomic weapon'. The Chinese took Seoul by January 1951; the US recaptured it two months later, but the counter-offensive stopped just before the 38th parallel. While there were no further major changes on the ground, there was no armistice until 27 July 1953.
27 Pimlott (ed.), *Political Diary of Hugh Dalton 1918–40, 1945–60*, p. 489.
28 Ibid., p. 485.
29 Jennie Lee, *My Life with Nye* (London: Jonathan Cape, 1980), p. 221.

30 As quoted ibid., pp. 217–18.
31 CAB 129/44, CP (51) 22, 'Supply of National Service men to meet the needs of the forces: Memorandum by the Minister of Labour and National Service', 23 January 1951.
32 CAB 128/19, CM (51) 15, 22 February 1951.
33 See LAB 10/994.
34 CAB 128/19, CM (51) 4, 25 January 1951.
35 Hansard, HC (series 5), vol. 484, col. 738, 15 February 1951.
36 PREM 8/1480, note from Brook to Attlee, 28 May 1951.
37 CAB 128/19, CM (51) 22, 22 March 1951.
38 In the event, the Conservatives introduced prescription charges in 1952.
39 Pimlott (ed.), *Political Diary of Hugh Dalton 1918–40, 1945–60*, p. 520.
40 Hugh Dalton, *High Tide and After: Memoirs 1945–1960* (London: Frederick Muller, 1962), p. 368.
41 CAB 128/19, CM (51) 25–6, 9 April 1951.
42 It was a £23 million saving in a *full* financial year.
43 Williams (ed.), *Diary of Hugh Gaitskell*, pp. 246–7.
44 CAB 128/19, CM (51) 26, 9 April 1951, 6.30 p.m.
45 *The Times*, 11 April 1951.
46 Williams (ed.), *Diary of Hugh Gaitskell*, pp. 246–7.
47 James Callaghan, *Time and Chance* (London: Politico's Publishing, 2006), p. 110.
48 Williams (ed.), *Diary of Hugh Gaitskell*, p. 238.
49 Pimlott (ed.), *Political Diary of Hugh Dalton 1918–40, 1945–60*, p. 506.
50 There are a number of other examples: Canning, Aberdeen, Palmerston, Russell (though he had been prime minister once before) and Salisbury.
51 As quoted in Foot, *Aneurin Bevan*, vol. 2, p. 327.

Chapter 14: Resignation

1 Jennie Lee, *My Life with Nye* (London: Jonathan Cape, 1980), p. 223.
2 Sir Archie Lush, interviewed by Hywel Francis, 11 May 1973, in the material collected by Professor Dai Smith, Richard Burton Archives, Swansea University, SWCC/MND/13.
3 Hansard, HC (series 5), vol. 487, col. 40, 23 April 1951.
4 Author's interview with Tony Benn, 31 January 2012.
5 David Butler and Gareth Butler, *Twentieth-century British Political Facts 1900–2000* (London: Macmillan, 2000), p. 267.
6 Barbara Castle papers, MS Castle 230, folder 2, 'Keep Left Feb. 1951–Sept. 1953', Group Paper 85.
7 Crossman's phrase can be found in Janet Morgan (ed.), *The Backbench Diaries of Richard Crossman* (London: Hamish Hamilton and Jonathan Cape, 1981), p. 400.
8 *Tribune*, 13 December 1946.
9 Sir Richard Acland, et al., *Keeping Left: Labour's First Five Years and the Problems Ahead* (London: New Statesman and Nation, January 1950), p. 28.
10 *Daily Express*, 24 April 1951.
11 Ben Pimlott (ed.), *The Political Diary of Hugh Dalton 1918–40, 1945–60* (London: Jonathan Cape, 1986), pp. 536–7.
12 Lee, *My Life with Nye*, p. 223.
13 Ibid., p. 224.
14 Michael Foot, *Aneurin Bevan*, vol. 2: *1945 to 1960* (London: Davis-Poynter, 1973), p. 330.

15 Hansard, HC (series 5), vol. 487, col. 36, 23 April 1951.
16 Ibid., cols 38–9.
17 Ibid.
18 Hansard, HC (series 5), vol. 487, col. 41, 23 April 1951.
19 Ibid., col. 42.
20 Ibid., col. 43.
21 Pimlott (ed.), *Political Diary of Hugh Dalton 1918–40, 1945–60*, pp. 537–9.
22 Ibid., p. 130.
23 Lee, *My Life with Nye*, p. 305.
24 Pimlott (ed.), *Political Diary of Hugh Dalton 1918–40, 1945–60*, p. 532.
25 C. R. Attlee papers, 'Letters to Tom', 24 July 1951.
26 Letter from Mr Robert S. Cornish (great-nephew of Clement Attlee) to the author, 4 February 2012.
27 Barbara Castle, *Fighting All the Way* (London: Macmillan, 1994), p. 202.
28 Hansard, HC (series 5), vol. 487, cols 1253–4, 2 May 1951.
29 As quoted in Foot, *Aneurin Bevan*, vol. 2, p. 343.
30 Aneurin Bevan, et al., *One Way Only* (London: Tribune, 1951).
31 When a later article by Bevan appeared in the anti-British Egyptian newspaper *Al Gomhuria* on this point (the same article on imperialism generally that he had first published in India), he was criticised for being anti-British by the Tory MP Martin Lindsay. See Hansard, HC (series 5), vol. 522, cols 632–3, 17 December 1953.
32 Foot, *Aneurin Bevan*, vol. 2, p. 353.
33 Geoffrey Goodman, *The Awkward Warrior: Frank Cousins: His Life and Times* (London: Davis-Poynter, 1979), p. 238.
34 Ibid., p. 239.
35 Labour Party, *Report of the 50th Annual Conference* (London: Labour Party, 1951), p. 122.
36 D. E. Butler, *The British General Election of 1951* (London: Macmillan, 1952), pp. 110–11; for a list of radio broadcasts, see p. 63.
37 Clement Attlee, *As It Happened* (London: Heinemann, 1954), p. 208.

Chapter 15: The Bevanites, 1951–5

1   Author's interview with Geoffrey Goodman, 20 May 2013.
2   Janet Morgan (ed.), *The Backbench Diaries of Richard Crossman* (London: Hamish Hamilton and Jonathan Cape, 1981), p. 406.
3   Ian Mikardo, *Back-bencher* (London: Weidenfeld & Nicolson, 1988), p. 123.
4   Michael Foot, *Aneurin Bevan*, vol. 2: *1945 to 1960* (London: Davis-Poynter, 1973), p. 340.
5   Mark Jenkins, *Bevanism: Labour's High Tide, the Cold War and the Democratic Mass Movement* (London: Spokesman Books, 1977), pp. 152–3, drawing on the original Keep Left minutes; see p. 286 and associated appendix for the list of members given to Jenkins by Jo Richardson.
6   Brian Brivati, *Hugh Gaitskell* (London: Richard Cohen Books, 1996), p. 164.
7   P. M. Williams (ed.), *The Diary of Hugh Gaitskell 1945–1956* (London: Jonathan Cape, 1983), p. 337.
8   David Butler and Gareth Butler, *Twentieth-century British Political Facts 1900–2000* (London: Macmillan, 2000), pp. 158–9.
9   Jenkins, *Bevanism*, p. 297.
10 Morgan (ed.), *Backbench Diaries of Richard Crossman*, p. 53.

11 Hansard, HC (series 5), vol. 494, col. 2602, 6 December 1951.

12 Morgan (ed.), *Backbench Diaries of Richard Crossman*, p. 48.

13 Ibid., p. 49.

14 Ibid., p. 63.

15 Barbara Castle, *Fighting All the Way* (London: Macmillan, 1994), p. 202.

16 Morgan (ed.), *Backbench Diaries of Richard Crossman*, p. 53.

17 Sir Archie Lush, interviewed by Hywel Francis, 11 May 1973, in the material collected by Professor Dai Smith, Richard Burton Archives, Swansea University, SWCC/MND/13.

18 Author's interview with Geoffrey Goodman, 21 November 2011.

19 Jenkins, *Bevanism*, p. 306.

20 *The Times*, 4 April 1952.

21 Aneurin Bevan, *In Place of Fear* (1952; London: Quartet Books, 1978), p. 51.

22 Author's interview with Tony Benn, 26 April 2009, as quoted in Nicklaus Thomas-Symonds, *Attlee: A Life in Politics* (London: I.B.Tauris, 2010), p. 251.

23 Bevan, *In Place of Fear*, p. 58.

24 Ibid., p. 158.

25 Ibid., p. 172.

26 Ibid., p. 195.

27 *Tribune*, 4 April 1952.

28 Williams (ed.), *Diary of Hugh Gaitskell*, p. 312.

29 Ibid., p. 312.

30 Ben Pimlott (ed.), *The Political Diary of Hugh Dalton 1918–40, 1945–60* (London: Jonathan Cape, 1986), p. 598.

31 Ibid., p. 599.

32 *The Times*, 6 October 1952.

33 Foot, *Aneurin Bevan*, vol. 2, p. 380.

34 Ibid., p. 381, n. 21.

35 *The Times*, 2 March 1953.

36 Richard Crossman archive, MSS.154/3/AU/1/335, Crossman to Bevan, 'Report on Rome visit, June 13 to 15, 1953'.

37 Hansard, HC (series 5), vol. 526, col. 971, 13 April 1954.

38 Mikardo, *Back-bencher*, p. 154.

39 Morgan (ed.), *Backbench Diaries of Richard Crossman*, pp. 314–5.

40 Richard Crossman archive, MSS.154/3/BE/1, Crossman to Harold Wilson, 22 April 1954.

41 Ben Pimlott, *Harold Wilson* (1992; London: HarperCollins, 1993), p. 166.

42 Victoria Honeyman, *Richard Crossman: A Reforming Radical of the Labour Party* (London: I.B.Tauris, 2007), p. 26.

43 J. P. D. Dunbabin, *The Cold War* (1994; 2nd edn, Harlow: Pearson Education, 2008), pp. 217–8.

44 Castle, *Fighting All the Way*, p. 222.

45 Ibid., p. 221.

46 Dunbabin, *The Cold War*, p. 190.

47 Author's interview with Geoffrey Goodman, 25 June 2012.

48 Labour Party, *Report of the 53rd Annual Conference* (London: Labour Party, 1954), p. 101.

49 *Western Mail*, 7 July 1960.

50 Richard Crossman archive, MSS.154/3/BE/4, Crossman to Bevan, 12 October 1954.

51 Author's interview with Geoffrey Goodman, 22 August 2012.

52 Williams (ed.), *Diary of Hugh Gaitskell*, pp. 375–82.

53 Atom bombs rely upon the splitting of the nucleus of an atom (fission) to emit energy; the power of the hydrogen bomb relies upon the fusing of nuclei.
54 Richard Crossman archive, MSS.154/3/BE/7, Crossman to Ted Davies, 7 March 1955.
55 Hansard, HC (series 5), vol. 537, cols 2120–1, 2 March 1955.
56 Richard Crossman archive, MSS.154/3/BE/9, Crossman to Bevan, 31 March 1955.
57 Pimlott (ed.), *Political Diary of Hugh Dalton 1918–40, 1945–60*, p. 673.
58 HO 291/232, memorandum from Newsam to the Home Secretary, 10 May 1954; handwritten reply from Kendal to Newsam, 15 May 1954.
59 *Daily Sketch*, 19 April 1954; Patricia Hollis, *Jennie Lee: A Life* (Oxford: Oxford University Press, 1997), p. 214.
60 *The Times*, 16 June 1955.
61 Letter to Hugh Gaitskell, 20 March 1955, Trades Union Congress papers, Modern Records Centre, University of Warwick (MSS.292/752/2). The sender of the letter is unclear, but it is surrounded by correspondence to Sir Vincent Tewson.
62 Kenneth Harris, *Attlee* (London: Weidenfeld & Nicolson, 1984), pp. 530–1.
63 Eric Shaw, *Discipline and Discord in the Labour Party: The Politics of Managerial Control in the Labour Party, 1951–87* (Manchester: Manchester University Press, 1988), p. 43.
64 D. E. Butler, *The British General Election of 1955* (London: Macmillan, 1955), p. 69.
65 As quoted ibid., p. 78.
66 As quoted ibid., p. 33.
67 These newspaper extracts are quoted ibid., p. 159.
68 Ibid., p. 33.

Chapter 16: The Pragmatic Bevan, 1955–7

1 Bernard Donoghue and G. W. Jones, *Herbert Morrison: Portrait of a Politician* (1973; London: Phoenix, 2001), p. 541.
2 Ben Pimlott (ed.), *The Political Diary of Hugh Dalton 1918–40, 1945–60* (London: Jonathan Cape, 1986), p. 675.
3 P. M. Williams, *Hugh Gaitskell: A Political Biography* (London: Jonathan Cape, 1979), p. 363.
4 As quoted in Ben Pimlott, *Harold Wilson* (1992; London: HarperCollins, 1993), p. 167.
5 Interview with Mrs L. Jeger, quoted in Donoghue and Jones, *Herbert Morrison*, p. 540.
6 Pimlott (ed.), *Political Diary of Hugh Dalton 1918–40, 1945–60*, p. 677.
7 *Tribune*, 2 October 1955.
8 Pimlott (ed.), *Political Diary of Hugh Dalton 1918–40, 1945–60*, p. 677.
9 *The Times*, 6 February 1956.
10 Michael Foot, *Aneurin Bevan*, vol. 2: *1945 to 1960* (London: Davis-Poynter, 1973), pp. 498–500.
11 *The Times*, 9 June 1956.
12 Hansard, HC (series 5), vol. 550, col. 389, 14 March 1956.
13 Barbara Castle papers, MS Castle 174, folder 1, 'NEC April 1951–July 1960'. Castle took shorthand notes at the dinner, from which a report was compiled.
14 Hansard, HC (series 5), vol. 558, col. 1708, 1 November 1956.
15 As quoted in Brian Brivati, *Hugh Gaitskell* (London: Richard Cohen Books, 1996), p. 277.
16 As quoted ibid., p. 279.
17 Hansard, HC (series 5), vol. 561, col. 1570, 6 December 1956.
18 Hansard, HC (series 5), vol. 562, col. 388, 8 November 1956.

19 Ibid., col. 392.
20 Geoffrey Goodman, *The Awkward Warrior: Frank Cousins: His Life and Times* (London: Davis-Poynter, 1979), p. 109.
21 Jennie Lee, *My Life with Nye* (London: Jonathan Cape, 1980), p. 168.
22 As quoted in Patricia Hollis, *Jennie Lee: A Life* (Oxford: Oxford University Press, 1997), p. 199.
23 José Enrique Rodó, *Ariel*, trans. Margaret Sayers Peden (Austin, TX: University of Texas Press, 1988), p. 79.
24 It was 'up to sixpence in the pound'. There was no compulsion, but Bevan saw it as a step forward. See Lee, *My Life with Nye*, p. 187.
25 J. P. D. Dunbabin, *The Cold War* (1994; 2nd edn, Harlow: Pearson Education, 2008), p. 22.
26 Author's interview with Geoffrey Goodman, 22 August 2012.
27 Bevan to Tito, 1 February 1954, in box 4 of the material collected by Professor Dai Smith, Richard Burton Archives, Swansea University, SWCC/MND/13.
28 *Daily Sketch*, 3 December 1955.
29 Janet Morgan (ed.), *The Backbench Diaries of Richard Crossman* (London: Hamish Hamilton and Jonathan Cape, 1981), p. 609.
30 Ibid., p. 607, n. 3.
31 Ibid., p. 608.
32 Ibid., p. 612.
33 The 1955 pact including Britain, Iraq, Turkey, Iran and Pakistan.
34 Morgan (ed.), *Backbench Diaries of Richard Crossman*, pp. 613–4.
35 Ibid., p. 614.
36 Ibid., pp. 615–16.
37 *Reynold's News*, 10 July 1960.
38 Author's interview with Geoffrey Goodman, 20 February 2012.
39 The speech can be heard online. See 'Your favourite conference clips', *BBC* [website], 3 October 2007. Available at http://news.bbc.co.uk/1/hi/programmes/the_daily_politics/6967366.stm (accessed 15 May 2014).
40 Geoffrey Goodman, *From Bevan to Blair: Fifty Years of Reporting from the Political Front Line* (rev. edn, Brighton: Revel Barker Publishing, 2010), pp. 75–6.
41 Morgan (ed.), *Backbench Diaries of Richard Crossman*, p. 619.
42 Foot, *Aneurin Bevan*, p. 574.
43 As quoted in *Tribune*, 26 July 1957.
44 Peter Shore, *Leading the Left* (London: Weidenfeld & Nicolson, 1993), p. 66.
45 *Tribune*, 11 October 1957.
46 Kenneth O. Morgan, *Michael Foot: A Life* (London: HarperCollins, 2007), pp. 200–1.
47 Ibid., p. 177, n. 48.
48 Pimlott (ed.), *Political Diary of Hugh Dalton 1918–40, 1945–60*, p. 691.
49 Labour Party Archive, Michael Foot papers, T2, File L, Lee to Foot, 2 May 1959.
50 Morgan (ed.), *Backbench Diaries of Richard Crossman*, p. 751.
51 Author's interview with Geoffrey Goodman, 21 November 2011.
52 Barbara Castle, *Fighting All the Way* (London: Macmillan, 1994), p. 81.
53 Richard Crossman archive, MSS.154/3/AU/1/369, Crossman to all members of the NEC, 26 February 1960.
54 Richard Crossman archive, MSS.154/3/AU/1/403, Crossman to Tommy Balogh, 12 July 1960.

Chapter 17: The Final Years, 1958–60

1 Janet Morgan (ed.), *The Backbench Diaries of Richard Crossman* (London: Hamish Hamilton and Jonathan Cape, 1981), p. 673.
2 *Tribune*, 15 August 1958.
3 *Tribune*, 2 August 1957.
4 Hansard, HC (series 5), vol. 580, col. 1407, 19 December 1957.
5 Hansard, HC (series 5), vol. 580, col. 760, 20 December 1957.
6 J. P. D. Dunbabin, *The Cold War* (1994; 2nd edn, Harlow: Pearson Education, 2008), p. 248.
7 *Tribune*, 30 August 1957; *The Times*, 31 August 1957.
8 Morgan (ed.), *Backbench Diaries of Richard Crossman*, p. 574.
9 Jenny Nicholson's article in the *Spectator* was entitled 'Death in Venice'.
10 *Spectator*, 15 April 1978.
11 Quotes from the coverage of Bevan's visit in *The Times*, 30 October, 4, 6, 7, 13, 14, 15 and 20 November 1957.
12 *The Times*, 13 December 1957.
13 *The Times*, 14 December 1957.
14 Morgan (ed.), *Backbench Diaries of Richard Crossman*, p. 674.
15 Ungoed-Thomas was MP for Llandaff and Barry from 1945 to 1950, then for Leicester North East from 1950 to 1962.
16 Morgan (ed.), *Backbench Diaries of Richard Crossman*, p. 677.
17 Ibid., p. 726.
18 David Butler and Richard Rose, *The British General Election of 1959* (London: Macmillan, 1960), p. 46.
19 Author's interview with Lord Healey, 9 February 2011.
20 As quoted in Butler and Rose, *The British General Election of 1959*, pp. 54–5.
21 H. G. Nicholas, *The British General Election of 1950* (London: Macmillan, 1951), p. 124.
22 Butler and Rose, *The British General Election of 1959*, p. 39.
23 Speech in Nottingham on 1 October 1959, as quoted ibid., p. 62.
24 Geoffrey Goodman, *From Bevan to Blair: Fifty Years of Reporting from the Political Front Line* (rev. edn, Brighton: Revel Barker Publishing, 2010), p. 71.
25 Ibid., p. 81.
26 Author's interview with Geoffrey Goodman, 21 November 2011.
27 *Sunday Pictorial*, 29 November 1959.
28 Ibid.
29 Labour Party, *Report of the 58th Annual Conference* (London: Labour Party, 1959), p. 155.
30 Michael Foot, *Aneurin Bevan*, vol. 2: *1945 to 1960* (London: Davis-Poynter, 1973), p. 649.
31 *Western Mail*, 7 July 1960.
32 *Guardian*, 29 March 1960.
33 As reported in the *Western Mail*, 16 July 1960.
34 Foot, *Aneurin Bevan*, vol. 2, p. 652.
35 As reported in the *Daily Express*, 7 July 1960.
36 *Western Mail*, 7 July 1960.
37 Telegram is in PREM 11/2928.
38 PREM 11/2928, memorandum to the chief whip, 11 July 1960; letter from the chief whip to the prime minister, 11 July 1960; unsigned letter to the chief whip, 11 July 1960; letter from the prime minister to the Dean of Westminster Abbey, 11 July 1960; letter from the Dean of Westminster Abbey to the prime minister, 13 July 1960.

Conclusion

1   *Time*, 21 March 1949.
2   Aneurin Bevan, *In Place of Fear* (1952; London: Quartet Books, 1978), p. 35.
3   Hansard, HC (series 5), vol. 580, col. 1404, 19 December 1957.
4   Brian Brivati, *Hugh Gaitskell* (London: Richard Cohen Books, 1996), p. 138.
5   Clement Attlee, 'Bevan as hero', *Observer*, 6 November 1960, in Frank Field (ed.), *Attlee's Great Contemporaries: The Politics of Character* (London: Continuum, 2009), pp. 139–40.
6   Author's interview with Geoffrey Goodman, 21 November 2011.
7   Ralph Miliband, *Parliamentary Socialism: A Study in the Politics of Labour* (London: Merlin Press, 1972), pp. 288–9.
8   Bevan, *In Place of Fear*, p. 128.
9   Author's interview with Geoffrey Goodman, 21 November 2011.
10 Evan Durbin, *Problems of Economic Planning: Papers on Planning and Economics* (London: Routledge & Kegan Paul, 1949), p. 42.
11 Richard Toye, *The Labour Party and the Planned Economy* (Woodbridge, Suffolk: Boydell Press, 2003), p. 239.
12 Ibid., p. 241.
13 Steven Fielding, *The Labour Party: Continuity and Change in the Making of 'New' Labour* (Basingstoke: Palgrave Macmillan, 2003), pp. 32–3.
14 Labour Party, *Report of the 58th Annual Conference* (London: Labour Party, 1959), p. 153.
15 '[G]rowth will continue [...] the future is more likely to be characterised by inflation than by unemployment. This change in the economic climate, and hence in the starting-point for analysis about the future, would alone suffice to outmode the greater part of the pre-war literature.' See Anthony Crosland, *The Future of Socialism* (1956; London: Constable, 2006), p. 6.
16 Crosland, *Future of Socialism*, p. 6.
17 Brivati, *Hugh Gaitskell*, p. 332.
18 *Tribune*, 11 December 1959.
19 Bevan, *In Place of Fear*, p. 143.
20 Ibid.
21 Wm Roger Louis (ed.), *Resurgent Adventures with Britannia: Personalities, Politics and Culture in Britain* (London: I.B.Tauris, 2011), pp. 188–9.
22 Bevan, *In Place of Fear*, p. 71.
23 Dominic Sandbrook, *Never Had It So Good: A History of Britain from Suez to the Beatles* (London: Abacus, 2006), p. 107.
24 Janet Morgan (ed.), *The Backbench Diaries of Richard Crossman* (London: Hamish Hamilton and Jonathan Cape, 1981), p. 971.
25 Ibid., p. 973.
26 I am grateful to Megan Fox for taking me to interview Dai Price and Jack Thomas on 8 June 2011.

Bibliography

Public Records

Cabinet Papers 1915–1984 (CAB).
Dominions Office (DO).
Hansard, Parliamentary Debates, Fifth Series.
Home Office Records (HO).
Ministry of Labour records (LAB).
Prime Minister's Office (PREM).
Records of the Director of Public Prosecutions (DPP).

Private Papers

C. R. Attlee papers (Bodleian Library, University of Oxford).
Bevan family papers, originally those of Arianwen Bevan-Norris: cited with kind permission of Jaselle Williams, the great-granddaughter of Aneurin Bevan's brother William Bevan, and her parents, Councillor David Williams and Jane Williams (Aneurin Bevan's great-niece).
Barbara Castle papers (Bodleian Library, University of Oxford).
Richard Crossman archive (Modern Records Centre, University of Warwick).
Hugh Gaitskell papers (University College, London).
Jennie Lee papers (Open University, Milton Keynes).
Herbert Morrison papers (Nuffield College Library archives, University of Oxford); the extracts here reproduced with the kind permission of the Warden and Fellows of Nuffield College.

Other Papers

BMA, Negotiation Committee Minutes, 1947–1948 (BMA House, Tavistock Square, London).
BMA, Minutes of Special Representative Meetings, 1948 (BMA House, Tavistock Square, London).
Labour Party Archive (People's History Museum, Manchester); including General Secretary's papers and Michael Foot papers.
Monmouthshire County Council Minute Books (Gwent Archives, Ebbw Vale, Blaenau Gwent).
Richard Burton Archives (Swansea University); including material collected in course of writing a biography of Aneurin Bevan by Professor David Smith, cited with his kind permission.

South Wales Miners' Library (Swansea University).
Tredegar Urban District Council Minutes (Gwent Archives, Ebbw Vale, Blaenau Gwent).
Trades Union Congress papers (Modern Records Centre, University of Warwick).

Newspapers and Periodicals

British Medical Journal
Daily Express
Daily Herald
Daily Mirror
Daily News
Daily Sketch
Daily Telegraph
Forward
Guardian
Independent
Lancet
Merthyr Express
Municipal Journal
New Statesman
Observer
Partisan Review
Plebs
Reader's Digest
Reynold's News
Socialist
South Wales Argus
Spectator
Sunday Pictorial
Time
The Times
The Times Magazine
Tredegar Valley District Monthly Report
Tribune
Western Mail

Books, Articles and Pamphlets

Addison, Paul, *The Road to 1945: British Politics and the Second World War* (London: Pimlico, 1994).
——— 'By-elections of the Second World War', in Chris Cook and John Ramsden (eds), *By-elections in British Politics* (London: UCL Press, 1997), pp. 130–50.
Anderson, Paul (ed.), *Orwell in Tribune: 'As I Please' and Other Writings 1943–7* (2006; London: Methuen, 2008).
Attlee, Clement, *As It Happened* (London: Heinemann, 1954).
Beckett, Clare, and Francis Beckett, *Bevan* (London: Haus Publishing, 2004).
Bevan, Aneurin, 'Plan for work', in G. D. H. Cole, et al., *Plan for Britain: A Collection of Essays Prepared for the Fabian Society* (London: Routledge, 1943), pp. 34–52.

———— *Why Not Trust the Tories?* (London: Victor Gollancz, 1944).

———— *In Place of Fear* (1952; London: Quartet Books, 1978).

Bevan, Aneurin, et al., *One Way Only* (London: Tribune, 1951).

Bevan, Aneurin, et al., *It Need Not Happen: The Alternative to German Rearmament* (London: Tribune, 1954).

Bevan, Aneurin, with John Strachey and George Strauss, *What We Saw in Russia* (London: Hogarth Press, 1931).

Beveridge, Sir William, *Social Insurance and Allied Services*, Cmd 6404 (London: His Majesty's Stationery Office, 1942).

Brivati, Brian, *Hugh Gaitskell* (London: Richard Cohen Books, 1996).

Brockway, Fenner, *Inside the Left* (Leicester: Blackfriars Press, 1942).

Brome, Vincent, *Aneurin Bevan* (London: Longmans, 1953).

Brooks, David, *The Social Animal* (New York, NY: Random House, 2011).

Bullock, Alan, *The Life and Times of Ernest Bevin*, vol. 1: *Trade Union Leader: 1881–1940* (London: Heinemann, 1960).

———— *The Life and Times of Ernest Bevin*, vol. 2: *Minister of Labour 1940–1945* (London: Heinemann, 1967).

———— *Ernest Bevin: Foreign Secretary 1945–1951* (London: Heinemann, 1983).

Butler, D. E., *The British General Election of 1951* (London: Macmillan, 1952).

———— *The British General Election of 1955* (London: Macmillan, 1955).

Butler, David, and Gareth Butler, *Twentieth-century British Political Facts 1900–2000* (London: Macmillan, 2000).

Butler, David, and Richard Rose, *The British General Election of 1959* (London: Macmillan, 1960).

Callaghan, James, *Time and Chance* (London: Politico's Publishing, 2006).

Campbell, John, *Roy Jenkins: A Biography* (London: Weidenfeld & Nicolson, 1983).

———— *Nye Bevan and the Mirage of British Socialism* (London: Weidenfeld & Nicolson, 1987).

———— *Roy Jenkins: A Well-rounded Life* (London: Jonathan Cape, 2014).

Castle, Barbara, *Fighting All the Way* (London: Macmillan, 1994).

Ceadel, Martin, *Thinking about Peace and War* (1987; Oxford: Oxford University Press, 1989).

Citrine, Walter, *Men and Work: The Autobiography of Lord Citrine* (London: Hutchinson, 1964).

Clarke, Peter, *The Cripps Version: The Life of Sir Stafford Cripps* (London: Allen Lane, 2002).

Cohen, Gidon, *The Failure of a Dream: The Independent Labour Party from Disaffiliation to World War II* (London: I.B.Tauris, 2007).

Coleman, Stephen, *Daniel De Leon* (Manchester: Manchester University Press, 1990).

Colville, John, *The Fringes of Power: Downing Street Diaries, 1939–1955* (London: Phoenix, 2005).

Coppard, Audrey, and Bernard Crick (eds), *Orwell Remembered* (London: Ariel, 1984).

Corthorn, Paul, *In the Shadow of the Dictators: The British Left in the 1930s* (2006; rev. edn, London: I.B.Tauris, 2013).

Craig, F. W. S. (ed.), *British Parliamentary Election Results 1918–1949* (Chichester: Political Reference Publications, 1969).

———— (ed.), *British Parliamentary Election Results 1950–1970* (Chichester: Political Reference Publications, 1971).

Craik, W. W., *Bryn Roberts and the National Union of Public Employees* (London: Allen & Unwin, 1955).

———— *The Central Labour College, 1909–29* (London: Lawrence & Wishart, 1964).

Crosland, Anthony, *The Future of Socialism* (1956; London: Constable, 2006).

Crowcroft, Robert, *Attlee's War: World War II and the Making of a Labour Leader* (London: I.B.Tauris, 2011).

Dale, Iain (ed.), *Labour Party General Election Manifestos, 1900–1997* (London: Routledge and Politico's Publishing, 2000).

Dalton, Hugh, *The Fateful Years: Memoirs, 1931–1945* (London: Frederick Muller, 1957).

———— *High Tide and After: Memoirs 1945–1960* (London: Frederick Muller, 1962).

Davidson, Peter (ed.), *The Complete Works of George Orwell*, vol. 17: *I Belong to the Left (1945)* (London: Secker & Warburg, 2001).

Demont, Susan E., 'Tredegar and Aneurin Bevan: A society and its political articulation 1890–1929', DPhil thesis, University of Wales, March 1990.

Donoghue, Bernard, and G. W. Jones, *Herbert Morrison: Portrait of a Politician* (1973; London: Phoenix, 2001).

Dunbabin, J. P. D., *The Cold War* (1994; 2nd edn, Harlow: Pearson Education, 2008).

Durbin, Evan, *Problems of Economic Planning: Papers on Planning and Economics* (London: Routledge & Kegan Paul, 1949).

Eagleton, Terry, *Why Marx Was Right* (New Haven and London: Yale University Press, 2011).

Eckstein, Harry, *Pressure Group Politics: The Case of the British Medical Association* (London: Allen & Unwin, 1960).

Edwards, Ness, *History of the South Wales Miners' Federation*, vol. 1 (London: Lawrence & Wishart, 1938).

Field, Frank (ed.), *Attlee's Great Contemporaries: The Politics of Character* (London: Continuum, 2009).

Fielding, Steven, *The Labour Party: Continuity and Change in the Making of 'New' Labour* (Basingstoke: Palgrave Macmillan, 2003).

Finch, Harold, *Memoirs of a Bedwellty MP* (Risca: Starling Press, 1972).

Fishman, Nina, *Arthur Horner: A Political Biography*, vol. 1: *1894–1944* (London: Lawrence & Wishart, 2010).

Foot, Michael, *Aneurin Bevan*, vol. 1: *1897 to 1945* (London: MacGibbon & Kee, 1962).

———— *Aneurin Bevan*, vol. 2: *1945 to 1960* (London: Davis-Poynter, 1973).

———— *Debts of Honour* (1980; London: Pan Books, 1981).

Foot, Michael, Richard Crossman and Ian Mikardo, *Keep Left* (London: New Statesman and Nation, 1947).

Fort, Adrian, *Archibald Wavell: The Life and Times of an Imperial Servant* (London: Jonathan Cape, 2009).

Foster, Margaret, *Good Wives? Mary, Fanny, Jennie and Me, 1845–2001* (London: Vintage, 2002).

Francis, Hywel, and Dai Smith, *The Fed: A History of the South Wales Miners in the Twentieth Century* (1980; 2nd edn, Cardiff: University of Wales Press, 1998).

Francis, Hywel, and Kim Howells, 'The politics of coal in South Wales, 1945–48', *Llafur: The Journal of the Society for the Study of Welsh Labour History* iii/3 (1982), pp. 74–85.

Golant, W., 'The emergence of C. R. Attlee as leader of the Parliamentary Labour Party in 1935', *Historical Journal* xiii/2 (June 1970), pp. 318–32.

Goodman, Geoffrey, *The Awkward Warrior: Frank Cousins: His Life and Times* (London: Davis-Poynter, 1979).

———— *From Bevan to Blair: Fifty Years of Reporting from the Political Front Line* (rev. edn, Brighton: Revel Barker Publishing, 2010).

———— (ed.), *The State of the Nation: The Political Legacy of Aneurin Bevan* (London: Victor Gollancz, 1997).

Grigg, John, *Lloyd George: The People's Champion 1902–1911* (London: Penguin, 2002).

Hando, Fred J., *The Pleasant Land of Gwent* (1944; Newport: R. H. Johns, 1949).

Harris, Kenneth, *Attlee* (London: Weidenfeld & Nicolson, 1984).

Hastings, Max, *All Hell Let Loose: The World at War 1939–45* (London: HarperPress, 2011).
——— *Finest Years: Churchill as Warlord 1940–45* (London: HarperPress, 2011).
Hattersley, Roy, *David Lloyd George: The Great Outsider* (London: Little, Brown, 2010).
Hayhurst, Mark, 'Duty bound', *Guardian*, 28 May 2005. Available at http://www.theguardian. com/books/2005/may/28/thinktanks.politicalbooks (accessed 22 May 2014).
Hennessy, Peter, *Cabinets and the Bomb* (Oxford: Oxford University Press for the British Academy, 2007).
Hollis, Patricia, *Jennie Lee: A Life* (Oxford: Oxford University Press, 1997).
Honeyman, Victoria, *Richard Crossman: A Reforming Radical of the Labour Party* (London: I.B.Tauris, 2007).
Horner, Arthur, *Incorrigible Rebel* (London: MacGibbon & Kee, 1960).
Jay, Antony (ed.), *The Oxford Dictionary of Political Quotations* (Oxford: Oxford University Press, 1996).
Jefferys, Kevin, *Anthony Crosland: A New Biography* (London: Richard Cohen Books, 1999).
Jenkins, Mark, *Bevanism: Labour's High Tide, the Cold War and the Democratic Mass Movement* (London: Spokesman Books, 1977).
Jenkins, Roy, *Churchill* (London: Macmillan, 2001).
Krug, Mark M., *Aneurin Bevan: Cautious Rebel* (New York, NY: Yoseloff, 1961).
Labour Party, *Report of the 31st Annual Conference* (London: Labour Party, 1931).
——— *Report of the 34th Annual Conference* (London: Labour Party, 1934).
——— *Report of the 37th Annual Conference* (London: Labour Party, 1937).
——— *Report of the 42nd Annual Conference* (London: Labour Party, 1943).
——— *Report of the 44th Annual Conference* (London: Labour Party, 1945).
——— *Report of the 46th Annual Conference* (London: Labour Party, 1947).
——— *Report of the 48th Annual Conference* (London: Labour Party, 1949).
——— *Report of the 50th Annual Conference* (London: Labour Party, 1951).
——— *Report of the 58th Annual Conference* (London: Labour Party, 1959).
Lee, Jennie, *To-morrow Is a New Day* (London: Cresset Press, 1939).
——— *Our Ally Russia: The Truth* (London: W. H. Allen, 1941).
——— *This Great Journey: A Volume of Autobiography 1904–45* (London: MacGibbon & Kee, 1963).
——— *My Life with Nye* (London: Jonathan Cape, 1980).
London, Jack, *The Iron Heel* (Stilwell, KS: Digireads.com, 2007).
Louis, Wm Roger (ed.), *Resurgent Adventures with Britannia: Personalities, Politics and Culture in Britain* (London: I.B.Tauris, 2011).
McCallum, R. B., and Alison Readman, *The British General Election of 1945* (London: Frank Cass, 1964).
McKibbin, Ross, 'The economic policy of the second Labour government', in Ross McKibbin, *The Ideologies of Class: Social Relations in Britain, 1880–1950* (Oxford: Clarendon Press, 1994), pp. 197–227.
Marquand, David, *Ramsay MacDonald* (London: Jonathan Cape, 1977).
Martineau, Lisa, *Politics & Power: Barbara Castle: A Biography* (2000; London: Andre Deutsch, 2011).
Middlemas, Keith, and John Barnes, *Baldwin: A Biography* (London: Weidenfeld & Nicolson, 1969).
Mikardo, Ian, *Back-bencher* (London: Weidenfeld & Nicolson, 1988).
Miliband, Ralph, *Parliamentary Socialism: A Study in the Politics of Labour* (London: Merlin Press, 1972).

Mitchell, L. G., *Charles James Fox* (Oxford: Oxford University Press, 1992).

Morgan, Janet (ed.), *The Backbench Diaries of Richard Crossman* (London: Hamish Hamilton and Jonathan Cape, 1981).

Morgan, Kenneth O., *Rebirth of a Nation: Wales 1880–1980* (1981; Oxford: Oxford University Press, 1982).

———— *Labour in Power 1945–1951* (1984; Oxford: Oxford University Press, 2002).

———— *Labour People: Leaders and Lieutenants, Hardie to Kinnock* (1987; rev. edn, Oxford: Oxford University Press, 1992).

———— *The Red Dragon and the Red Flag: The Cases of James Griffiths and Aneurin Bevan: The Welsh Political Archive Lecture 1988: 4th November 1988* (Aberystwyth: National Library of Wales Press, 1989).

———— *Michael Foot: A Life* (London: HarperCollins, 2007).

Morrison, Herbert, *Socialisation and Transport* (London: Constable, 1933).

———— *Herbert Morrison: An Autobiography* (London: Odhams Press, 1960).

Mowat, C. L., *Britain between the Wars, 1918–1940* (London: Methuen, 1968).

Nehru, Jawaharlal, *An Autobiography* (New Delhi: Penguin Books India, 2004) [edition with foreword by Sonia Gandhi].

Nicholas, H. G., *The British General Election of 1950* (London: Macmillan, 1951).

Nicolson, Nigel (ed.), *The Harold Nicolson Diaries 1907–1963* (London: Weidenfeld & Nicolson, 2004).

Orwell, George, *Essays* (London: Penguin and Secker & Warburg, 2000).

Page Arnot, Robin, *The Miners: A History of the Miners' Federation of Great Britain 1889–1910* (London: Allen & Unwin, 1951).

———— *A History of the South Wales Miners' Federation 1898–1914* (London: Allen & Unwin, 1967).

Pelling, Henry, *Popular Politics and Society in Late Victorian Britain* (London: Macmillan, 1968).

Perkins, Anne, *Red Queen: The Authorized Biography of Barbara Castle* (London: Macmillan, 2003).

Pimlott, Ben, *Labour and the Left in the 1930s* (Cambridge: Cambridge University Press, 1977).

———— *Harold Wilson* (1992; London: HarperCollins, 1993).

———— *Hugh Dalton* (London: HarperCollins, 1995).

———— (ed.), *The Political Diary of Hugh Dalton 1918–40, 1945–60* (London: Jonathan Cape, 1986).

———— (ed.), *The Political Diary of Hugh Dalton 1940–45* (London: Jonathan Cape, 1986).

Rao, Nirmala, and Ken Young, *Local Government since 1945*, Making Contemporary Britain series (Oxford: Blackwell, 1997).

Rodó, José Enrique, *The Motives of Proteus*, trans. Angel Flores (New York, NY: Brentano's, 1928).

———— *Ariel*, trans. Margaret Sayers Peden (Austin, TX: University of Texas Press, 1988).

Sandbrook, Dominic, *Never Had It So Good: A History of Britain from Suez to the Beatles* (London: Abacus, 2006).

Schneer, Jonathan, *Labour's Conscience: The Labour Left 1945–51* (London: Unwin Hyman, 1988).

Shaw, Eric, *Discipline and Discord in the Labour Party: The Politics of Managerial Control in the Labour Party, 1951–87* (Manchester: Manchester University Press, 1988).

Shore, Peter, *Leading the Left* (London: Weidenfeld & Nicolson, 1993).

Sieff, Israel, *Memoirs* (London: Weidenfeld & Nicolson, 1970).

Skidelsky, Robert, *Politicians and the Slump: The Labour Government of 1929–1931* (1967; London: Papermac, 1994).

Smith, Dai, *Aneurin Bevan and the World of South Wales* (Cardiff: University of Wales Press, 1993).

Smith, J. Beverley, et al., *James Griffiths and His Times* (Ferndale, Rhondda: Labour Party Wales and the Llanelli Constituency Labour Party, 1979).

Taylor, A. J. P., *Beaverbrook* (New York, NY: Simon & Schuster, 1972).

Thomas-Symonds, Nicklaus, 'Michael Foot's handling of the Militant Tendency: A reinterpretation', *Contemporary British History* ixx/1 (Spring 2005), pp. 27–51.

———— *Attlee: A Life in Politics* (London: I.B.Tauris, 2010).

Thomas, Gwyn, *The Alone to the Alone*, Library of Wales (1947; Cardigan: Parthian, 2008).

Toye, Richard, *The Labour Party and the Planned Economy* (Woodbridge, Suffolk: Boydell Press, 2003).

Unofficial Reform Committee, *The Miners' Next Step: Being a Suggested Scheme for the Reorganisation of the Federation* (1912; repr., London: Germinal & Phoenix Press, 1991).

Webster, Charles, *The Health Services Since the War*, vol. 1: *Problems of Health Care: The National Health Service before 1957* (London: Her Majesty's Stationery Office, 1988).

———— *The Health Services since the War*, vol. 2: *Government and Health Care: The British National Health Service, 1958–79* (London: Her Majesty's Stationery Office, 1996).

———— *The National Health Service: A Political History* (Oxford: Oxford University Press, 1998).

———— (ed.), *Aneurin Bevan on the National Health Service* (Oxford: University of Oxford Wellcome Unit for the History of Medicine, 1991).

Wheen, Francis, *Tom Driberg, His Life and Indiscretions* (London: Chatto & Windus, 1990).

Williams, Charles, *Harold Macmillan* (London: Weidenfeld & Nicolson, 2009).

Williams, Francis, *A Prime Minister Remembers: The War and Post-war Memoirs of The Rt. Hon Earl Attlee KG, PC, OM, CH: Based on His Private Papers, and on a Series of Recorded Conversations* (London: Heinemann, 1961).

Williams, P. M., *Hugh Gaitskell: A Political Biography* (London: Jonathan Cape, 1979).

———— (ed.), *The Diary of Hugh Gaitskell 1945–1956* (London: Jonathan Cape, 1983).

Williamson, Philip, *National Crisis and National Government: British Politics, the Economy and Empire, 1926–1932* (1992; Cambridge: Cambridge University Press, 2003).

Worley, Matthew, *Labour inside the Gate: A History of the British Labour Party between the Wars* (2005; London: I.B.Tauris, 2008).

———— *Oswald Mosley and the New Party* (Basingstoke: Palgrave Macmillan, 2010).

Internet Links

The Bevan Foundation [website]. Available at http://www.bevanfoundation.org (accessed 15 May 2014).

'Bevan is ultimate Welsh hero', *BBC News* [website], 1 March 2004. Available at http://news.bbc.co.uk/1/hi/wales/3523363.stm (accessed 15 May 2014).

Bogdanor, Vernon, 'Aneurin Bevan and the socialist ideal' [lecture at Gresham College, 16 October 2012]. Available at http://www.gresham.ac.uk/sites/default/files/16oct12vernonbogdanor_aneurinbevan.doc (accessed 15 May 2014).

'The NHS in England', *NHS* [website]. Available at http://www.nhs.uk/NHSEngland/thenhs/about/Pages/overview.aspx (accessed 15 May 2014).

'Your favourite conference clips', *BBC* [website], 3 October 2007. Available at http://news.bbc.co.uk/1/hi/programmes/the_daily_politics/6967366.stm (accessed 15 May 2014) [includes Bevan's 'naked into the conference chamber' speech from the 1957 Labour Party Conference].

Index